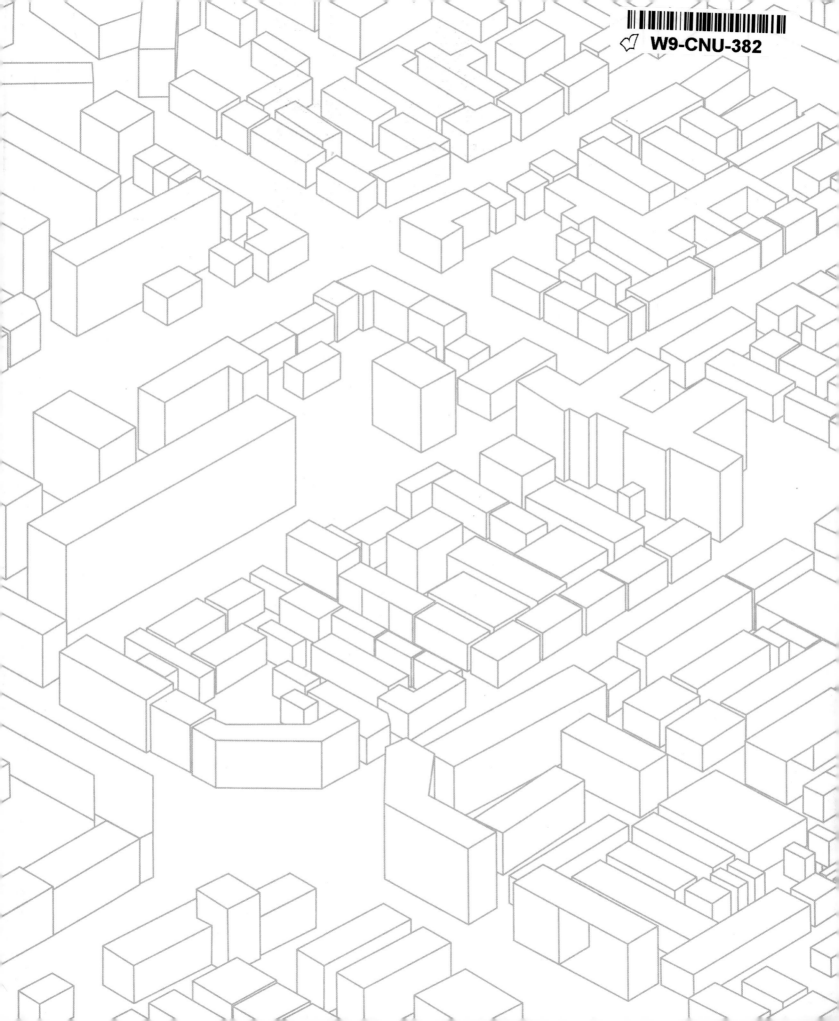

ATLAS
OF
CITIES

ATLAS OF CITIES

EDITED BY **PAUL KNOX**

PRINCETON UNIVERSITY PRESS

PRINCETON AND OXFORD

DEDICATION

This book is dedicated
to the memory of
Guido Martinotti

First published in the United States
of America and Canada in 2014 by

Princeton University Press
41 William Street
Princeton, New Jersey 08540
press.princeton.edu

Library of Congress Control Number:
2013954981

ISBN: 978-0-691-15781-8

This book was conceived,
designed, and produced by
Ivy Press
210 High Street
Lewes, East Sussex
BN7 2NS, UK

CREATIVE DIRECTOR   Peter Bridgewater
PUBLISHER   Jason Hook
EDITORIAL DIRECTOR   Caroline Earle
ART DIRECTOR   Michael Whitehead
DESIGNERS   JC Lanaway
ILLUSTRATOR   Nick Rowland

Color origination by Ivy Press Reprographics

Printed in China

10 9 8 7 6 5 4 3 2 1

Contents

Foreword
RICHARD FLORIDA

Ours is a world of cities. It has become a cliché to point out that more than half the world's population now lives in cities, but that doesn't make it any less true. What is even more important is that we will put millions more people into cities over the next generation or two, and spend trillions upon trillions of dollars rebuilding old cities and raising new ones all over the world.

It has also become a cliché to say that cities are humanity's greatest invention, but they are. From the dawn of human history, cultural and technological development have been closely linked to rising population densities. The congregation and conurbation of people into progressively larger and more complex cities is what propelled the rise of tool making, agriculture, art, and religion in prehistory; great thinkers, artists, and entrepreneurs—the Leonardo Da Vincis, William Shakespeares, Benjamin Franklins, Albert Einsteins, and Steven Jobs of the world—have almost always come of age in cities. This is even more the case today, as cities have become the key social and organizing units of the new knowledge-powered creative economy. *Homo creativus* is also *homo urbanus*.

It's time to put away the fiction that the world is flat. Cities shape and structure our increasingly interconnected planet. The world is spiky—its wealth is concentrated in the great cities that mass talent and enterprise, power innovation, structure trade, and shape commerce. Dense and interactive connectors, cities are economic and social organizing machines. They bring people and ideas together, providing the platform for them to combine and recombine in myriad ways. Cities are the basic motor of economic progress, driving artistic, technological, and economic growth at one and the same time.

They have also been fonts of democracy and freedom, since the days of classical Athens and Rome. The Paris Commune of 1871, the October Revolution of 1917 in St. Petersburg, the Chicago Convention in 1968, the Tiananmen Square uprising of 1989, the 2011 uprising in Cairo's Tahrir Square—each was urban to the core. Cities are places where people have always come together in the quest for a better world.

Cities are great palimpsests—as much as they are constantly changing, traces of their pasts bleed through in their built environments, their customs, and their political institutions. Wander through a European city and the old Roman street grid can be discerned amid bomb scars from the Second World War and the brownfields of post-industrialism; futuristic architecture soars alongside churches that people have worshipped in for more than a millennium.

This atlas takes us on a tour of great cities, ancient and modern, across the globe—from ancient Athens, Rome, and Alexandria to London, Venice, Bruges, and other medieval trading centers; from great imperial capitals like Constantinople to industrial capitals like Manchester, Düsseldorf, and Detroit; from modern global colossi like New York and London to Mumbai, Cairo, Jakarta, and other megacities of the emerging world; from smart cities and green cities like Freiburg and Tokyo to creative centers like Milan, Paris, Portland, and LA. Its essays, maps, charts, and illustrations reveal the likenesses, built and cultural, that unify the most diverse of cities and the incredible differences that divide them.

Richard Florida is director of the Martin Prosperity Institute at the University of Toronto's Rotman School of Management and global research professor at NYU. He is senior editor of the Atlantic *and co-founder and editor-at-large of* Atlantic Cities.

Introduction

1: The decision-making capacity of cities
Because cities bring together the decision-making machinery of public and private institutions and organizations, cities are centers of political and economic power.

Cities have always been central to the development of societies and the growth of their economies. Towns and cities in every historical period and in every geographical context have been engines of economic innovation and centers of cultural expansion, social transformation, and political change. This remains true today, even as cities around the world have inherited very different physical settings and have adapted to different roles and specializations in an increasingly integrated global system. Although they often pose social and environmental problems, towns and cities are essential elements in human economic and social organization. In this context, we can identify four fundamental aspects of the dynamism of cities:

4: The generative functions of cities
The concentration of people in cities makes for much greater interaction and competition, which promotes innovation and facilitates the generation and exchange of knowledge and information.

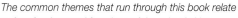

The four fundamental functions of cities
The common themes that run through this book relate to four fundamental functions of the role of cities, whose development can be traced historically and uncovered in cities across the globe. Each of the city types in this book illustrates different emphases and combinations of these functions and of creating and maintaining the infrastructure and social context to support them.

Cities, in other words, are not just concentrations of people. Nevertheless, the numbers are impressive. Cities now accommodate more than half the world's population. Between 1980 and 2010, the number of city dwellers worldwide rose by 1.7 billion. Much of the developed world has become almost completely urbanized, and in many less-developed regions the current rate of urbanization is without precedent. Metropolitan areas like Mexico City and São Paulo have been adding half a million people to their population each year: nearly 10,000 every week, even taking into account losses from deaths and out-migration. It took London 190 years to grow from half a million to 10 million. It took New York 140 years. By contrast, Buenos Aires, Kolkata (Calcutta), Mexico City, Mumbai (Bombay), Rio de Janeiro, São Paulo, and Seoul all took less than seventy-five years to grow from half a million to 10 million inhabitants. Urbanization on this scale is a remarkable geographical phenomenon—one of the most important processes shaping the world's landscapes.

Many of the world's big cities are the product of long periods of development; of a "golden age" of wealth or creativity; or, more often, of successive waves and cycles of development and of demographic, social, cultural, political, and administrative change. Each chapter in a city's history leaves its mark, for better or worse, in the layout of its streets, the fabric of its buildings, the nature of its institutions, and the cultural legacies of its residents. The layering and imprint of these are, of course, uneven; some elements are more durable than others, some are more cherished, and some are simply bypassed or left unchanged. This book charts the diversity of the world's cities, focusing on the different types of cities produced by patterns and processes of urbanization, past and present.

Foundations

In many ways, the foundations for today's cities were laid by the Greek and Roman empires. Their legacy is described in Chapter 1. The ancient Greeks developed a series of fortified city-states along the Mediterranean coast, and by 550 BCE there were about 250 such colonies, some of which subsequently grew into thriving cities, centers of rational inquiry and open-mindedness. The Roman Republic was established in 509 BCE and by 14 CE the Romans had conquered much of Europe. Most of today's major European cities had their origin as Roman settlements, which introduced innovations in civil society, urban administration and governance, and infrastructure. In many of these cities it is possible to find traces of the Roman street layout, as well as city walls, paved streets, aqueducts, sewage systems, baths, and public buildings.

The traces and echoes of Greek and Roman urbanism survive in many of today's cities, but their heyday was followed in Europe by the Dark Ages: decidedly rural, introverted, and not at all urban-oriented. From the 11th century onward, however, the feudal system of the Dark Ages faltered and disintegrated in the face of successive demographic, economic, and political crises. These crises arose because limited amounts of cultivable land could not cope with even modest population growth in the absence of significant technological improvements. To bolster their incomes and raise armies against one another, the feudal nobility began to levy increasingly higher taxes. Peasants were consequently obliged to sell more of their produce for cash in local markets. Gradually, a more extensive money economy

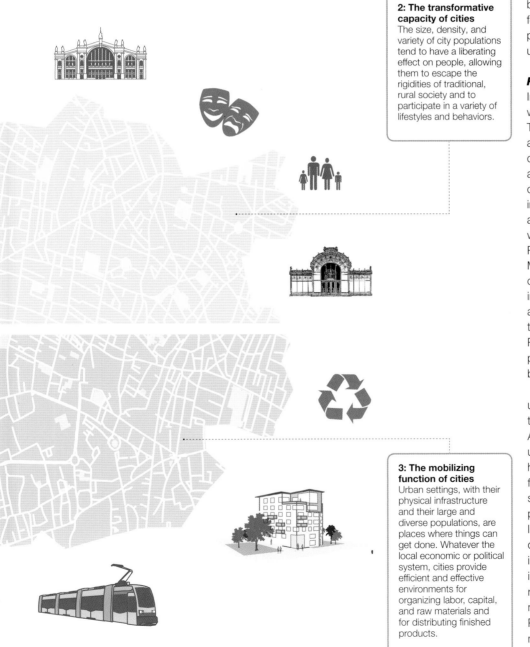

2: The transformative capacity of cities
The size, density, and variety of city populations tend to have a liberating effect on people, allowing them to escape the rigidities of traditional, rural society and to participate in a variety of lifestyles and behaviors.

3: The mobilizing function of cities
Urban settings, with their physical infrastructure and their large and diverse populations, are places where things can get done. Whatever the local economic or political system, cities provide efficient and effective environments for organizing labor, capital, and raw materials and for distributing finished products.

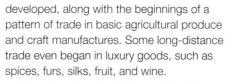

developed, along with the beginnings of a pattern of trade in basic agricultural produce and craft manufactures. Some long-distance trade even began in luxury goods, such as spices, furs, silks, fruit, and wine.

The regional specializations and trading networks that emerged provided the foundations for a new phase of urbanization based on merchant capitalism. One such network is charted in Chapter 2: the Hanseatic League, a federation of city-states around the North Sea and Baltic coasts. Inter-city trade became an engine of growth, and cities became cultural crossroads and political powerhouses. Among the legacies of late medieval urbanism were craft guilds, the codification of urban governance and the democratic process, and the creation of key public institutions. In some cases, the core of the old town remains as a beautifully preserved example of medieval European urbanism, attracting tourists and presenting some interesting issues associated with historic preservation.

In sharp contrast to cities based on trade are those whose *raison d'être* has been the administration of imperial power. At different times, and in different world regions, the likes of Athens, Beijing, Budapest, Constantinople,

Kyoto, London, Moscow, Mexico City, Rome, and Vienna became an expression, in brick and stone, of imperial power and grandeur. As Chapter 3 illustrates, the layout, principal buildings, and neighborhoods of such cities all reflect the centralized power of the imperial era. The imperial city exemplifies some of the generative functions of cities in terms of the exchange of knowledge and ideas, while its declarative built form expresses the relationships between art, power, and the city.

Industrialization

Industrialization rewrote the landscapes of many cities and prompted the emergence of an entirely new kind of city—the industrial city—whose fundamental reason for existence was not, as earlier, to fulfill military, administrative, ecclesiastical, or trading functions but, rather, to gather raw materials and to fabricate, assemble, and distribute manufactured goods. Industrial economies could be organized only through the large pools of labor, the transportation networks, the physical infrastructure of factories, warehouses, stores, and offices, and the consumer markets provided by cities. In addition to their new infrastructure and economic activities, industrial cities brought significant

Urban growth across the world

Urbanization is a global phenomenon, but the way cities are developing, the experience of city life, and the prospects for the future of cites vary widely from region to region. While much of the developed world has become almost completely urbanized, in Africa and Asia the current rate of urbanization is without precedent. North America is the most urbanized continent in the world, with more than 80 percent of its population living in urban areas. In contrast, Africa is less than 40 percent urban. To put these figures in perspective, only 30 percent of the world's population was urbanized in 1955. Currently, some 200,000 people are added to the world's urban population every day. By 2030, six out of every ten people worldwide will live in a city, and by 2050 this proportion will increase to seven out of ten people.

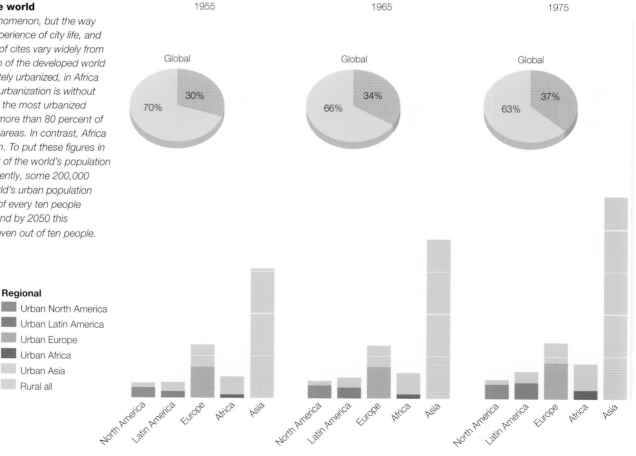

social, cultural, and environmental impacts: new class structures, urban poverty and inequality, pollution, socio-economic segregation; and philanthropy and liberal reform. Manchester, the focus of Chapter 4, was the shock city of 19th-century industrialization, growing from a small town of 15,000 in 1750 to a city of 70,000 in 1801, a metropolis of 500,000 in 1861, and a world city of 2.3 million by 1911. Today's industrial cities include the likes of São Paulo, Brazil, and Guangzhou, China; while many of the industrial cities that sprang up in Europe and North America in the 19th and early 20th centuries have experienced deindustrialization as the economy has globalized and jobs moved offshore.

The unintended consequences of industrialization, together with the progressive possibilities of new technologies, saw the birth of city planning. Meanwhile, city-based education and communications saw the advance of reason, rationality, and science over tradition, myth, superstition, and religious absolutes. As Chapter 5 shows, cities everywhere began to modernize, but Paris was the acknowledged capital of modernity in terms of both physical and cultural expression. Nineteenth-century Paris acquired wide boulevards, new bridges, a new water supply system, a gigantic system of sewers and street lighting, public buildings, and extensive improvements in urban parks that turned them into places of leisure. Within this new framework, modernized industry flourished, along with significant new artistic and cultural movements, mass entertainments, and new spaces of consumption. Amid the revolutionary ferment of ideas, Paris attracted and developed an unrivaled artistic and cultural scene.

Globalization

By the mid-20th century, economic globalization had resulted in the creation of an international urban system in which certain cities—"global cities"—acquired key roles in areas such as transnational corporate organization, international banking and finance, supranational government, and the work of international agencies. Global cities, the subject of Chapter 6, are the control centers for the flows of information, cultural products, and finance that collectively sustain economic and cultural globalization. They provide an interface between the global and the local. They contain the economic, cultural, and institutional apparatus that channels national and provincial resources into the global economy, and that transmits the impulses of globalization back to national and provincial centers. The rise of globalized consumer societies has meanwhile meant that cities are increasingly the setting for mega-events and spectacle; for the promotion of celebrity culture; for innovative and daring statements in architecture; for developments in fashion, theater, film, music, and art; for the rejection of tradition and convention in favor of the new, the challenging, the trashy. In this context, Chapter 7 features Los Angeles, a city that is widely viewed as the paradigmatic automobile city and the precursor of the postmodern city, where spectacle and consumption have become the dominant characteristics of urban life. At the same time, and for some of the same reasons, it is held up as an exemplar of dystopian urbanism.

Cities in less-developed regions stand in sharp contrast to all this. Whereas urbanization in developed countries was driven largely by economic growth, the urbanization of less-developed regions has been a consequence of demographic growth that has preceded economic development. Large increases in population, well in advance of any significant levels of industrialization or rural economic

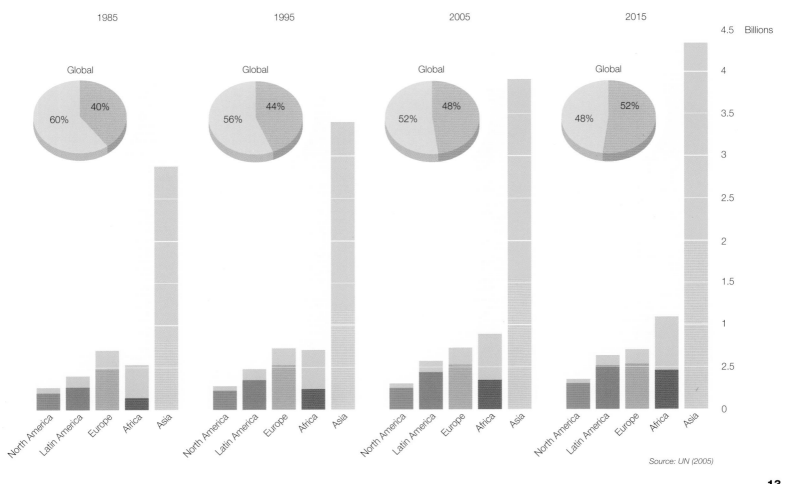

Source: UN (2005)

development, have resulted in "uncontrollable urbanization" and "overurbanization." For fast-growing rural populations, the limitations of agricultural development often mean an apparently hopeless future of drudgery and poverty. Emigration is no longer a demographic safety valve, as more affluent countries have put up barriers to immigration. The only option for the growing numbers of impoverished rural residents is to move to the larger towns and cities, where at least there is the hope of employment and the prospect of access to schools, health clinics, piped water, and the kinds of public facilities and services that are often unavailable in rural regions. Cities also have the lure of modernization and the appeal of consumer goods—attractions that rural areas are now directly exposed to via satellite TV.

Megacities

One dramatic outcome of this, described in Chapter 8, is the "megacity": a city of 10 million or more in population. Megacities not only link local and provincial economies with the global economy but also provide a point of contact between the traditional and the modern, and between formal and informal economic sectors. The slums and squatter settlements of megacities are often associated with severe problems of social disorganization and environmental degradation. Nevertheless, many neighborhoods are able to develop self-help networks and organizations that form the basis of community amid dauntingly poor and crowded conditions.

In some countries, governments and planning authorities have sought to avoid the

Thirteen city-types

Each chapter explores a distinct type of city, with a core case study supported by secondary examples to demonstrate the patterns of production, consumption, generation, and decay of the 21st century's defining form.

New York

Manchester

Paris

Bruges

Bruges

Ghent

Manchester

Lübeck

London

Freiburg

Paris

Augsburg

Innsbruck

Milan

Venice

Florence

Rome

Istanbul

Athens

Los Angeles

New York

Los Angeles

Miami

Mumbai

- Foundational
- Networked
- Imperial
- Industrial
- Rational
- Global
- Celebrity
- Megacity
- Instant
- Transitional
- Creative
- Green
- Intelligent

Brasilia

Miami

Brasilia

London

Athens

problems associated with urbanization by creating planned settlements on greenfield sites. In France and Britain, new towns were created in the second half of the 20th century to accommodate "overspill" population from the slums of big cities, and to create poles of new urban development in economically depressed regions. "Instant" cities have also been created as capital cities or administrative centers in some countries, sometimes to sidestep regional political rivalries, and sometimes to seek to take advantage of the efficiencies expected to result from the close proximity of government agencies in new, purpose-built settings. Chapter 9 focuses on Brasilia. Brazil's new capital city, on a cleared site in the Amazon, was intended to symbolize a new age in Brazilian history. The city is self-consciously rich with messages meant to

Freiburg

Istanbul

Mumbai

Milan

transform Brazilian society through new and radical forms of architecture that were planned as exciting, soaring, and uplifting symbols of modernization. As an "instant" city, Brasilia embodies innovative approaches to infrastructure and spatial organization; however, it also exemplifies some of the unintended consequences of planting a new city.

Contemporary patterns and processes of urbanization are heavily influenced by the economic and cultural globalization that has gathered pace since the 1980s. Some cities—Hong Kong, Miami, and Vancouver, for example—have become regional crossroads, and in the process have acquired a distinctively transnational character. Chapter 10 shows how Miami has become a financial and a cultural capital as well as an important hub for various illegal activities for a transnational region that extends beyond the southeastern United States to the Caribbean, Central America, and South America. As a result the city has developed a unique cultural mix, in many ways more temperamentally like the Mediterranean European coast or parts of Latin America. This cosmopolitanism is reflected in entertainment and cuisine: Colombian discos; European club scenes; traditional American bars; Cuban cafés; and restaurants specializing in "Eurasian," "New World," and "Nuevo Latino" cuisine have displaced the kosher delis and seafood shacks.

Chapter 11 details another aspect of economic and cultural globalization: the increasing importance of design. Cities in developed countries, initially a product of the manufacturing era, have been thoroughly remade in the image of consumer society. Competitive spending among affluent households has intensified the importance of style and design at every scale, and design professions have grown in size and importance, locating disproportionately in cities most intimately connected with global systems of key business services. Milan has a long history of specialization in certain aspects of design but it was only in response to the deindustrialization of the 1970s that the city embarked on a deliberate strategy of remaking and rebranding itself as a design city. Already evident in its built environment, its politics, its educational institutions, its design districts, and its fashion weeks, the city has revamped its infrastructure in preparation for hosting the World Exposition of 2014.

Sustainability

Meanwhile, worldwide awareness of the unintentional and unwanted side effects of urbanization has created an interest in the possibility of sustainable urban development. The world's cities consume 80 percent of global energy and produce 75 percent of global CO_2 emissions. Sustainable urbanization requires compact, transit-oriented development, adaptive reuse, pedestrian- and bicycle-friendly settings, co-housing, landscaping that preserves and enhances wetlands and natural habitat, and the inclusion of ecological goals and criteria in governance and policy. As Chapter 12 shows, a good example of this approach is Freiburg, Germany, where two districts—Vauban and Rieselfeld—represent advanced examples of a commitment to sustainable urbanism. Other cities, as charted in Chapter 13, have taken a different approach to the unintentional and unwanted side effects of urbanization, investing in "smart" technologies. Digital technologies are beginning to change the ways that cities and their buildings operate, along with the ways that their inhabitants behave. The Internet and social networking are changing both the commercial and the socio-cultural organization of cities. "Smart" buildings, vehicles, traffic systems, and water and power supplies have the potential to make cities more efficient and more resilient.

There is, of course, a great deal of geographical diversity and variety in the world's cities. Certain features of many cities are unique: the broad sweep of change always involves some degree of modification as it is played out in different environments. Every city has its own distinct character and story, yet many important generalizations can be made about different types of cities, with similar legacies, common sets of challenges, and parallel approaches to solutions. The essays and infographics in this book not only reveal the fascinating diversity of cities but also draw out important commonalities in their roles in economic, social, and cultural development and the ways in which technological, demographic, and political changes are reflected in their buildings and infrastructure.

THE FOUNDATIONAL CITY

LILA LEONTIDOU
GUIDO MARTINOTTI

Core cities
ATHENS _____
ROME _____

Secondary cities
KNOSSOS _____
SANTORINI _____
SPARTA _____
PELLA _____
SYRACUSE _____
MARSEILLE _____
ALEXANDRIA _____
CONSTANTINOPLE _____
BABYLON _____

Left: Athens, Greece

The Foundational City: Introduction

> **"The classical Greek city-state and the Roman urban civilization represent two distinct, albeit close and overlapping, cycles of ancient urbanization."**

At a time when much that we take for granted today was unknown, when the Earth was a flat disk at the center of the universe and there were no state borders but only tribal territories, the city emerged as both an idea and a material reality. The *polis* was the ancient Greek city-state, from which we get the terms politics and policy. Athens deserves the name "foundational city" for creating these concepts, for laying the foundations for democracy (*democratia*), and for its broader intellectual contribution. Rome deserves the same status for its cosmopolitanism and for administrative innovation over so large a territory that it was virtually a global city.

Athens and the Greek colonies

The Greeks established flourishing colonies, apoikies or paroikies. Hellenic urbanization expanded to the east, with Ionian cities along the Mediterranean shores of Asia Minor and the Greek islands of the Aegean archipelago, and to the west in southern Italy and Sicily (Magna Graecia). Colonies were part of the city-state.

Athenian city-state and Greek colonies

Sources: Toynbee (1967), Dimitrakos & Karolides (1950s)

The classical Greek city-state and the Roman urban civilization represent two distinct, albeit close and overlapping, cycles of ancient urbanization. A comparison between Athens and Rome reveals their similarity as eternal cities, cities of destiny that established the most important principles of European civilization, and their role as colonial cities. However, there were important differences: in the words of the sociologist Henri Lefebvre, "The Greek unification of form with function and structure … the city-state … identified mental with social … and thought with action, in a way that was destined to degenerate. … By contrast, did Roman diversity, governed as it was by an external constraining principle rather than by an internal unity, contain the seeds of further growth? It seems reasonable to suppose so." (Lefebvre 1991.)

In fact, the markedly different timelines of these two foundational cities have been attributed to several differences between them. Classical Athens excelled for only a century,

though the city existed at least from the 4th millennium BCE and survived long after that under Roman and later Ottoman rule, while Rome was dominant for over five centuries. Roman resilience can be attributed to its openness to a multicultural empire, a wise decentralized administrative system that integrated secondary cities in governance and defense, thus fragmenting the huge empire into several semi-autonomous cells, with a multicultural army to defend them: in other words, Rome respected local cultures, cultivating the *inclusive* principle which we detail later. By contrast, the vulnerability of the Athenian state was greatly due to its exclusion of non-citizens and "barbarians." Athens, as all the other *poleis*, was based on *jus loci* and had a substantial population of non-citizens (*metics*), which constituted the main weakness of the Athenian democracy and its difference from both the Macedonian and Roman empires. Rome had no distinction of this kind, though there was an important divide between *plebs*

and *patritiate*. The exclusion of the "others" from the Athenian army created vulnerability, which would cause disaster during the Peloponnesian wars.

Further, we should contrast the Athenian contribution to reason, knowledge, art, political culture as well as myth and mercantile expansion with Roman military, trade, political, and administrative innovation. The collective spectacles of each city illustrate the remarkable contrast: processions, rituals, and theater in Athens, where temples abounded and whose open-air theaters are still used today, vs. Roman pageants, *thermae*, and bloody sports in arenas, of which the Coliseum remains an impressive tourist landmark. The *thermae* and the *arenae* of Rome were probably the first examples of mass culture.

There were quite important differences within the so-called slave mode of production, which both societies shared. The decision-making process in ancient Greek *poleis* was based on an individual vote, after the exclusion of *metics*, women, slaves, and non-adults. In Rome, by contrast, political democracy and the whole institutional setting was based on collective units, tribes, and *centuriae*, and the vote was collective—a powerful tool for creating consensus and reducing conflict. This, combined with the Roman rule of law and the inclusiveness of the Roman system, allowed the empire to absorb different cultures. Athens, however, shaped individual voting in today's democracies, and indeed offered the theory, the practice, and the word *democratia*, democracy, which is derived from *demos/demoi*, the local communities surrounding the city-state.

Athens and Rome had a peculiar relationship of "cousins and strangers," which is the title of a book on modern relations between Britain and the USA; however, they were more strangers than cousins, because of the different languages and other distinctions. The cultural Hellenization of Rome, even after the defeat of Athens, brings to mind the European cultural imprint on the expanding USA. Athens and Rome shared the same gods, imported from Greece and renamed in Rome, though attitudes toward religion were different. Although the two empires were sometimes at war and competing for spheres of influence particularly in southern Italy, direct clashes between them were never as clear-cut and brutal as the confrontations between the Greeks and the Persians or the Romans and the Phoenicians. When in 41 BCE Rome conquered Athens, transforming it into a Roman province but giving back its independence, a high degree of integration followed.

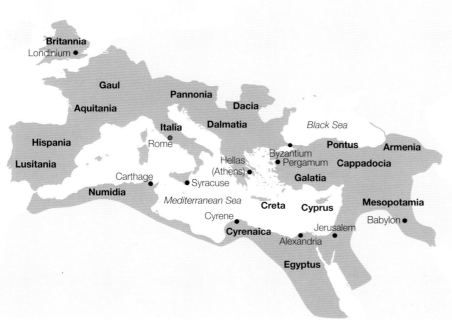

Sources: Benevolo (1993), Pounds (1990)

■ Extent of Roman Empire 117 CE

The Roman Empire

Between the Greek and Roman civilizations, a very important transition took place: from the city-state in classical antiquity to capital cities in the Macedonian period, and the Roman Empire with its important regional capitals in the course of its expansion to the east and the west. The inclusiveness of the Roman administration, which allowed a degree of local autonomy within the universal Roman law, meant that the empire could exercise influence over a wide area while permitting regional variations.

Athens: *Polis*, *Demos*, Colonies, and the Rise from Tyranny to Direct Democracy

Athens lives in the global imagination as a foundational city standing between Occident and Orient, the hegemonic city-state of classical antiquity that inspires collective memory; and yet, although its discontinuous history spans six millennia, Athens flourished for a mere century, the 5th century BCE. The first traces of life in Athens date from the 4th millennium BCE, the late Neolithic period, when among the four settlements the largest one was built around the rock of the Acropolis. After the 6th century BCE, following a first flowering of Greek civilization in the Ionian cities in Asia Minor, classical Athens rose from a sea of tyranny, first defeating the Assyrians and then expelling its tyrant, Hippias, in 510 BCE. Democratic civilization then continued until the Peloponnesian wars. Athens surrendered to the Spartans in 404 BCE and democracy was shattered by the regime of the thirty tyrants.

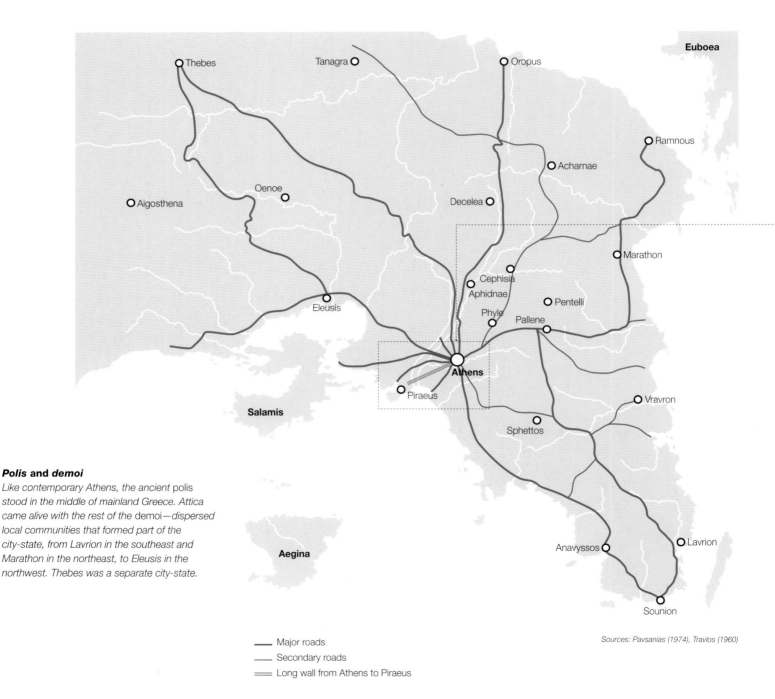

Polis and *demoi*

Like contemporary Athens, the ancient polis stood in the middle of mainland Greece. Attica came alive with the rest of the demoi—dispersed local communities that formed part of the city-state, from Lavrion in the southeast and Marathon in the northeast, to Eleusis in the northwest. Thebes was a separate city-state.

—— Major roads
—— Secondary roads
══ Long wall from Athens to Piraeus

Sources: Pavsanias (1974), Travlos (1960)

The birth of European civilization has been traced to this short-lived city-state. Athenian intellectual enquiry, science, philosophy, theater, art, and architecture were unparalleled until the 14th century, and were adopted as a foundational influence by Macedonian and Roman cities. Athens was the city of Socrates; of Plato's Academy, established in 387 BCE; of the peripatetic school of Aristotle, the Lyceum, established in 335 BCE; of Euripides' and Sophocles's tragedies and Aristophanes' comedies; and of philosophers and scientists whose intellect illuminated the ancient world and was rediscovered during the Renaissance.

There were also activities lost today, like music, and mysticism practiced in Athens and its surrounding settlements, like Eleusis.

In his well-known introduction to his *Politics*, Aristotle orders the state as the highest level of community that embraces, in turn, the individual, the family, and the village. Within these hierarchies, *kratos*, the state (the city-state at the time), was essentialized by Aristotle as a "creation of nature." The *polis* was not one city but a network of *demoi* and these, in turn, were the natural extension of the family and coincided with the state, according to Aristotle. The city, *polis*, was therefore also a

society, a community, an assemblage of *demoi* and *apoikies* (i.e. colonies), and a state, the realm of the citizen (*politis*), the person participating in public life, who was distinguished from *idiotis*, the private person (and the etymology for idiot, as in Marx's "rural idiocy"). Athenians were *polites* on multiple spatial levels—the local, the urban, and the national (state), as at the European level today—despite the etymology based on the *city*. Citizenship and participation in a real, natural city were considered a precondition of civilization and the essence of democracy—with tyranny or autocracy as its opposite.

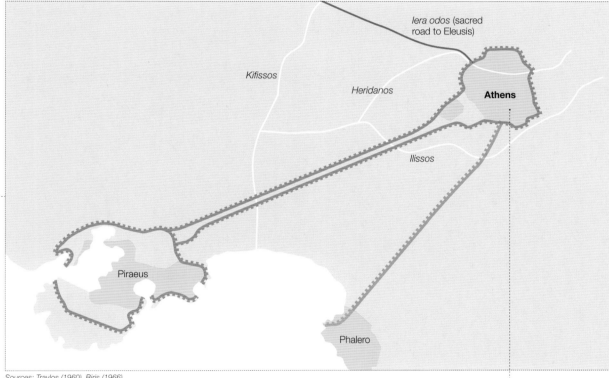

- - - - Walls

Iera odos (sacred road to Eleusis)

Kifissos

Heridanos

Athens

Ilissos

Piraeus

Phalero

Sources: Travlos (1960), Biris (1966)

Goddess Athena

The Athenian Acropolis

Gateway to the sea
Piraeus was the port of Athens and the most important demos, *located to the southwest. It was connected with Athens via the Long Walls, which were built in the classical period as a protection from flooding and for wartime communication between the city and the port. Traces of a wall to Phalero have also been found. They were demolished after the Peloponnesian wars.*

Acropolis, Agora, Architecture, Infrastructure

For Athens, the most significant of the myths of the twelve Gods of Olympus, who were personifications of animate nature, was that of the contest for the patronage of the city between Athena, the goddess of wisdom, and Poseidon, the god of the sea. Athena won this privilege by offering a sacred olive as a gift to the city, which was subsequently named after her. The contest is depicted in several sculptures and drawings, notably on the western pediment of the Parthenon. This temple was built on the sacred rock of the Acropolis by Ictinos and Callicrates and inaugurated by Pericles in 432 BCE. It was dedicated to Athena and contained a large statue of her, as well as evocative representations of myths and processions in her honor on the marble friezes. The Acropolis sculptures are today scattered around various European museums, notably the British Museum, and a movement for their reunification in the new Acropolis Museum in Athens is gaining ground. The overwhelming presence of the Parthenon as an icon of European civilization and American republicanism was exemplified during the Renaissance in Europe, in the USA through the buildings of Thomas Jefferson, and in the European movement of neoclassical architecture which flourished from the 18th century and was re-imported to Athens after 1834 when it was declared the capital of Greece.

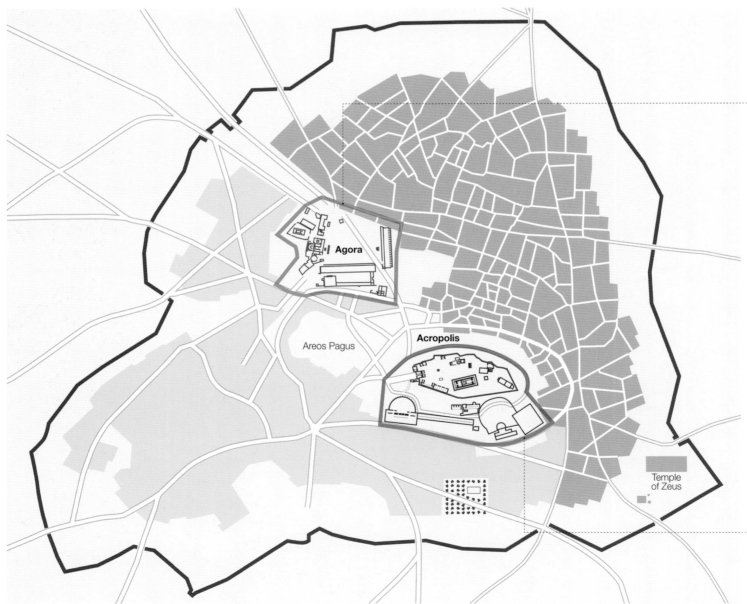

Agora

Areos Pagus

Acropolis

Temple of Zeus

Sources: Travlos (1960), Biris (1966)

The ancient city-state was centered on the *agora*, which combined nature with all kinds of public economic, political, and cultural activity. *Agora* literally meant "marketplace," since commerce was centered here, but it was actually a complex space of mixed uses and intense social interaction, a multifunctional or *hybrid* space where citizenship was forged, an active "public" realm open to political participation (Leontidou, 2009). It was a space between the individual and the state, where civil society emerged, and this was continued in the Roman forum.

Urban public space was the place where democracy and citizenship were concretized, and was not simply physical space (*urbs*).

In the *agora*, ideas and policies were debated in the citizens' assembly without any censorship. This was the forum for direct democracy, which in Athens meant that decisions were taken by all eligible "citizens" rather than just their representatives. Leaders were elected to office only in order to carry out the people's will: Pericles was not a ruler, but the city's leading citizen, elected annually. Decisions were taken after debates in the *agora*, where every man participated irrespective of income, property, or rank. However, Athens was a weak democracy in many senses. Citizenship was bounded by territoriality, gender, and social exclusion—of slaves, women, and a substantial population of non-citizen residents (*metics*). Women moved

in domestic spaces and worked, in a society where work was not valued as highly as in later Europe, while men moved in the public realm and had the privilege of talking in the *agora*, voting, and traveling. It should be recognized, however, that compared to earlier despotisms and later to Rome, slaves were few in Athens and Sparta: there was one slave to two citizens. As to women, they did mobilize the collective imagination in art, drama, and mythology, as goddesses and heroines. Works written by men often had women as protagonists.

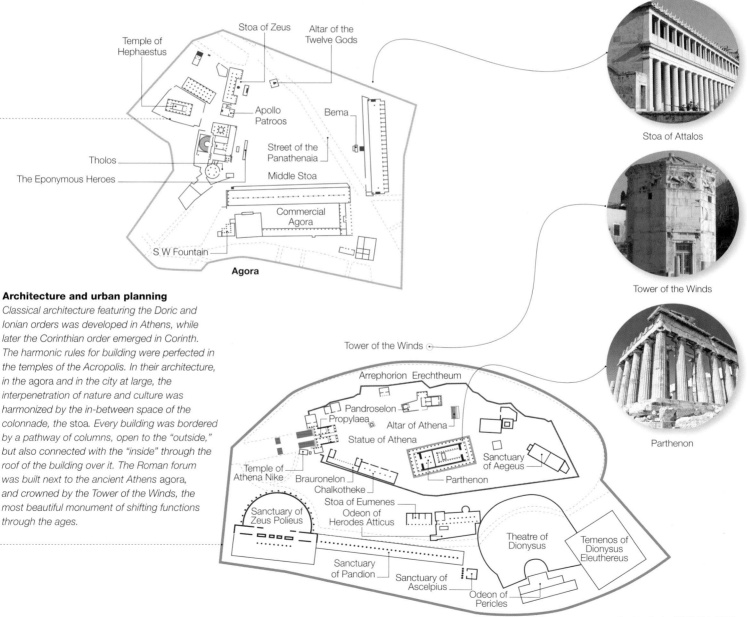

Stoa of Attalos

Tower of the Winds

Parthenon

Agora

Architecture and urban planning

Classical architecture featuring the Doric and Ionian orders was developed in Athens, while later the Corinthian order emerged in Corinth. The harmonic rules for building were perfected in the temples of the Acropolis. In their architecture, in the agora and in the city at large, the interpenetration of nature and culture was harmonized by the in-between space of the colonnade, the stoa. Every building was bordered by a pathway of columns, open to the "outside," but also connected with the "inside" through the roof of the building over it. The Roman forum was built next to the ancient Athens agora, and crowned by the Tower of the Winds, the most beautiful monument of shifting functions through the ages.

Sources: Travlos (1960), Biris (1966)

European Legacies and the Passage from Ancient to Modern Athens

The global imagination connects modern and classical Athens through their cultural landscapes of evocative symbolism. Over a very long period, Athens has enchanted personalities from Roman emperors like Hadrian to modern intellectuals like Gustav Flaubert and Sigmund Freud, Le Corbusier and Jacques Derrida. Europe "constructed" Hellenism through selective reinterpretations of classical Athens. It "borrowed" its conceptual apparatus and its architecture, at the same time trying to forge a modern Hellenic identity as imagined by Europe. Given the discontinuity of Athens's urban history, a snapshot approach to the several metamorphoses of the city would "visit" five important periods since the 19th century during which Athens became a prototype for urban geography:

1. After four centuries of Ottoman rule, Athens was declared the capital of the new Greek kingdom in 1834, and was rebuilt with modern urban design and monumental architecture mostly funded by diaspora Greeks, celebrating a classicism re-imported to Athens via European neoclassicism. This project was aimed at forging a modern Greek identity as imagined by Europe, in one of the most successful experiments in the creation of an artificial capital (Bastea, 2000; Loukaki 2008; Leontidou, 2013).

2. The interwar prototype of Mediterranean fast urbanization: interwar Athens grew rapidly during the 1920s and the 1930s in a spontaneous fashion after the arrival of refugees from Asia Minor in 1922 (Leontidou, 1990/2006).

3. The postwar agglomeration that has definitely not developed out of the ancient city-state: Athens grew by construction through

The expansion of Athens

The planned redevelopment of the early 19th century was overtaken by spontaneous urban development from the beginning of the 20th century. This is evident in piecemeal urban expansion, mixed land use, and social segregation which is vertical as well as horizontal, and has created a cityscape that is antithetical to the Anglo-American one, as workers and the poor live on the urban periphery. Popular suburbanization and semi-squatting solved problems of homelessness and unemployment, even if temporarily, for the better part of the 20th century.

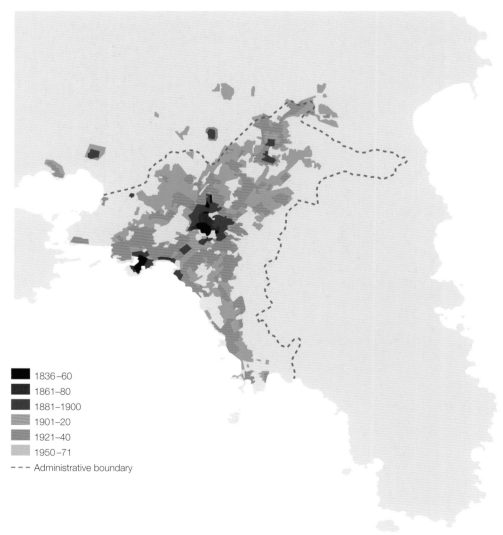

- ■ 1836–60
- ■ 1861–80
- ■ 1881–1900
- 1901–20
- 1921–40
- 1950–71
- – – – Administrative boundary

Athens urban residential area

Source: Leontidou-Emmanuel (1981)

destruction of its neoclassical heritage and many layers of history. It has been living its own history, retaining a postmodern collage in its landscape of spontaneous urbanization and informality (Leontidou, 1990/2006).

4. The post-Olympic entrepreneurial city of the new millennium: Athens entered global neoliberal urban competition, trying to attract mega-events and restructure its image with a combination of innovative urban design and postmodernity, on the one hand, and the valorization of the heritage of past ages, on the other. Athens clumsily adopted entrepreneurial city marketing in pursuit of mega-events for almost two decades, starting in the 1990s (with the unsuccessful bid for the 1996 "Golden Olympics" to "return to their homeland"), and culminating with the 2004 Olympics (Couch et al., 2007; Leontidou, 2013).

5. The debt crisis: the fourth period ended abruptly and Athens fell into the abyss of the debt crisis and urban degeneration, which has continued until today, when its population has declined. Outward movement to villages and the "brain drain" abroad have caused disurbanization and a sharp decline in the urban core, which suffers from blight, immiseration, and political upheaval. This brought to life the Athenian public spaces during the "movement of the piazzas" in the 2010s, which revived the spontaneity and direct democracy of the ancient Greek *agora* (Leontidou, 2012).

In the European imagination, and even the global one, Athens remains the essence of civilization in the abstract sense, but only on the basis of antiquity. Today's city is not considered up to the standards of European modernity and has become victim to a peculiar Orientalism emerging in northern Europe. In the neoliberal imagination, Athens is no longer a foundational city.

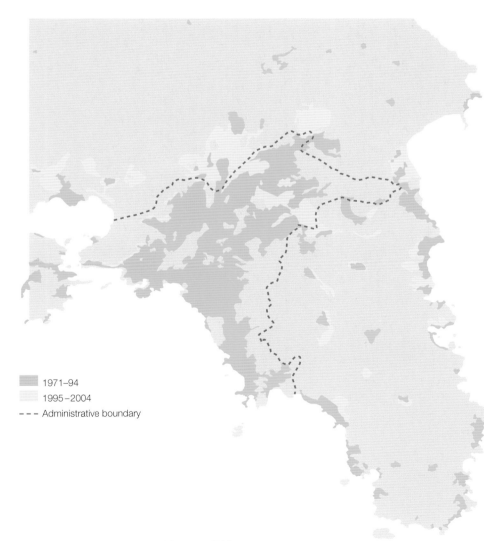

1971–94

1995–2004

– – – Administrative boundary

Sources: Leontidou-Emmanuel (1990, 2006), Couch et al. (2007)

Olympic stadium designed by Santiago Calatrava

Students protest against austerity measures outside Athens University in 2013

A city in decline?

A major transition in the development of Athens occurred with the 2004 Olympics. By 2001 Greater Athens had attracted 3,187,734 inhabitants (29 percent of the Greek population), most of whom were internal migrants. After this the city stopped growing. The population in 2011 had dropped to 3,122,540 inhabitants (28.9 percent of Greece), and this reduction was focused on the urban core, one-third of its population since EU accession (885,737 inhabitants in 1981) and remained at 467,108 inhabitants in 2011. The financial crisis curbed urbanization and the real estate bubble, but urban sprawl continued.

Rome: From Huts to New Towns

Town planning

*Roman society was a society of go-getters and builders. The blueprint of Roman urban planning was the "grid," grounded on the north/south and east/west main streets (*cardo *and* decumanus*) originally based on the* castrum, *the army camp often built by the* milites *themselves.*

A crucial mobilizing factor for Roman society was the *inclusive* character of an in-migrant society of people from different ethnic backgrounds. The kings of Rome were from the surrounding cities, the last three being Etruscans, and Rome was one of a cluster of settlements. The inclusive hybrid principle was a strength of Roman society, similar *mutatis mutandis* to the North American one. It accounted for the extraordinary transformative capacity displayed by Roman civilization over its long history from 759 BCE, the foundation of Rome, to 476 CE, the fall of the Western Roman Empire.

Rome developed from the original small settlement of outlaws in the wetlands around the River Tiber to the opulent global capital of one of the largest empires of world history, with a powerful capability in architecture and the planning of public places. The accumulation of building material in Rome (as well as in other cities) was so huge that it fueled urban building and rebuilding through the centuries. Romans were builders and organizers, with skills and effective mobilizing capacity, which included the ability to subjugate entire populations, exterminate opponents, but also to establish a complex system of relations with allies (*socii*) playing skillfully with different degrees of integration in the Roman *civitas*. This mobilizing

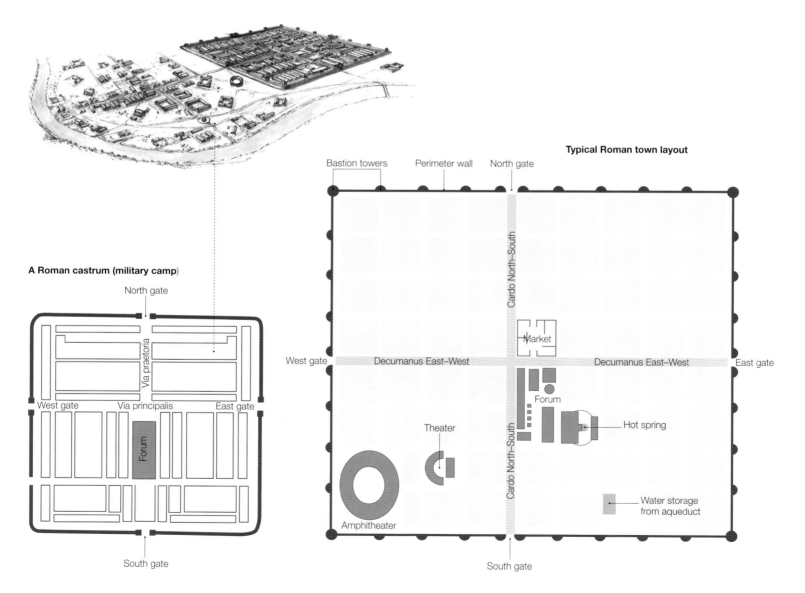

A Roman castrum (military camp)

North gate

Via praetoria

West gate — Via principalis — East gate

Forum

South gate

Typical Roman town layout

Bastion towers   Perimeter wall   North gate

Cardo North–South

Market

West gate — Decumanus East–West   Decumanus East–West — East gate

Forum

Theater

Hot spring

Cardo North–South

Amphitheater

Water storage from aqueduct

South gate

capacity was reflected in the sustainability of the Roman economy, through the construction of important infrastructures, roads, bridges, aqueducts, but also in the greater communicative power and diffuse literacy of the Roman world. It translated also into the generalized importance of the Roman rule of law, the monumentality of Roman public spaces, and, last but not least, the military organization that provided the material leverage for the transformation of Rome from local power to global city (caput mundi).

The concentration of power and wealth which derived from imperial expansion brought with it riches, but also tensions. In addition to slaves, the domestic economy needed a growing number of service classes of artisans, merchants, providers, go-betweens, and workers in transportation, which also meant a substantial animal population to be fed and taken care of. These developments put pressure on the poorer parts of the city, the insulae, with relatively high-rise, dense, and unsanitary buildings. As wealth increased, and Rome became dense and noisy, dirty and dangerous, the upper classes moved out to provincial towns like Pompeii or villas in the surrounding areas, including fairly distant islands like Ventotene where Augustus had an imperial residence (Martinotti, 2009, 2012).

Roman society believed in planting its imprint wherever possible. The concept of potestas romana found its counterpart in the architectural and monumental standardization of a vast area of urban settlements. It is strange that a civilization that was so ruthless in quashing revolts, and so firm in providing a common model, was on the other hand flexible in letting the locals govern themselves. This was part of their inclusive pragmatism, which gave the Romans strength and resilience.

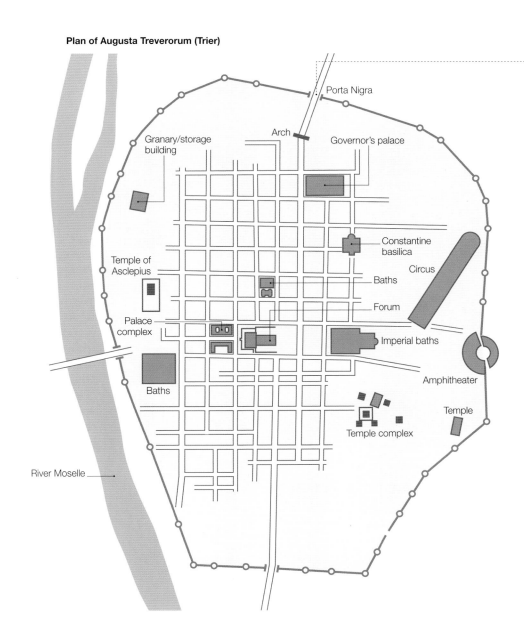

Plan of Augusta Treverorum (Trier)

Porta Nigra
Arch
Granary/storage building
Governor's palace
Temple of Asclepius
Constantine basilica
Circus
Baths
Forum
Palace complex
Imperial baths
Baths
Amphitheater
Temple
Temple complex
River Moselle

Porta Nigra

Roman Trier (Augusta Treverorum)

This Roman city grid can still be seen as the basis of the semis urbain of large parts of Europe: Naples, Pompeii, Syracuse, Mediolanum, Augusta Taurinorum (Turin), and Augusta Praetoria (Aosta) in Italy, Saguntum, Augusta Treverorum (Trier), Lutetia, Massalia, Aix-en-Provence, Bath, Alba Iulia in Romania, and literally hundreds of other places (sometimes difficult to identify because of changes of name) as far as Apamea or Palmyra in Syria.

Organization of the Built Environment

The generative capacity of the Roman civilization is evident in its organization of the built environment. One of the bulwarks of Roman power was extraordinary skill in public works. Ancient societies were by no means backward from the technological point of view. Roman aqueducts are a feat of planning and construction and the system of imperial roads is still the backbone of modern transportation beyond the Italian peninsula. Some of the Roman bridges withstood millennia of use. Not surprisingly the major

religious authority, the *Pontifex*, was literally a "bridge builder," probably more in the physical than in the symbolic sense. The building capacity shared synergies with military power and military personnel, and the rank and file of the army participated in civil building works.

Roman temples were a landmark in all cities and they still provide the foundation above which Christianity built its churches and basilicas. The Duomo in Ortigia (Syracuse) is but one of many cases in which the original

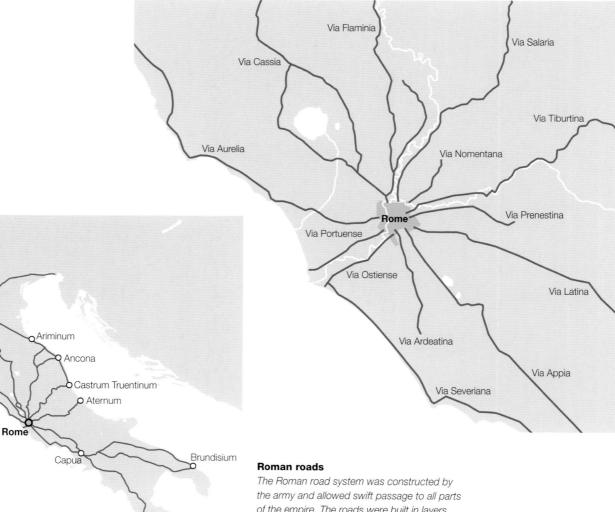

Roman roads

The Roman road system was constructed by the army and allowed swift passage to all parts of the empire. The roads were built in layers of graded materials and surfaced with cobbles or gravel. The surface was cambered to drain water away into side channels so that the roads could be used in all weathers. Mileposts were set up every 1,000 paces, and were frequently inscribed with the distance to Rome.

temple dedicated to Athena evolved into a Catholic cathedral and then an Arab mosque.

Anthropologists have underlined the importance of rites for social cohesion. The Romans were not an austere people: *otium*, the reflexive leisure of the upper classes, and *thermae*, the bath system open to everyone, were basic parts of urban life. The *circus* or *arena* was the major collective landmark of all the Roman cities, as the theater was in Greek ones. Eating well was valued. The populace had bread, though maybe not much else, although wine was always present in a land originally called *Enotria*, the land of wine. The upper classes had the banquet, derived from or kin to the Greek *symposium*, but much more opulent. The relation between the original frugality (bread, cheese, and onions) of a pastoral society that characterized the first centuries and the growing centrality of the luxury connected with leisure was a matter of debate, probably in large part ideological, between the *laudatores temporis actis* ("praisers of times past") and those who embraced new opulent habits. This public debate was accompanied by transformations in the urban landscape, with ever more splendid monuments and *fora*, temples and services like the *thermae* were supplied for private, but also public use, somewhat regulated in their use by different sexes. Mass leisure in the form of *circenses*, or performances in the arenas, became part of the welfare needed to keep the populace happy and quell social tensions. Roman aqueducts throughout Europe, from Britain to Greece, witness the technological sophistication of the Roman Empire. Baths were dense in the cities. The suburban *thermae* recently excavated in Pompeii by Luciana Jacobelli are a good example of the expansion of these ludic activities.

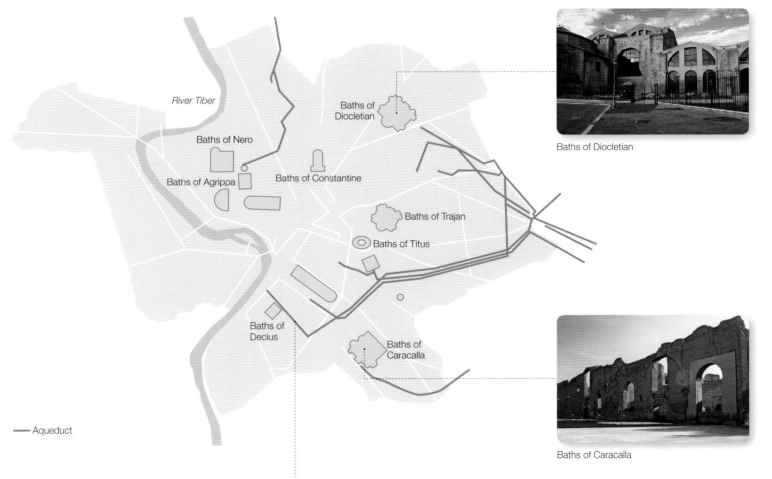

River Tiber

Baths of Diocletian

Baths of Nero

Baths of Constantine

Baths of Agrippa

Baths of Trajan

Baths of Titus

Baths of Decius

Baths of Caracalla

—— Aqueduct

Baths of Diocletian

Baths of Caracalla

Aqueduct

Baths and aqueducts

By the 5th century CE Rome had 11 monumental thermae, built by a succession of emperors. More than just a place to wash, the Roman bath was an important social center where people would come to relax and meet friends. Even the poorest could afford the nominal charge to use the baths, and they played a significant role in spreading Roman culture. The Baths of Caracalla could hold 1,500 people and they used around 4 million gallons of water each day.

Roma caput mundi:
The First Global City

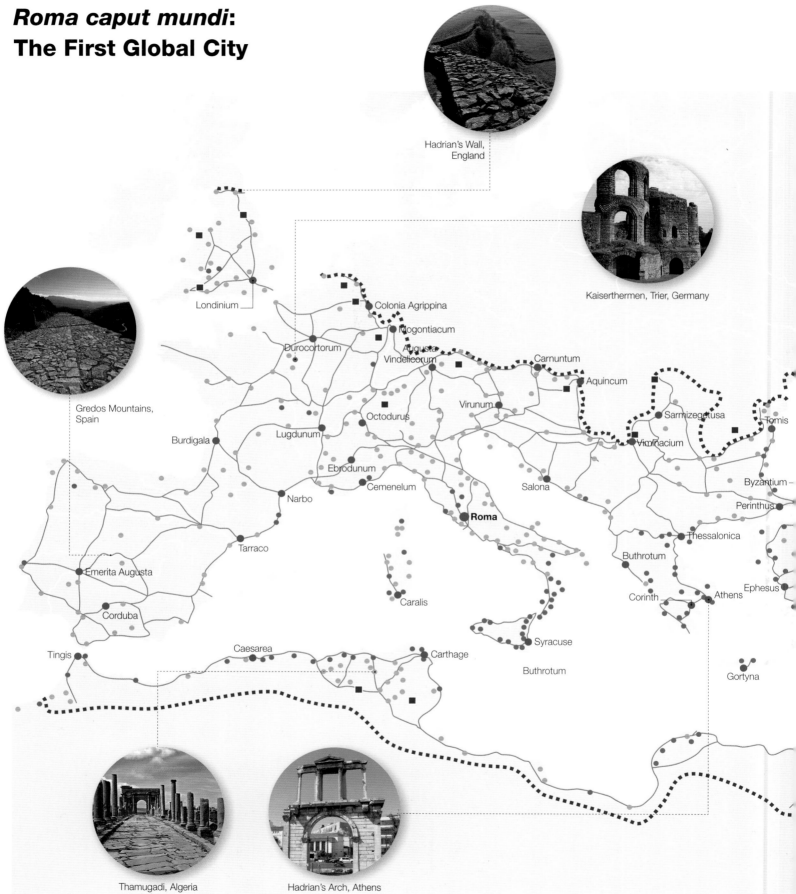

Hadrian's Wall, England

Kaiserthermen, Trier, Germany

Gredos Mountains, Spain

Londinium

Colonia Agrippina

Mogontiacum

Durocortorum

Augusta Vindelicorum

Carnuntum

Aquincum

Virunum

Octodurus

Sarmizegetusa

Tomis

Burdigala

Lugdunum

Ebrodunum

Viminacium

Byzantium –

Cemenelum

Salona

Perinthus

Narbo

Roma

Thessalonica

Buthrotum

Tarraco

Emerita Augusta

Caralis

Corinth

Athens

Ephesus

Corduba

Buthrotum

Tingis

Caesarea

Carthage

Gortyna

Syracuse

Thamugadi, Algeria

Hadrian's Arch, Athens

It may sound preposterous to equate present-day globalization with the Roman Empire centered around the Mediterranean *Mare nostrum*. However, the "megasystème" of Roman dominance was based not only on material power but also on the immaterial or organizational prowess that created the necessary ruling capacity. Roman dominance spread from the network of Roman centers at the apex, through the flows of communications and transportation, the location of specialized centers and their strategic importance, the location of major hinterland resources (agricultural, mining, and others), but above all through an efficient system of norms and practices that provided both the means to control internal social conflicts and long-lasting institutional arrangements for decision making. Allowing for differences of scale, this is not dissimilar from aspects of contemporary globalization (Martinotti, 1993).

Communications and logistical support were provided by the network of roads that accompanied the expansion of Roman power, and the speed of armies' transfer was regulated by the Roman martial pace. Communication was essential for Roman organization and culture, not only among different citizens, but also between the capital city and each town of the complex network of centers that constituted the Roman system. Roads were used for conveying messages, but other types of

communications were also known, such as an ingenious system of optical relays. Written messages circulated among the aristocratic classes, but domestic slaves in charge of administration were also literate, and women were entrusted with the formal education of the youngsters. The "tablet" was an essential device almost as it is now, though in clay rather than touchscreen form.

With the development of an imperial centralized power, begun by Augustus, the bureaucratic organization in Rome became increasingly important, and the number of norms and regulations promulgated by the emperor and his offices grew. These came to constitute a huge corpus that later had to be reorganized systematically together with the general *corpus juris romani*. The written legal system of norms provided a systematic and detailed description of social interactions of all sorts, and an understanding of their sociological meanings. This legal system had to be sustained by a consistent apparatus of judges, lawyers, law enforcers, bureaucrats, and the particular and important profession of the *jureconsulti*, private experts who counseled in law and who provided legal support to elected magistrates and later on to the *princeps*. The legal system with its elaborate sociology provided an important collective organizational knowledge passed on from generation to generation, and was in itself a substantial part of the literacy that characterized Roman culture and gave enormous strength to its economic and administrative organizations. The public spaces where these activities took place were part of the monumentality of the Roman city.

An ancient superpower

The Roman Empire developed an admirable network of towns, with hierarchies of major centers, regional capitals, and other cities. This was held together by advanced transport and communications. Monuments throughout Europe and West Asia bear witness to the global expansion of the Roman civilization.

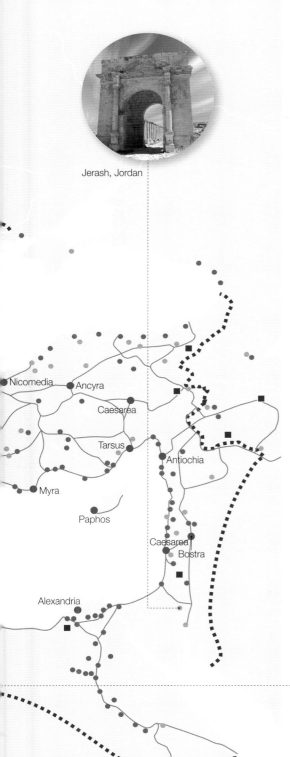

Jerash, Jordan

Aphrodisias, Turkey

- ● Imperial capital
- ● Provincial capital
- ● Roman-founded cities
- ■ Main legionary encampment
- ● Pre-Roman cities
- —— Road
- ▪▪▪▪ Extent of imperial frontier

Sources: Wikimedia (Andrei Nacu), Benvolo (1993), Pounds (1990/2007)

Cradles of Urbanism: Colonies and Capitals

Ancient civilizations were associated with urbanism and the sea. They had been remarkably urban since the pre-classical period, and several European concepts, ideas, and life patterns were conceived within their walls. Athens and Rome developed in an area marked by substantial existing urban civilizations, from the Mycenaean in the Peloponnese to the Phoenician in Carthage, from the Ionian in the Aegean to *Magna Graecia* in southern Italy and the Etruscan in central-northern Italy. Cosmopolitanism and learning created a rich culture in several cities, which were by no means "secondary," except perhaps from our modern perspective. They were significant in their own right, and challenged Athens and Rome in different respects.

The myth of Europa, the Phoenician princess abducted by Zeus in the form of a bull, which for millennia stirred popular imaginations in Greece and the Roman Empire, recognizes that civilization came to Greece from the Orient, from Phoenicia and beyond, and flourished first in Crete, in the Minoan cities. This was the advanced Bronze Age civilization in Europe, established about 5,000 years ago, and based on the civic center of Knossos, a palace-city without walls because it was naturally fortified.

Ancient civilizations of the Mediterranean

There were a number of centers of civilization around the Mediterranean apart from Rome and Athens, some of which were arguably as significant in laying the foundations of modern urbanism. The cities shown here flourished before the 8th century BCE, with the exception of Alexandria (since 331 BCE) and Constantinople (between 395 and 1453 CE, previously Byzantium).

Urban civilizations and areas of influence 1800–600 BCE

- Minoans c. 27th–15th centuries BCE
- Mycenaeans c. 16th–10th centuries BCE
- Cities of *Magna Graecia* 8th century BCE
- Ionian cities and Aegean islands 7th–6th centuries BCE
- Greek colonies in the Western Mediterranean 6th century BCE
- —— Macedonia 4th century BCE

Massalia (Marseille)

Naples

Mediterranean Sea

Messina

Syracuse

Mediterranean Sea

Minoans—
Knossos Palace in Crete

Mycenae—
The Lion Gate

Ionian cities and Aegean islands—
Temple of Apollon, Didyma
(present-day Turkey)

These undefended Minoan palace-cities were eventually conquered by the Mycenaeans, who by 1450 BCE controlled the Aegean archipelago as far as Troy. They were based in important cities of the Peloponnese like Argos, Mycenae, Epidaurus, and Corinth, and flourished until 1200 BCE. Then they collapsed, along with the Aegean civilizations, possibly as a result of natural disaster such as a volcanic eruption, or from wars.

The period between the 13th and the 9th centuries BCE is lost in the dark ages between the decline of the civilization around the Aegean archipelago and the beginnings of the classical period. During the 8th century BCE a first scientific revolution took place in constellations of glamorous Ionian cities, the port cities on the shores of Asia Minor, and the nearby Aegean islands, where Greeks had established colonies: Melitos, Efesos, Alikarnasos, Amaseia, and cities of the Aegean islands such as Samos, Lesbos, Kos, and Rhodes. On mainland Greece there was Athens but also Sparta, the other pole of urban structure, based on military power.

Greek colonies were also established as towns of *Magna Graecia*—south Italy and Sicily (Syracuse, Agrigentum, Messina)—and farther from those, in southern France (Marseilles) and eastern Spain, up to Gibraltar. But the really glamorous major cities were in the eastern Mediterranean: Babylon, the celebrated Mesopotamian city; Alexandria, established in Egypt in 331 BCE as one of several new cities of the same name by Alexander the Great and outshining the Macedonian capitals of Aegae (today associated with Vergina), Pella, and Dion as an uncontested center of knowledge; and Constantinople, the earlier Byzantium, re-established in 395 CE as the capital of the East Roman Empire, and called simply Polis, i.e. the City; its later Turkish name, Istanbul, is derived phonetically from the Greek "*is tan Polin*," "to the City."

Magna Graecia
Temple of Concord, Agrigento

Babylon
Ishtar Gate

Alexandria
sphinx statue on the hill

Constantinople
Golden Gate

Black Sea

Constantinople

Aegae (Vergina)

Lesbos

Troy

Samos

Amaseia

Mycenae

Corinth

Epidaurus

Ephesus

Miletus

Halicarnassus

Argos

Knossos

Kos

Rhodes

Crete

Cyprus

Mediterranean Sea

Babylon

Alexandria

Sources: Leontidou (2011), Demand (1990), Dimitrakos & Karolides (1950s)

THE NETWORKED CITY

RAF VERBRUGGEN

MICHAEL HOYLER

PETER TAYLOR

Core cities

AUGSBURG _____

LONDON _____

VENICE _____

FLORENCE _____

INNSBRUCK _____

LÜBECK _____

BRUGES _____

PARIS _____

GHENT _____

Left: Bruges, Belgium

The Networked City: Introduction

After the demise of the western Roman Empire in the 5th century, urban growth came to a standstill in most parts of western Europe. Only in the course of the 11th century did a new phase of urbanization begin. Although improvements in agriculture played a significant part in this urban renewal, it was primarily the revival of trade—especially with the more developed and urbanized economies of the Near East in the wake of the crusades—that caused cities to spring up again in many parts of Europe. The development of strong trade links between the cities of Latin Christian Europe (which were further intensified as a consequence of the commercial revolution of the 13th century) warrants the introduction of a specific typology to describe the late medieval and 16th-century European city: the networked city.

The cities of late medieval Europe were, of course, not the only ones that could be branded as networked cities. In the history

The principal Old World trading circuits around 1300

During the late medieval period, western Christian Europe was not isolated from the rest of the world. Various goods (including spices, silk, and precious metals) were regularly exchanged between Asia, Europe, and Africa, and from c. 1500 also with the Americas. However, until the discovery of direct sea routes to Asia (and America) at the end of the 15th century, late medieval merchants rarely traveled all the way between China and Europe (although there were exceptions, such as Marco Polo). Until then, the Old World trade network was divided into a number of overlapping commercial circuits which were dominated by particular groups of merchants (among them Chinese, Mongol, Indian, Persian, Arab, and European traders). The westernmost of these circuits, which at that time was not the most urbanized or economically advanced part of the Old World network, was controlled by different groups of Latin Christian traders.

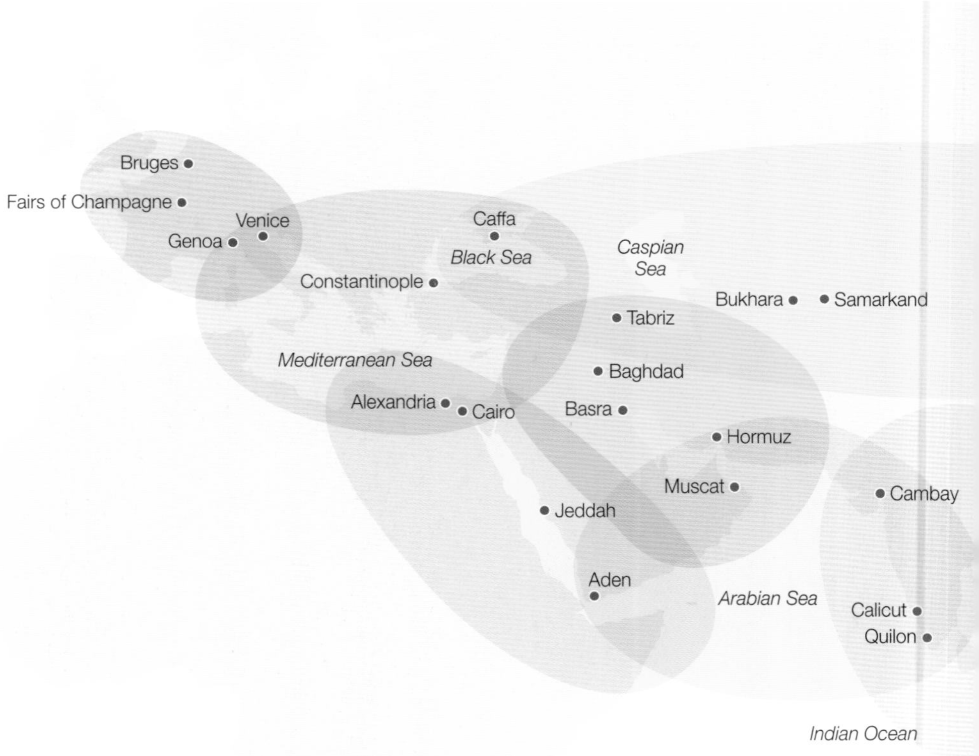

Western European circuit
Trans-Mediterranean circuit
Central Asian caravan circuit
Persian Gulf circuit
Red Sea circuit
Western Indian Ocean circuit
Central Indian Ocean circuit
Eastern Indian Ocean circuit

Source: Abu-Lughod (1989)

> **"From the 11th century, the cities of Latin Christian Europe became progressively connected in a Europe-wide trading network."**

of urbanism, myriad examples can be found of cities that had strong interconnections. In fact, the first known cities appear to have been linked together in dynamic trading networks. The geographer Ed Soja has described an early city network in the Ancient Near East, stretching across a T-shaped region from western Anatolia to the upper reaches of the Tigris and southward into the southern Levant between 9000 and 5000 BCE, including settlements such as Jericho, Çatal Hüyük, and Abu Hureyra. Another example is the silk road, with its various and changing routes connecting east, south,

and western Asia with Mediterranean Europe and north and east Africa from the late 3rd century BCE until c. 1400 CE, when the rise of sea trade diminished its importance.

These examples are by no means exceptional, and one could reasonably argue that all cities past and present are networked in one way or another. In fact, it is a generic characteristic of cities to be connected with the outside world, and this occurs through two different but related urban processes. The first defines how urban settlements are connected at the local level with a hinterland to which they provide central goods and services. The medieval towns of Europe, for instance, acted as commercial, administrative, religious, or educational centers, not only for their own inhabitants but also for those of the surrounding smaller towns, villages, and countryside. Many towns hosted weekly markets where a variety of regionally produced goods could be purchased. Some featured as the seats of princely or episcopal courts. A minority of big European cities (such as Florence, Venice, or Milan) even established formal political control over their hinterlands and developed into independent city-states.

The relations between such central places and their service areas are vertical in nature and typically generate a settlement hierarchy. This process has been called *town-ness*.

The second process determines how cities are linked with each other beyond their hinterlands by means of a mutual exchange of goods, capital, information, and so on, creating horizontal rather than vertical inter-urban relations. The result of this process, which has been termed *city-ness*, is not a settlement hierarchy but a city network. Thus, from the 11th century, the cities of Latin Christian Europe became progressively connected in a Europe-wide trading network through a variety of long-distance flows consisting of travelers, trade goods, money, letters, etc. This incipient city network was originally structured around two core zones, the commercial and banking centers of north-central Italy and the textile-producing cities of the southern Low Countries, which were connected through the great trading fairs of Champagne in northeastern France. These indirect links through France transmuted into direct links with the opening of a maritime route between Italy and Bruges and a more easterly route via the southern German cities, which resulted in the decline of the Champagne fairs around 1300. Another fundamental change took place in the 16th century, when the center of gravity within the European city network shifted toward northwestern Europe. One can conclude that in contrast to *town-ness* (which is a stable and static process), *city-ness* is very dynamic and prone to change.

Although *city-ness* will be the focus of this chapter, it should not be forgotten that *city-ness* and *town-ness* are not mutually exclusive but can and do occur in one and the same place at the same time: virtually every node in the late medieval European city network simultaneously featured as a central place for a hinterland. However, *city-ness* is relatively more important for understanding the economic dynamics of late medieval and 16th-century Europe.

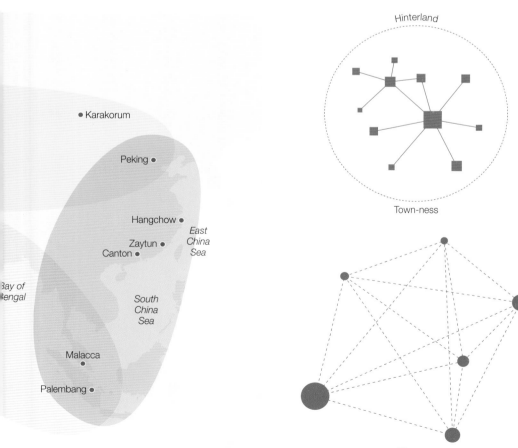

Hinterland

Town-ness

City-ness

Town-ness and city-ness
Cities are connected to the outside world through two generic processes, town-ness *and* city-ness, *that can and do occur simultaneously in one and the same place.* Town-ness *produces hierarchical, local, and rather static urban–hinterland relations, which traditionally have been described by central place theory.* City-ness, *on the other hand, generates dynamic, non-local inter-urban network relations, which have gained a lot of attention in contemporary global cities research.*

The Commercial Revolution of the 13th Century

In the course of the 13th century, a new way of organizing long-distance trade simultaneously developed in the networked cities of Italy and the Baltic, spreading to the rest of Latin Christian Europe during the following centuries. Before this so-called commercial revolution the European merchant typically was a traveling merchant, moving back and forth between different markets in order to purchase and sell merchandise. However, during the 13th century the merchants of Italy and the Baltic increasingly became sedentary, exchanging trade goods via their representatives who were established in various other European cities, thereby interlocking these cities into a city network through their commercial practices.

Although travel remained important, the commercial revolution broadly resulted in two types of medieval business organizations, which dominated European trade from the late 13th century to the end of the 16th century. On the one hand, in the inland cities of Italy and southern Germany a type of hierarchical company developed which in some cases could become very large by medieval

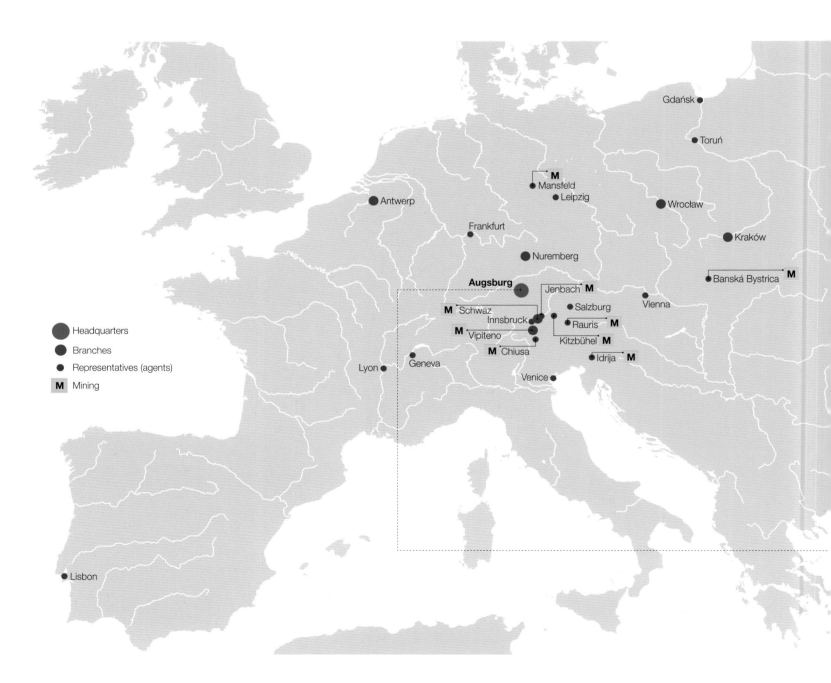

Headquarters

Branches

Representatives (agents)

M Mining

standards (firms such as the Bardi, Peruzzi, and Medici of Florence, or the Fugger and Welser of Augsburg, all had more than sixty employees). These hierarchical firms established branches or factors abroad which were directed from and employed by the headquarters.

On the other hand, in the maritime harbors of the Mediterranean, Atlantic, North Sea, and Baltic a countless number of small, flexible, and more network-like business organizations could be found, which were held together by mutual trust between the members. Some of these networks consisted of rather informal family partnerships with different family members residing in different cities, while others were formed of firms or individual merchants making use of correspondents abroad working for a commission. Of course many intermediate forms between these two prototypes existed.

One of the reasons for the transition from the traveling merchant to the sedentary merchant was the growing political power of the merchants in their home towns, which necessitated their presence at home in order to take care of local city politics. It resulted, however, in a more efficient organization of long-distance commerce in Europe, and in a progressive strengthening and expansion of the European city network. For more than three centuries European trade was organized according to the foundations laid during the 13th-century commercial revolution. It was not until the end of the 16th century that joint-stock companies such as the Dutch and English East India companies arose as a new type of business organization and again changed the nature of European long-distance trade.

The firm of Matthias Manlich of Augsburg

Matthias Manlich (1499–1559) was one of the most important merchants of 16th-century Augsburg. His firm traded mostly in copper and other metals, and was directly involved in copper mining thanks to privileges in the mining industry (especially in Tirol), which were obtained in exchange for loans to the Habsburgs. In addition to the headquarters in Augsburg, offices or warehouses of the firm were installed in those centers that were of major importance for the family business (branches probably existed in Antwerp, Nuremberg, Kraków, and Wrocław, the mining towns Schwaz and Vipiteno in Tirol, and perhaps also elsewhere). In many other places, the interests of the Manlich were represented by agents who also worked for other firms or on their own account. In 1581 the firm of Matthias Manlich was dissolved by his heirs.

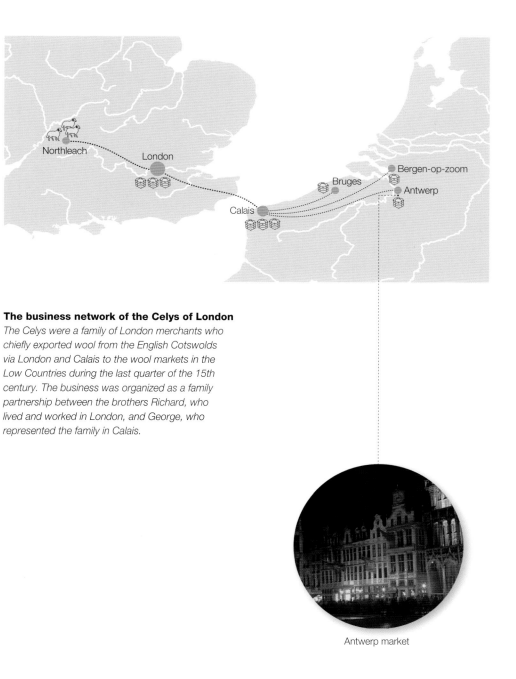

The business network of the Celys of London

The Celys were a family of London merchants who chiefly exported wool from the English Cotswolds via London and Calais to the wool markets in the Low Countries during the last quarter of the 15th century. The business was organized as a family partnership between the brothers Richard, who lived and worked in London, and George, who represented the family in Calais.

Augsburg

Antwerp market

Transport in Late Medieval Europe

Without some sort of transport infrastructure networked cities cannot function properly. Transport is the backbone of a city network, allowing for the traffic of people and goods within as well as between cities. Our present-day global cities are strongly dependent upon airline traffic for maintaining regular connections between them. In late medieval Europe, this was not so different. Cogs, galleys, and various other types of ships sailed from harbor to harbor across the European seas, while transport on the inland waterways, roads, and mountain passes of the

Continent took place via barges, carts, and pack animals. Without these indispensable means of transport, the European cities would have been much more isolated from each other.

By present-day standards, the quality of medieval roads was poor. Moreover, the insecurity of roads and the proliferation of tolls and customs dues were considerable obstacles to overland transport. Nevertheless, especially during the so-called road revolution of the 13th century, improvement works were carried out to many roads and bridges, resulting in a boom in overland transport. During the same period,

Major medieval European cities

This map shows the European cities with a population of 20,000 inhabitants or more around 1400. As can be seen, most of the big cities of Europe at the dawn of the 15th century were situated along the coast or on a navigable river (such as the Rhine, Seine, or Rhône). Many others were located on one or more important land routes. Good transport connections were vital to urban development in late medieval Europe.

Replica of a Hanse cog from 1380

land transport was facilitated by the rise of regional transport services. Such services were organized by local guilds or corporations of carriers and watermen, who often obtained a monopoly over the transport along a specific stretch of road or river, for example from their own town to the next town or port. However, specialized transport firms and long-distance carriers transporting goods over much longer distances emerged only at the end of the 15th century. The carters of Hesse in Germany who transported goods across the entire distance between Antwerp and southern Germany in their four-wheeled Hesse carts are a particularly notable example.

Despite these improvements, overland transport was more costly than maritime transport. Consequently, transport by ship was preferred in late medieval Europe, especially during the 14th and early 15th centuries, when the Hundred Years' War between France and England and the wars on the Italian peninsula made road transport particularly hazardous. By the end of the 15th century, however, overland transport had recovered, while maritime transport—in particular in the Mediterranean—became less and less safe as a result of an increase in piracy, especially between Muslims and Christians, and the conquests of the Ottomans in the eastern

Mediterranean. Piracy was a considerable threat to medieval maritime transport. In order to guarantee some protection against this danger ships often sailed in convoys, especially on long voyages with valuable cargoes. The organization of such convoys was sometimes controlled by the state, as in the case of the galley fleets of the Venetian and Florentine city-states.

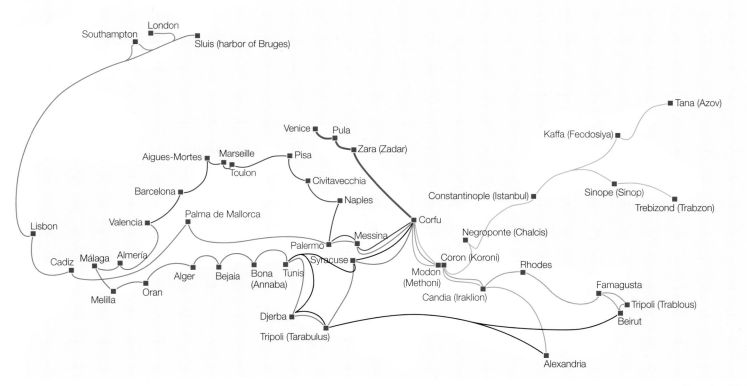

Source: Lane (1973)

Venetian merchant fleets in the 15th century
This map, based on a map by Frederic Lane, shows the extent of the Venetian galley fleets in the 15th century. The system of the galere da mercato came into existence by the end of the 13th century. Originally it was largely organized by private merchants, but from the 1330s it came under the strict control of the Venetian senate, which decided the itinerary of the galleys. The responsibility for navigation and transport of the galleys was auctioned annually by the Venetian state to private entrepreneurs.

—— Galleys of Flanders
—— Galleys of Aigues-Mortes
—— Galleys of Barbary
—— Galleys of Romania
—— Galleys of Beirut
—— Galleys of Alexandria
—— Galleys al trafego
—— Principal Venetian galleys

Late Medieval Communication Technologies

Present-day globalization would be unthinkable without the existence of modern communication technologies. In a similar way the networked cities of late medieval Europe were dependent upon the existence of a communications infrastructure which made it possible to obtain information about what was happening elsewhere in the city network. Governments and businessmen relied on these flows of information in order to make informed decisions.

Long-distance communication between the late medieval networked cities of Europe was based initially on face-to-face contacts, which required travel—often a hazardous and cumbersome undertaking. A valuable alternative to this was the use of postal correspondence. The preserved archives of a number of business companies vividly testify to the crucial role played by correspondence in late medieval society. The business archives of Simon Ruiz, for instance, a 16th-century merchant established in the Castilian town of Medina del Campo, hold about 50,000 letters, while the surviving records of the Tuscan merchant Francesco Datini (c. 1335–1410)

Postal speeds in late medieval Europe

Correspondence did not travel equally fast in all parts of Europe. This table shows the modal travel times in days for more than 200,000 letters sent between twenty of the most important commercial centers of late medieval Europe. Letters traveled faster from Italy to the eastern Mediterranean than to western Europe. On the one hand, this could be explained by differences in physical geography (from Italy, western Europe could only be reached by crossing the Alps or by sailing all the way around the Iberian peninsula, while cities to the east could be reached by direct sea routes). On the other hand, this suggests that communications infrastructures between Italy and the eastern Mediterranean were better developed than those with the west.

	Alexandria	Ancona	Avignon	Barcelona	Bruges	Constantinople	Florence	Genoa	Lisbon	London	Lyon	Palma de Mallorca	Milan	Naples	Palermo	Paris	Pisa	Ragusa (Dubrovnik)	Rome	Venice
Alexandria	0	35		35	60			46				32					40			38
Ancona	35	0		34	28	9						40		7			11	6		4
Avignon			0	8	10		14	9		16	5	10	8	22		9	14		17	16
Barcelona	35	34	8	0	23	41	23	17	24	27	18	2	18	33	33	20	22		30	21
Bruges	60	28	10	23	0	54	27	24	18	6	9	29	22	35		4	25		31	26
Constantinople				41	54	0	45	41					35				42	30		38
Florence		9	14	23	27	45	0			30	16	22	6	12	19	21	2	19	5	6
Genoa	46	9	17	24	41		6	0	32	30	12	20	3	12	15	18	4		18	15
Lisbon				24	18			32	0		20			40		31				
London			16	27	6		30	30		0		34	26	39		10	32		34	33
Lyon			5	18	9		16	12			0		10	26		7	14		17	11
Palma de Mallorca	32	40	10	2	29		22	20	20	34		0	19	27	26	26	19		28	24
Milan			8	18	22		6	3		26	10	19	0	16		16	7		11	4
Naples		7	22	33	35	35	12	12	40	39	26	27	16	0	6	29	14	20	4	15
Palermo				33			19	15				26		6	0		15		16	16
Paris			9	20	4		21	18		10	7	26	16	29		0	20		26	20
Pisa	40	11	14	22	25	42	2	4	31	32	14	19	7	14	15	20	0		8	8
Ragusa (Dubrovnik)		6				30	19							20				0		10
Rome		17	30	31			5	18		34	17	28	11	4	16	26	8		0	10
Venice	38	4	16	21	26	38	6	15		33	11	24	4	15	16	20	8	10	10	0

- 0–5 days
- 6–10 days
- 11–20 days
- 21–30 days
- 31–40 days
- 41–50 days
- 51 or more days

London · Bruges · Paris · Lyon · Milan · Venice · Avignon · Genoa · Florence · Pisa · Ancona · Rome · Naples · Barcelona · Ragusa (Dubrovnik) · Constantinople · Palma de Mallorca · Palermo · Lisbon · Alexandria

contain no fewer than 120,000 letters. Not only was information transferred via mail, but payments could also be carried out through correspondence: credit instruments such as bills of exchange were sent between the financial centers of Europe in the same way as ordinary letters.

The dispatch of letters over land was organized by courier services. From the 1260s onward, evidence can be found for the existence of regular courier services—named *scarselle* after the Italian word for purse— between Tuscany and the fairs of Champagne. Such courier services between different cities were either organized by merchant communities (or even individual firms), cities, religious institutions (such as the Teutonic Order), universities, or states. Postal services organized by the state developed relatively late compared to private initiatives, and their appearance was closely related to the establishment of foreign ambassadors in the 15th century. One of the most extensive postal networks of early modern Europe was created by the Milanese Tassis family for the Habsburg emperor Maximilian I.

At a time when newspapers were non-existent, the letters sent by diplomats or businessmen had a high "news" value, since they contained a lot of information about the political or market situation abroad. With the development of the first handwritten newsletters (such as the Venetian *avvisi*) in the 16th century, knowledge of foreign places improved greatly. Likewise, the correspondence system of the Augsburg Fugger firm developed in the second half of the 16th century into the so-called *Fuggerzeitungen*, providing regular news of economic and political matters for a large readership. These communication infrastructures were essential to the functioning of the networked cities of late medieval Europe.

A German postage stamp depicting the Tassis posthouse in Augsburg

— Primary routes
— Secondary routes

Source: Laveau (1978)

The Tassis postal network

The postal system of the Habsburg emperors was created by the Tassis (or Taxis) family of Bergamo at the end of the 15th century. It was established by Janetto de Tassis in Innsbruck for the German Emperor Maximilian I, and initially connected the Habsburg court to the Burgundian territories of the Habsburgs. Around 1500, the center of the Habsburg postal network was transferred to Brussels by Franz von Taxis, Postmaster-General of Philip the Handsome, who also extended the postal network to Spain and Italy, large parts of which had come under Habsburg control. Unlike the older courier services, the postal services of the Habsburgs were characterized by the establishment of fixed relay stations where horses and even riders could be swapped, whereas couriers used to travel themselves all the way from origin to destination, often on foot rather than on horseback.

The Merchant Nations

The networked cities of late medieval Europe housed a significant number of strangers: vagabonds, students, mendicant friars and other clergymen, traveling craftsmen, foreign merchants, diplomats, soldiers, etc. Some of these were given a hearty welcome by the local population, while others were looked upon with suspicion. Among these strangers, the foreign merchants were among the most numerous and influential. In most cities, fellow merchants originating from the same city or region organized themselves in communities or merchant *nations*.

The nations were extensions abroad of the corporations or guilds of local merchants which existed in many cities and towns of Europe. These associations of merchants were formed in order to promote and protect local trade privileges granted to the members of the corporation and to restrict external competition. Analogously, fellow merchants from a particular city or region staying in the same commercial center abroad began to organize themselves in foreign merchant communities or guilds. These consisted of independent merchants and their families, factors, and apprentices, not only those permanently residing abroad, but also temporary residents and even short-term visitors. In medieval Europe, such merchant guilds were widespread by the 11th century, and perhaps were formed as early as the 8th century. They finally disappeared from most parts of Europe in the late 18th century.

Often foreign merchant communities were rather loose associations, being nothing more than informal gatherings. Sometimes they existed in the form of religious fraternities, whereby the members assembled in the convent of a mendicant order, for example. In several cases, however, foreign merchant communities evolved into more formal

The German Hanse

The German Hanse originated c. 1160 as an association of German merchants who traveled regularly to the island of Gotland in the Baltic Sea. It originally comprised merchants from Lübeck and a number of Westphalian and Saxon cities, but was gradually joined by merchants from the new German cities established in the Slavic lands along the Baltic coast. It is not entirely clear which cities were members of the Hanse, but about 200 cities are known whose citizens could make use of the Hanseatic trade privileges abroad. For a century and a half from the middle of the 14th century the Hanse cities had a near-monopoly on the east–west trade between the Baltic and northwestern Europe, especially trading in furs, amber, and wax from Russia, fish from Norway and Iceland, wool and cloth from Flanders and England, Prussian grain and timber, as well as metals, beer, and salt. Hanseatic merchant communities could be found from Portugal to Russia, with the four Kontore (London, Bruges, Bergen, and Novgorod) being the principal trading partners of the Hanse. Due to increasing competition from southern German and Dutch merchants, the Hanse finally went into decline in the 16th and 17th centuries.

■ Head of the Hanse

● Important Hanse towns

● Kontore (principal foreign trading settlements of the Hanse)

Wool from England

Fish from Norway and Iceland

Grain from Prussia

Fur from Russia

organizations with their own regulations, headed by consuls or aldermen with judicial powers over the members of the community. The consuls were the official representatives of their nation, and they corresponded regularly with the government at home. Some foreign merchant nations, such as those of Venice, stood under the strict control of the mother city, while others (e.g., the Genoese colonies) were relatively independent.

Economically speaking, organization in merchant nations had several advantages. The nations obtained trading privileges and guaranteed solidarity among their members, reducing transaction costs and increasing market power. But nations also had important social, political, cultural, religious, and charitable functions. Merchants of the same nation worshiped together in chapels dedicated to the patron saints of their home town or country (such as Saint Mark for the Venetians, the *Volto Santo* for the Lucchese, Thomas Becket for the

English), and collectively participated in processions and other ceremonies. Finally, belonging to a community of individuals speaking the same language and having the same customs and cultural background gave merchants living abroad a sense of home.

Although foreign merchant communities were from time to time subjected to violence from the local population or from the government, many of these communities were considered to be a normal part of the city. They regularly participated in urban rituals like processions, religious festivities, or royal visits for instance, and in several cases they even took part in the urban politics of their new home town.

At all times successful cities have been cosmopolitan cities, and in medieval Europe this cosmopolitanism was indexed to a large degree by the number and size of nations organized within the city. The nations directly reflected the intensity of a city's external relations, its *city-ness*.

The trade network of the Catalan nation
Although Mediterranean trade in the late Middle Ages was dominated by Italian merchants, the importance of Catalan commerce, especially from Barcelona, cannot be overlooked. From the late 12th century, the principal trade route leaving from Catalonia was directed toward the eastern Mediterranean, from where chiefly spices were imported in exchange for textiles produced in the kingdom of Aragón and elsewhere in western Europe. Other connections, such as those with Flanders, northern Africa, or the western Mediterranean, can be considered as side-tracks from this main route. As long as trade with the eastern Mediterranean remained successful, Catalan commerce in general bloomed (especially between c. 1350 and c. 1435), but the decline of the route to the east in the 15th century also meant the demise of Catalan trade.

Band width approx. 800 miles

◎ Principal Catalan trading center ◉ Other important Catalan trading centers ● Principal destinations of Catalan foreign trade

The Cityscape of the Networked City

Being part of a city network has a strong impact upon the urban landscape of a networked city. The skylines of our contemporary global cities, with their high-rise tower blocks containing the headquarters and offices of multinational companies, are a vivid testimony to this. The cityscapes of the networked cities of late medieval Europe could be equally impressive, and to this day the beauty of the historic centers of cities such as Venice, Florence, Bruges, or Lübeck captures the imagination.

The concentration of international commerce and banking in medieval networked cities generated economic growth and created jobs. Many people were attracted by these opportunities, resulting in rising urban populations, especially from the 11th to the 13th centuries. New residential quarters—often housing poor immigrants—developed on the outskirts of the cities, necessitating the construction of new stretches of city walls. This urban growth could come to a sudden standstill, however, due to disruptions resulting from war, plague, or economic crisis, all of which occurred frequently during the 14th and

The trading quarters of late medieval Bruges
Bruges was the most important commercial metropolis of late medieval northwestern Europe. It was the gateway for textiles produced in the Low Countries, and a meeting place for merchants from northern Europe and the Mediterranean. A large number of foreign merchants resided for shorter or longer periods in the city, preferably in the vicinity of the harbor, which was located along a network of canals northeast of the market (Lange Rei, Goudenhandrei, Spiegelrei, and Kraanrei). In this neighborhood, the different merchant nations also established their nation houses or consulates. For various reasons, most merchant nations left Bruges for Antwerp around 1500.

Nation house of Florence
Used by the Florentines by 1420 at the latest.

Guild house of the brokers
The Bruges brokers played a crucial role in the international trade of the city as intermediaries between foreign merchants of different merchant nations.

Inn "Ter Buerse"
The inn "Ter Buerse" was an important meeting place for the international merchants of Bruges, and a center for trade in bills of exchange.

Nation house of Venice
Used by the Venetian merchant nation by 1397 at the latest.

Nation house of Lucca
Purchased by the Lucchese in 1394.

Nation house of Genoa
Built in 1399. The Genoese were the first Mediterranean nation to sail directly to Flanders around 1277.

Waterhalle (water hall)
The Waterhalle was a building used for loading and unloading of ships and for storage of merchandise. The construction of this building started in 1284.

Stadskraan (crane)
The crane was constructed just before 1292, and was used for loading and unloading of ships.

● Harbor infrastructures
● Commercial infrastructures
● Nation Houses of foreign merchant nations
- - Course of former Kraanrei canal

Nation house of the Basque (or Biscay) merchants
In 1494 the Biscay merchant nation received two houses from the city of Bruges. At the same location, they constructed a new building in the early 16th century.

15th centuries. The effects of these late medieval crises on urban population figures were felt most heavily in those cities that for various reasons lost their central position in the city network.

The cityscape of the late medieval networked city typically included purpose-built public infrastructures such as marketplaces and halls; a harbor infrastructure with canals, quays, and storage spaces; a customs house; a mint; weighing-houses; etc. Often these were impressive constructions meant to display the wealth of the city and its merchant elites. Among the most awe-inspiring of these

buildings were the town halls, from where the commercial elites governed the city. At least as imposing were the gothic churches and cathedrals, the construction of which was regularly sponsored by the merchants. A similar beauty could be found in the private merchant residences, some of which were among the first stone-built houses of the late medieval city.

The presence of foreign merchant communities also left its traces in the cityscape. Foreign merchants of the same merchant nation tended to live together in a particular neighborhood, where they resided in private houses or inns. They gathered in one of the

churches or chapels located in this neighborhood to worship the patron saint of their home town. After a while, the merchant nations began to build or obtain their own nation houses or consulates. In some cities the neighborhoods in which the foreign merchants resided formed separate quarters (called *funduk* in the Islamic ports of the Mediterranean, *fondaco* in Italian, and *Kontor* in German), which sometimes were detached by a wall from the rest of the city. In these quarters they built their own offices, warehouses, quaysides, living quarters, and churches.

Nation house of Castile
The Castilians owned a house here in 1483, probably on the west side of the street. In 1494 they received a new house on the east side. Until 1705 this house retained its function as the Castilian consulate: the Castilians remained much longer in Bruges than the other foreign merchant nations.

Nation house of the English merchants
Although English merchants traded with Bruges during the Middle Ages, it is not certain whether they had a nation house in Bruges before the late 16th century.

Engels Weeghuis (English weighing-house).
First mentioned in 1315. The street in which the Engels Weeghuis was located is still called Engelsestraat (England Street).

Stadswaag (weighing-house)
In the Stadswaag goods were weighed under public scrutiny, in order to promote fairness of trade.

Spaanse Waag (Spanish weighing-house)
Especially used by the Biscay merchants. It was destroyed in 1556 or 1557.

Oosterlingenhuis (nation house of the German Hanse)
The Oosterlingenhuis was used by the German Hanse from 1457. The house was a gift from the city of Bruges.

Tolhuis (toll-house)
At the Tolhuis, customs on interregional and international merchandise were collected.

Nation house of the Portuguese
This house was given by the city of Bruges to the Portuguese in 1494. Soon after, however, the Portuguese left Bruges for Antwerp.

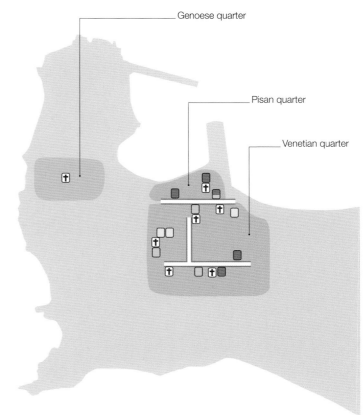

Genoese quarter

Pisan quarter

Venetian quarter

✝ Church

⬛ Merchant lodgings, warehouses, markets

⬜ Public oven

⬜ Bath house

The Venetian, Genoese, and Pisan quarters in 13th-century Tyre
Tyre (in present-day Lebanon) was one of the principal commercial and cultural centers of the crusader kingdom of Jerusalem. The history of the Italian communes in Tyre started with the conquest of the city by the crusaders in 1124. In that year, the Venetians were granted one-third of the territory of the city, together with various legal and commercial privileges, in exchange for their naval support during the conquest. The Pisans and Genoese, who only later obtained autonomous territories in the city, were much less privileged in comparison with the Venetians. The Italian quarters each contained a nation house, one or more churches, private houses, merchant lodgings, warehouses, markets, public ovens, shops, and bath houses. The three quarters were finally lost after the collapse of the crusader states in 1291.

Centers of Production and Consumption

The networked nature of the cities of late medieval Europe found its most clear expression in the domains of trade and banking. Some cities developed into veritable commercial empires, as epitomized by Genoa and Venice with their numerous Mediterranean trade colonies. However, a thriving commerce was not possible without production on the one hand and consumption on the other. Consequently, it should not be a surprise that many of the key cities in the late medieval European city network were also important centers of production and/or consumption.

Many of the commercial and financial capitals of Europe were among the chief centers of production. Florence, for instance, was a considerable producer of a variety of woolen and silk textiles, while Venice produced not only textiles, but also ships, glass, mirrors, and various other luxury goods. However, unlike Florence or Venice, many production centers did not have a strong internationally oriented commercial sector for marketing their products abroad. Instead, their goods were exported through a gateway city that formed the link between the production region and the larger trade network. The textiles produced in the industrial cities and towns of Flanders (for

Legend:
- Wool—international
- Wool—regional
- Specialized linen
- Specialized fustian
- Duchy of Milan c. 1420
- Duchy of Milan c. 1535

The Lombard textile industries between 1350 and 1550

With the exception of the southern Low Countries, north-central Italy was the most important textile-producing region of late medieval Europe. In Lombardy, export-oriented textile production was not limited to its capital Milan, but was dispersed across various cities and towns. Each of these was specialized in the production of one or more particular varieties of linens, fustians, or woolen cloths. A polycentric city-region developed, whereby the bigger cities offered specialized commercial skills and services linking the various industries in the smaller towns to regional and international markets. Similar developments could be observed in other highly urbanized industrial regions including the Low Countries and Swabia.

Source: Epstein (2000)

example Ghent, Ypres, Kortrijk) were exported through Bruges, while the yields of the silver- and copper-mining towns of central Europe (Banská Bystrica, Schwaz, Kutná Hora) passed through gateways such as Nuremberg and Augsburg. Moreover, production was not limited to the big cities: the development of proto-industries in rural and small town settlements was a significant characteristic of the late medieval economy of Europe.

The principal consumption centers of late medieval Europe were the capital cities, where royal and princely courts were significant consumers of luxury goods of all kinds. Moreover, capital cities attracted large numbers of servants, administrators, noblemen, artists, craftsmen, merchants, bankers, and a variety of other people who resided at or worked for the court. As a result, capital cities—such as Paris, London, Venice, Naples, and Prague—were among the biggest cities of late medieval Europe, and these concentrations of population generated particularly high levels of consumption.

The networked cities of late medieval Europe could therefore incorporate a variety of different functions: production, consumption, commerce, education, administration, etc. Sometimes these functions were concentrated in a single metropolis. Sometimes, however, they were dispersed across a number of cities within a region, each with its own specialization. Such regions consisting of one or more industrial cities, commercial gateways, and consumption centers in various constellations, with different cities fulfilling different but complementary functions, can be characterized as polycentric city-regions. Like polycentric metropolises today, these multinodal regions constituted dynamic networks on their own, which on a higher level were linked into the overarching city network.

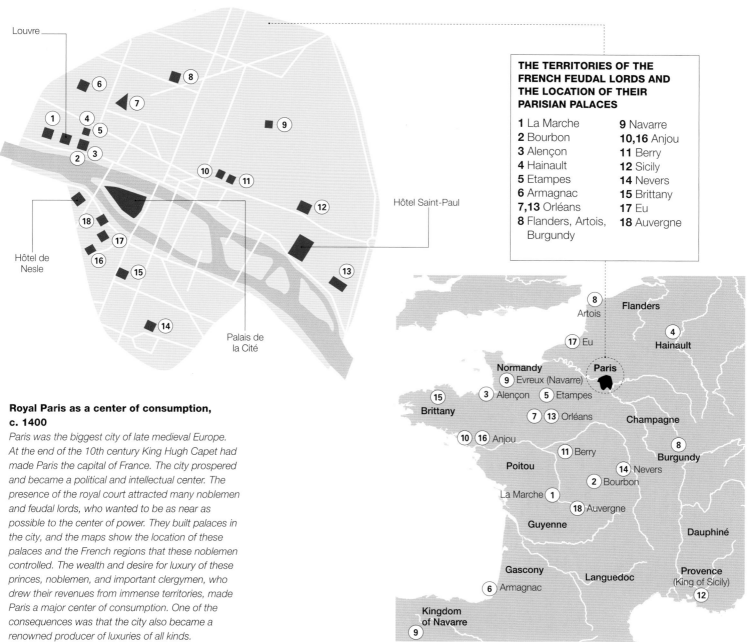

THE TERRITORIES OF THE FRENCH FEUDAL LORDS AND THE LOCATION OF THEIR PARISIAN PALACES

1 La Marche	**9** Navarre
2 Bourbon	**10,16** Anjou
3 Alençon	**11** Berry
4 Hainault	**12** Sicily
5 Etampes	**14** Nevers
6 Armagnac	**15** Brittany
7,13 Orléans	**17** Eu
8 Flanders, Artois, Burgundy	**18** Auvergne

Royal Paris as a center of consumption, c. 1400

Paris was the biggest city of late medieval Europe. At the end of the 10th century King Hugh Capet had made Paris the capital of France. The city prospered and became a political and intellectual center. The presence of the royal court attracted many noblemen and feudal lords, who wanted to be as near as possible to the center of power. They built palaces in the city, and the maps show the location of these palaces and the French regions that these noblemen controlled. The wealth and desire for luxury of these princes, noblemen, and important clergymen, who drew their revenues from immense territories, made Paris a major center of consumption. One of the consequences was that the city also became a renowned producer of luxuries of all kinds.

Source: Spufford (2002)

The Dispersal of Innovations

The existence of a city network with a relatively well-developed transport and communications infrastructure allowed for the exchange of people, goods, money, and information between the cities of the late medieval European network. One tragic marker of the existence of this dense network was the spread of the plague, which was facilitated by these exchanges: in the middle of the 14th century, this devastating epidemic reappeared in Europe via an Italian ship coming from Kaffa in the Crimea, and then spread from the Mediterranean through the rest of the city network to affect almost all of Europe.

A more beneficial effect of the existence of strong interrelations between the networked cities of late medieval Europe was the spread of innovation. Technical innovations and skills in manufacturing, for instance, spread through the permanent migration of skilled craftsmen from one center to another, or circulated between places through the tramping of highly mobile journeymen. The main source of innovation in late medieval Europe was Italy, and many innovations spread across Europe through the migration of Italian technical experts. Examples are the diffusion of public clocks from Italy to the rest of Europe between 1370 and 1500, or the transfer of fustian weaving from northern Italy to upper Germany during the second half of the 14th century.

The spread of the plague
After its disappearance in the 8th century, the plague or Black Death remained absent from Europe for about 600 years. The disease vigorously reasserted its presence in the middle of the 14th century, however. It broke out in 1346 among the troops of a Mongol prince besieging the Genoese trading colony of Kaffa on the Black Sea. The epidemic spread across the city, and from there it was transferred to Genoa by ship in 1347. By June 1348 most of the Mediterranean was affected, and by the end of 1350 the disease had also spread to western and northern Europe. With an estimated average mortality rate of more than 30 percent in Europe between 1346 and 1348, the effects of the Black Death on the European population were enormous. Not all parts of the continent were equally affected, however.

December 1350

June 1350

Dec. 1349

June 1349

December 1348

June 1348

December 1347

Partly or completely plague-free area

The recruitment of foreign technical experts was an established mechanism for transferring technology, and this occurred across territorial and linguistic barriers. Sometimes such migration was forced, however, as in the case of the diaspora to the Protestant areas of Europe of specialized textile artisans from the southern Low Countries during the religious wars of the second half of the 16th century.

Technical knowledge and skills, which were often tacit and as such hard to identify, were also transferred through journeyman tramping. Late medieval and early modern European journeymen were highly mobile. Many of them traveled around in order to gain valuable technical experience before returning home and setting up their own businesses. During

their travels, they worked in one or more workshops, cooperated with other craftsmen, and learned about regional differences in technology and work organization. Especially in the smaller, more specialized crafts, like book binding, belt making, gold beating, and harness making, it was a common practice for journeymen to tramp across long distances. In these economic sectors, a particular city could gain a reputation for technological capital, and become a pole of attraction for journeyman tramping.

According to Jane Jacobs it is thanks to this dispersal of innovations through city networks that economic expansion takes place. Through a mechanism of import replacement local production replaces imports from other cities,

resulting in an expansion of urban economic life based upon a more varied division of labor. Consequently, city networks were—and still are—vital to economic growth.

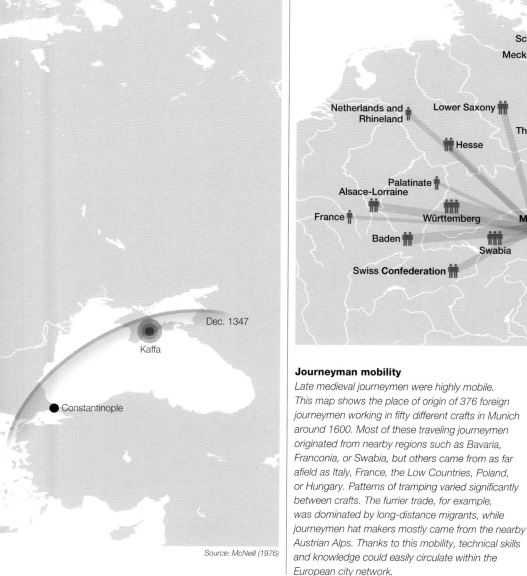

Source: McNeill (1976)

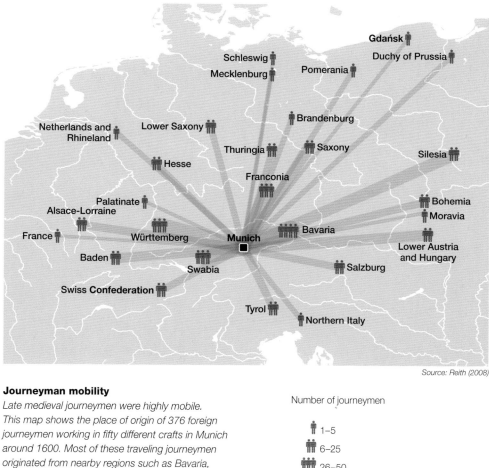

Source: Reith (2008)

Journeyman mobility

Late medieval journeymen were highly mobile. This map shows the place of origin of 376 foreign journeymen working in fifty different crafts in Munich around 1600. Most of these traveling journeymen originated from nearby regions such as Bavaria, Franconia, or Swabia, but others came from as far afield as Italy, France, the Low Countries, Poland, or Hungary. Patterns of tramping varied significantly between crafts. The furrier trade, for example, was dominated by long-distance migrants, while journeymen hat makers mostly came from the nearby Austrian Alps. Thanks to this mobility, technical skills and knowledge could easily circulate within the European city network.

Number of journeymen

1–5
6–25
26–50
51 and above

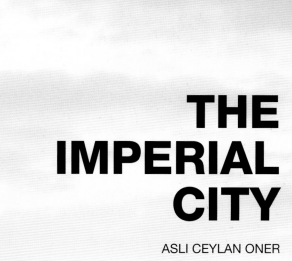

THE IMPERIAL CITY

ASLI CEYLAN ONER

Core city
ISTANBUL _____

Secondary cities
ROME _____
ST. PETERSBURG _____
VIENNA _____
LONDON _____
BEIJING _____
MEXICO CITY _____
MOSCOW _____

Left: Istanbul, Turkey

The Imperial City: Introduction

"Building on their historic significance, imperial cities remain important in the present."

Imperial cities were the epicenters of political, cultural, economic, and military power for the empires they represented, and each had its golden age in accordance with the standing of the empire of which it stood at the head. These cities have provided the setting for victory celebrations, great works of art, and monumental architecture as well as riots, internal political struggles, and war. The intense economic and cultural activity in imperial cities led to innovation and exchange of knowledge and ideas, exemplifying the generative function of cities. Building on their historic significance, imperial cities remain important in the present. Some, such as London, Rome, Amsterdam, Tokyo, Beijing, Madrid, Mexico City, Moscow, and Istanbul, are significant world cities acting as the command and control centers of the global economy. Some former imperial cities have capitalized on their heritage as important historical cultural centers, including St. Petersburg, Kraków, Salzburg, and Kyoto.

Imperial cities are often strategically located for access to, and protection of, major trade routes. In some instances the location of the city required a compromise between strategic advantage and infrastructural challenges. For example, in the case of Rome, although the site offered a protected inland location and access to the sea via the River Tiber, the location also faced problems with water supply, flooding, and river pollution. Mexico City's location in a closed drainage basin surrounded by mountains on the Lake Texcoco always caused flooding problems for the city. In Amsterdam, a major trading port with a booming population after the 17th century, there was a need to develop advanced water management and construction technologies to establish a city around a canal system. In general, access to water, trade routes, and protection are the most important determinants of imperial city locations. Salzburg, Budapest, and Vienna are situated on major rivers that provide trade access. Beijing's imperial city status was advanced by its proximity to the sea. Amsterdam and St. Petersburg are significant port cities and their imperial city status was derived from this.

The growth of a city from a small settlement to a large imperial center often required a remarkable level of planning. Examples of large-scale planning activities to create infrastructure and a grand sense of space in imperial cities include Vienna's 19th-century Ringstrasse, which surrounds historic buildings, open spaces, and monuments; Haussmann's mid-19th-century plan for Paris; the planning of Amsterdam's canals to facilitate trade and protection; and the first permanent bridge over the Danube that links Buda and Pest.

Connected to large-scale planning, monumental buildings and architecture, especially religious buildings and palaces, played a significant role in demonstrating the power of imperial cities. The planning and organization is often oriented toward these buildings. Open spaces and gardens are also

Roman Empire

BRITANNIA
Londinium

GAUL
PANNONIA
AQUITANIA
DACIA
DALMATIA
Italia   *Black Sea*
Rome   Thrace   **Byzantium**
HISPANIA   Pontus
LUSITANIA   ARMENIA
Athens   Pergamum   CAPPADOCIA
Carthage   MESOPOTAMIA
NUMIDIA   Syracuse   CYPRUS
Mediterranean Sea
Cyrene   Babylon
CYRENAICA   Jerusalem
Alexandria
EGYPTUS

Extent of Roman Empire 117 CE

important elements that reflect the ideals of imperial cities. The Baroque gardens in Vienna and Salzburg are as impressive as their royal palaces and concert halls.

Imperial cities were the focus of political and military conflicts. Since these cities defined strategic locations as well as being command and control centers, their conquest mostly brought about the demise of their empires. Imperial cities had cosmopolitan populations from many different ethnic and religious backgrounds. Different religious groups maintained their own traditions, but sometimes this created struggle and internal conflicts. Today, former imperial cities have become important world cities with cosmopolitan populations. Their density and large population have a major transformative impact on their national and regional cultures. Imperial cities still carry the traces of history in their physical, economic, social, and cultural environments.

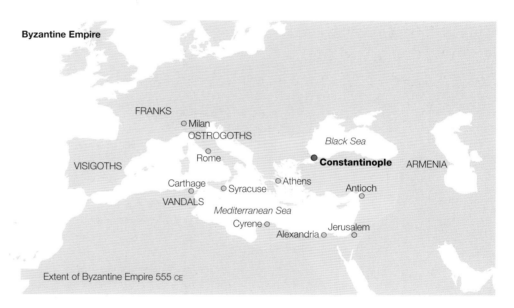

Byzantine Empire

FRANKS
Milan
OSTROGOTHS
Black Sea
Rome
VISIGOTHS   **Constantinople**   ARMENIA
Carthage   Athens
VANDALS   Syracuse   Antioch
Mediterranean Sea
Cyrene
Jerusalem
Alexandria

Extent of Byzantine Empire 555 CE

Commanding three empires

As a former imperial center, Istanbul offers an interesting case study of the framework of the imperial city. For almost two millennia Istanbul has been a global center. It was the imperial capital of the Roman, Byzantine, and Ottoman Empires for more than 1,700 years, and today it is the economic capital of the Turkish Republic. Istanbul was initially designed by Constantine the Great to be a world center, and today, with a population of around 11 million, Istanbul is the largest metropolis in Turkey and the only city that serves as a bridge between Europe and Asia. Istanbul is currently rebuilding its glory as a global city, while its imperial past still has an important impact on its urban development.

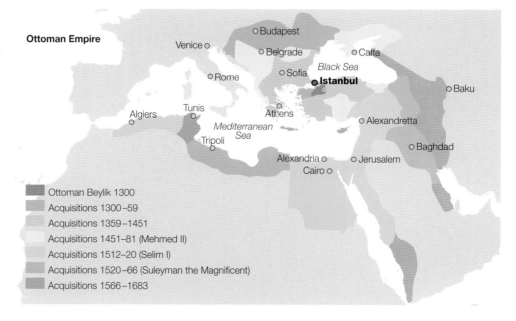

Ottoman Empire

Budapest
Venice
Belgrade   Caffa
Black Sea
Sofia
Rome   **Istanbul**
Baku
Algiers   Tunis   Athens
Alexandretta
Mediterranean Sea
Tripoli
Baghdad
Alexandria
Jerusalem
Cairo

Ottoman Beylik 1300
Acquisitions 1300–59
Acquisitions 1359–1451
Acquisitions 1451–81 (Mehmed II)
Acquisitions 1512–20 (Selim I)
Acquisitions 1520–66 (Suleyman the Magnificent)
Acquisitions 1566–1683

Byzantium: Foundations of an Imperial City

One of the common elements of imperial cities is the significance of their location. Factors such as easy access, protection, and control of important trade routes have defined the locations of imperial cities throughout history. Imperial cities like London, Amsterdam, and Rome are all strategically located according to these ideals, and Istanbul is no exception. Istanbul was founded as the city of Byzantium on Seraglio Point by the Greek colony of Megarian Dorians in the 7th century BCE. The colony consulted the Oracle at Delphi about where to locate their new city. At that time, there was also a city on the opposite shore of the Marmara Sea called Chalcedon (present-day Kadikoy). It was known as the "city of the blind" because it had overlooked the valuable location of Seraglio Point.

The city's name was derived from the leader of the colony, Byzas. The ancient Greek city of Byzantium had the characteristics of a typical Greek city. The acropolis located in the

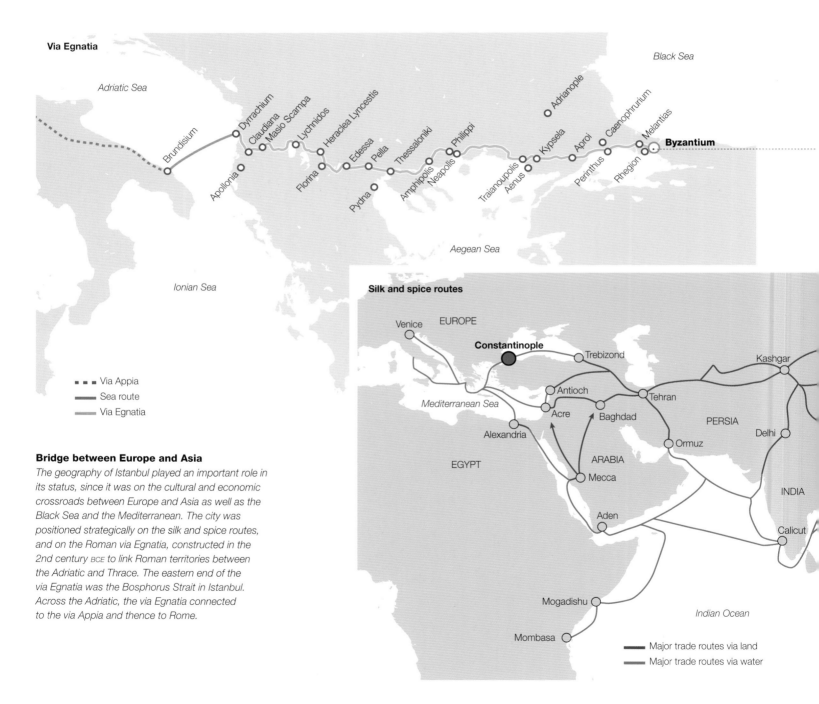

Via Egnatia

Legend:
- - - - Via Appia
——— Sea route
——— Via Egnatia

Silk and spice routes

Legend:
——— Major trade routes via land
——— Major trade routes via water

Bridge between Europe and Asia

The geography of Istanbul played an important role in its status, since it was on the cultural and economic crossroads between Europe and Asia as well as the Black Sea and the Mediterranean. The city was positioned strategically on the silk and spice routes, and on the Roman via Egnatia, constructed in the 2nd century BCE to link Roman territories between the Adriatic and Thrace. The eastern end of the via Egnatia was the Bosphorus Strait in Istanbul. Across the Adriatic, the via Egnatia connected to the via Appia and thence to Rome.

courtyard of today's Topkapi Palace area contained the royal palace and temples dedicated to various gods. The agora was located in today's Hagia Sophia Square and the amphitheater, Kneigon, was in the area overlooking the Bosphorus. The city was well protected by the sea on the Marmara and the Bosphorus side, but a defensive wall was necessary on the western side. Protective walls have always been one of the most important concerns in this city. The walls of Byzantium played a significant role in the city's defense and were fine examples of military engineering.

Many invaders tried to capture this important location. In the 5th century BCE, after the Persian invasion, both Byzantium and Chalcedon came together under the leadership of the allied Greek city-states against the Persians. In 489 BCE the Spartan commander Pausanias took Byzantium from the Persians and governed the city until 477 BCE. After this the city became a member of the Delian League of cities led by Athens. When the Delian League was dissolved Byzantium became independent, but after the Peloponnesian War, Byzantium was again ruled by the Spartans until 390 BCE.

Throughout the Hellenistic period, Byzantium remained independent. The city was at the crossroads of the trade routes between the Black Sea and the Mediterranean as well as Asia Minor and the Balkans. At the end of the Hellenistic period, Byzantium had a formal alliance with Rome; although it was under Roman protection, it remained a free city. Byzantium was linked to Rome by the via Egnatia, a road that went all the way from the Adriatic coast to Thrace. The Romans even built an aqueduct to bring water to the city during Emperor Hadrian's rule.

Seraglio Point

Seraglio Point is in the intersection of the Marmara Sea and the Bosphorus Strait, which provides the only access to the Black Sea. Seraglio Point also has a natural harbor called the Golden Horn, which provides invaluable opportunities for sea trade and defense.

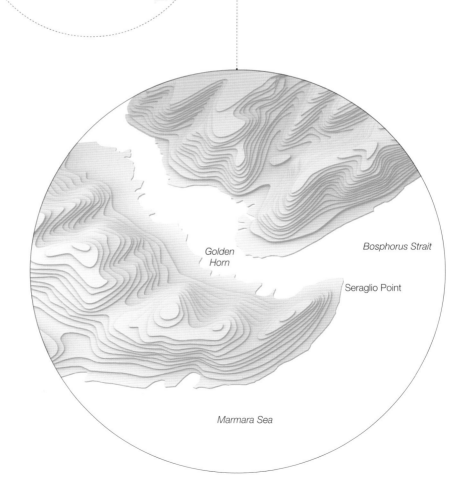

Byzantium to Constantinopolis: Planning for Greatness

Grand planning schemes were frequently employed in imperial cities as a demonstration of power and prestige. For example, the imperial city area in Beijing is a separate planned sector behind walls, with gardens, shrines, and the Forbidden City in the center. Initially, St. Petersburg was developed according to a plan in which the city center was shaped by a rectangular grid of canals. In Moscow, especially since 1300s, the Kremlin has been a fortified complex that symbolized imperial power and prestige through the palaces, cathedrals and towers. In Vienna, the Ringstrasse was established around the city center as a prestigious boulevard. As an imperial city of 1,700 years' standing, Istanbul's planning process is unique.

Toward the end of the 2nd century, Byzantium was captured by the Roman emperor Septimius Severus, having supported Pescennius Niger, Severus's rival for the imperial throne. The city was badly damaged in the war and Severus's son, Caracalla, persuaded his father to rebuild the city because of its geostrategic importance. Severus repaired the defensive walls, in the process encompassing an area twice the size of the original city. The construction of the

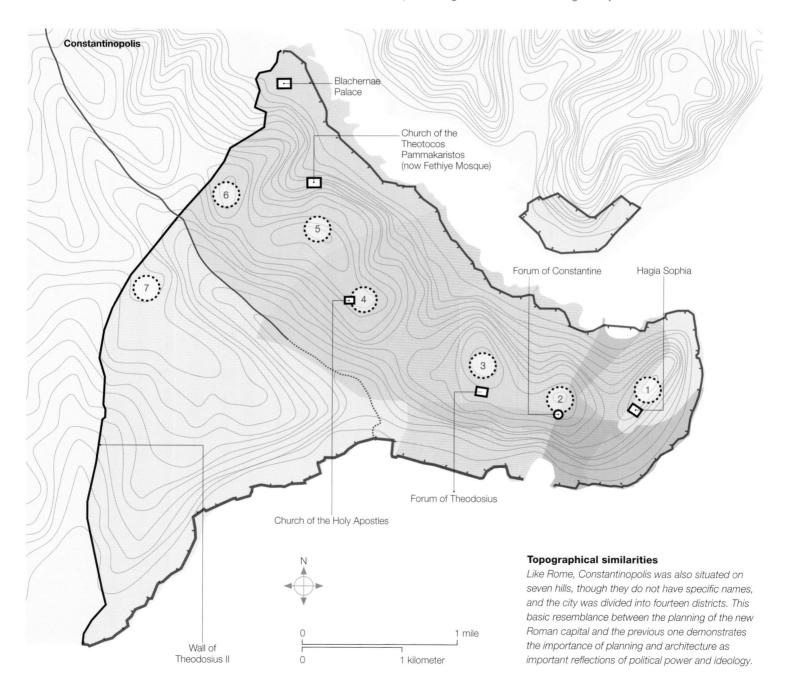

Constantinopolis

Blachernae Palace

Church of the Theotocos Pammakaristos (now Fethiye Mosque)

Forum of Constantine

Hagia Sophia

Forum of Theodosius

Church of the Holy Apostles

Wall of Theodosius II

N

0   1 mile

0   1 kilometer

Topographical similarities

Like Rome, Constantinopolis was also situated on seven hills, though they do not have specific names, and the city was divided into fourteen districts. This basic resemblance between the planning of the new Roman capital and the previous one demonstrates the importance of planning and architecture as important reflections of political power and ideology.

Hippodrome in front of today's Blue Mosque and large public baths also took place in this period. There was also a colonnaded way erected around the main avenue known as Mese.

In 324 Constantine I became the emperor of Rome. Constantine made Byzantium the capital of the Roman Empire with the name Constantinopolis, or Nova Roma Constantinopolitana (New Rome, the City of Constantine). Constantine granted tolerance to Christianity within the empire and offered his patronage to the Christian faith. Consequently many churches were built, including the first Hagia Sophia and the Church of the Holy Apostles, although pagan religion and temples persisted. Works of art and statues were brought to the new capital from different parts of the empire. Constantine built new walls to enclose a larger area, and also built the Grand Palace of the Byzantine Emperors. The forum of Constantine housed the senate and other important religious and ceremonial buildings. Mese, connecting important buildings and forums, was still the main street, and new streets covered with porticos were added. Constantine the Great turned the city of Byzantium into one of the largest cities of Christendom, comparable to Jerusalem.

After Constantine's death in 337, the history of Constantinople and the Roman Empire was marked by religious conflicts as well as political struggles and wars, particularly with the Persians. The city was still the imperial capital of the Roman Empire and the marks of this could be seen in the economic trade links, busy harbors, large population, great buildings, and monuments. By 395 when the emperor Theodosius the Great died the population had grown to about 300,000. Theodosius's death marked the permanent division of the Eastern and Western Roman Empire. The capital of the Eastern Roman Empire remained in Constantinople and the Western Roman Empire's capital was moved to Ravenna.

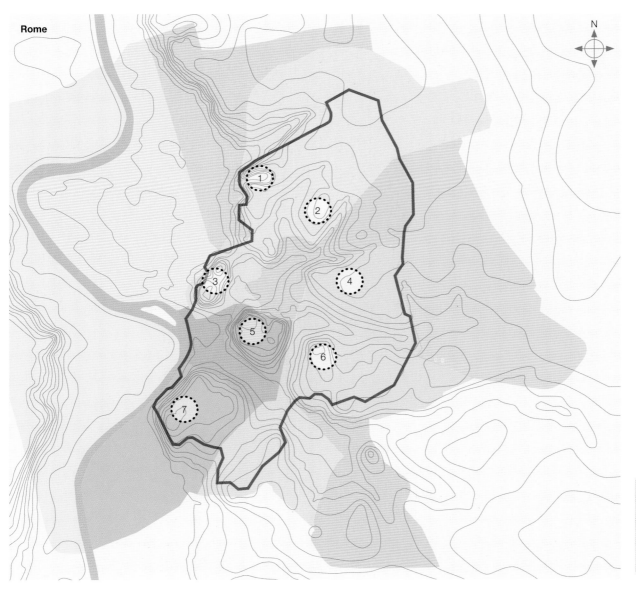

Rome

1 Quirinal Hill
2 Vimina Hill
3 Capitoline Hill
4 Esquiline Hill
5 Palatine Hill
6 Caelian Hill
7 Aventine Hill

0   1 Mile

0   1 Kilometer

A Focus of Power and Control

As overt symbols of political and imperial power, imperial cities had to be prepared for threats both from outside and from within. The defensive walls were symbolic of imperial grandeur, but also performed an obvious military function. In Europe, walls had been used to protect cities against attacks and artillery since medieval times. The walls of Vienna were the most significant factor in preventing the Ottomans from penetrating further into Europe in the 17th century.

Internal threats were exemplified by the riots in Paris that started the French Revolution, and Bloody Sunday in St. Petersburg in 1905, which threatened the Tsarist regime. As the capital of the Byzantine Empire, Constantinople was the scene of numerous struggles for political supremacy.

The period between 527 and 565 under the emperor Justinian is recognized as the zenith of the Byzantine Empire; during this period the population reached more than 500,000. Its

Hagia Sophia

Hagia Sophia interior

City walls

At the end of the 4th century, threats from the Goths and the Huns resulted in the construction of another set of walls by the emperor Theodosius II, enlarging the borders of the city by 40 percent more than the area enclosed by the Constantinian walls. These walls marked the western borders of the city in the Byzantine period and are still visible today.

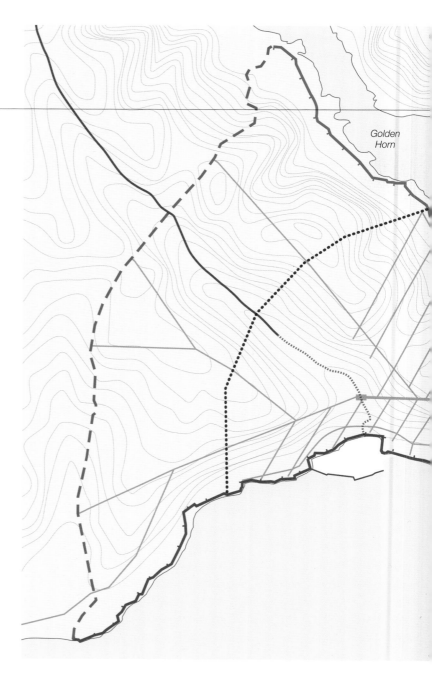

—— Golden Horn Wall
—— Propontis Wall
– – – Wall of Byzantium
–·–·– Severan Wall
······· Wall of Constantine
— — Wall of Theodosius II
—— Roads

Golden Horn

imperium extended throughout Asia Minor to the Persian borders, and included the Balkans, Italy, and North Africa. However, these were also times of great struggle. The biggest internal crisis was the Nika Revolt, which demolished much of the historic imperial settlement, including the first Hagia Sophia. Justinian's palace was under virtual siege for a week before he succeeded in putting down the revolt. The reconstruction of the city included the great Hagia Sophia as it stands today, which was finished in 537 and dedicated to Divine Wisdom.

The Byzantine Empire was characterized by violent political upheavals. Between 330 and 1204, around seventy emperors reigned in Constantinople, and over half of them were overthrown by violent revolts. From the 7th century, the Arabs and Sassanid Persia became a threat for the city. These threats diminished the empire and Constantinople shrank in size, although after 750 the empire began to recover. By 1050 the population of Constantinople was around 375,000.

The Fourth Crusade sacked Constantinople in 1204, the culmination of the long religious and political rivalry between the Holy Roman Empire and the Byzantine Empire. Fires and looting destroyed many historic buildings, and important Greek Orthodox churches like Hagia Sophia were converted to Roman Catholicism. The crusade resulted in the destructive Latin rule in the city, until in 1261 the Greeks regained control, restoring the Byzantine Empire. However, Constantinople was fatally weakened by the Latin occupation, and the population of the city in 1453 when it was taken by the Ottomans was around 25,000–50,000.

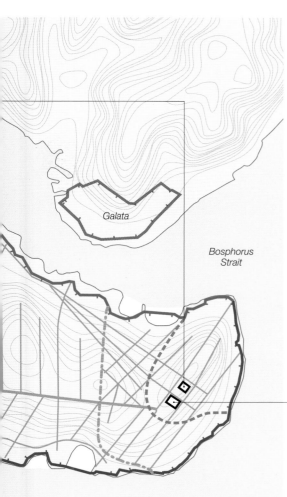

Galata

Bosphorus Strait

Marmara Sea

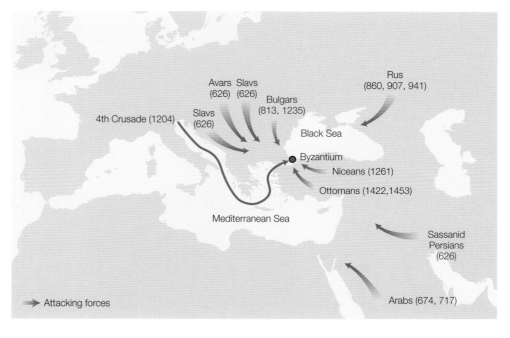

Avars (626) Slavs (626)

Slavs (626)

Bulgars (813, 1235)

Rus (860, 907, 941)

4th Crusade (1204)

Black Sea

Byzantium

Niceans (1261)

Ottomans (1422,1453)

Mediterranean Sea

Sassanid Persians (626)

Arabs (674, 717)

 Attacking forces

City under attack

Despite the strong walls of Constantinopolis, there were many attacks on the city by those hoping to capture this important strategic location. The attack in 1453 by the Ottomans was the most significant. The Byzantine fleet chained the entrance to the Golden Horn, and the defenders used Greek fire to repel the attackers. However, the Ottomans made a deal with the Genoese population in the Galata area, on the opposite side of the Golden Horn, and carried their ships overland to the harbor. On May 29, after a siege that had lasted almost two months, the city fell.

Hagia Irene

Architectural Splendor

Architecture has always been an important indicator of political power in imperial cities. As power shifted between different groups, important buildings would be symbolically converted or demolished altogether. For example, when the Moors were expelled from Madrid in 1085, the new king ordered the main mosque to be converted to a Catholic church. Templo Mayor, a major Temple of Aztec Civilization, was destroyed in 1521 when Spanish started to rule Mexico City. During the Nazi occupation in Poland, many Jewish monuments and synagogues in Kraków were either destroyed or neglected. During Stalin's time, in Moscow, many historic buildings, especially religious ones, were demolished to open grand-scale avenues. After the conquest of Constantinople in 1453 by Fatih (Conqueror) Sultan Mehmet, the building of another imperial capital began and

Fatih Mosque

Sulemaniye Mosque

Nurvosmaniye Mosque

Blue Mosque

architecture was the focal point of this development. From this time, although the city was still called Constantinople in the west, it was known in the east as Kostantiniyye or, increasingly, Istanbul.

The city walls were repaired and Hagia Sophia was converted into a mosque. The sultan decided to increase the ethnic mix of the city. Turks, Jews, Greeks, and Armenians were brought from different parts of the Ottoman Empire. Former Greek inhabitants of the city were encouraged to return. Each ethnic group had its own quarters, religious leaders, and places of worship, although many churches were converted to mosques. Ten years after the conquest, Fatih ordered the building of a large religious complex under his name in the place of the Church of the Holy Apostles. The complex, or *kulliye*, included the Fatih Mosque together with a religious school (*medrese*), a public kitchen, a hospital, a library, public baths, a marketplace, tombs, a hospice, and a *caravanserai* (inn for travelers). This idea of the *kulliye* as a religious complex became an important pattern in Ottoman city planning.

Kulliyes and mosques formed the centers of different neighborhoods. Topkapi Palace, the imperial palace of the Ottoman sultans until 1856, and the Grand Bazaar, the world's largest covered bazaar, were also constructed during Fatih's time.

Between 1453 and 1923 thirty Ottoman emperors reigned in Istanbul. The longest ruling emperor was Suleyman the Magnificent, who was in power for forty-six years between 1520 and 1566. During his time, the empire reached its largest extent and Istanbul became an imperial capital that reflected Ottoman political power. The chief architect of Sultan Suleyman was Sinan, who designed truly monumental mosques and other buildings that are still important features in the skyline of the city. The most important of his buildings are the Sehzade and Suleymaniye mosques, the latter dedicated to Suleyman the Magnificent himself. Both of these mosques are part of larger *kulliye* complexes. After Suleyman, the Ottoman Empire went into a period of stagnation and then decline. However, the glory of Istanbul as an imperial capital was never lost.

In the 1850s, the Tanzimat Reform Movement, which was heavily influenced by European ideals of urbanization, made considerable efforts to turn Istanbul into a modern European metropolis by introducing new public services including police, fire, and transport as well as building new squares, streets, and sidewalks. The establishment of the Istanbul Municipality and the City Planning Council also took place under this movement. In the 1860s a new palace for the Ottoman sultans, Dolmabahce Palace, was built on the Bosphorus shore. After the First World War, the Ottoman Empire came to an end. Ankara was chosen as the capital of the new Turkish Republic, although Istanbul remained the economic capital of the country.

Taksim Square

Dolmabahce Palace

Galata Tower

Yeni Mosque

Topkapi Palace

Hagia Sophia

Ottoman monuments
The Ottomans added a number of important religious and political complexes to the city. Fatih Mosque, Suleymaniye Mosque, Nurosmaniye Mosque, Yeni Mosque, and Blue Mosque are among the most important religious complexes. The grand architectural schemes of the royal palaces of Topkapi and Dolmabahce were a concrete demonstration of imperial power.

Cosmopolitanism

Imperial cities are characterized by a diverse ethnic and cultural mix, a result of both the historical development of the city and the geographical reach of the empire. London's population still reflects the colonial past of the British Empire. In Vienna, the 1890 Census showed that 65.5 percent of the population was born outside the city, with an ethnic mix that included Balkan Muslims, Jews, and Hungarian gypsies. Thus, diversity is an important element of imperial cities.

Greek Constantinople and Ottoman Istanbul were both regarded not only as imperial cities, but also as holy ones. Before Constantine the Great, paganism was the dominant religion in Constantinople. As Christianity grew in importance within the Roman Empire, Constantinople became one of the largest Christian cities of its time. Together with Rome, Alexandria, Antioch, and Jerusalem, Constantinople was one of the five cities whose bishops were given the title of patriarch. From early times, the Byzantines saw themselves as the guardians and upholders of correct Christian belief, as is reflected in the word "Orthodox," derived from the Greek words *orthos* ("right") and *doxa* ("belief").

321
. 2

1,025

143

17

Sveti Stefan Church
(Bulgarian Orthodox church)

The Phanar Greek Orthodox College

Religious buildings

Istanbul metropolitan area has numerous places of worship distributed across its thirty-nine municipalities. The most important religious complexes are located in the historic peninsula and in the municipalities along the Bosphorus Strait.

Sulymaniye Mosque

When the Ottomans conquered the city in 1453, they fulfilled one of the central desires of the Islamic world, a desire which had been embraced since the time of the Prophet Mohammed. After this conquest, the Ottoman Turks were seen as significant leaders of Islam. The non-Muslim population of the city was divided into "millets" (nations) and each millet had its own religious leader.

People from many different religious faiths have lived together in Istanbul for centuries. Each of these groups maintains their own traditions and customs, making Istanbul a melting pot of different religions. Istanbul currently has two dominant religious minorities: Christians and Jews. There are different

Christian sects such as the Armenian Christians, the Greek Orthodox, and the Catholic Levantines. The Armenians are the largest ethnic religious minority with around 60,000 people. The Armenian Patriarchate is located in the Kumkapi area, which is one of the historic settlement areas for the community. The Greek Orthodox community has historically been an important element in Istanbul, though it has shrunk from 70,000 people in the 1950s to the current 2,000. However, as the home to the Orthodox Patriarchate, Istanbul is still regarded as an important center for Orthodox Christians. Since the beginning of the 17th century, the Orthodox Patriarchate has been located in the Fener district in the Church of St. George. The

Greek population is distributed across various parts of Istanbul such as Nisantasi, Sisli, and Kadikoy. The Roman Catholic Levantines are mostly of Italian or French origin and are settled chiefly in the Galata area. Most of the Jewish population in Istanbul are Sephardic Jews. The history of the Sephardic Jewish community in Istanbul goes back to 1492, when Jews who had escaped from the Spanish Inquisition came to the Ottoman Empire. Today there are around 20,000 Jewish people in Istanbul and the city has twenty-two active synagogues.

Greek Orthodox church in Kuzguncuk

230
1

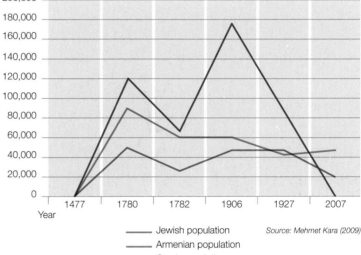

Population size of ethnic minorities in Istanbul

Year

—— Jewish population
—— Armenian population
—— Greek population

Source: Mehmet Kara (2009)

Religious demographics

In the era of Suleyman the Magnificent, the population of Istanbul reached 500,000, similar to that in the era of Justinian. In 1535 it was reported that there were 80,000 households in Istanbul (including the Galata district) of which 58 percent were Muslim, 32 percent were Christian, and 10 percent were Jewish. In the 17th century, Istanbul's population was 700,000 and the Jewish and Christian population formed around 40 percent of the total, Greeks being the largest minority and Jews making up 5 percent of the population.

Bet Yaakov Synagogue in Kuzguncuk

987

Mosque

Church

Synagogue

30
4

Source: Istanbul City Guide

From Imperial City to Global City

Former imperial capitals such as London, Paris, Tokyo, Rome, Beijing, Mexico City, Moscow, and St. Petersburg are today seen as important global cities with command and control functions in the global economy. They attract flows of capital and are magnets for immigrants. The historical importance of these imperial cities has played an important role in their current global city status.

At the beginning of the 20th century, Istanbul was in economic and political decline following the transition from the Ottoman Empire to the Republican era. Ankara was the capital city of the Turkish Republic, although Istanbul maintained its importance as Turkey's industrial and economic center. As a result of this, since the 1950s Istanbul has been a magnet for migration from rural areas, which has resulted in an increase in unplanned developments and vast urban sprawl. In the 1980s globalization pushed the city and national governments to find new ways to revive the global city status of Istanbul. Important city marketing efforts and urban renewal projects promoted Istanbul's image. Since the 1990s, Istanbul has developed as a global city and the financial center of the Middle East. As the Turkish economy entered a more liberal phase from the 1980s, the number of foreign firms locating

A new city

Urban transformation projects are intended to result in a modern makeover for Istanbul's urban realm. However, there are questions regarding the impact on the people and local businesses that will be displaced as a result of these projects, as well as concerns about historic preservation and the prospect of increased land prices.

Basaksehir
Residential development conforming to new earthquake-resilience standards.

Eyup
A proposal for a new university.

Esenler
Social housing scheme in which existing householders will move to new housing. The value of their old houses will be counted as down payment, and they will pay the rest in installments.

Esenyurt
A proposal to create a neighborhood that is a revival of the Ottoman neighborhood.

Gungoren
A project to create better social housing for the Roma population.

Kucukcekmece
Slums replaced with social housing projects.

Zeytinburnu
Mixed use development that references the existing neighborhood fabric.

Beyoglu
The Tarlabasi area in Beyoglu is to be transformed into an urban space like the Champs Élysées in Paris. 278 buildings have been surveyed and restoration projects are in preparation.

Source: Vatan (2010)

their offices in Istanbul has increased.

In regaining global city status, Istanbul has also suffered problems related to congestion, pollution, traffic, transportation, housing, and natural resources. With existing trends, Istanbul's population may reach up to 22 million people in 2025. Thus, like London, Barcelona, Tokyo, Shanghai, and Paris, planning for the future as well as the present is extremely important for Istanbul with regard to globalization-related concerns and impacts.

Around 60 percent of the employed population of Istanbul work in the service sector. With the impact of current planning and development efforts, by 2023 employment in the service sector is expected to rise to 70 percent. In order to plan for this forecast growth in both population and service-sector employment, the current administration in Istanbul has focused its development efforts on polycentric growth and "urban transformation projects." These include slum clearance, bringing buildings up to standard in terms of earthquake regulations, and large-scale urban design projects that include business districts with iconic buildings, shopping malls, residential areas, and waterfront developments.

Since the designation of Istanbul as the European Capital of Culture in 2010, urban development efforts have gained momentum. In 2004 Istanbul Metropolitan Municipality established a separate planning unit, the Istanbul Metropolitan Planning and Urban Design Center (IMP), which directly reports to the mayor and brings together architects, city planners, and engineers from both academia and professional practice. When established, with 550 employees, IMP was the largest planning office in Europe. IMP's planning efforts focused on decentralizing the existing central business district to ensure more balanced economic growth and urban development and creating designated subcenters with more high-quality office space for the service sector. Current developments in this former imperial city are now moving in the direction of making Istanbul an important global city.

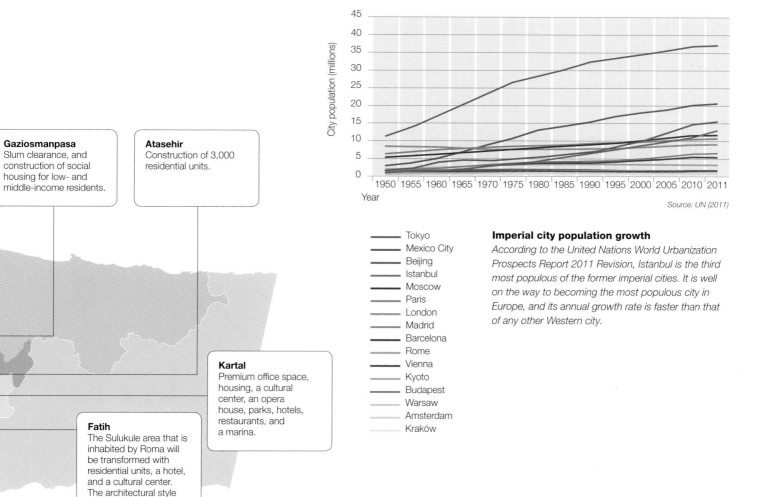

Population growth since 1950

City population (millions) / Year

Source: UN (2011)

Tokyo
Mexico City
Beijing
Istanbul
Moscow
Paris
London
Madrid
Barcelona
Rome
Vienna
Kyoto
Budapest
Warsaw
Amsterdam
Kraków

Gaziosmanpasa
Slum clearance, and construction of social housing for low- and middle-income residents.

Atasehir
Construction of 3,000 residential units.

Kartal
Premium office space, housing, a cultural center, an opera house, parks, hotels, restaurants, and a marina.

Fatih
The Sulukule area that is inhabited by Roma will be transformed with residential units, a hotel, and a cultural center. The architectural style will be an eclectic mix of Ottoman and Turkish styles.

Imperial city population growth
According to the United Nations World Urbanization Prospects Report 2011 Revision, Istanbul is the third most populous of the former imperial cities. It is well on the way to becoming the most populous city in Europe, and its annual growth rate is faster than that of any other Western city.

Rediscovering the Layers of the Imperial City

The past of imperial cities, marked by political and economic changes, social transformations, monumental works of architecture, and planning ideas, plays an important role in the shaping of their current urbanization. Different eras have left distinctive marks in the urban environment. Many of these imprints are visible and become part of the city culture, but some are hidden beneath the current layer of development. In Istanbul, 9,000 years of history has left many layers to be discovered.

Since Byzantine times, Istanbul's water had been stored in underground cisterns. The biggest is the Basilica Cistern or Yerebatan Sarayi (the Sunken Palace), built in the 6th century by the emperor Justinian. When the Ottoman Turks came to the city in 1453, nobody showed them these cisterns. The Basilica Cistern was forgotten until the 1540s, when people started to fish from the basements of their houses. This secret chamber has another hidden layer that relates to paganism. Some of the 336 columns supporting the cistern feature pagan statues like Medusa. This

Archeological discoveries

Thousands of archeological artifacts were discovered during the construction of the Marmaray project. Archeological excavations started in 2004 and lasted for seven years. During the excavations, project construction was temporarily put on hold.

Yenikapi

The Byzantine Theodosian Harbor, built in the 4th century and in use until the 13th century, was found to contain thirty-six wooden ships. This discovery is believed to be the world's largest sunken ship collection. Beneath this layer was found an 8,500-year-old Neolithic settlement with residential foundations, tombs, around 2,000 footprints, utensils, and pottery. These discoveries are to be exhibited in a special archeology park in the station area.

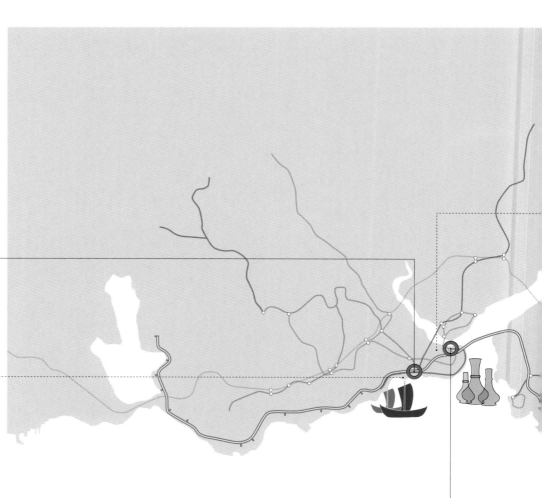

Marmaray tunnel

A mobile crane ship working on the construction of the Marmaray tunnel project. This immersed tube tunnel is almost a mile long with a maximum depth of 184 feet. The tunnel is part of a 45-mile rail project connecting forty stations on the Asian and European side of the Bosphorus Strait. The tunnel opened for passenger use on October 29, 2013.

Sirkeci

Architectural remains were found here from Byzantine and Ottoman times; glass from the Roman, Byzantine, and Ottoman eras; and pottery and remains dating back to pre-Roman times.

was Justinian's way of showing that paganism had been superseded in the city, literally driven underground. Another discovery was made in 1912, when a fire destroyed the Sultanahmet Square, revealing the walls and mosaics of the 4th-century Grand Palace of the Byzantine emperors. Today, the remains of the mosaics of the Grand Palace are on display and it is likely that many more are waiting to be revealed.

Recently there have been new discoveries as a result of a mega-transportation project that is seen as the long-term solution to Istanbul's overwhelming traffic problems. Transportation has always been a major issue in Istanbul, especially between the European and Asian side. In 2004 the Turkish Ministry of Transportation launched the "Marmaray Project," a $2.5 billion scheme funded by the national government, the European Investment Bank, and the Japan International Cooperation Agency. The Marmaray Project is expected to have a capacity of 75,000 passengers per hour in each direction and to decrease pollution and carbon dioxide emissions. The project includes the world's deepest immersed tube tunnel under the Bosphorus Strait, and also focuses on upgrading the commuter rail system. The project was expected to be finished by 2009; however, when the remains of the imperial city started to resurface from many different eras, the project was delayed for four years.

Since the excavations started in 2004, around 40,000 historic artifacts have been discovered in various locations including Yenikapi, Sirkeci, Fikirtepe, and Pendik. These excavations uncovered Istanbul's history dating back to Neolithic times. The most important discovery came from the Yenikapi area, which is the ancient Theodosian Harbor from the 4th-century Byzantine Empire era: thirty-six ships were found dating back to different times. Another surprising discovery came from the Pendik district, where archeologists discovered an 8,500-year-old Neolithic settlement with house foundations, tombs, footprints, and various tools. These archeological findings are expected to add more depth not only to the history of Istanbul, but also to the history of urbanization in Europe.

Underground cisterns

With 336 columns the underground Basilica Cistern or Yerebatan Sarayi (the Sunken Palace) is the biggest of several hundred cisterns that lie beneath modern Istanbul. A number of column bases are upside-down Medusa heads.

Pendik

Neolithic settlement from 6400 BCE with houses and tombs (containing many utensils and pottery).

Tram route

Light rail route

Bus route

Marmaray rail route

Underground train route

THE INDUSTRIAL CITY

JANE CLOSSICK

Core city
MANCHESTER _____

Secondary cities
BERLIN _____
CHICAGO _____
DETROIT _____
DÜSSELDORF _____
GLASGOW _____
SHEFFIELD _____

Left: Manchester, England

Industrial City: Introduction

"In Manchester urban form altered rapidly over a thirty-year period and the city was completely transformed. An urban revolution on this scale had not happened previously in human history."

The "Industrial Revolution" brought a half-century or so of immense social and economic change to the world. This was expressed in urban terms with the evolution of a new kind of city: the industrial city. The raison d'être of the city up to this point was to fulfill military, political, ecclesiastical, or trading functions. Now the industrial city would gather raw materials and fabricate, assemble, and distribute manufactured goods. This was the culmination of

forces which had gathered pace during the 18th and early 19th centuries, beginning in Britain (Manchester, Glasgow, Sheffield, and Birmingham) and spreading within a few decades to western Europe (for example Berlin and Düsseldorf) and the USA (notably Chicago and Detroit).

Improvements in water power, chemical engineering, and metallurgy prompted the production of machine tools, which in turn began the process of mechanization of both manufacturing and agriculture. The need for labor on the land and for the hand-working of goods was dramatically reduced, leaving a huge pool of unemployed workers who were forced to migrate to find work. In a self-reinforcing cycle, they migrated to the industrial city, which needed people to man its factories, warehouses, railway stations, and ports. The more the people came, the more the city and its production capacity overwhelmed the old ways. Daily life for both the rural and urban populations had changed beyond all recognition, and the industrial city grew faster than any city had before.

Iron smelting

Population loss in major industrial cities 1951–2013

After population explosion associated with industrialization many industrial cities in the Western world have shrunk dramatically, some by as much as half. New industrial cities in the developing world are rising in their place.

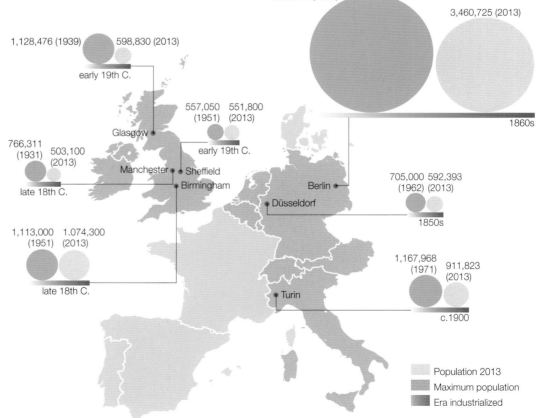

1,128,476 (1939) 598,830 (2013)
early 19th C.

766,311 (1931) 503,100 (2013)
late 18th C.

Glasgow

557,050 (1951) 551,800 (2013)
early 19th C.

Manchester • Sheffield
Birmingham

1,113,000 (1951) 1.074,300 (2013)
late 18th C.

4,338,756 (1939)

3,460,725 (2013)

1860s

Berlin
Düsseldorf

705,000 (1962) 592,393 (2013)
1850s

Turin

1,167,968 (1971) 911,823 (2013)
c.1900

Population 2013
Maximum population
Era industrialized

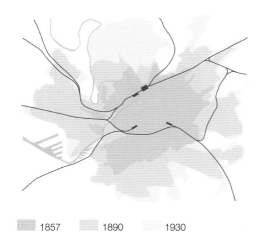

1857   1890   1930

The first industrial city: urbanization of Manchester 1857–1930

Massive population expansion was matched with rapid urbanization of the surrounding country, with the city proper rapidly swallowing surrounding villages and towns as it grew.

Industrial cities are also centers of banking, markets, and transport, because industry tended to be sited in existing centers of trade with easy access to distribution networks. For example, Düsseldorf was long-settled and thriving prior to industrialization. It is adjacent to the Rhine, and had been the focus of regional markets and culture since the 14th century, when its market square was constructed. In the USA, Detroit successfully industrialized for similar reasons. Its location in the Great Lakes region made it a center for global trade and the ideal location for Henry Ford to set up his car manufacturing business at the beginning of the 20th century, taking advantage of metal-working, machine tool-making, and coach-building industries already in the area. In terms of transport, the Industrial Revolution also brought with it tremendous technological advances. Like migration, the construction of new transport networks both underpinned and reinforced the growth of industrial cities, which soon became the hubs of local, inter-urban, and national railways.

A new kind of society emerged, one that was fundamentally urban in character. The industrial city has long been associated with dreadful conditions for the working classes, but it also produced a whole new socio-economic group, the middle class. This group was made up of industrialists, as well as the new professionals who dealt with the vast amount of administration and control required by the emerging economic system (for example, managers, clerks, officials, statisticians, and members of local government). Although power had traditionally been held by the landed gentry, parliamentary reforms that extended the franchise and the movement toward local governance in the 19th century redistributed power into the hands of the middle classes, who had a profound effect on the shape of the city and the buildings to be found there. Suburbanization of wealth changed the shape of the city as a whole, and consumerism and the pursuit of leisure, as well as industry, structured the shape of the buildings at its center. An excellent example can be found in Glasgow, where stately stone buildings such as the City Chambers were constructed, funded by industrial wealth and embodying its power.

Here, we unpick what happened during the Industrial Revolution, and consider its relationship with urban form. Although the discussion looks at the common qualities of industrial cities, it is worth remembering that no city type exists in isolation from its national, global, political, social, and cultural context. Cities are a palimpsest of overlaid structures (both physical and social), with a depth and specificity that is impossible to accommodate through typology alone. For this reason Manchester, the first and archetypal industrial city, is the focus of this chapter, which draws in relevant examples from other cities to illustrate particular ideas. Manchester was a center for weaving from the 16th century, but the forces of industry converged and it became "Cottonopolis," the world center of cotton production. Cities generally evolve slowly, and great changes cannot be seen clearly over the lifetime of one individual, yet in Manchester urban form altered rapidly over a thirty-year period and the city was completely transformed. An urban revolution on this scale had not happened previously in human history, and it introduced the idea of the city as something which could and should be changed and reformed by human agency. It is not easy to conceptualize cities as metamorphosing, shaping and being shaped by society. Over the 19th and 20th centuries few corners of the earth have been unaffected by industrialization, and industrial cities are everywhere, shaping the lives and livelihoods of the individuals who walk their streets.

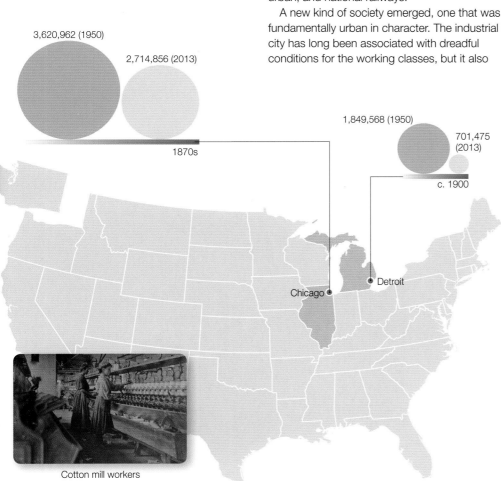

3,620,962 (1950)

2,714,856 (2013)

1870s

1,849,568 (1950)

701,475 (2013)

c. 1900

Chicago

Detroit

Cotton mill workers

Mechanization of Production

The technology that is intertwined with the existence of the industrial city came into being during the 18th and 19th centuries and would reformat the urban landscape of Britain, and subsequently the world. Wrought iron, steam power, and machines for manufacture were all invented during this critical period, and had far-reaching social, economic, and physical effects. Interdependent with these inventions was the culmination of the "agricultural revolution," which increased the productivity of the land and reduced the number of people required for farming. This meant that there was both a pool of surplus labor as well as the capacity to feed growing industrial cities such as Manchester, Sheffield, Birmingham, and Glasgow.

At first cottage industries blossomed, as unemployed laborers and smallholders who had lost their land to new "enclosure" laws sought to earn a living. In Lancashire, families of spinners and weavers worked at home and were both the owners and operators of the means of production. The spinning jenny, the water-frame, and subsequently the spinning mule were to change all that. When Bolton barber Richard Arkwright opened his factory at Shudehill in Manchester, it was the first time that a building had been constructed specifically

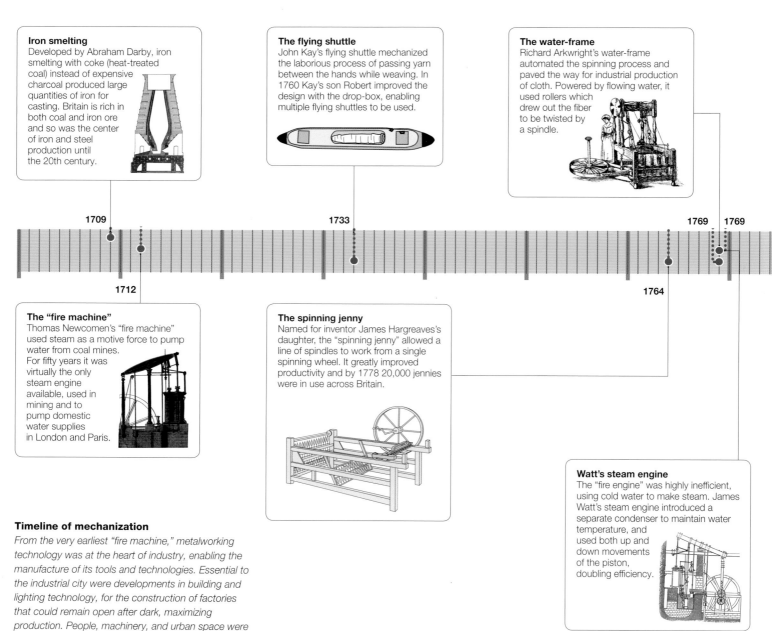

Iron smelting
Developed by Abraham Darby, iron smelting with coke (heat-treated coal) instead of expensive charcoal produced large quantities of iron for casting. Britain is rich in both coal and iron ore and so was the center of iron and steel production until the 20th century.

The flying shuttle
John Kay's flying shuttle mechanized the laborious process of passing yarn between the hands while weaving. In 1760 Kay's son Robert improved the design with the drop-box, enabling multiple flying shuttles to be used.

The water-frame
Richard Arkwright's water-frame automated the spinning process and paved the way for industrial production of cloth. Powered by flowing water, it used rollers which drew out the fiber to be twisted by a spindle.

The "fire machine"
Thomas Newcomen's "fire machine" used steam as a motive force to pump water from coal mines. For fifty years it was virtually the only steam engine available, used in mining and to pump domestic water supplies in London and Paris.

The spinning jenny
Named for inventor James Hargreaves's daughter, the "spinning jenny" allowed a line of spindles to work from a single spinning wheel. It greatly improved productivity and by 1778 20,000 jennies were in use across Britain.

Watt's steam engine
The "fire engine" was highly inefficient, using cold water to make steam. James Watt's steam engine introduced a separate condenser to maintain water temperature, and used both up and down movements of the piston, doubling efficiency.

1709   1733   1769   1769

1712   1764

Timeline of mechanization
From the very earliest "fire machine," metalworking technology was at the heart of industry, enabling the manufacture of its tools and technologies. Essential to the industrial city were developments in building and lighting technology, for the construction of factories that could remain open after dark, maximizing production. People, machinery, and urban space were all essential components of the Industrial Revolution.

to house the machinery of production, rather than the producers. Once iron was cheaply available in large quantities, it was used for the framed construction of "fire-proof" factories and warehouses that did not require internal supporting walls, so that large interior expanses could be filled with machinery or used for storage. The industrial metropolises in the north of England were studded with these new, technologically advanced buildings.

By the 20th century, the assembly-line system had similarly transformed American industry in cities such as Detroit. Now, even complex machines like cars could be constructed en masse, and a new economic model had come into play. In the early days,

workers were not seen as potential consumers but rather as a pauperized pool of readily available labor. "Fordist" principles led to workers earning higher wages (the "$5 dollar day"), so that they became potential consumers of the goods they produced. As in Manchester, the scale of production and the requirement for access to distribution networks meant that the industrial city was the only place where competitive mechanized manufacture could take place. Industry had fundamentally linked capitalism to urban spaces, with a new skyline that owed its very existence to the mechanization of production.

Gas lighting
Invented by William Murdoch, gas lighting was established in London, allowing factories and stores to remain open after dark.

Sheet glass
The Chance Brothers developed sheet glass, which allowed the construction of large and cheap industrial buildings. The culmination of this technology was the Crystal Palace constructed in Hyde Park, London, for the Great Exhibition in 1851.

1812

1832

1779

1784

Puddling and rolling iron
Henry Cort developed puddling and rolling of iron, producing a malleable material much purer and easier to work than brittle pig iron.

The spinning mule
Samuel Crompton's spinning mule, a combination of the jenny and the water-frame, produced fine, even thread strong enough to be woven into cloth which could, for the first time, compete with imported fabrics from India.

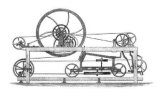

Rapid growth of cotton mills
In 1782, there were only two cotton mills in Manchester, both powered by water; in 1792 there were fifty-two steam-powered mills, and by 1830 there were 100.

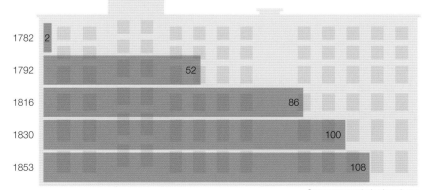

1782 2
1792 52
1816 86
1830 100
1853 108

Source: www.spinningtheweb.org

Innovations
in Transport

Big cities are hungry cities and by the early 19th century industrial cities were consuming ever larger quantities of coal. The swathes of brick dwellings which housed the vast workforce had coal fireplaces, and a ten horse-power factory used one ton of coal per day. Although the concentration of industry in the north of England at this time was linked to the presence of rich coal seams, coal was expensive and impractical to move by road, even though turnpikes had improved conditions for wide-wheeled vehicles.

As a result, mill-owners and prospectors invested in canals on which coal could be shipped for half the price. Cheap imports of building materials, limestone, and lime allowed rapid construction of warehousing and factories and as the population increased, fast boats were used to deliver perishables and passengers from the countryside.

Manufacturing was undoubtedly at the heart of early industrial cities, yet of equal importance were transport networks which brought fuel to feed the steam engines, raw materials to feed

Lancashire

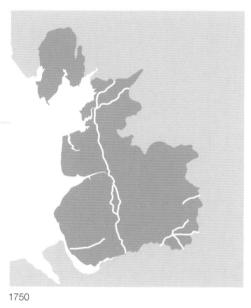

1750

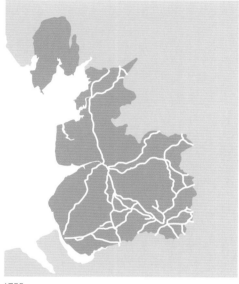

1755

Turnpike map of Lancashire

Turnpikes were toll roads, introduced piecemeal in Britain throughout the 18th century, and revenue from tolls was used for maintenance. This, combined with the use of the McAdam system of road building (where hardcore is used to support packed stones), meant that through-routes were reliably maintained, and journeys between cities in wheeled vehicles which had previously taken days took only hours to complete. This facilitated more efficient communication, movement of people, goods, and food, and was a key factor precipitating the Industrial Revolution.

1800

1836

Source: Lancashire County Council

the factories, and food to feed the people. Rapidly following the major canals, the railways came to Manchester in 1830, plowing without care through the city's working-class districts, destroying homes and communities. In 1844 there were six lines that connected Manchester to London, Liverpool, Birmingham, Leeds, Sheffield, and Bolton, and journey times had been slashed, making England a much smaller place. By 1851 railways were carrying huge numbers of passengers, and London's Great Exhibition at the Crystal Palace saw 6 million people visit from all over the country, many arriving by train.

Transport was also fundamental to the Industrial Revolution in the USA. From modest beginnings, Chicago had by the 1830s become a booming metropolis after the construction of a long-distance canal connecting it to the Ohio–Mississippi river basin. From the 1850s the railroad connected it to the eastern seaboard and by 1854 it was the world's largest grain port. Railways ensured centralization of trade and production, but subsequently also allowed for their dispersal to neighboring cities such as Denver, Minneapolis, and Omaha when the costs of trade in Chicago became prohibitive. Canals also continued to

be useful throughout the 19th century. The Sanitary and Ship Canal reversed the flow of the Chicago River, pushing industrial waste away from the city, and in England the Manchester Ship Canal brought sea-going ships to the city. This is the signature of the industrial city: it is a "geographic plexus" at the center of a vast hinterland of satellite towns and a much wider national and international network of trade.

Chicago steam railway network, 1855

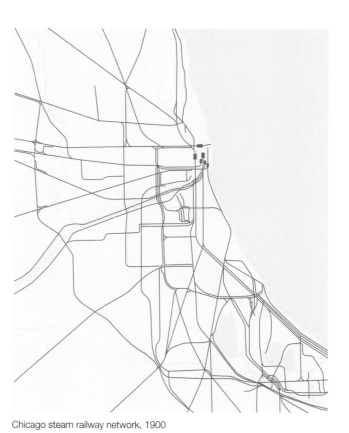

Chicago steam railway network, 1900

Source: Lake Forest College Library special collections

Chicago urban transport network

In 1900 the population of Chicago was 1.7 million people, making it the fifth- or sixth-largest city in the world, and transportation was a major problem. The 1890s saw the first elevated railway system, and at the end of the decade inter-urban lines connected steam-powered railroads to the suburbs. Electric traction allowed trams to replace horse-drawn and cable cars. Urban rail links encouraged suburbanization, as the more affluent moved to greater and greater distances from the industrial core of the city.

Electric trams on the streets of Chicago, 1893

Chicago's elevated railway system in 1900

Migration and Human Suffering

Population growth in industrial cities was explosive. Manchester's population increased tenfold between 1811 and 1911, as did Birmingham's. In the USA Chicago saw its population rise from 4,000 in 1837 to 110,000 in 1860. But the better life people sought was hard to find in the booming cities, which had grown in an uncontrolled, unregulated way. Wages were barely above subsistence, and there was a surplus of workers, so the majority of the labor force was casual, powerless, and expendable. Working hours and conditions were pitiless, with loud, dangerous machinery regularly maiming and killing workers. The average working week in Manchester in 1830 was sixty-nine hours for men, women, and children.

Living conditions were no better. In English cities like Liverpool, cheap "jerry-built" housing was constructed around narrow alleys and courts without sanitary infrastructure. Overcrowding was endemic, with the worst conditions in areas populated by Irish immigrants. Here, where the poorest, most desperate sector of the population lived,

Clean water
In 1831 less than half the population of Manchester had access to clean water. Cholera, a pathogen spread when contaminated feces comes into contact with drinking water, killed 32,000 people across Britain in 1832 and 62,000 in 1848. In Soho, London, John Snow had noted clusters of cholera cases around infected pumps, and was the first to identify that the disease is waterborne and that it was associated with specific, contaminated pumps.

Privies
There were insufficient privies; in one example 250 people shared a single toilet. Those that existed drained into open sewers. Above Ducie Bridge on the Irk, Engels noted that "In one of these courts there stands directly at the entrance, at the end of the covered passage, a privy without a door, so dirty that the inhabitants can pass into and out of the court only by passing through foul pools of stagnant urine and excrement."

Overcrowded conditions

River Irk

Living conditions in the new industrial city
The worst housing, the "back-to-backs," filled the interiors of blocks, hidden from genteel view by businesses fronting the streets. Narrow alleyways and courts without drainage or ventilation were rife with overcrowding, disease, and suffering.

conditions were such that people often lived more than one family to a room. As a result of the extreme poverty and dreadful conditions, there were frequent epidemics of cholera, typhus, influenza, and typhoid. In 1841 working-class life expectancy in England was just 26.6 years with 57 percent of children dying before their fifth birthday. Vegetables were expensive, so the population subsisted on bread, potatoes, and occasional meat. The conditions were noted with horror by contemporary observers, most famously by Friedrich Engels in *The Condition of the Working Classes in England* in 1844: "350,000

working people of Manchester and its environs live, almost all of them, in wretched, damp, filthy cottages … the streets which surround them are usually in the most miserable and filthy condition, laid out without the slightest reference to ventilation, with reference solely to the profit secured by the contractor."

Some migrants were from the countryside, put out of work by technical innovations such as the use of fertilizers (often by-products of industrial processes) and the invention of new iron farming implements. Artisans were no match for the powerful and efficient new factories which made the same goods at a

fraction of the cost. Other migrants were from overseas, like the Irish escaping to Great Britain and America from the ravages of successive years of potato famine between 1845 and 1852, and Jewish immigrants from central and eastern Europe. While there had been resistance to industrialization in some quarters, with "Luddite" protesters destroying machinery and marching against change in England, it was ultimately futile; the industrial city needed a workforce and found it in the very people whose previous livelihoods it had destroyed.

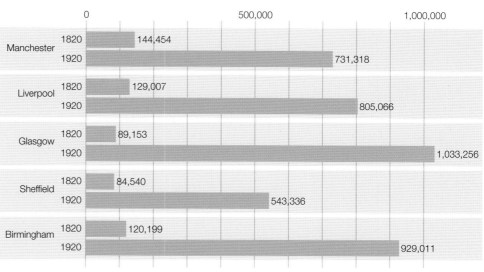

Source: UK census data

Rented cellars
Even cellars were rented, and the Manchester Statistical Society's survey found in 1835 that 3,500 cellar dwellings contained 12 percent of the population, or 15,000 people.

Population growth in key industrial cities
A massive shift in population distribution from 80 percent rural in 1780 to 80 percent urban in 1900 led to desperately overcrowded conditions in industrial cities. The most dramatic increase was in Glasgow, with the population increasing tenfold.

Back-to-back houses
Cheap back-to-back houses were thrown up by unscrupulous developers, with walls just a single brick thick. They were damp, unventilated, and severely overcrowded, like the weavers' houses in Back Irk Street, Manchester, one of which contained twenty-two people.

- Mill or works
- Warehousing/business
- Public houses
- Chapel/church/school
- Housing
- Housing back-to-back
- Pavement area

Governance and Social Reform

Local governance of industrial cities in their earliest incarnation was nonexistent, and they grew unchecked. Cities like Manchester were presided over by an oligarchy of merchants, for whom the proliferation of squalor and the suffering of the populace were of no concern. In the early 19th century five separate local authorities were involved in governing Manchester, resulting in competition and confusion. Acts of the 1830s endorsed local government, and Manchester led the way with the establishment of Manchester Corporation and the election of its first mayor. Town halls were a response to urban growth and the need for centralized organization of service provision, but they were also a statement of the "new corporatism" of the Victorian era, in which the self-governing city was seen as both the source of and a prerequisite for local creativity under a utilitarian and laissez-faire regime of central government.

Timeline of urban reform
Manchester led the way in reforms that simultaneously improved and controlled the city fabric, although such acts frequently increased the suffering of the very poorest in society, destroying their slum homes and the communities that lived there.

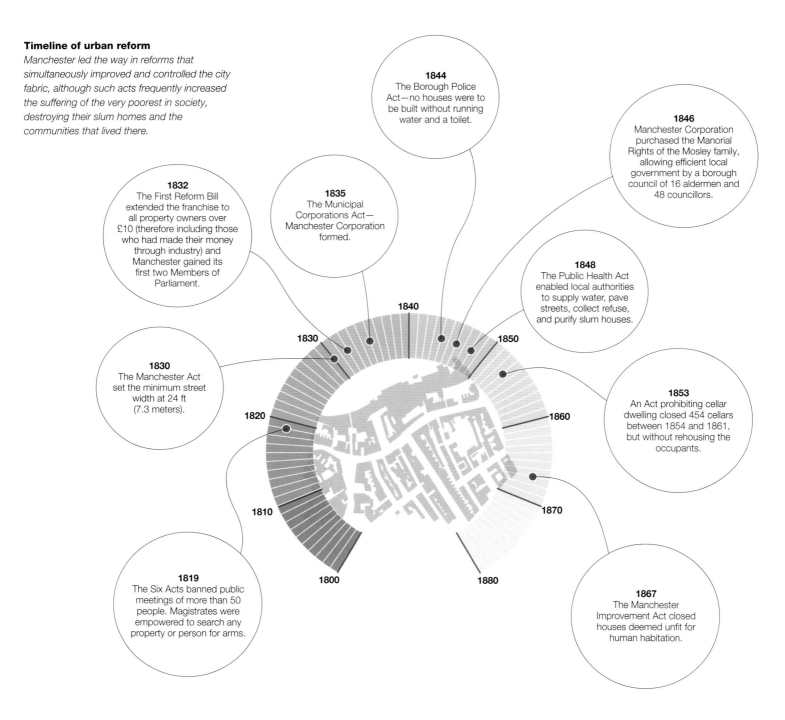

1844
The Borough Police Act—no houses were to be built without running water and a toilet.

1846
Manchester Corporation purchased the Manorial Rights of the Mosley family, allowing efficient local government by a borough council of 16 aldermen and 48 councillors.

1832
The First Reform Bill extended the franchise to all property owners over £10 (therefore including those who had made their money through industry) and Manchester gained its first two Members of Parliament.

1835
The Municipal Corporations Act—Manchester Corporation formed.

1848
The Public Health Act enabled local authorities to supply water, pave streets, collect refuse, and purify slum houses.

1830
The Manchester Act set the minimum street width at 24 ft (7.3 meters).

1853
An Act prohibiting cellar dwelling closed 454 cellars between 1854 and 1861, but without rehousing the occupants.

1819
The Six Acts banned public meetings of more than 50 people. Magistrates were empowered to search any property or person for arms.

1867
The Manchester Improvement Act closed houses deemed unfit for human habitation.

1800 · 1810 · 1820 · 1830 · 1840 · 1850 · 1860 · 1870 · 1880

Initially, central government in Britain was ill-equipped to cope with the urban revolution, and until the 1830s many new industrial metropolises had no representation in the House of Commons. This was a politically repressive period, as the government became aware of the growing power of urban populations and feared revolution. Attempts were made to stamp out dissent and prevent free speech, but the new urban space was antagonistic to control. It was easy for networks to form and for radicals to meet subversively. The concentration of people in industrial cities made them hotbeds of political unrest where people could form groups to combat their powerlessness in the face of industrial capitalism. Manchester was also to become the source of the trade union movement, since political and social unrest went hand in hand with the repeated economic crises (boom and bust) of the Industrial Revolution.

Industrial urban reform brought new approaches to studying and understanding urban society. In response to virulent epidemics of disease, the new science of epidemiology emerged; the "fathers of sociology" observed social relations in industrial cities before establishing their new paradigms of thought: Marx in Manchester, Weber in Berlin, and Durkheim in Berlin and Bordeaux. The Manchester Statistical Society was formed in 1833, the first organization to systematically study and document social issues such as child labor and overcrowding. Later, theorists at the Chicago School in the early 20th century viewed the city as a living organism with its own metabolism. For the first time, the city was an entity which could be both studied and solved, and a series of liberal reforms were introduced during the latter half of the 19th century to ameliorate the worst excesses of industrial capitalism.

Urban protests—"Peterloo"

Government repression famously came to a head at a protest on August 16, 1819 in St. Peter's Field, Manchester, an urban open space. The new urban culture enabled 60,000 people to gather to protest against the lack of suffrage in northern England, and in favor of parliamentary reform. Eleven people were killed and 400 injured when soldiers and cavalry stormed through the crowd. Soon after it became known as the "Peterloo" massacre after the Battle of Waterloo, which had taken place in 1815.

Peterloo massacre

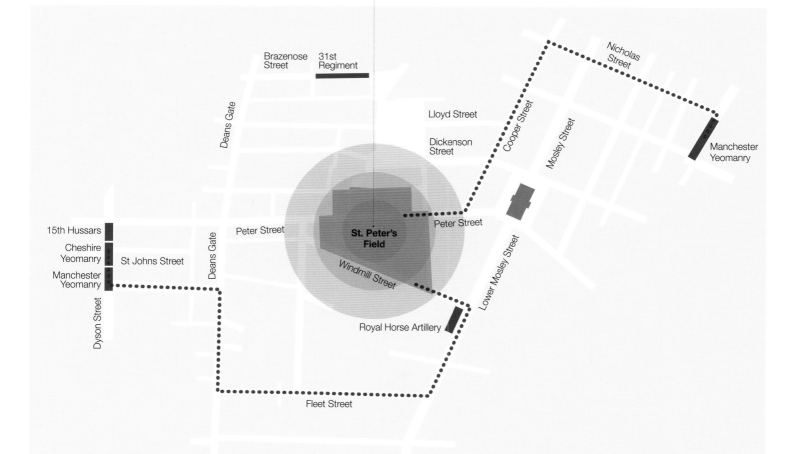

Architecture of Industry

Industrial cities may have contained the machinery for production but they were also hubs of banking, trade, and transport. New kinds of buildings dominated the skyline, utilizing the technologies of wrought iron and sheet glass. Warehouses and factories with tall chimneys belched out smoke, and functionality dominated aesthetics. Manchester, although a symbol of manufacturing, was in fact largely filled with warehouses, with only 18 percent of the labor force employed in the mills in the first part of the 19th century. There were wrought iron edifices built by architect-engineers: huge civic, transport and trade buildings, as well as viaducts and bridges. Yet these were uncertain times, and for civic buildings neo-classical styling lent historical weight and authority to the governance of the new urban population. This reference to classical history in architecture found its way into the design of a great many of Manchester's buildings. Philanthropic and liberal reformist organizations built libraries and workers' housing; the corporation built public buildings and the town hall. Private corporations made their authority concrete by cladding their buildings in stone, with columns and porticoes.

Architecture of the new city

The growth of the city of Manchester correlated with innovations and construction of the transport network, which allowed the city to expand since people could live farther afield yet still travel by train or stagecoach for work. Later, these transport links included an extensive network of electrically powered buses and trams. Because transport was expensive, this resulted in "suburbanization of the bourgeoisie," explored on pages 84–85.

Royal Exchange

Liverpool and Manchester Railway

1 *St Ann's Square*
2 *Bridgewater canal*
3 *Warehouses from canal to Deansgate*
4 *Arkwright's first steam-powered mill*
5 *Manchester Bolton & Bury canal*
6 *Rochdale canal*
7 *Portico Library*
8 *Royal Exchange*
9 *Murray Mills in Ancoats*
10 *First Town Hall*
11 *Merchants' Warehouse, Castlefield*
12 *Liverpool and Manchester Railway*
13 *Brunswick Mill*
14 *Theatre Royal*
15 *New neo-Gothic Town Hall*

Theatre Royal

The industrial city was a new type of economic system, an urban industrial capitalism that produced and consumed both locally and globally. The size of the new urban population and the cultural milieu in which it existed resulted in the provision of a range of new urban amenities. Entertainment, leisure, and educational buildings were constructed, which had previously only existed in the largest mercantile cities such as London. Even the circus, which had roamed through small villages and towns, now had a home in the city. Theaters, museums, and other places of entertainment sprang up to cater for the masses, and the Education Acts of the late 19th century saw the construction of public state schools for the cities' children. New manufacturing processes were used to make goods for export, but also to make everyday objects for local consumption: iron cookware, crockery, stoneware, and glass. Consumer society was in its infancy, but a new kind of food shopping had come into being as a result of manufacturing. Markets had previously been the site of food shopping, but customers ran the risk of food being adulterated, of poor quality, or even perished. Branding both of foods and of the shops which sold food came into being, and a new city form appeared to accommodate the new shops, the high street, which replaced the market square as the center for local trade during the 19th century.

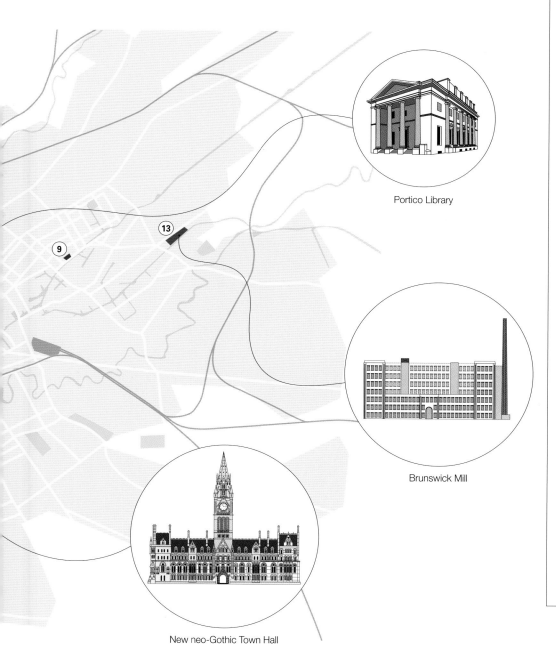

Portico Library

Brunswick Mill

New neo-Gothic Town Hall

TIMELINE OF NEW INFRASTRUCTURE

1735–53 *St Ann's Square*—fashionable part of town, with elegant brick houses.

1759–77 *Bridgewater canal* constructed connecting Manchester to Liverpool and the Midlands by way of the Grand Trunk Canal.

1770–1829 *Warehouses from canal to Deansgate* (formerly Alport Street) designed by James Brindley (also the engineer for the aqueduct across the Irwell for the Bridgewater canal).

1782 *Arkwright's first steam-powered mill*, Miller Street, Shudehill (destroyed 1940) in which steam was used to raise water from a waterwheel.

1791 *Manchester Bolton & Bury canal* joined Leeds–Liverpool canal near Bolton.

1804 *Rochdale canal* joined Bridgewater canal at Castlefield linking Manchester and Hull and opening Manchester to the east coast.

1802–06 *Portico Library*, Mosley Street, designed by Thomas Harrison.

1806 *Royal Exchange* designed by Thomas Harrison.

1798–1806 *Murray Mills* in Ancoats. Old Mill 1798, Union (now Redhill) Street, powered by Boulton & Watt steam engine, is the oldest extant mill in Manchester, and typical of purpose-built mills

1822–25 *First Town Hall*, King Street, designed by Francis Goodwin.

1827–28 *Merchants' Warehouse*, Castlefield—the oldest extant canal warehouse with arched shipping holes allowing goods to be loaded direct from the water (converted to studios and offices 1996).

1830 *Liverpool and Manchester Railway* opens.

1840s *Brunswick Mill*, Bradford Road, on the banks of the Ashton canal constructed by Davis Bellhouse. One of the largest mid-19th-century mills in the country.

1844 *Theatre Royal*, Peter Street, designed by Chester & Irwin.

1868–77 *New neo-Gothic Town Hall* designed by Alfred Waterhouse, embodying the self-governance of the industrial city and the power of the empire.

City Shaped by Industry

The industrial city was physically unlike any that had existed before. The polarization of wealth and poverty was stark, and this division was etched into the city fabric. Previously, cities had contained some manufacturing, as well as trading in goods manufactured in their environs. As the capital of Prussia, Berlin was a center for small-scale manufacturing with numerous small workshops, and Manchester had a specific 18th-century typology, the workshop house, where one or more families would reside below a shared attic workshop space. Wealthy merchants lived centrally in the fashionable streets around St. Ann's Square, close to the thriving trading area of Market Street. But mechanized industry also tended to be drawn toward centers of mercantile trade, so factories were sited in the center of towns and cities that were already centers of finance and transport.

As populations exploded, the streets around the industrial cores rapidly became slums and rookeries, in which the poorest people were densely packed. This was a new kind of poverty, an urban poverty which was linked inextricably to the physical conditions of the city. Politically, the placing of the worst slums

The suburbanization of wealth in Chicago

In 1870, 49 percent of Chicago's population were immigrants. People from Ireland and Germany arrived in the mid-19th century and were followed by large numbers of Russian Jews, Slavs, and Italians. Concentric zonation was observed by the geographers of the Chicago School, who mapped the influx of migrants who began at the city center and gradually worked their way outward as they gained wealth and power. The maps below, based on Chicago census data, show the export of wealth to the suburbs, reflected in property ownership, economic class, and lower urban densities.

Population density per sq. mile, 1930

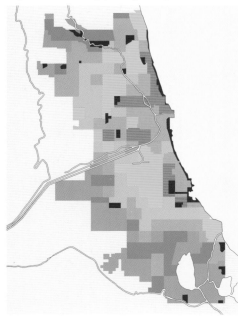

■ 50,000 and above	■ 10,000–19,999
■ 40,000–49,999	■ 5,000–9,999
■ 30,000–39,999	■ Under 5,000
■ 20,000–29,999	■ Parklands

Economic status of families, 1934

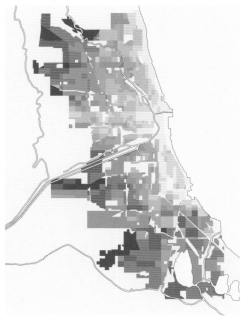

■ Highest economic class	■ Lowest economic class
■ High economic class	
■ Middle economic class	
■ Low economic class	

Percentage of total homes owned, 1934

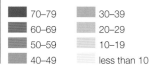

■ 70–79	■ 30–39
■ 60–69	■ 20–29
■ 50–59	■ 10–19
■ 40–49	■ less than 10

nearest to the factories served as a warning to slightly better-off workers of the dire fate that would befall them should they attempt to upset the status quo.

The dirt, squalor, and disease at the industrial center prompted those who could afford it to move to the suburbs, forcing the city's boundaries outward. In Manchester, the merchants' dwellings were quickly abandoned to be converted into warehousing and the workshop houses which had previously been the good-quality homes of skilled craftsmen became multiple-occupancy tenements. Urban transport connections enabled the suburbanization of the bourgeoisie, further polarizing wealth and poverty into concentric rings around the core. Industrial workers' suburbs sprang up and quickly became slums, as the city was flipped in terms of prestige. Whereas in the 18th century the rich had lived in the center, in the 19th century they clamored to live at the edge. Engels noted that the shape of the city concealed the true nature of working-class poverty from middle-class eyes. "The town itself is peculiarly built so that a person may live in it for years and go in and out daily without coming into contact with a working people's quarter or even with workers, so long as he confines himself to business or to pleasure walks."

Polarization of poverty and wealth

As in Chicago, Manchester was also zoned concentrically by wealth. Arterial routes into the city center were lined with stores for middle-class consumption, a new urban form: the high street. It was in the interests of storekeepers to maintain an outward appearance of cleanliness and wealth, and the avenues of storefronts effectively concealed the jumbled working-class districts behind. The poor could not shop on such streets and were thus invisible to many middle-class occupants of the city; the two worlds were very close, but never collided.

Housing conditions in Manchester, 1904

Suburb housing with gardens

Housing complying to later bye-laws

Housing complying to early bye-laws

Converted back-to-back properties

Slum housing/ back-to-back

Railway/canal land

Warehouses/offices

Works/factories

River/canal ways

Railways

Public parks, recreation grounds, and cemeteries

Source: Marr Map of Manchester Housing (1904)

Deindustrialization

The phenomenon of the "shrinking city" is evident throughout the industrial areas of western Europe and the USA, as automation of manufacture, containerization of ports, and efficient communication has reduced the need for a large labor force. In the northwest of England, the number of industrial jobs halved between 1960 and 1980, and this had a clear, negative effect on population numbers. In the USA, Detroit was formerly the leading city for automobile and weapons manufacture, reaching its peak population of 1.8 million in 1950, but by the year 2000 its population had fallen to just 700,000. In the late 20th century, the heart of

industrial production has moved to mega-cities in the developing world, such as Guangzhou or São Paulo. Thus, city centers that had been packed with warehousing and manufacturing emptied, and the unpopular residential areas near the core were left largely uninhabited. The process of suburbanization of wealth continued apace, with out-of-town offices, business and retail parks taking trade away from the unfashionable centers where vacant and derelict plots deterred investment. By the early 1990s, industrial city centers were deserted; Liverpool's center, for example, had just 2,300 inhabitants.

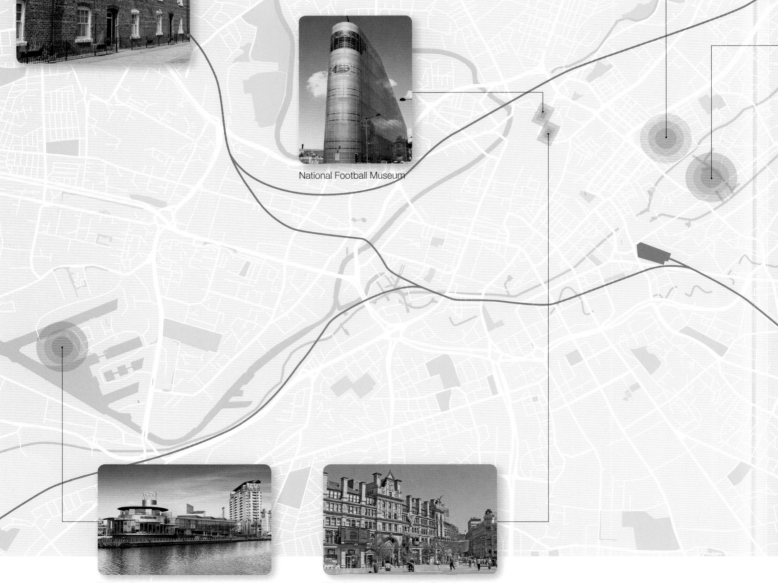

Georgian terraced housing in Ancoats

National Football Museum

Salford Quays

The Printworks (27 Withy Grove)

Diversification has been a solution for many industrial cities. The cotton industry peaked in Britain in 1913, but slow take-up of new technologies and the unionization of the workforce meant that competition from the Far East quickly took its toll, and by the 1960s mills were closing in Lancashire at the rate of one per week. Yet Manchester's economy was diverse enough to absorb the loss, with manufacturing in other, more technologically advanced sectors on the rise. In the late 20th century, neoliberal and conservative economic policy had emphasized the global marketability of the city-region, and Manchester employed several strategies, including hosting the Commonwealth Games, reorganizing the city center as a place of heritage and leisure (after the 1996 IRA bombing), and encouraging the redevelopment of former industrial buildings as dwellings for the affluent. Universities have played a key role in this process in many industrial cities; Liverpool's center now has around 23,000 inhabitants, many of them students. In the USA other factors, such as climate, also play a part. In the mid-20 century populations shifted between the "Frost Belt" (northeastern) cities to the "Sun Belt" (southern) cities, facilitated by the advent of air conditioning, but the trend is now reversing, as drought and water shortages are having an impact.

Not all industrial cities have succeeded in the competition for global investment, and many continue to suffer from entrenched poverty and spatial segregation. In Detroit people continue to abandon the city center. Liverpool has regenerated its docklands, yet redundant spaces, "obsolete" buildings, and associated urban blight continue to be problematic and the population as a whole is still falling. In many cases, former industrial metropolises which came into being as a result of specific economic, social, and political circumstances have not adapted well to the globalization of markets. Their future in the 21st century remains uncertain.

Industrial decline
Primary industries in the UK began to disappear overseas, as markets became global. However, although heavy industry has declined, manufacturing is still an important part of the British economy.

Regeneration at New Islington

Successful regeneration projects
Since the mid-1980s, Manchester has been re-marketed as a global "destination" through preservation and regeneration of its historic industrial fabric. Examples of new iconic projects include the National Football Museum (formerly Urbis) by Ian Simpson Architects and the development at Salford Quays. The formerly uninhabited industrial quarter of Ancoats is now among the most expensive and prestigious city center locations.

City of Manchester Stadium

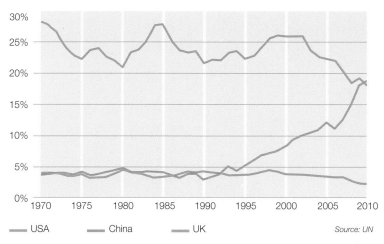

UK import and export of cotton piece goods 1951–64

Millions square yards

UK imports: cotton piece goods   UK exports: cotton piece goods

Source: www.spinningtheweb.org

Manufacturing output as shares of world total

USA   China   UK   *Source: UN*

THE RATIONAL CITY

ANDREW HEROD

Core city
PARIS _____

Secondary cities
VIENNA _____
NEW YORK _____
LONDON _____
BUDAPEST _____
WASHINGTON, D.C. _____

Left: Paris, France

The Rational City: Introduction

A city of layers

Paris's built environment is a palimpsest constructed over two millennia. Roman Paris is still visible in the street patterns of modern Paris, illustrating how the spatial structures of one period can continue to shape those that follow them centuries later.

Rulers have frequently designed urban landscapes to promote society's functioning along more rational lines— that is to say, they have used spatial engineering for the purposes of social engineering. Although such thinking has been implemented in numerous places— as with Roman towns or Manhattan's street grid—it was perhaps in 19th-century Paris that it reached its zenith. This chapter, then, principally explores Paris's redevelopment in the 1800s along rationalist lines.

Settlement of the Paris area began around 4200 BCE. According to most scholars, by about 250 BCE the Parisii tribe, for whom the city is named, had established an *oppidum* (defensive position) on an island in the River Seine to control trade along it. After conquering the area, the Romans built the Gallo-Romano city of Lutetia, on the Seine's left bank. In the 6th century the focal point moved back to what is today the Île de la Cité, around which modern Paris would grow.

From these humble origins has emerged one of the globe's most influential cities. The Paris region has the world's sixth-largest urban GDP

━━━ Roman streets
▬ ▬ ▬ Presumed continuation of Roman streets
▬▬▬ Roman buildings
▪ ▪ ▪ ▪ Aqueduct

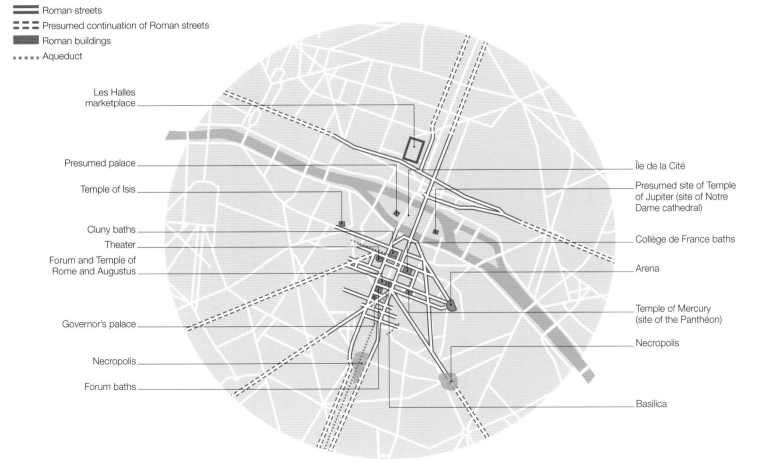

Les Halles marketplace

Presumed palace

Temple of Isis

Cluny baths

Theater

Forum and Temple of Rome and Augustus

Governor's palace

Necropolis

Forum baths

Île de la Cité

Presumed site of Temple of Jupiter (site of Notre Dame cathedral)

Collège de France baths

Arena

Temple of Mercury (site of the Panthéon)

Necropolis

Basilica

($813 billion in 2012) and is the planet's most visited tourist spot. The region has Europe's largest commercial office market at about 50 million square yards of space and Europe's second-largest inland port. In 2012 A.T. Kearney and the Chicago Council on Global Affairs ranked Paris the planet's third-most important city. Paris, then, is a major engine of the global economy.

Paris's purposeful planning has allowed the city to mobilize for economic and other purposes, with such efforts continuing to shape it long after their originators' deaths. Les Halles—established in the 12th century by King Philippe-Auguste and called *Le Ventre de Paris* ("the Belly of Paris") by Émile Zola—served Parisians as a marketplace until the 1970s. Several major streets follow Roman ones while defensive walls constructed by Charles V (built 1356–83) and Louis XIII (built 1633–36) were later demolished to become the pathway for Louis XIV's 17th-century *grands boulevards*. Widespread reconstruction in the 19th century continues to shape how the city functions.

Paris as an economic, political, and cultural center

Paris has long been an important decision-making center. In 508 Clovis I, King of the Franks, made it his capital. Charlemagne subsequently moved the capital to Aachen/Aix-la-Chapelle, but in 987 Hugh Capet, Count of Paris, was crowned king and once again made Paris the capital. Although Louis XIV removed the seat of power to his chateau at Versailles in 1682, in 1789 French revolutionaries returned it to Paris, where,

" Paris was home to the third-largest number of Fortune 500 company headquarters worldwide in 2013, behind only Beijing and Tokyo."

Walls of Paris

Paris's earliest walls were erected to defend the city. However, the Wall of the Farmers-General (built between 1784 and 1791 at what was then the city limits) and its sixty-two toll barriers principally served to control the movement of goods into Paris so that they could be taxed.

except for brief periods of conflict, it has remained. Today Paris is the undisputed focal point of France's highly centralized political system, to the point that many declare that "*Quand Paris éternue, la France s'enrhume*" ("When Paris sneezes, France catches a cold"). Its political position as a "hypertrophic city" (the enlarged "head" of a nation-state's "body") is reflected in the large number of buildings devoted to government functions. Such primacy is even manifested in telephone area codes—France is broken into five regions, with the code for Paris being "01."

Historically, Paris's role as an economic and political center has driven its population growth. By 1300 Paris's population was 225,000, the largest in western Europe. In 1500 it was still western Europe's most populous city, though by 1800 it was second to London. Such population concentration led to the establishment of the University of Paris in the mid-12th century and the city soon became a center of learning for scholars from across Europe. Paris's importance as an educational center continues, as its more than seventy institutions of higher learning give it one of the greatest concentrations of students in Europe. The Paris region has five "competitive clusters" established under government aegis linking

hundreds of software, healthcare, multimedia, automotive, and other companies with universities and research laboratories. Globally, Paris is second only to Brussels for hosting international organizations, including the OECD, UNESCO, and the European Space Agency.

Long an important architectural trendsetter—Notre Dame established the city as a leader in Gothic architecture in the mid-12th century—Paris produced the Beaux Arts style in the 19th century and High Modernism in the 20th. More recently the hi-tech/postmodern Centre Georges Pompidou has inspired architectural designs across the planet. Indeed, such has been its creativity in music, philosophy, art, architecture, and literature that Walter Benjamin called Paris "the capital of the 19th century" and Gertrude Stein claimed that it was "where the 20th century was." Today, Paris is a multicultural city, with significant immigrant and gay populations. This diversity continues to produce an urban environment of considerable cultural vibrancy.

——— Louis XIV's *grands boulevards* (late 17th century)
——— Louis XIII (early 17th century)
– · – · Charles V (14th century)
– – – Philippe Auguste (12th century)
• • • • 10th–11th century
······· Gallo-Roman

The Rationalization of Space after the French Revolution

French geographer Henri Lefebvre once remarked that "new social relationships call for a new space, and vice versa." The revolutionaries of 1789 certainly thought so: one of the first things they did was create a new architectural and planning department, the *Conseil des Bâtiments Civils*, that would turn the royalist and clerical landscape of Paris into a rationally planned republican and secular landscape.

The idea that the built environment should reflect the tenets of the Age of Reason was central to the revolutionaries' goals. Hence, they repurposed many old buildings, turning Notre Dame cathedral into a "Temple of Reason" and converting the Panthéon from a church to a place of final rest for France's great and good. But new social institutions also required new types of buildings. Consequently, courts and prisons were redesigned to reflect the new rights of the accused—the right to trial in open court rather than in secret, for instance,

A new city for a new society

Ideas of rational planning stemming from the Enlightenment were embodied in Paris's urban landscape both before and after the French Revolution. For instance, fears that corpses buried in myriad churchyards across Paris constituted a health hazard resulted in a 1786 law banning cemeteries from the city. Over the next few years some 6 million bodies were dug up and stored in the city's mine shafts, which had been created in the Middle Ages when rock to build Paris had been quarried. In the early 1800s the new Père-Lachaise, Montmartre, and Montparnasse cemeteries were opened, located beyond what was then Paris's outskirts. These cemeteries affirmed a new vision of order, one which impacted both the living and the dead. The revolutionaries also planned to rebuild parts of Paris. A more orderly urban fabric, they believed, was both a manifestation of new social mores and would also provide the foundations out of which a new society would emerge.

Plans to improve the area around the Les Halles market were drawn up by the Commission des Artistes, which met between 1793 and 1797 to explore ideas for redesigning Paris

Montmartre (Cimetière du Nord)

Site of Cimetière des Saints-Innocents, the oldest and largest cemetery in Paris, which closed in 1780 and was emptied of bodies in 1786

Montparnasse (Cimetière du Sud)

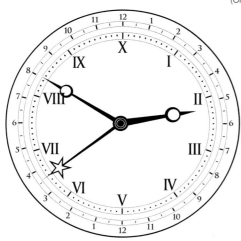

Rationalization of time

Urban planning was not the only arena in which the revolutionaries hoped to foster more rational ways of living. They also created a new calendar with ten-day weeks, ten-hour days, and hundred-minute hours. Under this decimal system, one "revolutionary second" was 0.864 standard seconds, one "revolutionary minute" was one standard minute and 26.4 standard seconds, and one "revolutionary hour" was two standard hours and twenty-four standard minutes. Several clockmakers built time pieces that displayed such a decimal system.

The square in front of the church of Saint-Sulpice was to be redesigned as part of a plan to transform the church into a place for the deist worship of the "Supreme Being" necessitated new floorplans. The revolutionaries also emphasized equality in death as in life—whereas previously the privileged had been buried inside churches and the rest outside them, now rich and poor were buried side by side in the new municipal cemeteries. Cemeteries were also presented as secular, rather than religious, places.

For his part, Napoléon Bonaparte wanted to turn Paris into "the most beautiful city that has ever existed," both to create work for unemployed Parisians but also to bring order to its narrow, snaking medieval streets. Thus, the rue de Rivoli in central Paris was built as an elegant east–west axis to which a series of perpendicular streets would connect, providing pedestrian-friendly arcades for luxury shops. To facilitate transportation he had three river bridges and several canals built, as well as two-and-a-half miles of stone quais to prevent flooding.

Similar efforts to plan space rationally were also implemented at this time in other cities, as with Frenchman Pierre L'Enfant's 1791 plan for Washington, D.C., and the street grid developed for Manhattan in New York City. Such ideas were also taken up in the 1920s by the Russian revolutionaries, who set about building "Soviet cities" whose layouts they viewed not only as reflecting greater social equality—land use would be based on rational planning rather than market forces—but also as providing an environment in which people would adopt new, "socialist" cultural and political identities. For them, the built environment both mirrored developing social relations and was also constitutive of them.

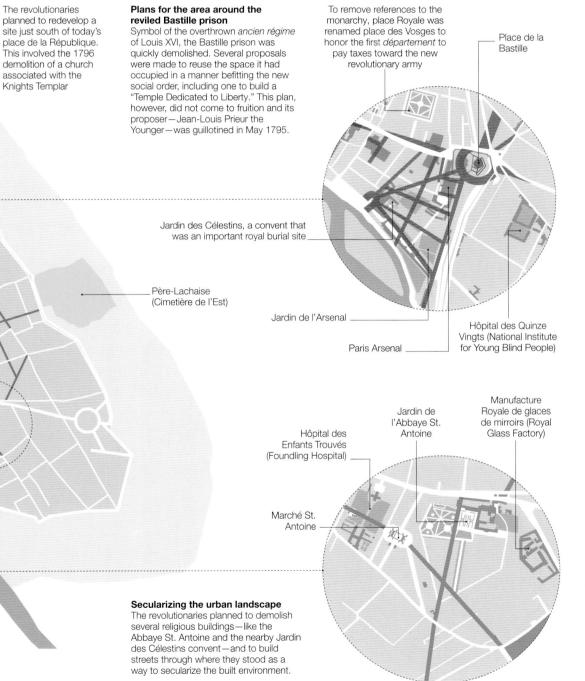

The revolutionaries planned to redevelop a site just south of today's place de la République. This involved the 1796 demolition of a church associated with the Knights Templar

Plans for the area around the reviled Bastille prison
Symbol of the overthrown *ancien régime* of Louis XVI, the Bastille prison was quickly demolished. Several proposals were made to reuse the space it had occupied in a manner befitting the new social order, including one to build a "Temple Dedicated to Liberty." This plan, however, did not come to fruition and its proposer—Jean-Louis Prieur the Younger—was guillotined in May 1795.

To remove references to the monarchy, place Royale was renamed place des Vosges to honor the first *département* to pay taxes toward the new revolutionary army

Place de la Bastille

Jardin des Célestins, a convent that was an important royal burial site

Père-Lachaise (Cimetière de l'Est)

Jardin de l'Arsenal

Paris Arsenal

Hôpital des Quinze Vingts (National Institute for Young Blind People)

Manufacture Royale de glaces de mirroirs (Royal Glass Factory)

Jardin de l'Abbaye St. Antoine

Hôpital des Enfants Trouvés (Foundling Hospital)

Marché St. Antoine

Secularizing the urban landscape
The revolutionaries planned to demolish several religious buildings—like the Abbaye St. Antoine and the nearby Jardin des Célestins convent—and to build streets through where they stood as a way to secularize the built environment.

The Haussmannization of Paris

Soon after seizing absolute power in a coup on December 2, 1851, Emperor Napoléon III set about fulfilling both his own and his uncle Napoléon Bonaparte's dream of turning medieval Paris into a modern city worthy of an empire. Although several rulers had previously attempted some wholesale urban redevelopment, such that by the 1830s there were already a few open boulevards like the rue des Italiens and the Champs-Élysées, much of the cityscape remained crowded and disorderly. Paris had the smallest streets of any major European city, with its thoroughfares primarily designed for pedestrians rather than vehicles. These narrow streets not only made commerce more difficult but also made it easier for workers to challenge imperial rule because they could readily build barricades to block troop movements. Consequently, the emperor hired Georges-Eugène Haussmann to redesign the city through the *éventrement* (gutting) of central Paris. In planning the city to be more rational Napoléon and Haussmann hoped to facilitate both trade (allowing goods to get more easily to central markets from outside the city) and social control. As Haussmann put it: "*la destruction des vieux quartiers enlèverait un camp à l'émeute*" ("the destruction of the old neighborhoods should remove a training ground for rioting").

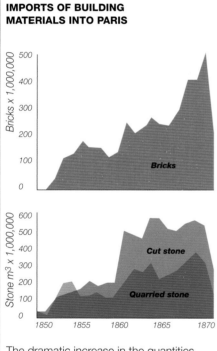

IMPORTS OF BUILDING MATERIALS INTO PARIS

Bricks x 1,000,000

Bricks

Stone m³ x 1,000,000

Cut stone

Quarried stone

1850　1855　1860　1865　1870

The dramatic increase in the quantities of bricks (top) and quarried stone and cut stone (bottom) coming into Paris after 1850 is an indication of the scale of the construction work generated by Haussmann's plans.

The Haussmann network

Although Haussmann is often credited with transforming the city, in many instances he simply implemented earlier plans. However, he accelerated the process dramatically, establishing three principal networks to ease traffic circulation. The first (1854–58) improved north–south movement in central Paris by constructing the boulevard de Sébastopol. The second network (1858–60) allowed the easier flow of traffic out from the center. This included roadworks around what would become the place de la République in central Paris, the rue de Rome linking the new gare Saint-Lazare with northwestern Paris, and the boulevards around the Arc de Triomphe. The third network aimed to better link the old suburbs with the rest of the city. Thus, the eastern working-class neighborhood of Belleville was linked to the industrial district Bercy to its south, while the southern part of the wealthy 16th arrondissement in the west was connected to the area around the Arc de Triomphe.

Bridges

In addition to building roads and housing, Haussmann constructed or reconstructed many bridges across the Seine. These were essential to connecting the emerging road network on the two sides of the river.

New and reconstructed streets of Paris

■ Second Empire, 1852–70
■ Third Republic, post-1870

Pont des Invalides

Pont de l'Alma

With a knowledge of architecture, planning, the law, and finance, Haussmann set about implementing a comprehensive transformation of the city that would regulate the design of buildings, roads, and boulevards, establish green spaces, modernize the sewer and water systems, and create terminating vistas suitable for public monuments emphasizing the empire's glory. It is estimated that some 60 percent of Paris's buildings were rebuilt in the process, with about 20,000 houses being demolished and over 40,000 built between 1852 and 1872. These developments led to an increase in rents, which forced poorer people toward Paris's outer neighborhoods and led to the "bourgeoisification" of its center.

Such efforts to remake medieval cities into modern, more rationally planned ones were not confined to Paris. In 1857 Emperor Franz Joseph I of Austria decreed that Vienna's old city walls be demolished and a new ringroad (the *Ringstrasse*) be built, thus removing an impediment to the movement of traffic around and through the city. His plan to remake Vienna also involved constructing new buildings to showcase the Habsburg Empire's grandeur. Copying Haussmann, widening the streets likewise made it more difficult for crowds to erect barricades. This was an important consideration, given that Vienna had seen significant demonstrations during the 1848 revolutionary wave that had engulfed Europe.

Rue de Rivoli

The area around the rue de Rivoli and the Louvre saw some of the earliest large-scale demolitions. Although the rue de Rivoli was created by Napoléon Bonaparte, Haussmann extended it eastward into the Marais district. Below the street lies one of the new main sewer lines constructed during Napoléon III's reign.

Île de la Cité

The clearances on the Île de la Cité in the 1860s were extensive, even by modern-day standards. The goal here was to facilitate the speedy movement of goods across the Seine in Paris's center.

Boulevard de Sébastopol

Pont Louis-Philippe

Pont Saint-Michel

Pont National

Pont d'Austerlitz

City of Health: Sewers and Parks

During the Middle Ages Paris's sewage generally flowed straight into the Seine. However, as the population grew the smell of waste moving through open sewers became increasingly unbearable. Worse, these open sewers were a source of disease. Although there were early 19th-century attempts to improve the situation—Napoléon Bonaparte wanted to build "bubbling fountains at every road intersection so as to sanitize the air and clean the streets"—several cholera outbreaks finally pushed the authorities to act. Viewing disease as largely resulting from flawed urban design, Haussmann argued that creating a more salubrious city required better planning. Consequently, whereas in 1800 Paris only had about 12 miles of sewers and some 60 miles in 1840, Haussmann added over 300 miles. Heralded as an engineering marvel that brought Paris into the modern age, the new system transformed the city from one in which waste was *"tout à la rue"* ("all in the street") to *"tout à l'égout"* ("all in the sewer").

Parks of Paris

Together with Jean-Charles Adolphe Alphand, the city's Director of Promenades and Plantings, the horticulturist Jean-Pierre Barillet-Deschamps, architect Jean-Antoine-Gabriel Davioud, and Eugène Belgrand from the Water Department, Haussmann sought to improve public health and morals by planning Paris rationally. Not least among these efforts was the laying out of numerous parks and green spaces to encourage the citizens to take exercise "en plein air" (in the open air).

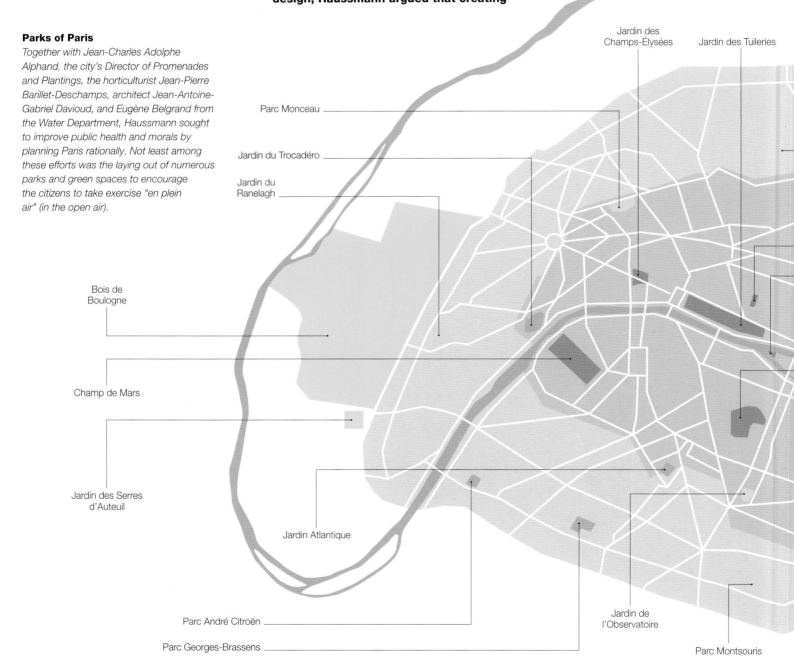

Jardin des Champs-Élysées

Jardin des Tuileries

Parc Monceau

Jardin du Trocadéro

Jardin du Ranelagh

Bois de Boulogne

Champ de Mars

Jardin des Serres d'Auteuil

Jardin Atlantique

Parc André Citroën

Parc Georges-Brassens

Jardin de l'Observatoire

Parc Montsouris

Reflecting bourgeois fascination with "progress," the sewers emblematized the new rational social and spatial order being imposed upon Paris and soon became a tourist attraction. This was quite a different view than previously—in his 1830 novel *Les Misérables*, for instance, Victor Hugo had linked the sewers to discord and revolution, seeing them as "the evil in the city's blood" but also "the city's conscience," the place where "all the dishonesties of civilization … fall into the pit of truthfulness." Concurrently, changing attitudes toward water and bathing meant that creating cleaner citizens became tied to ideas of modernity, and Haussmann built a second pipe network to bring potable water into the city.

In addition to water and sewer lines Napoléon III ordered the construction of numerous green spaces. Impressed with London's parks, the emperor viewed green spaces as bringing the countryside to the city. Not only would parks serve as a social safety valve by providing working-class Parisians spaces in which to relax rather than riot, but they were also imagined to "give Paris lungs." Such ideas presaged the garden city movement of the early 20th century that shaped other cities' development—Paris's parks influenced Frederick Law Olmsted (who designed New York's Central Park) and Béla Rerrich (who designed several parks in Budapest).

Extant ideas about the role played by air in spreading disease also shaped how streetscapes were constructed. According to the then-popular "miasmatic theory of disease," lack of air circulation and sunlight were considered bad for people's health. Consequently, many buildings acquired elaborate terraces, loggias, and dormers as Paris's bourgeoisie increasingly found upper floors desirable as places from which to enjoy cooling winds, access sunlight, and admire the views.

Pre-Haussmann

Designed by Haussmann and his associates

Post-Haussmann

Square Marcel-Bleustein-Blanchet

Parc des Buttes-Chaumont

Parc de la Villette

Jardins du Palais-Royal

Square du Vert-Galant

Square Louis XIII

Jardin du Luxembourg

Jardin des Plantes

Parc de Bercy

Bois de Vincennes

Parc Floral de Paris

The sewer network in 1837

Sewers constructed 1856–78

Source: Gandy (1999)

Sewerage system

Haussmann's energy, drive, and enthusiasm were nowhere more evident than in the expansion of the system of sewers in the city. In the space of thirty years the length of the sewerage system increased fivefold. Haussmann's new sewers were so wide and spacious that tours were arranged so that the bourgeoisie and visiting royalty could marvel at the scale of the achievement.

Paris as a City for Transportation in the 19th Century

The coming of the railways radically transformed Paris's relationship with the rest of France, as goods and people could now get to and from the capital more rapidly than ever before. The first mainline station—the gare Saint-Lazare—opened in 1837, followed by the gare d'Austerliz and gare Montparnasse (both opened in 1840), the gare du Nord (inaugurated in 1846 but rebuilt between 1861 and 1865), the gare de l'Est (1849), and the gare de Lyon (1855). But the railways did not just change the connections between Paris and the outside world. They also had impacts within the city. Thus, whereas during the Middle Ages the portals to Paris had been the city gates, now it was the train stations that largely served as the capital's entrance points. Accordingly, architects attempted to make them awe-inspiring for arriving visitors. Moreover, train stations became focal points for new road construction to link them to commercial and residential areas within the city, such that more than 60 percent of present-day Paris's streets were built after 1853.

Regions served today by Paris's 19th-century railway stations

- Gare du Nord
- Gare de l'Est
- Gare de Lyon
- Gare d'Austerlitz
- Gare Montparnasse
- Gare Saint-Lazare

Machines for nation-building

The railways facilitated the "annihilation of space by time" to make the geographical movement of goods and people to and from Paris easier. By transforming public perceptions of the relationship between what were formerly considered to be distant cities, railways were central players in spurring greater national economic, political, and social integration. Although several 19th-century stations no longer operate—including the gare de la Bastille (opened in 1859 but demolished in 1984 to make way for the new opera house on the place de la Bastille) and the gare du Champ de Mars (built to receive construction materials for the pavilions of the various Paris World's Fairs)—the six mainline stations built during the golden age of steam continue to tie the country together.

While the middle of the century saw the building of a web of above-ground lines, by its end the focus was on building an underground transportation network—the Métro. By the 1890s Paris's streets had again become crowded as the city's population had burgeoned and as the first motor cars had begun to appear. In response, and in an effort to match cities like London, Athens, and Budapest, which already had underground train systems, as well as to prepare for the 1900 World's Fair to be held in Paris, Fulgence Bienvenüe, an engineer with Paris's Bridges and Roads Department, convinced the municipal council to adopt a plan to build a new, subterranean rail system.

The first Métro line, connecting porte Maillot in the west with porte de Vincennes in the east, opened in time to shuttle people across Paris for the 1900 Summer Olympic Games. The following year Bienvenüe unveiled a plan to add additional lines so that nowhere would be more than 500 meters (547 yards) from a Métro station. By 1914 there were fifty-six miles of Métro rails in a ten-line network that carried 467 million travelers annually. Continuing the theme of nature in the city exemplified by Paris's new parks, the earliest Métro station designs made extensive reference to wildlife—entrances had two ornate lampposts resembling sprays of Lily of the Valley, while the entrance coverings looked like dragonfly wings.

Growth of the rail network

c.1850

c.1860

c.1870

c.1890

Source: Clout (1977)

Cathedrals of steam

The new railway stations were designed to project the magnificence of the Second Empire and to emphasize the power of the steam engine, which symbolized progress in the new era. For its part, the art nouveau architecture of the early Métro stations reflected the exuberance of the Belle Époque.

Art nouveau Métro stations

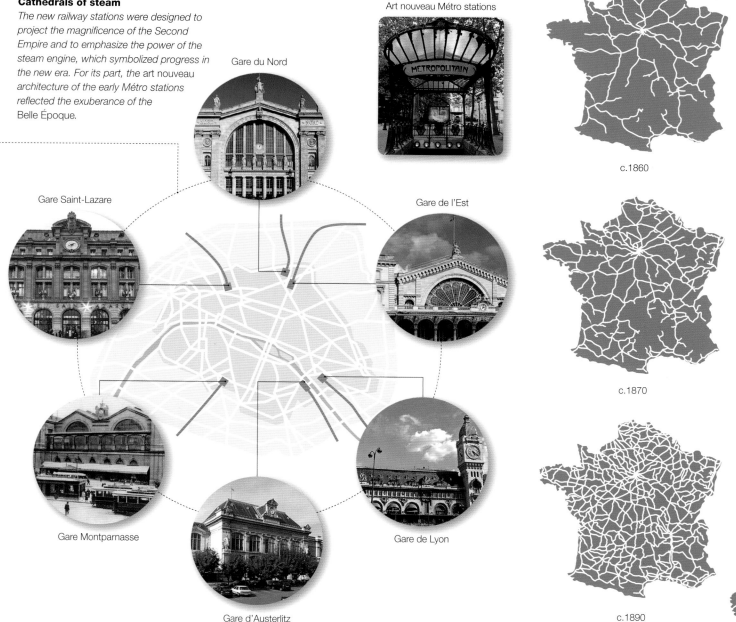

Gare du Nord

Gare Saint-Lazare

Gare de l'Est

Gare Montparnasse

Gare d'Austerlitz

Gare de Lyon

Paris as an Imperial Canvas

Understanding that, as French sociologist Jean Duvignaud has put it, "the city is a language," Napoléon III wanted to build a metropolis that would speak to and for the empire. He envisioned the new Paris as an imposing city of marble, one that would be a lasting symbol of French power. The city, then, would literally be a text, the architecture and landscape of which people could read as they passed by during their day-to-day activities.

Perhaps one of the most grandiose buildings intended for this purpose was the Garnier Opera House, built between 1861 and 1875. Viewed as a way of communicating with posterity, the building was replete with symbolism, not least of which was its physical location in the heart of a neighborhood that was itself in the center of bourgeois western Paris and therefore, metaphorically, of France and the empire. Covered with gilt, pastel colors, and imperial symbols like eagles and the initials of the emperor and his wife Empress Eugénie, the

Architecture fit for an empire

The Haussmann era left Paris with a distinctive architectural style. Thus, a typical Haussmannian boulevard is broad and lined on both sides by apartment buildings with uniform façades of cut stone. It generally opens on to a large monument or imposing building, which serves as a terminating vista designed to emphasize Napoléon III's power and splendor. Apartment buildings are no more than seven stories tall. The second and fifth floors usually have balconies. Several families of varying social classes were expected to live under the same roof. Normally, apartment buildings had a mansard roof (a double-pitched roof with a steep lower slope and dormers to provide light). Such roofs increased the living space in the attic, thereby providing an additional usable floor for servants. One of the most impressive buildings constructed as a terminating vista was the Opéra Garnier. Designed to rival the splendor of Louis XIV's palace at Versailles, it was the most expensive building initiated in Second Empire Paris. Its construction required clearing nearly three acres of land and building several new thoroughfares, including the avenue de l'Opéra that leads to its principal façade.

Société Générale bank

Gare du Nord train station

Opéra Garnier

Eiffel Tower

Théâtre de la Ville

Opéra Garnier's Beaux Arts style oozed imperial self-assurance while its symmetry spoke to the age's ideas about rational planning and progress. It inspired similar edifices elsewhere, including the Warsaw Philharmonic building and Kraków's Juliusz Słowacki Theatre, the Library of Congress's Thomas Jefferson Building in Washington, D.C., the Theatro Municipal do Rio de Janeiro, and opera houses in Hanoi and Ho Chi Minh City.

Paris also held several international exhibitions in the 19th and early 20th centuries designed to underscore French industrial prowess and cultural superiority—Gustave Eiffel, for instance, built his iconic tower for the 1889 Exposition Universelle (World's Fair). However, it was probably the 1931 International Colonial Exhibition in which the colonies "came to Paris" and one could "take a tour of the world in a day" which most expressed Paris's relationship with the empire. Turning the bois de Vincennes into a site to showcase colonial architecture populated with "natives" from the colonies, the exhibition was calculated to demonstrate the benefits that French colonialism was supposedly bringing to the "unenlightened peoples" of the world. This display was intended as a spectacular confirmation that, through its *mission civilisatrice* ("civilizing mission"), France was banishing irrationality and backwardness from its colonies across the globe. It also allowed Parisians to gawk at the empire's "exotic" peoples and their buildings with a sense of superiority.

Such imperial extravaganzas were not confined to Paris. Other French cities held similar fairs demonstrating the alleged virtues of French colonialism, and other imperial powers followed suit—Amsterdam and Berlin held exhibitions in 1883 and 1896, respectively, as did London in 1911 and 1924.

Second Empire architecture

1 *Opéra Garnier*
2 *Louvre (1852–57 additions)*
3 *Élysée Palace (renovation)*
4 *Champs-Élysées buildings*
5 *Saint-Augustin church*
6 *Les Halles*
7 *Gare du Nord train station*
8 *Théâtre de la Ville*
9 *Théâtre du Châtelet*
10 *Théâtre de la Gaîté*
11 *Hôtel du Louvre*
12 *Société Générale bank*
13 *Eiffel Tower*

Théâtre du Châtelet

EXHIBITIONS IN PARIS 1810s–1930s

France's first national trade fair to promote improvements in agriculture and technology was held in Paris in 1798. Its success spawned subsequent exhibitions highlighting the country's industrial progress, leading to a World's Fair in 1855. Other countries held similar events, each trying to outdo its rivals in claiming technological superiority.

1819	Fifth Public Fair for French Industrial Products
1823	Sixth Public Fair for French Industrial Products
1827	Seventh Public Fair for French Industrial Products
1834	Eighth Public Fair for French Industrial Products
1839	Ninth Public Fair for French Industrial Products
1844	Tenth Public Fair for French Industrial Products
1849	Eleventh Public Fair for French Industrial Products
1855	World's Fair
1865	Fair for the Fine Arts as Applied to Industry
1867	World's Fair
1878	International Exhibition of Marine and River Industries
1878	World's Fair
1881	International Electricity Exhibition
1889	World's Fair (construction of the Eiffel Tower)
1898	International Automobile Exhibition
1900	World's Fair (construction of Le Grand Palais)
1925	International Exhibition of Modern Industrial and Decorative Arts
1931	International Colonial Exhibition
1937	International Exhibition Dedicated to Art and Technology in Modern Life

City of Culture

The changes taking place in Paris in the late 19th and early 20th centuries proved a fertile environment for myriad writers, philosophers, painters, and sculptors. The city's physical transformation and the political struggles between, on the one hand, the religious and political establishment and, on the other, the increasingly alienated proletariat exposed contradictions that were increasingly reflected in art and literature. Thus, the bourgeoisification of central and western Paris—especially around the newly constructed Parc Monceau—contrasted with the appalling living conditions experienced by immigrant workers streaming in from the countryside to neighborhoods like the Marais and Belleville in eastern Paris. Paris, then, was a city full of beauty and wealth but also of poverty, alienation, and significant self-indulgence. Charles Baudelaire perhaps best captured the spirit of the age and its contradictions with a new term, *modernité* ("modernity"), which he used to describe the tensions between "the transitory, the fugitive, [and] the contingent, which make up one half of art, the other being the eternal and the immutable."

Artistic communities

Montmartre

Montparnasse

The Montparnasse scene

The cafés and bars close to Montparnasse's carrefour Vavin (today's place Pablo-Picasso)—establishments such as Le Dôme, La Closerie des Lilas, La Rotonde, Le Select, and La Coupole—were favorite watering holes for painters, writers, and intellectuals in the early 1900s. Immortalized as "les Montparnos" ("the Montparnassians") by Michel Georges-Michel in his 1923 novel of the same name, people like Picasso, Modigliani, Jean Cocteau, and Diego Rivera created an iconoclastic atmosphere in the neighborhood.

Chemin du Montparnasse

With an entrance located at 21, avenue du Maine, the little passageway chemin du Montparnasse contained many artists' studios where Braque, Matisse, Picasso, Juan Gris, Amedeo Modigliani, Max Jacob, Marc Chagall, and others came to work. Today there is a little museum that recalls the neighborhood's heyday.

Rue Delambre

This street contains several sites associated with the early 20th-century's cultural vibe. Japanese painter Léonard Tsugouharu Foujita lived at no. 5 from 1917 to 1926 while the American photographer and dadaïst Man Ray had a studio at no. 13. Several of the expatriate American writers living in Paris between the world wars would drink at the Dingo Bar (today called the Auberge de Venise), located at 10, rue Delambre. These included Hemingway, F. Scott Fitzgerald, Sinclair Lewis, John Dos Passos, Ezra Pound, Henry Miller, and Thornton Wilder.

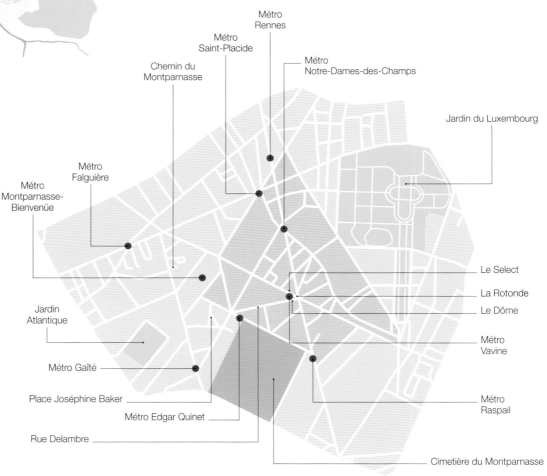

Métro Rennes

Métro Saint-Placide

Chemin du Montparnasse

Métro Notre-Dames-des-Champs

Jardin du Luxembourg

Métro Falguière

Métro Montparnasse-Bienvenüe

Jardin Atlantique

Le Select

La Rotonde

Le Dôme

Métro Vavine

Métro Gaîté

Place Joséphine Baker

Métro Raspail

Métro Edgar Quinet

Rue Delambre

Cimetière du Montparnasse

Within this environment many new forms of cultural expression were invented. The revolutionary art movements of Impressionism (associated with painters like Édouard Manet, Claude Monet, Pierre-Auguste Renoir, and Mary Cassatt), Fauvism (led by Henri Matisse and André Derain), and Cubism (pioneered by Pablo Picasso and Georges Braque) were all Parisian-born and the neighborhoods of Montmartre and Montparnasse became the heart of intellectual and artistic life in Paris and, arguably, the world. French writers like Marcel Proust (whose novel *In Search of Lost Time* explored the aristocracy's decline during the *fin de siècle*), musicians like Érik Satie, and poets like Guillaume Apollinaire (credited with coining the term "surrealism") were active in Paris. Many foreigners were similarly attracted to Paris, including Gertrude Stein, Ernest Hemingway, James Joyce, and Ezra Pound. A number of African-American performers and writers like Josephine Baker, Langston Hughes, and Gwendolyn Bennett likewise came to Paris, finding the city less restrictive than the Jim Crow United States. Paris was also an important early hub of cinema as Auguste and Louis Lumière made and showed short documentaries in the 1890s while Georges Méliès shot several fantasy films, probably the best known being his 1902 *A Trip to the Moon*.

Rue Cortot
During the Belle Époque *Renoir lived for a while at no. 12, while painters Émile Bernard, Suzanne Valadon, André Utter, and Maurice Utrillo later used a studio there. A 17th-century country house originally owned by Roze de Rosimond, an actor with Molière's theater company, the building is now home to the Musée du Vieux Montmartre. The composer and pianist Érik Satie, who played at Le Chat Noir, a nightclub frequented by Henri Toulouse-Lautrec and Claude Debussy, lived at no. 6.*

Rue Norvins
With its big houses and gardens, the rue Norvins is considered by many to be the "Champs-Élysées of Montmartre."

Avenue Junot
Built between 1910 and 1912, avenue Junot was home to writer Tristan Tzara (no. 15), film director Henri-Georges Clouzot (no. 37), and painter Maurice Utrillo (no. 11), one of the few well-known painters to have been actually born in Montmartre.

Cimetière du Montmartre

Rue Lepic

Métro Lamarck-Caulaincourt

Cimetière Saint-Vincent

Basilique du Sacré-Coeur

Métro Anvers
Square Louise Michel
Métro Abbesses

Métro Blanche
Métro Pigalle

Moulin Rouge
Opened in 1889, the Moulin Rouge nightclub, with its scantily clad dancers, encapsulated the bohemian lifestyle of Belle Époque *Montmartre. Located at the bottom of the Montmartre hill, the Moulin Rouge sat between the wealthier parts of Montmartre below and the poorer ones closer to the top and so served as a place for bourgeois Parisians to mingle with bohemians.*

Le Bateau-Lavoir
Located at no. 13, rue Ravignan, Le Bateau-Lavoir was a place where poor artists could access studio space. Numerous artists lived and worked there, including Picasso, who painted his proto-Cubist piece Les Demoiselles d'Avignon there. After 1914 many Bateau-Lavoir artists relocated to Montparnasse, feeling that Montmartre had become too commercialized.

Moulin de la Galette
The Moulin de la Galette, situated at the top of the Montmartre hill, was named for a type of French pancake. In the 1830s the windmill had been turned into a cabaret and was a favorite haunt of avant-garde artists like Toulouse-Lautrec, van Gogh, Émile Bernard, and Picasso. Renoir's 1876 Bal du moulin de la Galette is considered to be one of Impressionism's most important works.

Paris as a 20th- and 21st-century City

Although Haussmann has generally been seen as responsible for what Paris looks like today, there were also important 20th-century developments. In the 1950s the government began constructing an office center to the city's west. This area (La Défense) is now the largest purpose-built business district in Europe and its skyscrapers are visible across the city. In 1989 the Grande Arche de la Défense was opened. Resembling a hollowed-out cube, this was one of the *grands projets* ("great projects") commissioned by President François Mitterrand to celebrate the 200th anniversary of the French Revolution—others included the Louvre Pyramid, the Bastille Opera, and the Bibliothèque Nationale. In 1992 the Métro line was extended to the area, making it accessible to central Paris.

High migration from rural areas and overseas to Paris in the post-war periods and a lack of adequate housing meant that some neighborhoods became overcrowded—large numbers of immigrants escaping wars in southeast Asia coalesced near the place d'Italie in southeastern Paris and many North Africans made the streets near Saint-Denis in northern Paris their home. In this context in 1961 President Charles de Gaulle famously took Paul Delouvrier, the government's chief representative for the Paris region, up in a helicopter and ordered him to "*mettez-moi de l'ordre dans ce merdier*" ("bring me some order in this shithole"). Consequently, the French government initiated what British geographer Peter Hall has called the most "grandiose" plan ever attempted in the history of urban civilization by constructing several *villes nouvelles* ("new towns") on Paris's outskirts connected to the central city by large highways

La Voie Triomphale

As Paris begins the 21st century it carries in its built environment the marks of its Roman origins, its medieval walls, its 18th-century revolutionary conversions, its dramatic 19th-century reinvention in the age of steam and imperial domination, and its 20th-century redevelopment to accommodate the automobile. In all of this a key axis of growth has been the Voie Triomphale ("Triumphal Way"). Some five miles in length, the Voie stretches from the Louvre to La Défense. Linking several important monuments, historically the Voie was designed to promote French prestige. This continues to be a goal and the French government is moving forward with plans to push the Voie even further westward, with the construction of the Seine-Arche.

La Grande Arche

Arc de Triomphe

CNIT—Centre des nouvelles industries et technologies (Center for New Industries and Technologies)

Neuilly-sur-Seine

Palais des Congrès

La Défense

Bois de Boulogne

and express railway lines. However, the sense of anomie encouraged by these drab, modernist *grands ensembles* ("housing projects") and the high levels of youth unemployment suffered by their inhabitants have led to rioting in recent years.

Paris also expanded its transportation infrastructure. Aéroport Charles de Gaulle, opened in 1974 to replace Orly as Paris's main airport, is now Europe's second-busiest airport and a major international hub. Since 1994 high-speed Eurostar trains have run between Paris and London and Paris and Brussels. City planners are also looking to expand the city's Métro system as part of the *Grand Paris* ("Greater Paris") project unveiled in 2007 by President Nicolas Sarkozy to significantly upgrade Paris for the 21st century. This expansion will involve adding over ninety miles of new lines into the surrounding Île-de-France region.

The suburban rail system

Paris's suburbs and airports are connected to the city by the Réseau Express Régional (RER, "Regional Express Network") train system. Although its origins stretch to the 1930s and plans to create a metropolitan train grid, construction of the first lines did not begin until the 1960s. RER trains stop at several stations in Paris proper, including the gare du Nord, which is linked by the Eurostar train service to London. The RER is thus well integrated with the Paris Métro system.

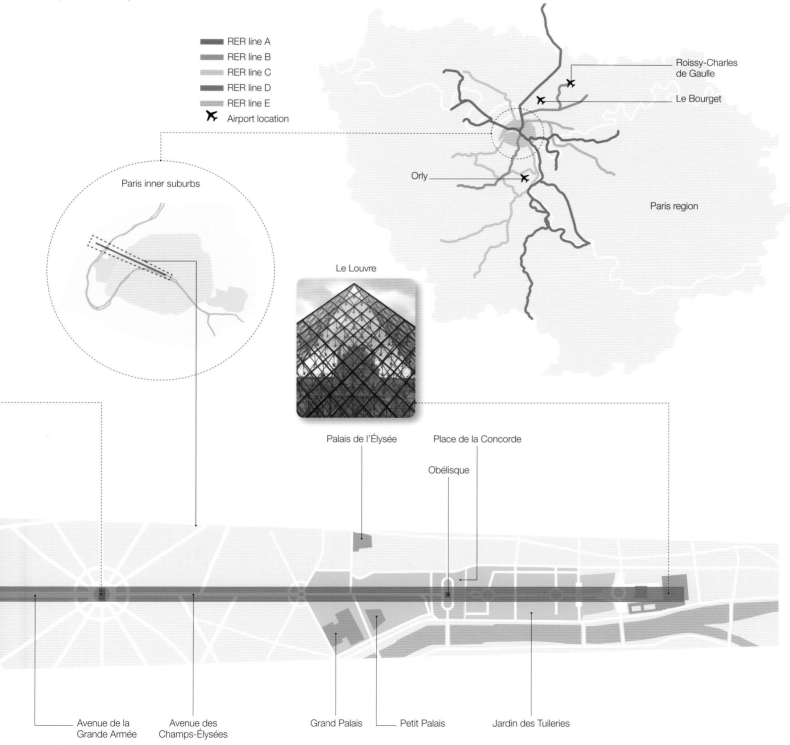

RER line A
RER line B
RER line C
RER line D
RER line E
Airport location

Paris inner suburbs

Roissy-Charles de Gaulle

Le Bourget

Orly

Paris region

Le Louvre

Palais de l'Élysée

Place de la Concorde

Obélisque

Avenue de la Grande Armée

Avenue des Champs-Élysées

Grand Palais — Petit Palais

Jardin des Tuileries

THE GLOBAL CITY

BEN DERUDDER
PETER TAYLOR
MICHAEL HOYLER
FRANK WITLOX

Core cities

LONDON
NEW YORK

Secondary cities

FRANKFURT

SAN FRANCISCO

GENEVA

MUMBAI

NAIROBI

Left: New York City, USA

The Global City: Introduction

Vancouver ● ○ Calgary

Toronto ● Montreal ●

Chicago ● ○ Boston / New York

San Francisco ○ Las Vegas ○ Washington, D.C.

Dallas ● ○ Atlanta

Los Angeles ●

Houston ● ○ Orlando / ○ Miami

● Mexico City

Rio de Janeiro ○ ●
São Paulo

● Buenos Aires

"Most studies of global cities focus on their economic capacities, but globalization involves much more than one sphere of activity."

The concept of the "global city" was invented in the 1990s by Saskia Sassen to describe a new type of city that specialized in transnational relations. Initially the focus was on London, New York, and Tokyo, but the idea was soon generalized by the sociologist Manuel Castells to include a broader range of cities that formed the nodes and hubs in his interpretation of contemporary society as a "network society." This notion was then expanded to suggest the existence of a "world city network," emphasizing the global scope of the services offered by contemporary cities. What we now call globalization originated from the combining of the computer and communication industries in the 1970s, which enabled new levels of worldwide contact and organization. This "shrinking" of the world has had profound implications economically, politically, and culturally. One unforeseen effect has been the increasing importance of cities. Although it was initially thought that globalization would reduce the functional importance of cities, the increased worldwide dispersal of human activities has in fact generated new organizational demands to manage, service, and generally facilitate the intensification of global relations.

There is a wide range of terminology used to analyze the concept of globalization and its impact on cities, though the terms "global city" and "world city" dominate and are commonly used interchangeably. Part of the problem of terminology arises from the fact that globalization is a complex and pervasive set of processes which affects all cities: there are really no "un-global cities."

The study of global cities can be divided into two parts: the global practices that take place within a particular city and the relations between cities that result from those practices. The study

Amsterdam
Brussels
Düsseldorf
Frankfurt
Stockholm
Moscow
Berlin
London
Warsaw
Paris
Prague
Zurich
Vienna
Geneva
Munich
Madrid
Rome
Istanbul
Barcelona
Milan
Monaco
Beijing
Seoul
Osaka
Tokyo
Tel Aviv
Amritsar
Shanghai
Jerusalem
Damman
Delhi
Manama
Taipei
Riyadh
Varanasi
Guangzhou
Hong Kong
Mecca
Macau
Mumbai
Bangalore
Bangkok
Kuala Lumpur
Singapore
Nairobi
Jakarta
Sun City
Johannesburg
Perth
Sydney
Melbourne

Legend:

- ◎ Archetypal global cities
- ● Economic cities
- ● Financial cities
- ● Cultural cities
- ● Political cities
- ● Entertainment cities
- ○ Religious cities
- ● Gateway cities
- ● Resource cities
- ● Other important global cities

of global practices entails a focus on topics such as, for instance, the design of large office towers and iconic buildings, the creation of services that enable firms to operate in a global marketplace, and the ways in which global cities are characterized by inequality and hyperdiversity. The study of relations between cities resulting from these practices involves, for instance, analyses of migration flows to global cities, airline and Internet connections between global cities, and the connectivity of global cities in the office networks of globalized firms. We consider both aspects in this chapter.

Global capacities

Most studies of global cities focus on their economic capacities, but globalization involves much more than one sphere of activity. London and New York are widely recognized as the model global cities and their capacities are importantly economic, especially financial, but they are also political and cultural. Other global cities also have a range of capacities, but there is a tendency for depth of influence in one sphere. In addition, there are specialist cities with a particular global reach in, for example, resources, entertainment, religion, or as global gateways.

Global Infrastructure Networks

One of the most noticeable manifestations of the worldwide connectivity of global cities is the central position they hold in global infrastructure networks. Air travel between the world's major urban centers has increased at an exponential rate over the last decade. Between 1970 and 2010 the number of people flying into and out of London's major airports (Heathrow and Gatwick) quadrupled to 125 million passengers. Similar, and sometimes even bigger, growth figures can be found in New York, Tokyo, Singapore, and Hong Kong.

Although perhaps less visible, the technological infrastructures that support the blizzard of communications flowing daily around the world are also tied to global cities. The Internet has obviously become an essential part of the lives and activities of businesses, governments, and individual users. Although these users meet and communicate in a "virtual" world that is distinct from their physical location, the Internet does have a very material geography of hardware infrastructures and material connections. For a large part, the geography of this "wired world" is that of global cities: cities such as London, Hong Kong, and San Francisco are home to, and connected by, the most sophisticated,

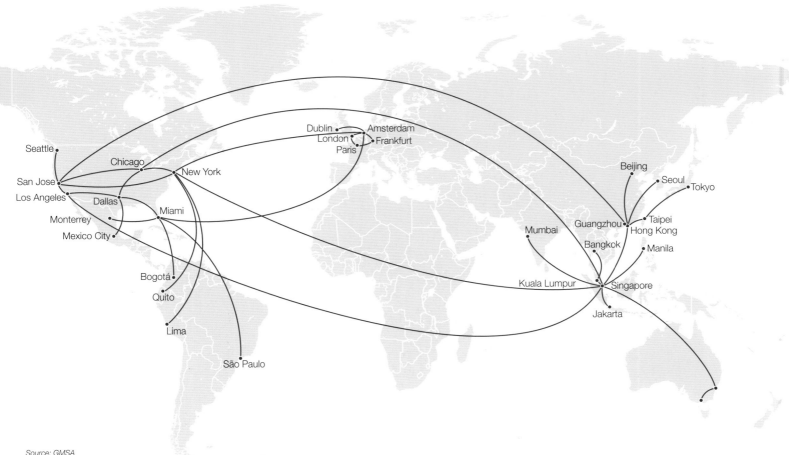

Source: GMSA

Global networks

A clear example of how electronic infrastructures facilitate interactions between global cities is the extensive fiber networks that support the Internet. This figure shows the geography of the network infrastructure in 2012 of Aicent, a "global" communications services provider. Each company will have its own, specific strategy, but in general the deployment of these networks closely follows demand, which is clearly driven by global city-formation.

diverse, and capable telecommunication infrastructures ever seen.

The relationship between infrastructure networks and global city-formation is symbiotic. On the one hand, the various connections between global cities logically create an enormous demand for air transport and telecommunication networks. For instance, the integration of the world's major financial markets, organized from global cities, helps explain the many direct flights and designated communication networks between, say, London, Hong Kong, New York, Tokyo, and Singapore: these infrastructures enable the circulation of information and knowledge, both disembodied (electronic flows) and embodied (business air travel). On the other hand, air transport and telecommunication networks themselves are sometimes perceived as levers toward attaining global city status. For instance, Hong Kong's airline Cathay Pacific boasts the slogan "Hong Kong: Asia's world city" as part of a broader boosterist policy in which connectivity in airline networks is mobilized to assert the city's "place" in the universe of global cities. Meanwhile, Hong Kong has also built itself into one of the most sophisticated telecommunications markets in the world through a range of liberal and supportive policies.

Global city connections

The geographies of airline networks have different drivers (business, tourism, colonial heritage, physical and cultural proximity), but a key element is linkages between global cities. Demand is biggest for connections between cities such as London, New York, Singapore, and Hong Kong, hinting at the integration of their globalized economies. The figure maps the twenty-five most important international connections of more than 1,000 nautical miles in 2009.

Greater than 1,500,000 passengers
1,000,000 to 1,499,999 passengers
900,000 to 999,999 passengers
750,000 to 899,999 passengers
Less than 749,999 passengers

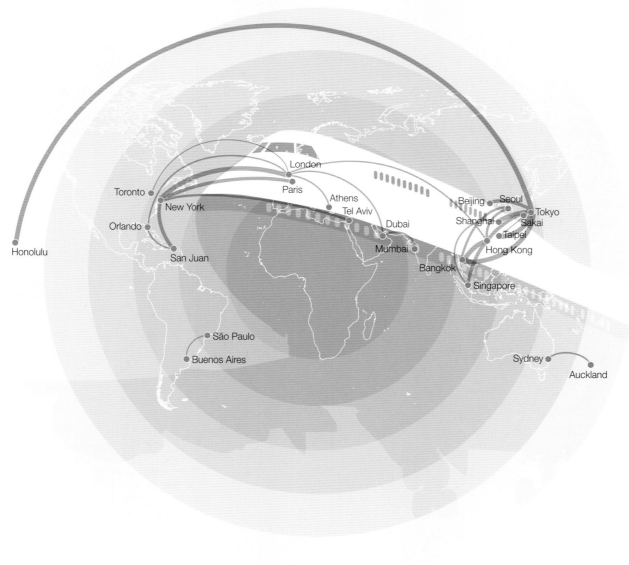

Source: CAPA (2010)

Global Networks of Firms

Infrastructure networks facilitate global city-formation, but they do not constitute its essence. Perhaps above all, it is the centrality of cities such as New York and London to transnational corporate organization that underlies their key position in contemporary globalization. One way of considering this is to focus on the hierarchical relationships within the corporate structure of the world's major multinational corporations.

The map below gives an overview of the networks of the *Fortune* top 100 companies for 2005, showing linkages between different levels of firms' corporate hierarchies—for example between global headquarters and regional headquarters, or between regional headquarters and subsidiaries. Overall, the city networks created by these companies through their location choices hint at the importance of *global* inter-city connections, but it is equally clear that these connections retain a strong *regional* dimension: a city's strongest

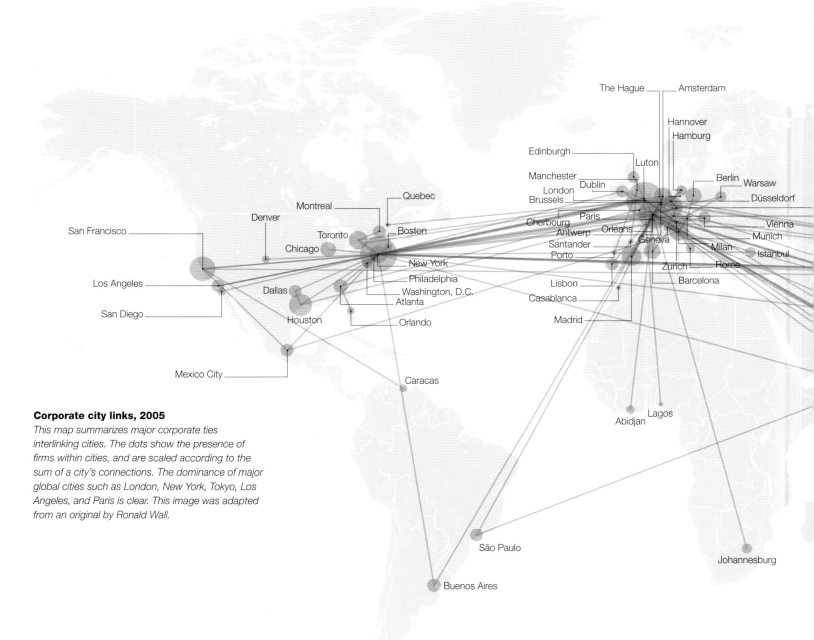

Corporate city links, 2005

This map summarizes major corporate ties interlinking cities. The dots show the presence of firms within cities, and are scaled according to the sum of a city's connections. The dominance of major global cities such as London, New York, Tokyo, Los Angeles, and Paris is clear. This image was adapted from an original by Ronald Wall.

Source: Wall and Knapp (2011)

connections tend to be with cities in the same region, with only a few cities having sizeable connections across the globe. Colonial heritages are also visible: the major connections of Lagos, Johannesburg, Melbourne, and Sydney are with London rather than New York.

Another way of looking at the position of cities in corporate networks is to focus on the provision of those services required to exercise global control. Firms such as those active in finance, management consultancy, law, advertising, accountancy, logistics, etc.,

provide these services. Indeed, it has been argued that the function of a global city is chiefly the management and governance of the global operations of companies. From this perspective, the connectivity of global cities can be measured by assessing the relative size and functions within the globalized network of business service companies' offices in a particular city.

Frankfurt
Strasbourg

Seoul
Shanghai
Osaka
Tokyo

Hong
Kong

Bangkok

Kuala Lumpur

Singapore

Sydney
Melbourne

COMMERCIAL INTER-CITY RELATIONS

An interesting symmetry can be seen in two tri-city structures on opposite sides of the world. In each case the political and commercial centers of a large national economy work in concert with a third closely integrated city. This third city acts as a global gateway, but its key characteristic is that it lies in a different economic jurisdiction. Quite simply, you can do things in London and Hong Kong that you cannot do in the USA and mainland China, respectively. For example, the critical precursor of financial globalization, the invention of the Eurodollar market for dollar-deficient Europe in 1957, operated through London because such a market was not allowed in the USA itself; and Hong Kong operated as a safe capitalist gateway for investing in China before its repatriation through the "one country–two systems" deal of 1997. The path to globalization of the two cities is reflected today in divisions of labor within each triad, with London and Hong Kong providing specialist global outreach. That the same structure has emerged in relation to the world's two leading national economies shows the importance of commercial cross-border maneuverability even at the very top of the international system.

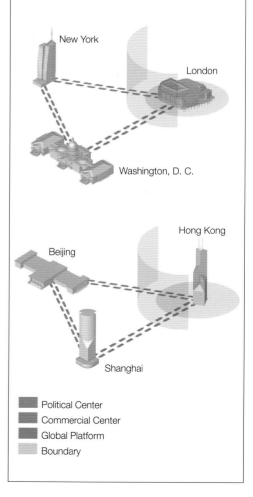

New York

London

Washington, D. C.

Hong Kong

Beijing

Shanghai

■ Political Center
■ Commercial Center
■ Global Platform
▨ Boundary

Global City Skylines

The association between global city-formation and the presence of tall buildings may seem a matter of straightforward economics. For instance, the construction of skyscrapers seems justified since the demand for land, and therefore its price, is so high that it makes economic sense to build a tall office block so as to minimize the building's footprint while maximizing the potential office space. But the story is more complicated than this, as the market for offices also actively shapes global cities' functions and futures: the size and quality of office markets *directs* corporations to global cities, so these office buildings function as sizeable investment assets linking global cities to international capital markets. For instance, there has been a marked shift in the ownership of offices in the City of London, which runs parallel to the city's connectivity in infrastructure and corporate networks.

Global skyline, 2013

This figure plots cities according to the visual impact of their skylines. It is based on statistics in the Emporis database, and reflects completed high-rise buildings where each building is assigned points based on its floor count.

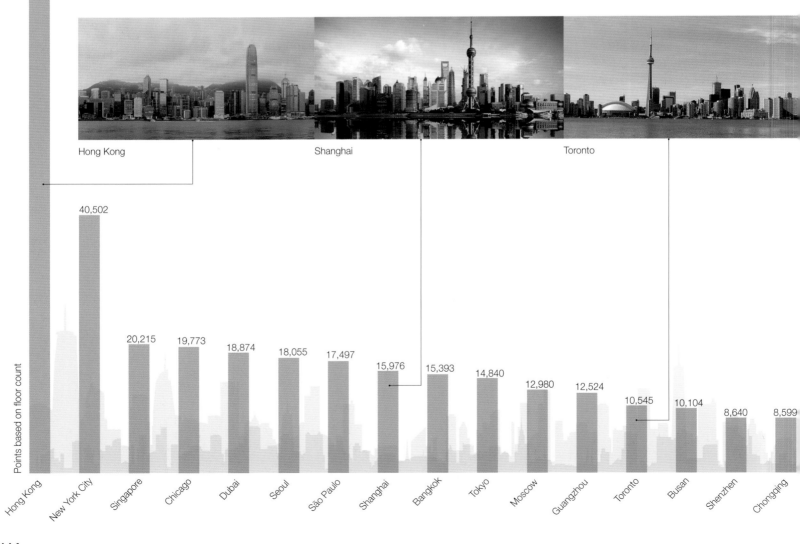

Points based on floor count

Hong Kong	130,459
New York City	40,502
Singapore	20,215
Chicago	19,773
Dubai	18,874
Seoul	18,055
São Paulo	17,497
Shanghai	15,976
Bangkok	15,393
Tokyo	14,840
Moscow	12,980
Guangzhou	12,524
Toronto	10,545
Busan	10,104
Shenzhen	8,640
Chongqing	8,599

Hong Kong Shanghai Toronto

However, the built environment of global cities is much more than a collection of buildings to enable the work of globally operating firms and institutions. Global cities are also prime examples of "designscapes": distinctive ensembles of buildings that convey a message to the world. Hence economistic readings should be complemented by considering what a building represents and signifies apart from its obvious function. For instance, the building of the 2,716-ft (830-meter) high Burj Khalifa in Dubai, or the transformation of London's Baltic Exchange into "the Gherkin," were intended above all to channel international recognition

and subsequently investment to these cities. Similarly, names such as "International Financial Center" (Hong Kong) or "World Trade Center" (New York) for skyscrapers are used to convey global cities' role and aspiration. The increasing entrepreneurialism of urban governance has made such rebuilding, repackaging, and rebranding of the urban landscape a common priority among (aspiring) global cities. In this context, the erection of signature skyscrapers and iconic buildings is but one aspect of a much broader makeover of global cityscapes: flagship cultural sites, conference centers, big mixed-use developments, waterfront

redevelopments, and major sports and entertainment complexes have appeared in many global cities. The broader economic rationale of global cities' designscapes is that these cities derive a kind of monopoly rent as a result of the image they acquire from their "front regions": the financial districts, cultural quarters, design and entertainment districts. Favorable images of these settings, reinforced and amplified by the media, help global cities to become tastemakers, where the valorization of the urban milieu extends to all sorts of products and activities through branding that simply invokes the city's name.

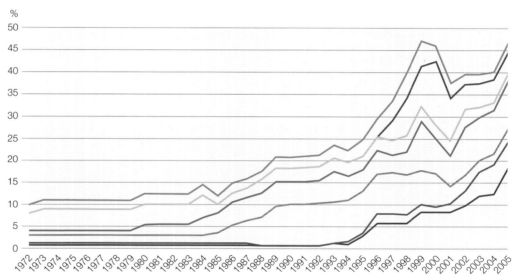

Panama City

Source: Lizieri and Kutsch (2006)

Office ownership

The above graph shows the combined percentage of international ownership of the office market in the City of London. Until the mid-1980s international ownership remained remarkably stable, at between 10 percent and 15 percent. The proportion of non-UK ownership then began to increase in parallel with financial deregulation across the late 1980s, reaching 25 percent in the second half of the 1990s and approaching 50 percent by 2005.

Other
International
Middle East
Western Europe
Japan
USA
Germany

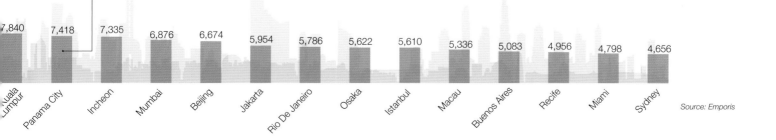

Kuala Lumpur	Panama City	Incheon	Mumbai	Beijing	Jakarta	Rio De Janeiro	Osaka	Istanbul	Macau	Buenos Aires	Recife	Miami	Sydney
7,840	7,418	7,335	6,876	6,674	5,954	5,786	5,622	5,610	5,336	5,083	4,956	4,798	4,656

Source: Emporis

Local and Regional Patterns of Economic Activity

Global cities are clusters of globalized business activity. On the local scale, these clustering processes are most pronounced in a restricted "space of centrality" within global cities. The City of London, for instance, is a prominent spatial agglomeration of banking, insurance, and other financial institutions, while advanced producer services, such as law, advertising, accountancy, and management consultancy have their own, partly overlapping, distinctive clusters in central London. This space of centrality indicates the importance of localized

productive relationships within and between global service firms, based on reputation, trust, face-to-face interactions, informal information, and social networks.

However, adjacent city-regions are increasingly being caught up in globalization processes. The expansion of globalizing cities into their regions has given rise to more spatially dispersed and varied global city-regions. These new landscapes of functionally interlinked urban settlements are characterized by complex geographies, combining aspects of a hierarchical division of labor between central city and wider

London's local clustering

The City of London and adjacent locations have developed specific clusters of advanced producer services, reflecting a long and successful history as the world's leading international financial center. These clusters of specialized services, together with regulatory institutions and a rich enabling infrastructure, encourage both planned and haphazard face-to-face contacts, and provide access to vital information and to competing interpretations of new knowledge. This is significant for the formation of trust between actors in global markets that are characterized by insecurity, fluidity, and the circulation of tacit knowledge.

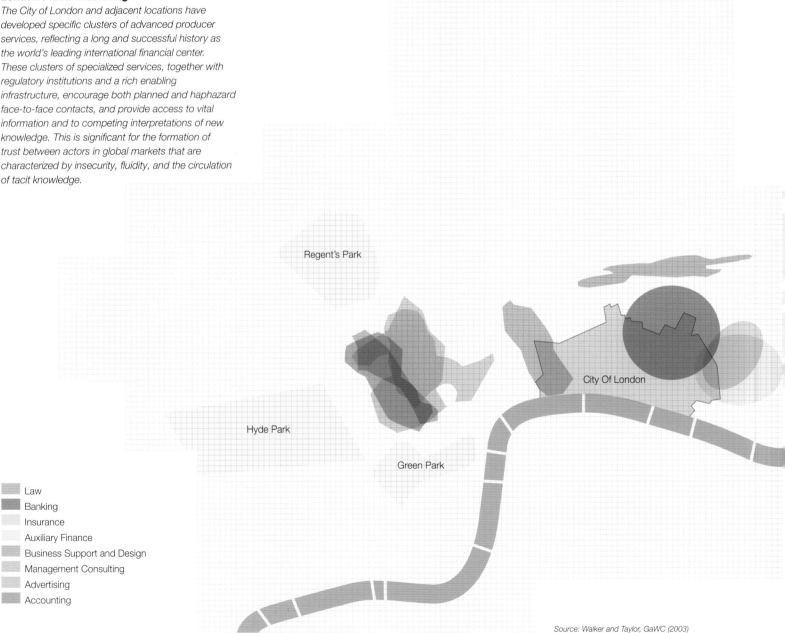

Regent's Park

Hyde Park

Green Park

City Of London

Law
Banking
Insurance
Auxiliary Finance
Business Support and Design
Management Consulting
Advertising
Accounting

Source: Walker and Taylor, GaWC (2003)

city-region (for example, between headquarters and back offices in business services) with the complementary coexistence
of different types of clustered economic activities in various parts of the global city-region.

London, for example, sits at the heart of the economically vibrant southeast of England, a polycentric "mega-city region" that has become increasingly interlinked through business service networks of global reach. This functional expansion of London connects the diversified global service complex of the City to a number of complementary smaller clusters of business services in the southeast, such as finance, management consultancy, accountancy, advertising, and IT services. These functional

interlinkages transcend traditional administrative boundaries and pose challenging questions about the appropriate scales of governance for these new economic spaces.

In contrast, a more pronounced sectoral specialization can be seen in the San Francisco Bay Area, where Silicon Valley's innovative IT cluster links up with finance in downtown San Francisco. In this case, high-tech firms in the global city-region are equally, if not more, integrated into global economic flows as the financial institutions in the major city in the region. The distinct business culture of Silicon Valley's globally integrated regional innovation system has become a model for emerging high-tech regions across the world, although

its unique historical and geographical context limits the scope for successful imitation.

The example of the San Francisco Bay Area shows that expansion of global city processes into the wider region gives way to the emergence of large polycentric regions with multiple connections into the world economy. One of the starkest examples is China's Yangtze River Delta: although the region has a major "global city" eye-catcher in the form of Shanghai, the region as a whole is densely urbanized with a host of large cities such as Nanjing, Hangzhou, and Suzhou that are proximately located, functionally integrated, and globally connected.

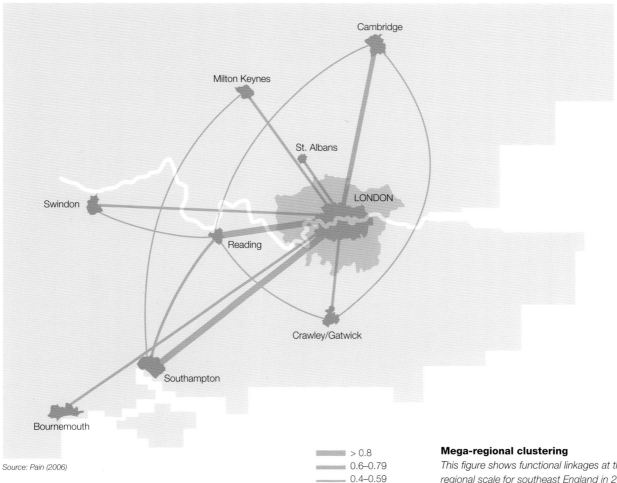

Source: Pain (2006)

▬▬▬	> 0.8
▬▬▬	0.6–0.79
────	0.4–0.59
────	0.2–0.39

Mega-regional clustering

This figure shows functional linkages at the mega-regional scale for southeast England in 2006, based on intra-firm office networks of advanced producer services. The dense network of connections that extend far beyond the administrative boundaries of the metropolis brings into question conceptualizations of London as a monocentric core in the European urban landscape.

Global Cities and Social Inequality

Global cities have highly divided labor markets. Inequality of earnings and income has been rising in much of the global economy over the last two decades, but this increase has been more marked in global cities. This inequality is commonly related to the economic structure of global cities: the more pronounced decline of manufacturing industries in these cities is associated with a decline in the number of middle-skill and middle-income jobs, while the growth of the management and service sectors is associated with growth both in professional and managerial jobs at the top of the ladder (bankers, management consultants, etc.), and in low-skill and low-wage service jobs at the bottom (e.g. hotel maids, waiters and waitresses, cleaners, security guards, etc.). Although there are ongoing debates as to how "universal" this rising inequality is in the context of different migration policies and welfare regimes at national level, the observations for New York City are broadly true for cities such as London and Tokyo as well.

Income inequality

Between the late 1980s and the mid-2000s, the top fifth of New York City families increased their relative share of total income. While income inequality grew in the United States as a whole over this period, New York City's grew more. The income of the top quintile grew by 32 percent between 1987 and 2006, while the average growth for the other four quintiles was 5.45 percent.

Top Fifth
Executives, senior
management, celebrities

First Fifth
Low-skill, low-wage
service positions

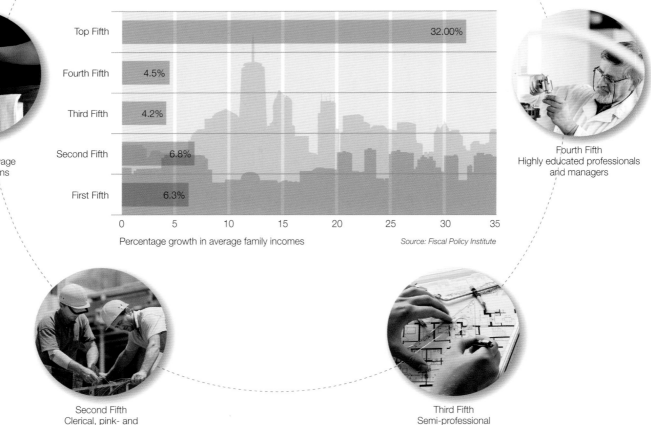

Top Fifth	32.00%
Fourth Fifth	4.5%
Third Fifth	4.2%
Second Fifth	6.8%
First Fifth	6.3%

0   5   10   15   20   25   30   35

Percentage growth in average family incomes

Source: Fiscal Policy Institute

Fourth Fifth
Highly educated professionals
and managers

Second Fifth
Clerical, pink- and
blue-collar workers

Third Fifth
Semi-professional
and craftsmen

This growing social division is visible in the housing market of global cities, which is characterized by extreme gentrification. Gentrification can be defined broadly as the social upgrading of an area by incoming high-income groups (which includes the reinvestment of capital), and results in both landscape change and the direct or indirect displacement of low-income groups. Although gentrification has been observed all around the world across the urban hierarchy, it is telling that the term was first coined in London in the 1960s, at a time when the city was emerging as a global city. London's gentrifiers turned their backs on suburbia at the same time as the city became the hub of a new fast-moving capitalism that was expanding across the globe. These processes were subsequently exacerbated by the housing requirements of new high-income earners, often working in the City, where jobs had expanded as a result of the deregulation of the Stock Exchange in 1986. A couple of years into the global financial crisis, this inequality remains in place: the effectively globalized top end of the London housing market remains largely buoyant, while the housing market in the rest of the UK has largely stagnated.

Housing market boom and bust

In the UK, property prices peaked in the third quarter of 2007, after huge rises from 1996 to 2007. In early 2007 interest rates were raised and lending conditions tightened. The fall in house prices accelerated in the second half of 2008, due to the global financial meltdown and the economic recession. However, the London housing market has rebounded faster than that in the remainder of the UK: average prices are back to the 2007 level, with a house in the global city of London costing on average twice as much as elsewhere in the UK.

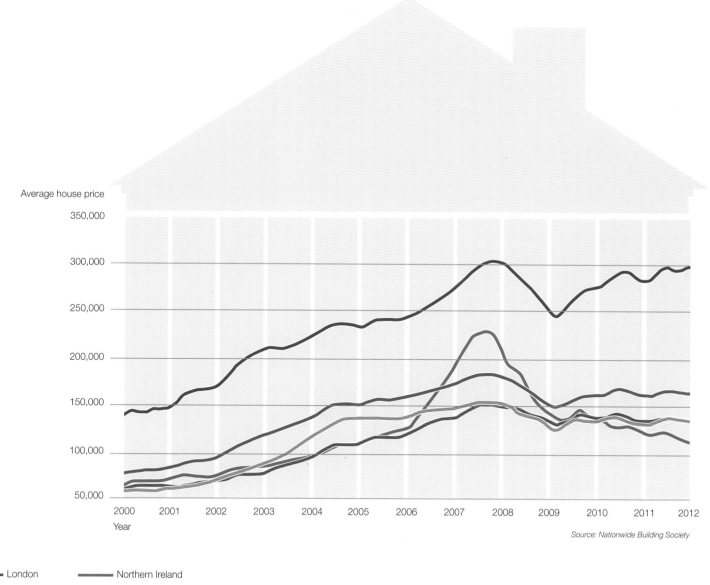

Average house price

Year

Source: Nationwide Building Society

London
UK
Wales
Northern Ireland
Scotland

Global Cities and Migration

As argued earlier, global cities' labor markets are characterized by increasing inequality whereby the significant surge in the proportion of highly skilled workers at the apex of the city's labor market has been accompanied by a smaller but still significant rise in the proportion of workers at the bottom end. However, perhaps even more significant is that migrant workers increasingly dominate both extremes: global cities' labor markets have increasingly come to depend upon migrant workers, both those who work in highly skilled jobs such as finance, management consultancy, and advertising, and those who work in bottom-end service-sector jobs such as cleaning, hospitality, care, construction, and food processing, jobs that literally keep global cities such as London "working." Thus we see the emergence of what may be termed a "migrant division of labor." Although this migrant division is often international, this need not be the case. China has recently been the arena of the largest rural–urban migration in history, producing new global cities out of communism, which curtailed city growth.

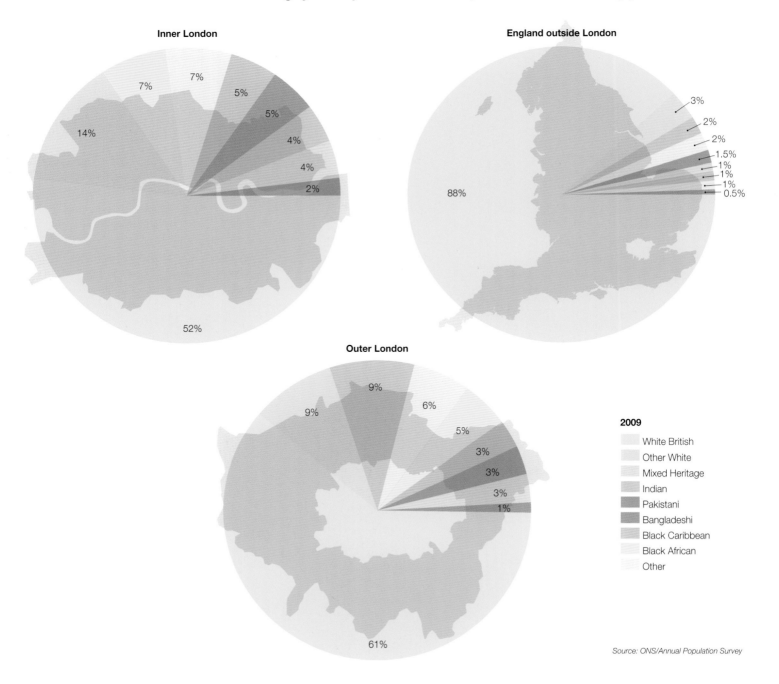

Inner London

England outside London

Outer London

2009
White British
Other White
Mixed Heritage
Indian
Pakistani
Bangladeshi
Black Caribbean
Black African
Other

Source: ONS/Annual Population Survey

In the mid-1990s the deregulation of the financial sector in the UK had been insufficient to invigorate the rather conservative British finance houses. These firms were taken over, largely by foreign, mainly US-based financial mega-players. This led to large numbers of very high salaries (comparable to their New York counterparts) and to the increased internationalization of the workers in these firms, which made up about a third of employment in the City. At the other end of the spectrum it was estimated that, in 2001, foreign-born workers occupied 46 percent of London's low-wage jobs. This reliance on migrant workers is even more significant in certain sectors such as cleaning where the numbers of foreign-born workers rose from 40 percent in 1993–94 to almost 70 percent in 2004–05. Similar rates are evident among chefs and cooks, catering assistants, and care assistants, such that it is increasingly evident that some parts of London's low-wage economy could no longer function without the labor of migrants.

What factors account for the emergence of this migrant division of labor in the case of London? Research has identified a number of processes, including labor market deregulation and reforms to the welfare system, which have meant that conditions of work have generally deteriorated, so that London's employers find it extremely difficult to attract domestic workers into these jobs. This process has been matched by a growth in mobility from the Global South, which has delivered a workforce that is filling these vacancies in an effort to try and improve their lives on the other side of the world.

Multicultural city

Migrant low-wage workers

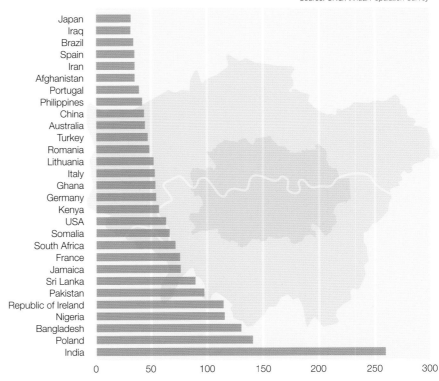

Migrant high-wage workers

Source: ONS/Annual Population Survey

Diverse city

London is often referred to as a "world within one city," a finding that was substantiated by the Global Cities at Work research which recorded some sixty-three different nationalities in the city's population. The majority of migrants came from Eastern Europe, sub-Saharan Africa, and Latin America. This reflects the fact that where once migration to the UK was dominated by nationals from the Commonwealth (the Indian subcontinent and the Caribbean), these flows are being diversified by migration from both an enlarged European Union as well as from parts of the world without strong historical colonial connections with the city or the country, especially Latin America. As a consequence, London's population is far more ethnically diverse than the population of the rest of England.

Number of foreign-born people resident in London (thousands), and country of birth (2011)

Global Cities and Tourism

The air transport infrastructures and designscapes of global cities are not meant only to help move professionals or attract investment; they are also intended to attract tourists. Indeed, tourism makes a significant contribution to the economic, social, and cultural fabric of these cities. New York City, for instance, ranks as a favored destination for international travelers to the United States. In 2010 the city welcomed almost 50 million visitors, including 9.7 million international travelers. In direct contrast to the United States' national average, international visitor spending dominates tourism receipts in New York City. The flagship cultural sites, large convention centers and/or trade fair grounds, waterfront redevelopments, and major sports and entertainment complexes that have appeared in many global cities are part of a deliberate, boosterist strategy to attract visitors and their spending.

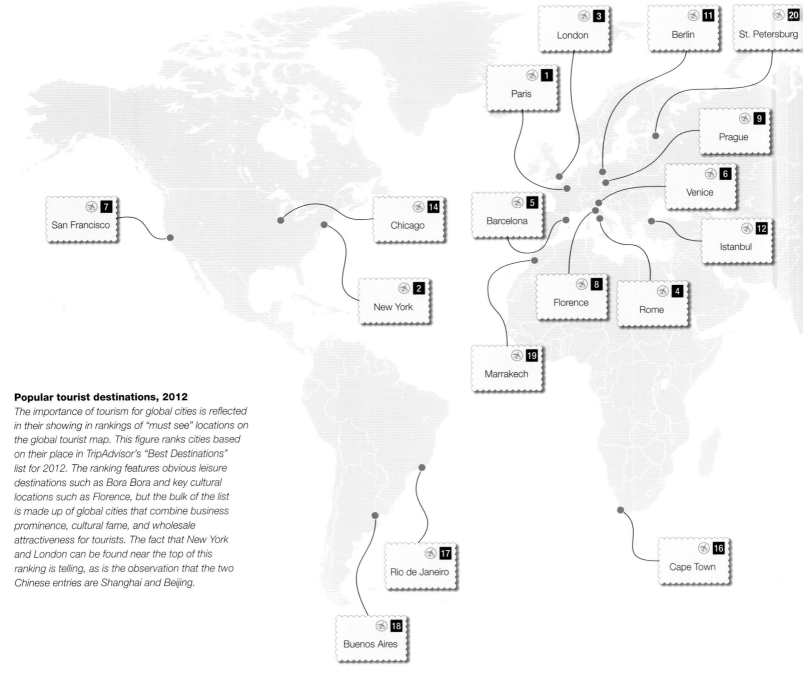

Popular tourist destinations, 2012

The importance of tourism for global cities is reflected in their showing in rankings of "must see" locations on the global tourist map. This figure ranks cities based on their place in TripAdvisor's "Best Destinations" list for 2012. The ranking features obvious leisure destinations such as Bora Bora and key cultural locations such as Florence, but the bulk of the list is made up of global cities that combine business prominence, cultural fame, and wholesale attractiveness for tourists. The fact that New York and London can be found near the top of this ranking is telling, as is the observation that the two Chinese entries are Shanghai and Beijing.

The economic significance of the tourism sector is enormous: total visitor spending in New York was more than US$30 billion in 2010, with international visitors contributing a disproportionate amount of that total during their stay. There is no question that travel and tourism is now a critical industry for New York City: total visitor spending (domestic and international) has doubled since 2001, and tripled over the past twenty years. It is important to stress that tourism should not be seen as a mere ancillary function of global cities, or some sort of byproduct of a city's prominence in other fields. Rather, tourism has become a key part and indeed a driver of global city-formation. For instance, a 2010 survey showed that 60 percent of the overseas travelers to New York City were there for leisure, recreation, or holidays, compared to 54 percent for the country as a whole. Perhaps somewhat counterintuitively, then, this makes New York City more of a leisure destination than a business destination in both absolute and relative terms.

Global attraction

This figure shows the rising importance of New York as a destination for international travel, most of which is for tourism. The percentage of travelers visiting New York as part of their trip to the USA continues to grow, as does the number of travelers for whom New York is their main destination.

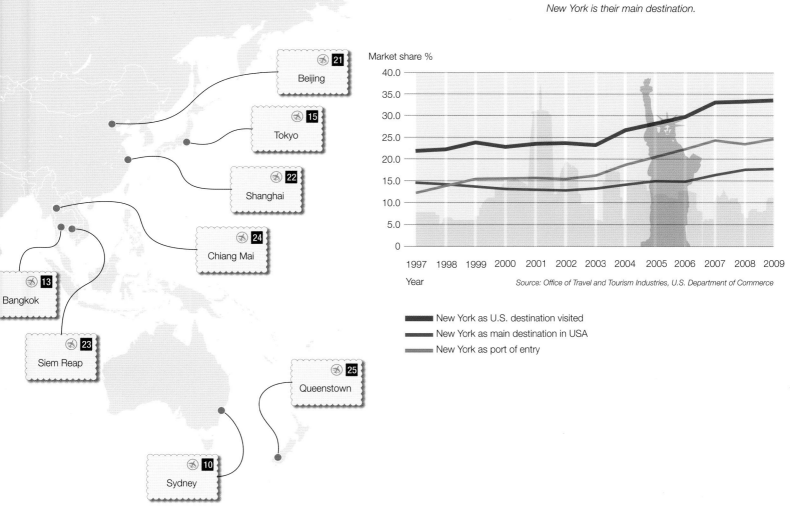

Source: Office of Travel and Tourism Industries, U.S. Department of Commerce

■ New York as U.S. destination visited
■ New York as main destination in USA
■ New York as port of entry

THE CELEBRITY CITY

ELIZABETH CURRID-HALKETT

Core city
LOS ANGELES _____

Secondary cities
NEW YORK _____
LONDON _____
MILAN _____
MUMBAI _____
LAS VEGAS _____

Left: Los Angeles, USA

The Celebrity City: Introduction

"In Hollywood, the golden rule is that gold rules."

The West in the 21st century is defined by technology, conspicuous consumption, and a post-scarcity *modus vivendi* that mass society embraces. We all have acquired lots of stuff, as well as the aspirational habits once reserved to the upper classes. We have become a society of spectacle, moving from post-scarcity to unfettered abundance—romantic capitalism, if you will, and the trappings associated with it.

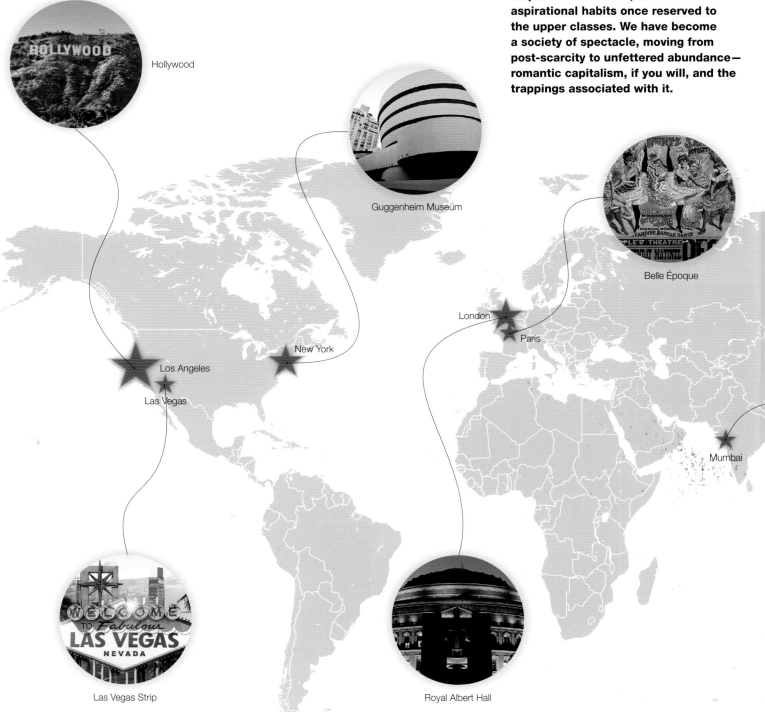

Hollywood

Guggenheim Museum

Belle Époque

London

Paris

New York

Los Angeles

Las Vegas

Mumbai

Las Vegas Strip

Royal Albert Hall

This situation is best exemplified by the phenomenon of celebrity, which is everywhere and everything. Our passion for celebrity information emerges, at least partially, from a desire to establish connections with others. Celebrity has become more important and ubiquitous as society fundamentally shifts. We live farther away from our families, we marry later, we have fewer children, and we don't know our next-door neighbors. Celebrities are people we form connections with, and form connections through—they give us something to talk about, they provide the glue in an otherwise anonymous globalized society. But more than that, celebrity offers us a way to live, one that involves spectacle and the embracing of capitalism. All of us partake in this, through the packaging of our lives, the identification and promotion of ourselves through what we buy, where we live, what we watch, whom we follow on Twitter or Facebook, and so forth.

Bollywood

Celebrity capitals

From a study of over 600,000 entertainment industry photographs, a picture of the global celebrity capitals emerges as portrayed in the adjacent world map. Over 80 percent of all the photographs were taken in just three places: New York, Los Angeles, and London. Additionally, Paris, Las Vegas, and Mumbai play crucial roles in the global network of celebrity cities. Mumbai, home to Bollywood, remains a unique and autonomous capital but perhaps the greatest producer of film celebrities in the world.

The Emergence of the Celebrity City

Celebrity, then, is a leitmotif for broader cultural trends of spectacle, dystopia, anonymity, and relentless surveillance. Equally, it emerges in particular places at particular times. Celebrity flourishes as a result of a global urban system, whereby a few cities uphold a larger culture distributed worldwide. The unpacking of celebrity demonstrates that, like other industries, it depends on agglomerative dynamics deeply embedded in particular places and globally connected to other hubs. Perhaps its distinguishing characteristic is its dependence on a geographic backdrop for success—there are fewer factories and more palm trees and nightclubs, but the effect on the industry is the same. The place and its image matter to the long-term development of the celebrity industry and the cities in which it resides. In fact, the backdrop may be the most important element of stardom. Celebrities come and go but their capitals remain fixed—Paris and the Belle Époque, Swinging London, and the modern urban dystopia of Los Angeles.

Partly this symbiosis is a function of the relationship between cultural industries and celebrity. Cultural industries, heavily concentrated in particular metropolises, tend to create our stars, whether Los Angeles' film industry, New York's fashion and art industries, or London's rich music scene. Thus, the cities' form and their economic concentrations produce particular types of interaction, information, and competition. These functional aspects of the city then become an intricate part of how we understand celebrity and the distinctions within it. In other words, the economic concentrations and prosaic functions of urban centers heavily influence their position within romantic capitalism and its accompanying global celebrity complex.

Cities, unlike rural towns, tend to offer a liberated and liberating culture as a result of their density, general acceptance of diversity, and eccentricity across lifestyle and behavior. In other words, there is the practical function of the colocation of cultural industries and media, but also celebrity's reliance on a dense and more liberated urban society to create the necessary backdrop and culture. Like the Chicago School's assessment of the new industrial city as dense, diverse, and tolerant, the celebrity city relies on a similar capacity for openness, whether it is the concentration of nightlife and music venues that allows for clusters of celebrities and their fans, the late-night restaurants and lax policies that allow for dancing in the streets, the live workspaces of artists, or simply the many thousands of people acting out their own spectacle.

Celebrity and the Global City

In his famous book *The Image*, the social critic and commentator Daniel Boorstin claimed: "Being known primarily for their well-knownness, celebrities intensify their celebrity images simply by becoming widely known for relations among themselves." As tautological as such a statement may appear, the recursive nature of celebrity is one of its defining characteristics. Cultural industries and their stars are visual phenomena, and a measure of their success is the frequency with which the people and places are photographed. We can consider photographs as the index of the cultural stock exchange for star power. Thus, we can see an economic geography of celebrity, of which Los Angeles is the very nexus, connecting a few other global hubs including London, New York, and Paris.

Using a unique dataset of caption information from over 600,000 entertainment photos taken by Getty Images, we have mapped out the geography of the celebrity city and the social, economic, and physical infrastructure that upholds it. The networks, events, people, and places that maintain the star system also tell us about their habitat and *habitus*. Glamorous or seedy, sprawling and dense, old architecture and new: all of these elements of urbanity are part of where celebrity is documented.

The Celebrity Industrial Complex

Celebrity-related jobs

"Star power" is a function of the intricate production chain headquartered primarily in New York and Los Angeles, where over 110,000 people in each city work in celebrity-related jobs. These numbers convey the extent and diversity of the various people, monies, and firms necessary to uphold even just a fleeting image.

The image of celebrity—a particular person or the flurry of people creating a glamorous milieu—is transmitted around the world. But it emerges from a particular place and an intricate network of people, businesses, and resources that are embedded in that place. Like technology's Silicon Valley or finance's Wall Street, celebrity has Los Angeles for its center of production and distribution. From the Jazz Age to the 21st century, West Hollywood has supplied images of beautiful people doing wildly glamorous things. The photographs, the ink-spillage, and the rapid news cycle create a spontaneous intimacy that obfuscates the intricate underpinnings of Los Angeles' celebrity industrial complex.

The successful process of building up stars and projecting their images around the globe hinges on the work of thousands of workers and firms devoted to the upkeep of celebrities as individuals and of celebrity as a phenomenon. Publicists, lawyers, and agents focus their entire careers on celebrities. Agencies have thousands of staff devoted to celebrity clients' endorsements, rights, and deals. Even the most mundane supporters—hairdressers, gyms,

represents approx 10,000 persons

Los Angeles

Celebrities 34,800

Handlers 5,320

Support staff 68,950

Preppers 35,670

Media machine 64,850

New York City

Celebrities 12,020

Handlers 7,980

Support staff 125,010

Preppers 73,360

Media machine 88,190

Sources: County Business Pattern Industry Data, BLS 2008; Currid-Halkett (2010)

department stores—are essential to the upkeep of the image and appearance of celebrities. All of these people and institutions work together to cultivate the image, profile, economic capital, and media attention that each individual star attains. Jennifer Aniston, Angelina Jolie, and David Beckham would not exude the same "star power" without the daily maintenance of the star machine. Nebulous and ephemeral as it appears, celebrity is dependent on agglomeration economies and economies of scale and scope that are geographically bound to Los Angeles and its fellow celebrity cities, New York, Paris, and London. More broadly, these various functions operate in situ,

simultaneously, and their concentration in one place enables the exchange of knowledge, ideas, style, and the competition for these ingredients. Thus Los Angeles' celebrity operates much like Detroit's automobiles, Pittsburgh's steel, and Seattle's aerospace. The density of its economic and social activities enables the celebrity city to regenerate itself constantly. As celebrity's form and function is inherently ephemeral, these capacities to create new knowledge, new ideas, new celebrities is all the more important.

There are five rungs on the ladder of occupations and businesses that comprise these cities' celebrity industrial complex. The

stars and aspiring stars, whether supermodels or actresses, are at the top, and they are responsible for everyone else having a job. The second rung involves those who work for the stars—their handlers, agents, publicists, and representation. Then there are the support staff—the lawyers, chauffeurs, and attendants—and then the preppers—manicurists, stylists, and fitness trainers. Finally, though perhaps most importantly of all, comes the media machine which anoints and appoints the stars and presents them to the world. Celebrities and their images come and go, but the celebrity industrial complex stays in place.

Numbers of celebrity-related businesses in NYC and LA

Numbers of celebrity-related businesses in NYC and LA

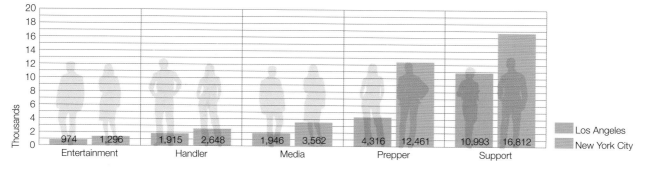

	Entertainment	Handler	Media	Prepper	Support
Los Angeles	974	1,915	1,946	4,316	10,993
New York City	1,296	2,648	3,562	12,461	16,812

Payrolls of celebrity related businesses in NYC and LA (US dollars)

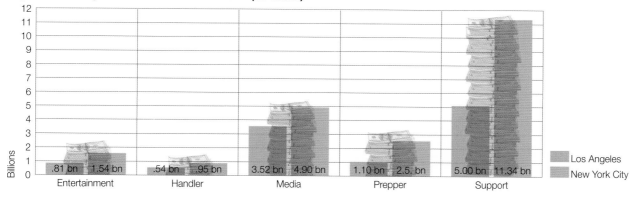

	Entertainment	Handler	Media	Prepper	Support
Los Angeles	.81 bn	.54 bn	3.52 bn	1.10 bn	5.00 bn
New York City	1.54 bn	.95 bn	4.90 bn	2.5 bn	11.34 bn

Sources: County Business Pattern Industry Data, BLS 2007 (businesses) and 2008 (payroll); Currid-Halkett (2010)

Celebrity city economy

In New York City, almost $1 billion in payroll is doled out to those working in public relations, while that figure is $536 million in Los Angeles. In Los Angeles, media drums up over $3.5 billion in payroll, while the city's celebrity occupations—actors, musicians, athletes—alone generate over $1.5 billion in payroll. Twenty-first-century celebrity is a real economy and a real place, even if it is its ephemeral and virtual presence that dominates our understanding.

The World City Network of Celebrity

Across the world, from Memphis to Mumbai, consumers of popular culture buy magazines, watch television programs, and follow blogs documenting the lives of celebrities—the elite cultural producers of the world's creative cities. From the frequency of the appearance of stars in *Vanity Fair*, *People* magazine, or *Hello!*, we might think that celebrities are everywhere. From Marshall McLuhan's perspective, they indeed are everywhere. The media is the message and the message is incessant.

Yet the empirical study of celebrities' comings and goings indicates that, while it may seem that they are everywhere, they are really only located in a few elite cities around the world. The media breeds the fiction of their accessibility even if they are truly miles away, tucked away in the bungalows of the Hollywood Hills and the roped-off restaurants of Sunset Boulevard and Bond Street. In fact, from our study of over half a million Getty photographs of stars attending different events, it turns out that stars spend most of their time in just three cities around the world: London, New York, and Los Angeles. Eighty percent of the photographs were taken in just these three

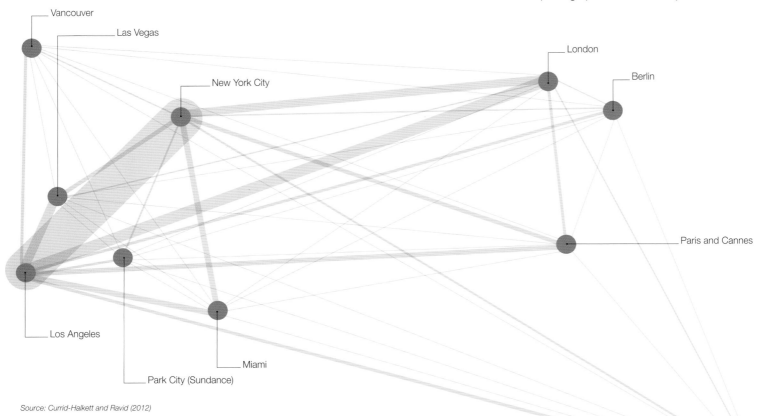

Vancouver
Las Vegas
New York City
London
Berlin
Paris and Cannes
Los Angeles
Miami
Park City (Sundance)
Sydney

Source: Currid-Halkett and Ravid (2012)

Celebrity city connections

Studying the social networks of the stars indicates that London, New York, and Los Angeles are not just the celebrity capitals of the world but are also significantly connected to each other through the flows of stars coming and going. In this diagram, the thickness of the line connecting two cities reflects the number of celebrity trips to and from them. New York and Los Angeles, for example, are the most connected celebrity cities in the world, followed by Los Angeles and London. Image adapted from an original by Gilad Ravid; data from March 2006 to February 2007.

Los Angeles

New York

London

places. In addition, a few other cities operate as ephemeral celebrity hubs: Cannes during its eponymous film festival, Miami during Art Basel, Park City Utah during the Sundance Film Festival. The celebrity city network highlights a very important, recurring aspect of 21st-century economic development: a globally connected urban system that generates winner-take-all geographies, often leaving the hinterlands behind.

Like other industries, the rationale for this finite number of cities can be explained by a simple fact: most industries rely on agglomerative social, economic, and physical infrastructure and a heavily connected system of knowledge. Celebrity, existential at its core, relies on a system of upholding stars and their milieus that sells magazines, movies, and tourist destinations. The stars themselves, not unlike Wall Street traders, rely on localized networks to maintain and advance their careers, to generate and attain knowledge and innovation. One cannot become a global star without being regularly present in the locations where the paparazzi have set up shop to take photos and send them round the world.

There is, however, an important missing aspect to this world city network. Bollywood, India's film capital and home to some of the biggest stars in the world, does not appear to be connected to any of the major Western celebrity hubs. The stars of Bollywood appear to be entirely removed from Western pop culture even though by absolute number of fans they are significantly more celebrated. Qualitative research done on Bollywood (Lorenzen and Taübe, 2008; Lorenzen and Mudambi, 2013) suggests that even if the Indian film industry shoots on location around the world and has booming exports, its celebrity is quite insular. Centering upon Mumbai and with its own sizable media machine, Bollywood's celebrity system finds little need to connect to the Western urban system.

Bollywood

Mumbai, as the location of Bollywood, is arguably the biggest celebrity city in the world but remains utterly disconnected from its Western counterparts. Bollywood produces 200–250 films a year and ticket sales are estimated to be on a par with those of Hollywood. Bollywood's industry is so economically and culturally robust it has little need or desire to connect up with the Western celebrity and entertainment network.

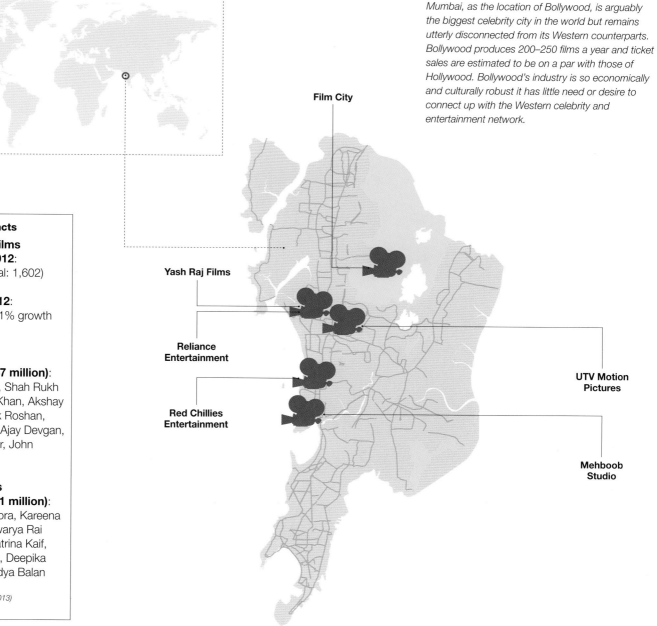

Film City

Yash Raj Films

Reliance Entertainment

Red Chillies Entertainment

UTV Motion Pictures

Mehboob Studio

Bollywood Facts

Number of films produced 2012: 221 (India total: 1,602)

Turnover 2012: $1.8 billion (21% growth since 2011)

Male stars (fees up to $7 million): Salman Khan, Shah Rukh Khan, Aamir Khan, Akshay Kumar, Hrithik Roshan, Saif Ali Khan, Ajay Devgan, Ranbir Kapoor, John Abraham

Female stars (fees up to $1 million): Priyanka Chopra, Kareena Kapoor, Aishwarya Rai Bachchan, Katrina Kaif, Bipasha Basu, Deepika Padukone, Vidya Balan

Source: Lorenzen (2013)

The Social Science of Celebrity Networks

Networking is essential to all our lives, but what exactly does this mean? What does the most elite of networks— Hollywood's A-list—tell us about their social behavior and where it is located? Can their social networks explain the difference between the A-list and the C-list, let alone the rest of us?

In recent years, social networks have been an important component in the study of economic development and urban prosperity. Early work on Silicon Valley noted informal personal relationships as being essential to the thriving of the industry (to the detriment of Boston's Route 128). Those who study creative industries remark upon the necessity of ad hoc clusters

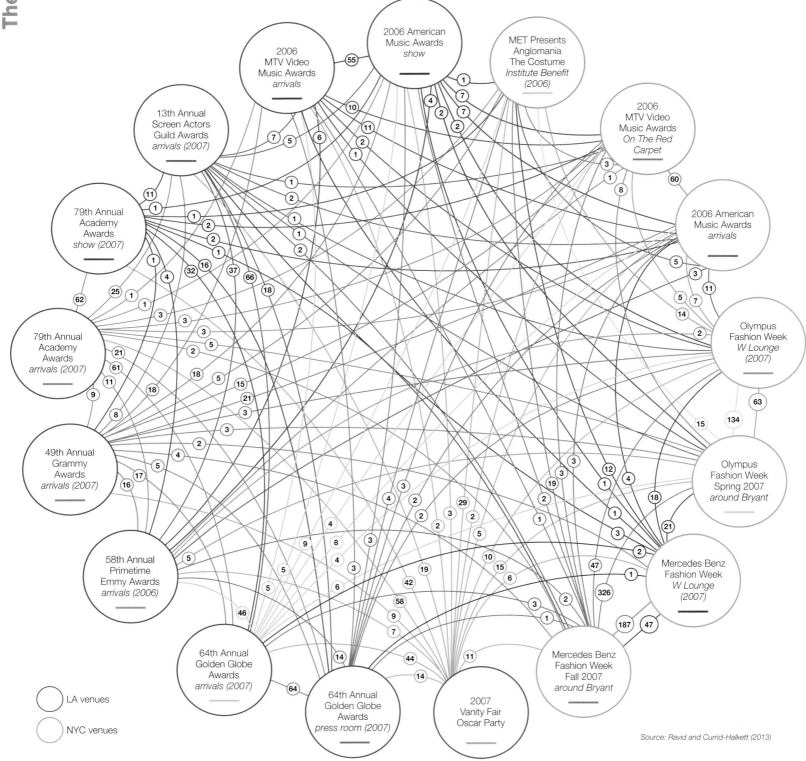

LA venues

NYC venues

Source: Ravid and Currid-Halkett (2013)

of people living, working, and bumping up against one another. More recently, the tracking of cell phone data suggests that diverse social networks are strongly linked to city prosperity.

Photographs of celebrities reveal important information about such connections. While celebrities are an elite population within cultural industries, their social dynamics may tell us something important about the role of social networks in the prosperity of other careers and industries. My colleague Gilad Ravid of Ben Gurion University in Israel and I conducted social network analysis of our Getty dataset that enabled us to analyze who was in each of the photos, who they were photographed with, at

what event, in what city, and how many photos were taken of each star. The caption information for these photographs reveals that the A-list has a meaningfully different network to everyone else in the entire photograph database.

To put the social networks of stars in perspective, consider that most of the world has six degrees of separation (this mythological number has been shown to be empirically sound). Those within the celebrity network have just 3.26 degrees of separation. Even celebrities who have no obvious linkage with other celebrities by virtue of occupation, location, or status are connected by just 3.26 people. The A-list is even more compact. Drawing from

Forbes Magazine's Star Currency rankings, we were able to study the social networks of stars based on where they show up in the rankings. While the Getty photographs include 7,000 people, members of the A-list spend time solely with the same twenty other A-list stars. One of the means by which elite celebrities perpetuate their exclusive status is by attending prestigious events where only other top stars are in attendance. These events themselves—the Oscars, Fashion Weeks, Art Basel Miami—transform the cities in which they are held. They become exciting centers of glamor and spectacle, which encourages their citizens to participate in the celebrity city milieu.

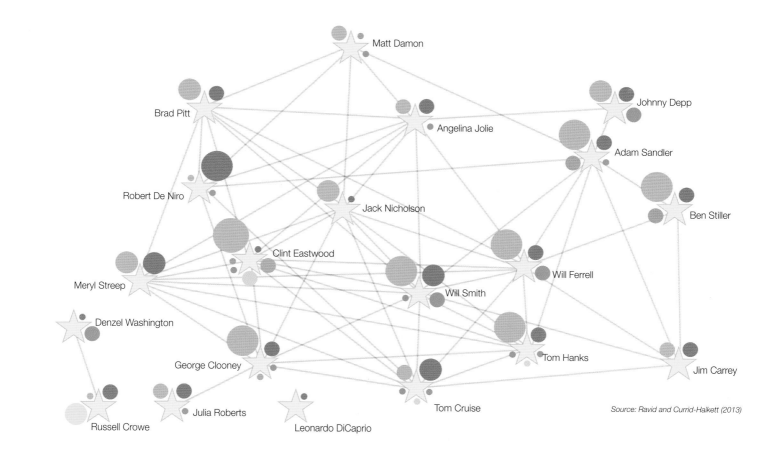

Source: Ravid and Currid-Halkett (2013)

Celebrity networks across events

Despite the spectacle of celebrity occurring at far-flung events across discrete cities around the world, patterns and connectivity emerge. Time and again, the same celebrities appear as players in the various celebrity spectacles. For example, those who attend the Vanity Fair Oscar Party also all show up at the Met's annual Costume Institute Gala. The image opposite portrays the connections across events that tie the global celebrity cities together. The lines show the connections between people, the numbers show the number of people who attended one event who also attended the other ones to which that event is connected.

Events attended

○ 1

○ 2–5

○ 6–10

○ 11–19

○ 20 and over

Location

Los Angeles
New York City
Las Vegas
London
Paris
Berlin
Tokyo
Sydney

The social network of celebrities across cities

Elite celebrities may move from city to city, event to event, but still maintain the same dense network regardless of location. While the Getty photographs include 7,000 people, this data from 2006 to 2007 shows that members of the A-list spend time solely with the same twenty other A-list stars.

The Geography of Talent

Celebrity cities are places of spectacle and fascination. Their success hinges on the media's and the public's fascination with particular people and events. Yet just as celebrities are not famous for the same reasons, neither are celebrity cities. These places possess different attributes—Las Vegas' seediness, Los Angeles' shallow glitter, the grit of New York and London. One element of these distinctions derives from the people who personify the urban form. The stars then—the human capital, so to speak—create our image of the celebrity city.

Some stars maintain their celebrity status through their talent, defined through Oscars, Golden Globes, and blockbuster films. Others pin their stardom to the thin reed of being personally interesting to the world. The means by which a celebrity maintains his or her star status is linked to the cities they spend time in, and the events they attend. Our photographic analysis revealed distinctly different patterns based on whether a star was an Oscar-winning, box-office juggernaut or whether they simply had a knack for spilling tabloid ink. As such, celebrity cities become aligned with the reputation of the stars that frequent them.

Theatre Royal, Haymarket

Metropolitan Opera House

Berlin

London

New York City

Las Vegas
Los Angeles

Berlinale—Berlin International Film Festival

We took *Forbes Magazine*'s Star Currency list of those stars who drove box-office receipts, won awards, and drew other stars to films, and mapped their geographical behavior around the world. Our analysis demonstrates that particular celebrity cities are negatively or positively associated either with talent or with fame pure and simple. Thus, while Paris Hilton spends most of her time in Los Angeles, the capital of all celebrity cities, talent-driven stars like Angelina Jolie rarely set foot into LA's media spotlight. Talent celebrities seldom appear in Los Angeles but do make appearances in more international locales.

Talent does not rely on being in the camera's flash, so simply being photographed in Los Angeles does not demonstrate anything unique or substantive about one's celebrity. Attending an event in a more distant locale, however, indicates global demand and the far-reaching impact of a star's film, music, or creative output. Going to cities in Australia or Germany is strongly associated with increases in star power. London is the city most associated with high-talent stars. Unsurprisingly, Las Vegas and Los Angeles are associated with the most primal aspects of celebrity—flashiness, ephemerality, more than a hint of tawdriness. Cities like London and Sydney are globally cosmopolitan destinations. Thus the stars and their cities are mirror images of one another.

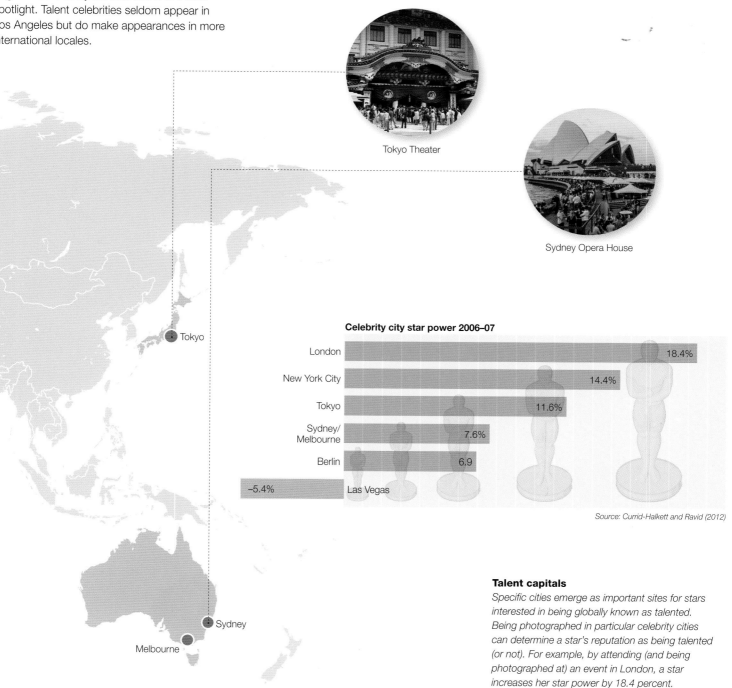

Tokyo Theater

Sydney Opera House

Celebrity city star power 2006–07

London	18.4%
New York City	14.4%
Tokyo	11.6%
Sydney/Melbourne	7.6%
Berlin	6.9
Las Vegas	−5.4%

Source: Currid-Halkett and Ravid (2012)

Talent capitals

Specific cities emerge as important sites for stars interested in being globally known as talented. Being photographed in particular celebrity cities can determine a star's reputation as being talented (or not). For example, by attending (and being photographed at) an event in London, a star increases her star power by 18.4 percent. Conversely, being photographed at an event in Las Vegas decreases star power by 5.4 percent.

Celebrity Cities and the "Famous for Being Famous"

Celebrity cities, like those that are centers of finance or technology or art, tend to focus on a particular aspect of the industry. Thus the talented stars migrate to those cities with particular attributes. While Los Angeles, London, and New York appear to be the epicenters of celebrity culture, in truth the geographical behavior of talented stars and simply famous stars shows remarkably different patterns.

Part of this can be explained by the "famous for being famous" star's need to be constantly in the spotlight in order to maintain their celebrity status. Thus, for these stars, being closely proximate to the media capitals is essential to their stardom. As such, while London is a magnet for talent stars, it is also essential for the Paris Hiltons of the world. Great Britain's concentrated media (only fifteen major daily newspapers) and the BBC juggernaut means that everyone consumes the same media. For those famous for being famous stars, attending an event in London will ensure wide distribution across the country.

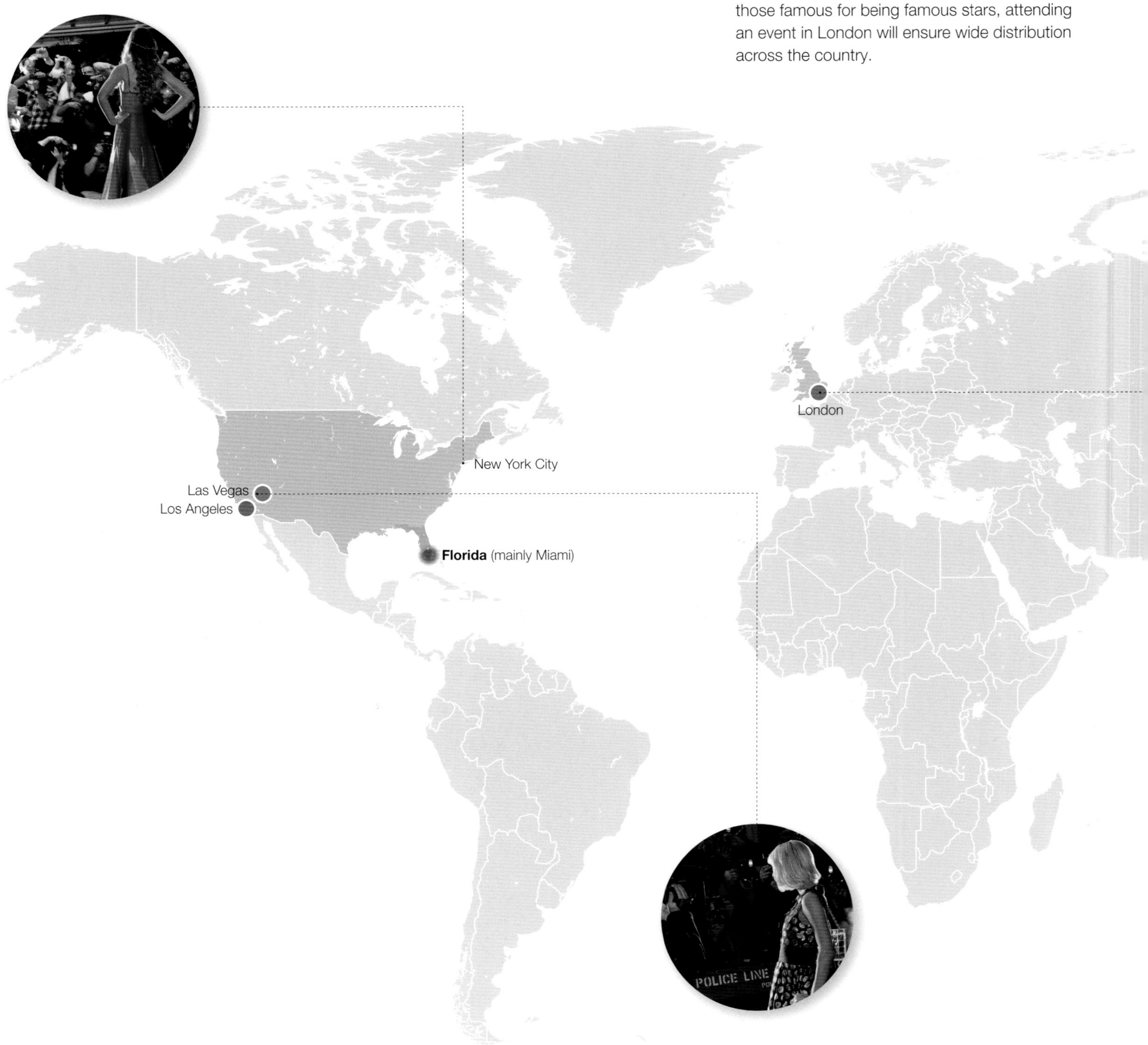

London

New York City

Las Vegas
Los Angeles

Florida (mainly Miami)

Simply famous stars spend extended periods of time in Los Angeles to maximize their exposure. However, the simply famous must also travel to more events so as to get their photos in the tabloids. Paris Hilton does not get the same attention per event as a talent-driven star like Angelina Jolie or Tom Cruise. Take the case of London celebrity events: in 2006 Angelina Jolie was photographed 100 times at a single event; Tom Cruise was photographed 111 times at his *Mission Impossible* film premiere; Paris Hilton attended ten London events in that same year and was photographed 173 times in total. This gives her a photo-to-event ratio of 17.3 versus 100 and 111 for Jolie and Cruise respectively. Additionally, the type of event is predictive of type of star. Talented stars tend to attend events exclusive to their industry or charity events, while simply famous stars show up at any type of event as long as a photographer is on hand.

Las Vegas is a problematic celebrity hub all around. Showing up in this desert simulacrum of a city is associated with a decline in star power of any kind. Las Vegas is only celebrity relevant when a star is hosting a birthday party. For the simply famous, the media is all that counts, and if such a star is in Vegas she's not likely to be in front of a camera reminding the world she exists.

Celebrity city media power 2006–2007

Los Angeles	25.2%
Florida (mainly Miami)	17%
London	15%
Sydney/Melbourne	13.1%
Tokyo	7.3%
New York City	6.6%
Las Vegas	−10.8%

Source: Currid-Halkett and Ravid (2012)

"Famous for being famous" capitals
Cities are sites of celebrity spectacle, and this spectacle is played out in the media, which upholds the famous and the celebrated through endless images. For stars who rely primarily on their fame (not their talent), attending events is important, but not in the same cities as the talented. For the "famous for being famous," Los Angeles remains the essential city of celebrity. Attending one event in Los Angeles increases media volume by 25 percent, compared to Las Vegas which decreases media volume by over 10 percent. Other cities, like New York and Tokyo, operate on a middle ground, supporting talented and just famous stars alike.

The Geography of Buzz

From the counterculture of Silicon Valley to the icy capitalism of Wall Street, the social milieu shapes the success of those working within a particular industry. Ideas are traded, job opportunities emerge, creativity flourishes "in the air," as the great economist Alfred Marshall once remarked of the clustering of industrial activity. In my book *The Warhol Economy*, I studied the creative industries of New York City. My research partially emerged from my perplexity as to why poor artists and design graduates flocked to New York City to live in cramped apartments, pay exorbitant rents, and face cutthroat competition

with every other creative person vying for a job or project. During my time traipsing from gallery opening to bar to fashion show, I realized that no amount of working hard in a studio in Ohio would replace the ad hoc, serendipitous social interaction that opened doors to new jobs, access to editors and curators, and put one on the frontier of new fashion, music, and art movements. In fact, penetrating the right networks and meeting the right people trumped endless nights working in solitude. What Marshall observed over one hundred years ago is still true in the age of technology and email—being in situ matters.

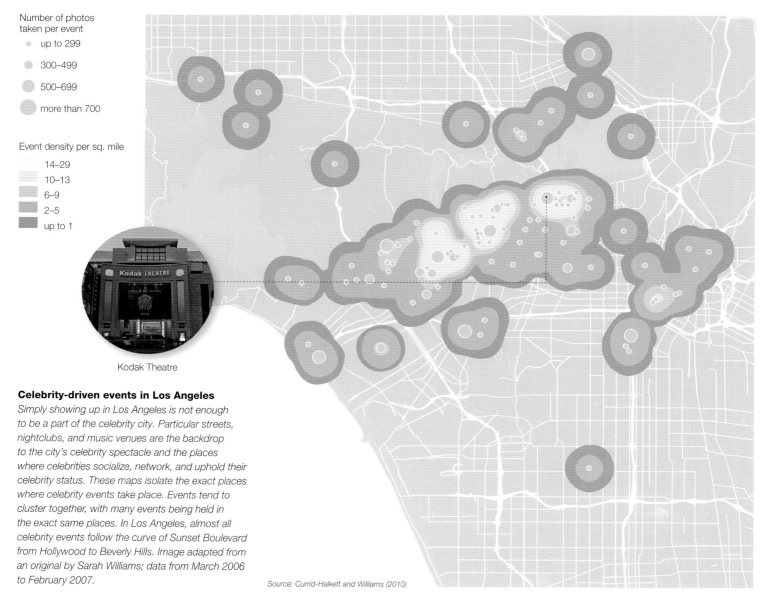

Number of photos taken per event
- up to 299
- 300–499
- 500–699
- more than 700

Event density per sq. mile
- 14–29
- 10–13
- 6–9
- 2–5
- up to 1

Kodak Theatre

Celebrity-driven events in Los Angeles
Simply showing up in Los Angeles is not enough to be a part of the celebrity city. Particular streets, nightclubs, and music venues are the backdrop to the city's celebrity spectacle and the places where celebrities socialize, network, and uphold their celebrity status. These maps isolate the exact places where celebrity events take place. Events tend to cluster together, with many events being held in the exact same places. In Los Angeles, almost all celebrity events follow the curve of Sunset Boulevard from Hollywood to Beverly Hills. Image adapted from an original by Sarah Williams; data from March 2006 to February 2007.

Source: Currid-Halkett and Williams (2010)

Could the story of New York City's creative scene apply more broadly to how social lives drive careers? My belief was that these patterns would be particularly profound in highly subjective, winner-take-all industries where being seen enables one to capture the attention of the media and hence the gatekeepers. To study the role of the social scene in economic success, my colleague Sarah Williams of MIT and I collected caption information from Getty Images entertainment photographs and geocoded all of the industry events in Los Angeles and New York, categorizing each event as fashion, art, film, music or "magnet" (for example, a charity gala, which is an event not aligned with a particular celebrity industry but which attracts many stars). We found that celebrity-driven social scenes tend to exhibit nonrandom, statistically significant clustering patterns, and that fashion, art, music, and film types tend to socialize in the same geographically concentrated areas that overlap across industries. In short, it's no accident that celebrities are spending time in the same restaurants, walking down the same streets, and smiling on the same red carpets.

Celebrity cities offer the necessary conditions to create the glamor and drama that draw audiences, tourists, and consumers to partake in this global spectacle. As ubiquitous as celebrity seems to be, when we look closely there are very few neighborhoods even within celebrity hubs where photographs are actually taken. In Los Angeles, Hollywood, Beverly Hills, West Hollywood, and Century City are the main nodes where celebrity events are photographed. Looking closely, these urban contexts offer the iconic infrastructure—the Kodak Theatre (renamed the Dolby Theatre in 2012), Times Square, the Beverly Hills Hotel—that makes celebrity culture so alluring. Such excitement would not be generated by a quiet street in Missouri.

Event density per sq. mile
- 131–450
- 74–130
- 18–73
- up to 17

Number of photos taken per event
- up to 20
- 21–50
- 51–100
- 101–200
- 201–10

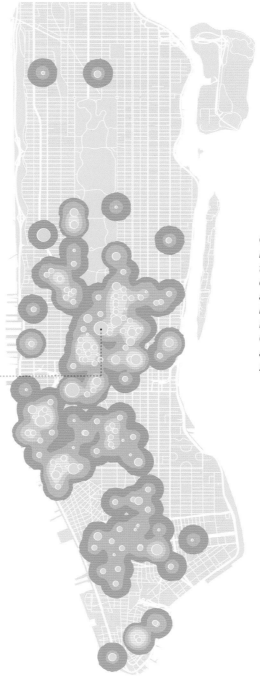

Times Square

Celebrity-driven events in New York City
New York City's geography is vastly different than that of Los Angeles, and yet the spectacle of celebrity follows a similar pattern of clustering and concentration. Almost all of the events are hosted below 59th Street, just south of Central Park. The dominant hubs for celebrity are Chelsea and Times Square. Image adapted from an original by Sarah Williams; data from March 2006 to February 2007.

Source: Currid-Halkett and Williams (2010)

THE MEGACITY

JAN NIJMAN
MICHAEL SHIN

Core city
MUMBAI _____

Secondary cities
CAIRO _____
MEXICO CITY _____
JAKARTA _____
KARACHI _____
SHANGHAI _____
SÃO PAULO _____
NEW YORK _____

Left: Mumbai, India

The Megacity: Introduction

"In 1970 there were only two megacities; in 1990 there were ten; and by 2013 there were twenty-eight."

If urbanization could be said to have taken the world by storm in the modern period, the arrival of megacities on the global scene in recent years has been even more explosive. Ancient Rome was the first city with more than a million people—its scale and density during Antiquity were unique and perplexing. Not until the 7th century did medieval Xian in China emerge as the second city in the world to reach the million-mark. In Europe, industrializing London was the first city to top 1 million, but not until about 1800. Today, two in five urban residents across the world live in cities of over a million and there are more than fifty such cities in the United States alone. Indeed, most places today are hardly considered a real city if they have fewer than a million residents.

Cities greater than 10 million in 2013
The world's twenty-eight megacities in 2013, defined as cities with more than 10 million inhabitants. Only six are located in the western hemisphere and most are found in South, East, and Southeast Asia. The megacity phenomenon is increasingly concentrated in the developing world where population densities tend to be higher and where urbanization is of more recent origins. In west Europe and North America, urban systems tend to be older and more dispersed.

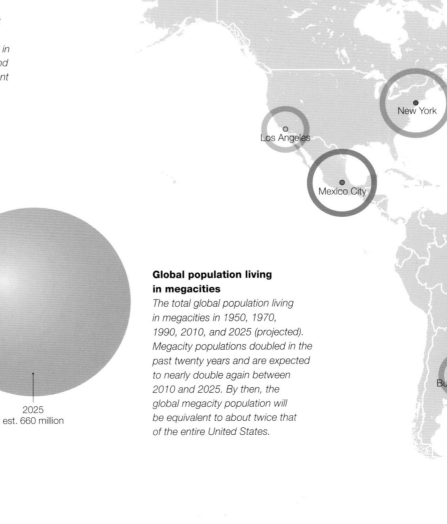

Global population living in megacities
The total global population living in megacities in 1950, 1970, 1990, 2010, and 2025 (projected). Megacity populations doubled in the past twenty years and are expected to nearly double again between 2010 and 2025. By then, the global megacity population will be equivalent to about twice that of the entire United States.

1950
zero

1970
39 million

1990
145 million

2010
350 million

2025
est. 660 million

Megacities, however, are in a different league. The common threshold is 10 million inhabitants across the metropolitan area or contiguous urban region (estimates tend to vary with spatial delineations). They are a very recent phenomenon. In 1970 there were only two megacities, New York and Tokyo; in 1990 there were ten; and by 2013 there were twenty-eight, led by the Tokyo–Yokohama urban region with an estimated 37 million people. If Tokyo–Yokohama were a country, it would be the 35th biggest in the world and outrank Canada both in terms of population and gross domestic product. More modest Mexico City, with 20 million people, is bigger than 180-plus countries in the world today and its GDP exceeds that of countries such as Denmark or Venezuela. At the present time, nearly 500 million people in the world live in these giant metropolises and their numbers are growing fast.

Megacities are unevenly distributed around the world. More than half, including the seven biggest, are located in Asia. Interestingly, there are only a few in the West: New York and Los Angeles in the United States, with Paris as the lone megacity in Europe, though it will soon be joined by London. The fact that the majority of megacities are found in what is generally considered the "developing world" raises some important questions about how megacities come about and how desirable they are.

Size matters. Cities are generally deemed beneficial because they offer economies of scale: it becomes cheaper and more efficient to provide a host of services or to engage in economic activity when people are close together. Thus, urbanization is commonly seen as part and parcel of modernization and progress. But is it possible that cities can get *too* big, and the advantages give way to diseconomies of scale? What if distances across the urban area are too extensive? What if commuting becomes too costly? What about the ecological footprint of megacities? How important is population density, apart from size? And what if megacities are not actually planned, as appears to be the case in much of the less developed world? This chapter highlights the emergence of megacities in recent times, the considerable variation among them, and some of their main features and challenges.

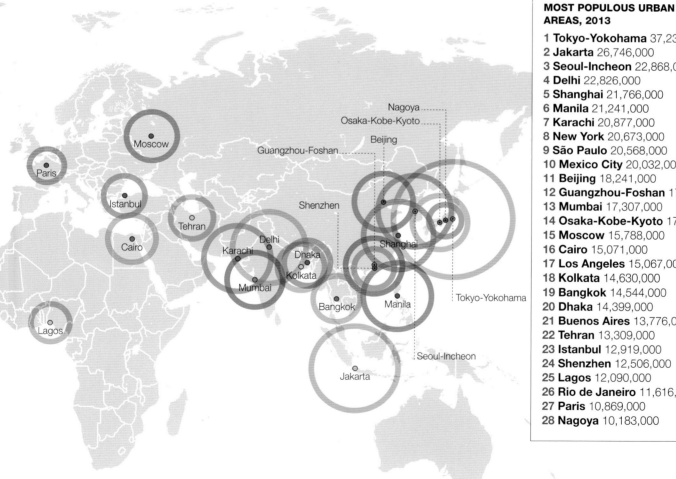

MOST POPULOUS URBAN AREAS, 2013

1 **Tokyo-Yokohama** 37,239,000
2 **Jakarta** 26,746,000
3 **Seoul-Incheon** 22,868,000
4 **Delhi** 22,826,000
5 **Shanghai** 21,766,000
6 **Manila** 21,241,000
7 **Karachi** 20,877,000
8 **New York** 20,673,000
9 **São Paulo** 20,568,000
10 **Mexico City** 20,032,000
11 **Beijing** 18,241,000
12 **Guangzhou-Foshan** 17,681,000
13 **Mumbai** 17,307,000
14 **Osaka-Kobe-Kyoto** 17,175,000
15 **Moscow** 15,788,000
16 **Cairo** 15,071,000
17 **Los Angeles** 15,067,000
18 **Kolkata** 14,630,000
19 **Bangkok** 14,544,000
20 **Dhaka** 14,399,000
21 **Buenos Aires** 13,776,000
22 **Tehran** 13,309,000
23 **Istanbul** 12,919,000
24 **Shenzhen** 12,506,000
25 **Lagos** 12,090,000
26 **Rio de Janeiro** 11,616,000
27 **Paris** 10,869,000
28 **Nagoya** 10,183,000

Megacity Growth

Megacities can emerge in different ways. In their present form, New York and Los Angeles are polycentric urban regions that are in fact made up of a number of bigger and smaller cities that have evolved into a single megacity. New York reaches into four states and besides New York City it includes places such as Newark, Scranton, and Stamford. Other major U.S. metropolitan areas such as the San Francisco Bay Area, or southeastern Florida, have also emerged as a result of this process of amalgamation. This is a reflection, among other things, of the high overall urbanization rate of

U.S. society, where urban growth is notably dispersed across space so that cities in certain regions sooner or later run into each other.

But this is not how most megacities in the so-called "Global South" have come into existence. There, growth has often been centered on a relatively small number of major cities with enormous hinterlands. This is obviously related to the history of urbanization in different places. Bombay, in its incipient stages, was very much the product of British industrial colonial policy in the latter part of the 19th century. The railroads were built to further this policy, as were the port and other

MUMBAI'S POPULATION GROWTH SINCE 1872	
	Mumbai population
1872	664,605
1881	773,196
1891	821,764
1901	812,912
1911	1,018,388
1921	1,244,934
1931	1,268,936
1941	1,686,127
1951	2,966,902
1961	4,152,056
1971	5,970,575
1981	8,227,382
1991	12,500,000
2001	16,369,084
2011	18,400,000

Source: Indian census records

Bombay around 1900

Bombay developed into an industrial city in the second half of the 19th century, occupying only the southern part of the peninsula that is now generally known as Greater Mumbai. The city included the port, a naval base, railroads, colonial offices and residential areas, textile mills, and separate residential areas for native Indians. The population at the turn of the century was around 800,000.

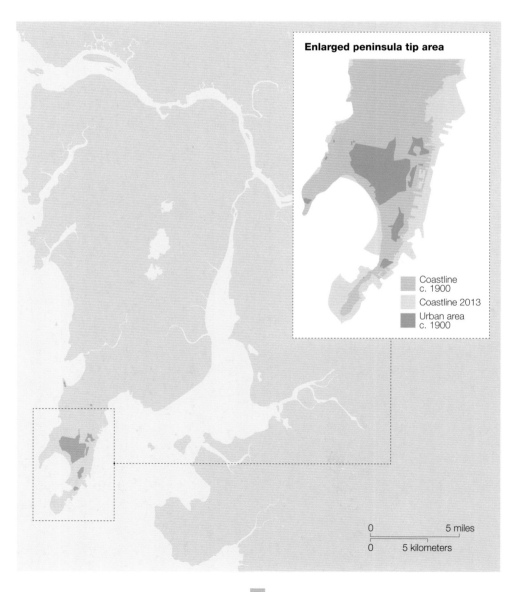

Enlarged peninsula tip area

Coastline c. 1900
Coastline 2013
Urban area c. 1900

0   5 miles
0   5 kilometers

Urban area c. 1900

infrastructures. Thus, while the United States witnessed urbanization across many regions and involving a wide range of cities, Bombay's growth acceleration at the dawn of the 20th century took place in the context of an otherwise overwhelmingly rural west India.

Bombay (renamed Mumbai in 1995 as a belated native reaction to colonial linguistic legacies) has grown into a megacity by gradually expanding from the center outward. Today, when Mumbai's population has grown to more than 20 million, there is still only one major focus, in South Mumbai, where the Portuguese first landed in the late 16th century, where the British subsequently built their fort and offices for the colonial government, and where the

Indians after Independence established the country's main stock exchange and set up the headquarters of the Indian Reserve Bank.

Megacity growth due to outward expansion rather than amalgamation suggests a more important rural–urban dynamic. In Mumbai and other megacities of the Global South, rural–urban migration has been a major driving force and this is shown by the high proportion of recent migrants in the more peripheral parts of the city. And most of that growth, in Mumbai and elsewhere (e.g., Jakarta, Lagos, Karachi), happened in the second half of the 20th century, after independence. Consider this: New York is a megacity of nearly 20 million in a nation that is about 85 percent urbanized;

Mumbai is a megacity of more than 21 million in a nation where two-thirds of the population still live in rural areas.

Growth due to expansion rather than amalgamation implies a constant process of adaptation by newcomers to urban life, but also a greater diversity among the city's population in terms of livelihoods, well-being, and communal attachment. And, importantly, megacities of the Global South, because they are less polycentric, tend to have more strained infrastructures. In Mumbai, this is a particular challenge because the main business district is at the southern tip of the peninsula, far from the topographical center of the metropolis and far from connections to the mainland.

The Mumbai megacity today

During the second half of the 20th century, the "Island City" expanded from the south upward, generally following the railroads built by the British in earlier times. Once the peninsula was "full," expansion continued on the mainland in what is Navi Mumbai (New Mumbai). Today, about 12 million people live on the peninsula known as Greater Mumbai while another 9 million live on the mainland in Mumbai urban region.

The Mumbai skyline

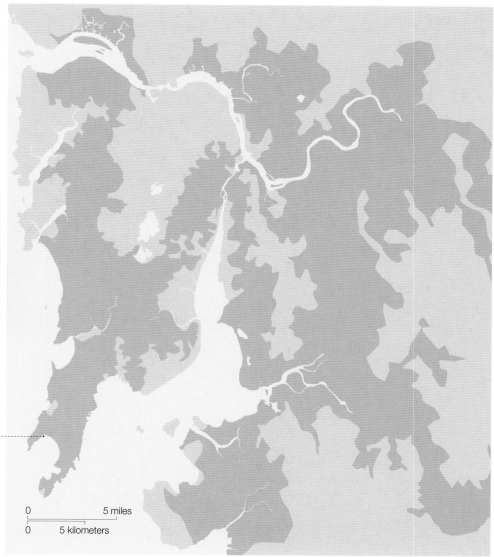

Urban area c. 2013

The Large and Crowded Spaces of the Megacity

The famous urbanist Louis Wirth wrote back in the 1930s that "great cities" combine three fundamental features: size, density, and diversity. Great cities, in his mind, were places with critical mass and combustible human energy; places of tension and friction at times, but also cradles of creativity and progress. Without density, there is not enough human contact; without diversity and difference, there is no chemistry; without size, there is not enough of anything. Wirth was one of a group of sociologists who became known as the

Chicago School. Back then, Chicago had over 3 million people (more than today); it was the second biggest city in the United States and one of the biggest in the world, and its population was a brew of ethnicities and nationalities.

If it makes intuitive sense that great cities require some minimum size, it is far from obvious what the upper threshold should be or indeed whether there is a linear relationship between size and "greatness." As noted earlier, economies of scale can at some point regress into *dis*economies of scale. The same could be

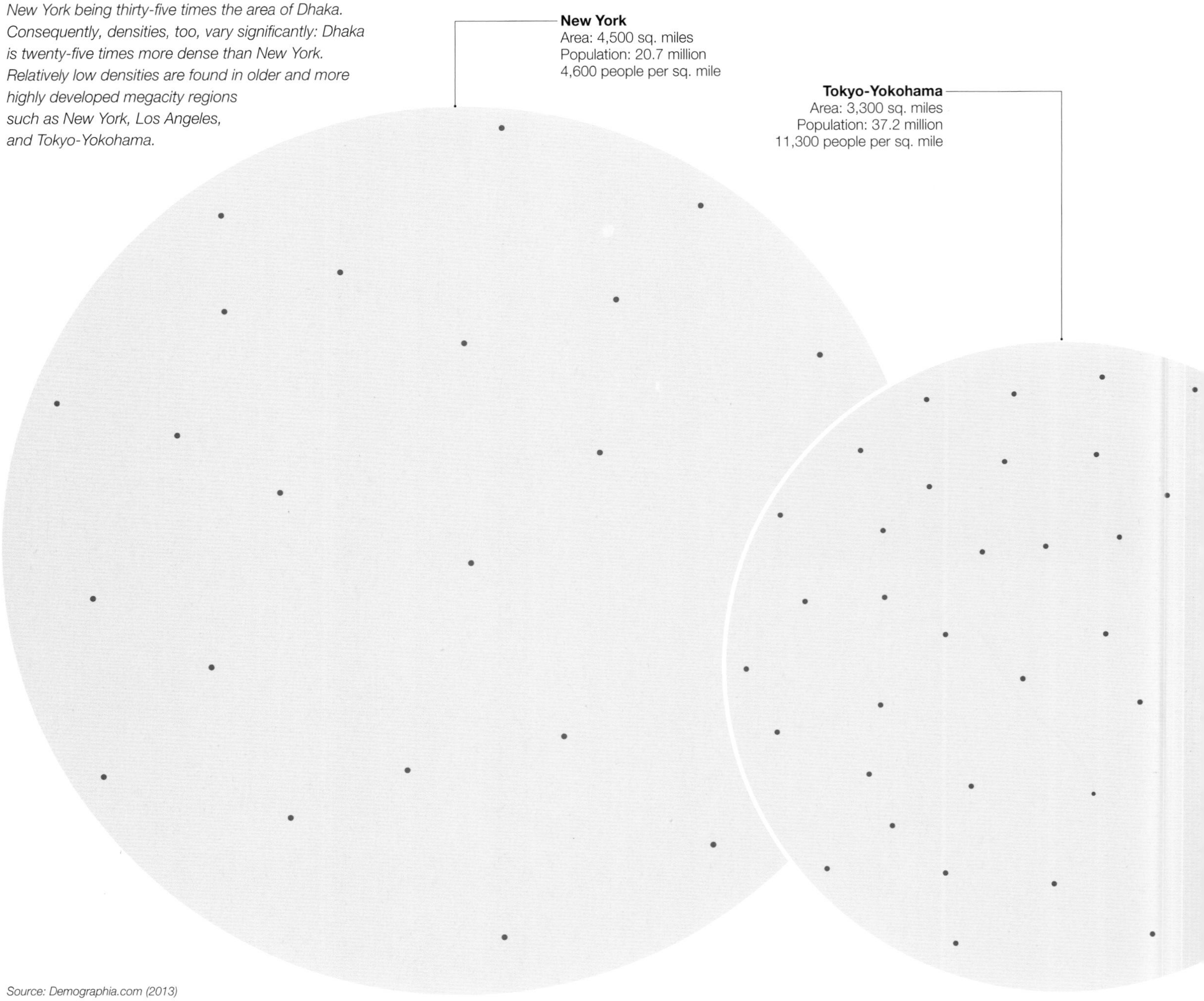

Megacity densities, 2013 estimates

All megacities have populations greater than 10 million but they vary tremendously in terms of area. New York and Dhaka are the two extremes with New York being thirty-five times the area of Dhaka. Consequently, densities, too, vary significantly: Dhaka is twenty-five times more dense than New York. Relatively low densities are found in older and more highly developed megacity regions such as New York, Los Angeles, and Tokyo-Yokohama.

New York
Area: 4,500 sq. miles
Population: 20.7 million
4,600 people per sq. mile

Tokyo-Yokohama
Area: 3,300 sq. miles
Population: 37.2 million
11,300 people per sq. mile

Source: Demographia.com (2013)

said about density: it is desirable and conducive to lots of wonderful things, but extreme density can certainly be a problem. Among megacities there is no clear correlation between population size and density. Tokyo–Yokohama is three times the size but only one-third the density of Lagos. Los Angeles and Kolkata are of similar size but Kolkata is five times as dense. And Mumbai is nearly eighteen times as crowded as New York even though they have comparable populations. Thus, the polycentric urban regions of the United States or Japan have substantially lower densities than the monocentric megacities of the Global South.

If city size and density do not correlate in a consistent way across all megacities, high density certainly does not suggest greater prosperity. Dhaka, the most crammed megacity of them all with an incredible 115,000 people per square mile, is also the poorest, while New York, Los Angeles, and Paris are among the megacities with the lowest densities and the highest per capita incomes. In poor megacities, population densities tend to be overwhelming and put enormous strains on housing, transportation, work-spaces, and public areas. When a garment factory building collapsed on the outskirts of Dhaka in 2013, more than 900 people were killed and more than 2,500 others were injured. That, too, said something about that megacity's extreme density.

Population density is a requirement for efficient public transportation and the provision of many other public and private services. It also makes for a dynamic, exciting, creative, and combustible urban environment. But most of us would like to sit rather than stand when we are traveling to work on the train and we all need some private space, at least sometimes. The sheer scale of present-day Dhaka or Mumbai would have been beyond Louis Wirth's imagination.

New York
2.6 people per 1,124 sq. ft

Los Angeles
2.8 people per 1,900 sq. ft

Tokyo
1.9 people per 800 sq. ft

Mumbai
4.5 people per 600 sq. ft

Household density, 2013 estimates

Megacities all have enormous populations but they vary widely in terms of density. Family or household sizes differ as well from one megacity to another and this implies a wide range in the size of an average home and the number of people living in it. In Mumbai, the average family of 4.5 people shares a mere 600 square feet. In Los Angeles, the average person has six times as much space in their home. One should keep in mind this is only an average: in all megacities, living conditions and individual living space vary substantially across the urban landscape.

Los Angeles
Area: 2,435 sq. miles
Population: 15.1 million
6,200 people per sq. mile

Mexico City
Area: 787 sq. miles
Population: 20 million
25,400 people per sq. mile

Cairo
Area: 643 sq. miles
Population: 15.1 million
23,500 people per sq. mile

Kolkata
Area: 464 sq. miles
Population: 14.6 million
31,500 people per sq. mile

Lagos
Area: 351 sq. miles
Population: 12.1 million
34,500 people per sq. mile

Mumbai
Area: 211 sq. miles
Population: 17.3 million
82,000 people per sq. mile

Dhaka
Area: 125 sq. miles
Population: 14.4 million
115,200 people per sq. mile

Megacity Geographies

Megacities display complex geographies and they are often difficult to traverse. Few of their inhabitants have a clear picture of the city's overall spatial dimensions and prevailing order (if there is any) and their mobility is often restricted to the neighborhoods where they live and work. The megacity as a whole remains little more than an abstraction even for its own inhabitants. This is as true for New York as it is for Cairo or Mexico City, and it certainly also applies to Mumbai. It is the chaotic jumble and density of the megacities of the Global South, not so much their extent, that makes them hard to know and to map.

Sanjay Gandhi national park

New industrial zone

Western suburbs

Airport

Eastern suburbs

Back office district

Dharavi

Old industrial zone

Dock areas

Global central business district

Port

The changing shape of Mumbai

Greater Mumbai is like a mega-jigsaw puzzle with a good number of pieces changing shape over time while the city as a whole continues to grow outward. Imagine a metropolis with eighteen times the population density of New York and half the people in slums. The airport that was once on the urban perimeter is now in the very center. Some of the most exclusive residential areas on the waterfront date back to colonial times and the main business districts are still at the southern tip of the peninsula, increasingly difficult to reach for commuters from the suburbs. Slum areas large and small are interspersed with new middle-class developments.

Marsh areas
Upper income residential districts
Slum areas
— Railways
— Roads

The Mumbai peninsula is bound by the Arabian Sea to the west, Thane Creek to the east, and Vasai Creek and Ulhas River to the north. It is connected to the mainland in the north and northwest. The area's dimensions are about thirty miles from north to south and an average of six miles from west to east. The population is over 12 million people and the average population density is about 86,000 people per square mile. The city grew spectacularly in the decades following Independence (1947) and its geography became increasingly dense. The last half-century has witnessed a shift of population from the south to the northern suburbs, initially closely clustered around the railways.

The geographical constraints of the Island City put a premium on space and have historically influenced land values and land use in the city. There has been a steep gradient in land values from the south to the north. In the mid-1990s, the unprecedented influx of foreign corporations (mainly in the south of the city) contributed to an extreme escalation of land values, making Mumbai for a time the most expensive city in the world. As India's commercial capital and largest city, Mumbai is sometimes referred to as "the City of Gold," a place where many have gone from rags to riches. It is a place, in other words, with plenty of opportunity for upward mobility.

But Mumbai is also known as a city of extremes, of very rich and desperately poor, of a relatively large and prosperous middle class, and as the site of some of the largest slums in Asia. In the past two decades, more new homes have been built for the upwardly mobile than in any comparable period before. The new middle class is carving out a conspicuous consumerist niche in the urban landscape but it is doing so in competition with about 6 million slum dwellers for whom living space is a matter of survival, not luxury. And their numbers have been growing, too.

There is a sense in which Mumbai is like two cities blended together and mixed up. Locals refer to the *pukka* city as the one that is planned, and meant to be; the *kucha* city, in contrast, is the city that is unfinished, unintended. Or, maybe, they are better thought of as different worlds, coexisting in the space of a single city.

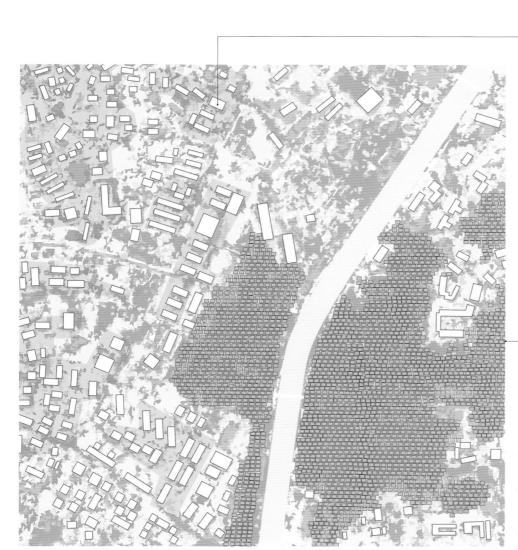

Middle-class high-rise

Slum area with middle-class housing in background

Tale of two cities

The pukka *and* kucha *city juxtaposed in Mumbai's northwestern suburbs. The fine-grained maze of the slum area along the Western Expressway stands in contrast to the generously spaced middle-class high-rise area to the west. This is a familiar pattern across this megacity's landscape.*

Mega-slums

One of the most striking characteristics of the megacities of the Global South is the conspicuous and ubiquitous presence of slums. In most cases, they have been part and parcel of the urban landscape for a century or more and their numbers, if anything, have increased over time. In contrast to the historical experience of cities like New York or London (which used to have substantial slum areas into the early 20th century but are now generally considered slum free), it is hard to avoid the impression that today's mega-slums are here to stay. Slum dweller numbers can only be estimated, but they are staggering, from 2.5 million in Manila to 5 million in Cairo to about 7 million in Mumbai.

The presence and persistence of slums are related to the drivers of urban growth in the megacities of the Global South: massive rural–urban migration in which push factors are disproportionately strong. Migration is fueled by rural poverty and the lack of opportunities in the countryside rather than demand for labor in the cities. And it is the lack of absorptive capacity

Slum dwellers in selected megacities

The exact slum populations of most megacities are unknown but there are some fairly reliable estimates—these are estimates for 2013. Rio de Janeiro, notwithstanding its popular image as a slum-ridden city, is with about 1.2 million slum dwellers the smallest of this select group. The slum populations of Lagos or Mumbai are nearly big enough to form a megacity by themselves. To put some of these numbers in perspective, Jakarta's slum population is greater than the entire population of Ireland.

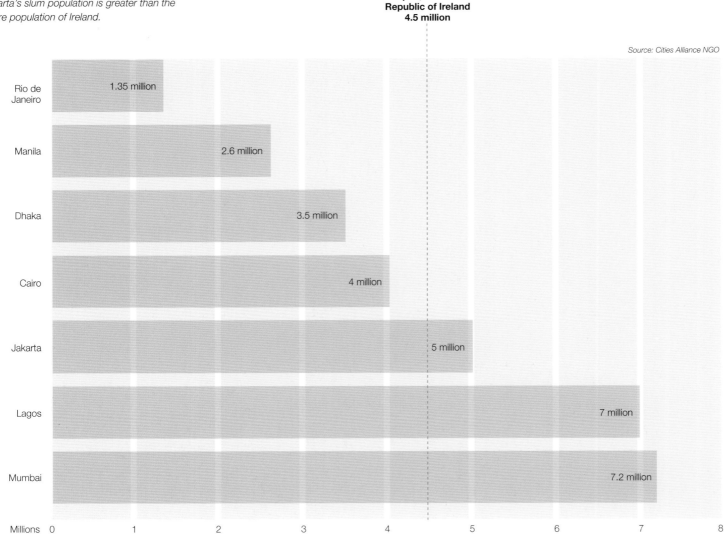

Population of the
Republic of Ireland
4.5 million

Source: Cities Alliance NGO

Rio de Janeiro — 1.35 million
Manila — 2.6 million
Dhaka — 3.5 million
Cairo — 4 million
Jakarta — 5 million
Lagos — 7 million
Mumbai — 7.2 million

Millions 0 1 2 3 4 5 6 7 8

for these new migrants (and, generally, their high rates of reproduction) that cause the proliferation of slums. Typically, the largest concentrations are found near the expanding urban perimeter but there is also lots of infill throughout the interior urban zones.

Slums come in different sizes and are often scattered across the city, but some contiguous slum areas are enormous and in some ways could be viewed as "cities" in themselves. Dharavi, a tightly packed area hemmed in between railroads near the topographical center of Greater Mumbai, holds about 600,000 people. Orangi Town's area in Karachi is far

bigger and spread out, and more diverse, and counts 1.5 million. Slums come in various shapes and sorts, from the makeshift and highly transient hutments made of tarp, cloth, or cardboard of the most recently arrived migrants to the more permanent and professionally constructed homes in longer established slums. The definition of what is and what is not a slum is highly contentious and often politically loaded.

Many slums are characterized by overcrowding, lack of sanitation, unsafe structural conditions, pollution, and high levels of psychological stress. In Dharavi, the average dwelling is a single room of 195 square feet

shared by a family of six. Three out of every four dwellings have no underground sewerage and three out of ten have no piped water. In Dharavi, there is one toilet for every 350 people (and this is a particularly serious problem for females). Yet slums often offer people a space of hope, relative comfort among kin and a support network, and sometimes they are sites of small-scale economic activity providing a range of job and livelihood opportunities. In Dharavi, only 5 percent of the heads of households say they are unemployed. Half of those who live in Dharavi also work there, and more than 90 percent say they have no plans to leave.

Dharavi density

Dharavi is one of Mumbai's best-known slum areas (it was featured in the 2008 movie Slumdog Millionaire*). The area covers about 0.66 square miles and houses an estimated 600,000 people. That translates into thirteen times the density of Manhattan—a figure that is particularly hard to comprehend as Dharavi has almost no high-rises.*

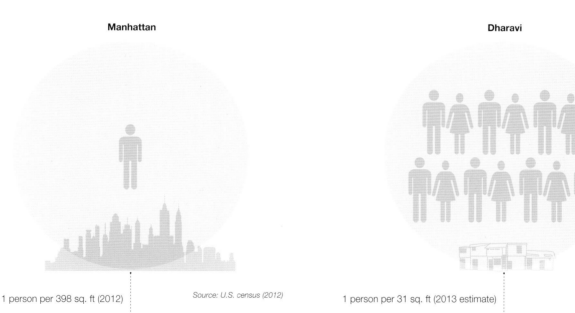

Manhattan

1 person per 398 sq. ft (2012)

Source: U.S. census (2012)

Dharavi

1 person per 31 sq. ft (2013 estimate)

Source: Nijman (2010)

Downtown Manhattan

Slum areas of Mumbai

Transportation Challenges

Cities are in constant movement. Commuters travel between home and work; goods move between production sites, wholesalers, retailers, and consumers; professionals traverse the city to provide services; people navigate to a wide range of service centers from hospitals to banks to supermarkets to restaurants; and people move around in their social networks.

Megacities must accommodate the movement of tens of millions of people. Or, to put it differently, it is through adequate transportation that the city mobilizes the productive and consumptive capacity of its large population. This is a massive challenge because the urban economy demands efficient mobility and because people have limited time and patience. Most megacities today are in the process of huge infrastructural investment projects and long-term improvements so as to increase efficient movement between key sites such as airports, main railway stations, central business districts, seaports, manufacturing areas, and markets.

Mumbai rail transport

The Greater Mumbai peninsula has only three major railway lines and they are vital to the functioning of this megacity. Workplaces are highly concentrated in the south near the two terminal stations and increasingly also near the city's topographical center, with many people facing a long commute from the eastern and western suburbs. The overcrowded trains are generally the fastest way to and from work but they are a stressful experience.

Mumbai rail statistics, 2013	
Number of major rail lines	3
Factor of overcapacity of the average train car	3
Number of railway stations	56
Number of passengers per day (millions)	7.2
Number of people that die in train accidents every day	12

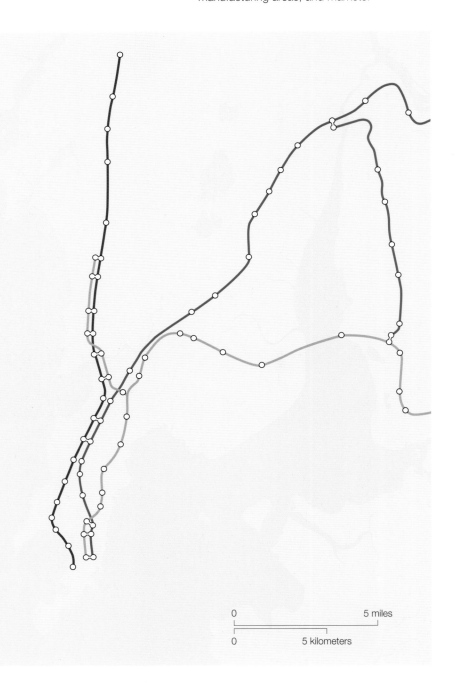

— Western
— Central
— Harbour
— Thane
○ Station
∞ Joining station

0   5 miles
0   5 kilometers

As the cities themselves have taken on massive proportions, there is continuous pressure to connect the outward-moving periphery to the center(s). This implies an ever-increasing need for fast long-distance connections (high-speed rail, flyovers, subways) in addition to continuous needs for short-distance connections (buses, taxis, rickshaws, pedestrian bridges). The megacity moves at various scales and multiple speeds.

What makes megacities different, too, is the intensity of all this movement. Every day in Mumbai there are 7.2 million people getting on the trains and another 4.5 million people riding on the buses. That is nearly 12 million uses of public transport per day. In addition, in 2013 the total count of four-wheeled motorized vehicles was 2 million. That is more than 950 cars per mile of road—and it explains the constant need to widen the main arteries in the city. And cars must share the roads with about 100,000 auto rickshaws and an equal number of motorcycles.

Mumbai commutes are not as long as in some other megacities, such as Mexico City or São Paulo, because as a peninsula Greater Mumbai is quite compact—but the commutes tend to be more intense because of the enormous population densities. Traveling on the local trains here is a memorable experience for any visitor, assuming that he or she manages to get on. The middle and upper middle classes from the suburbs increasingly choose to commute by car, which tends to be more comfortable but often takes longer. The proliferation of cars seems unstoppable but the price in terms of congestion (and pollution) is increasingly unaffordable.

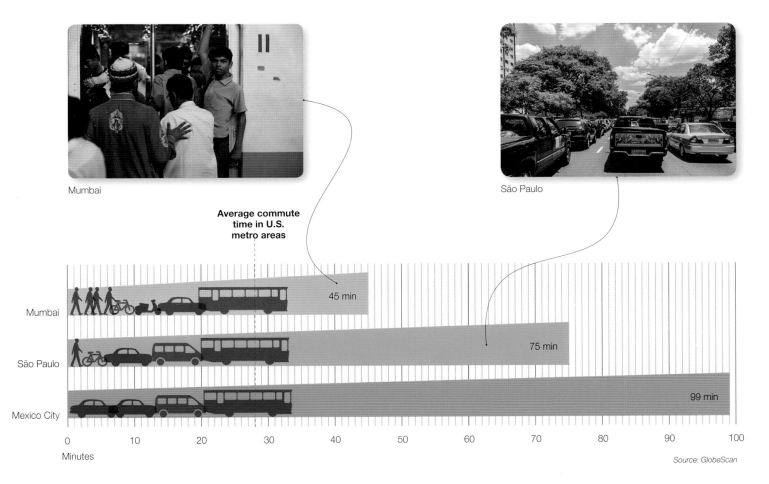

Mumbai

São Paulo

Average commute time in U.S. metro areas

Mumbai	45 min
São Paulo	75 min
Mexico City	99 min

0   10   20   30   40   50   60   70   80   90   100

Minutes

Source: GlobeScan

Megacity commuting times, 2013

Traffic in megacities in the global south can be nightmarish compared with Western megacities: commuting times are long, pollution is severe, and the economic costs drive governments to invest heavily in infrastructural improvements. Commutes tend to increase with sprawl and this explains why the figure for compact Mumbai is lower than for Mexico City or São Paulo. But the means of transportation differ as well: more than a third of Mumbai's commuters walk to work while in Mexico City people travel almost exclusively by car or public transport.

Megacity Metabolism

One of the most perplexing things about ancient Rome was how it managed to house a million inhabitants. The technologically proficient Romans invented cement and constructed the first multistory buildings, designed road systems that facilitated efficient movement of people and goods, and, perhaps most important of all, they invented the aqueducts that flushed the city with water from the nearby hills.

Cities can be thought of as organisms that live off their environment. They breathe oxygen and exhale carbon dioxide; they take in water and food and discharge sewage; they consume energy; they carry in an enormous range of products and materials and they produce substantial economic growth and piles of garbage. Megacities (must) do all of that at a scale that sometimes exceeds the imagination. They need vast infrastructures and the organizational skills to manage them effectively. And sometimes they fail.

The provision of water is a critical challenge to all megacities. Even for a city like Dhaka, located near the lower reaches of the Ganges River and having a monsoon climate, access to clean water is problematic. No less than 550 million cubic meters of drinking water is pumped into the Bangladeshi capital every year. But millions throughout the urban area have to

Mumbai's metabolism

Mumbai's functioning on a daily basis relies on massive inputs from the environment, from drinking water to food, from gasoline to construction materials. This requires not just availability of inputs but also a reliable infrastructure and enormous management efforts. The same goes for outputs, from wastewater to garbage. Some inputs remain in the city, including about 80 percent of construction materials, gradually adding to the "weight" of the urban built environment and to the city's growth and ecological footprint.

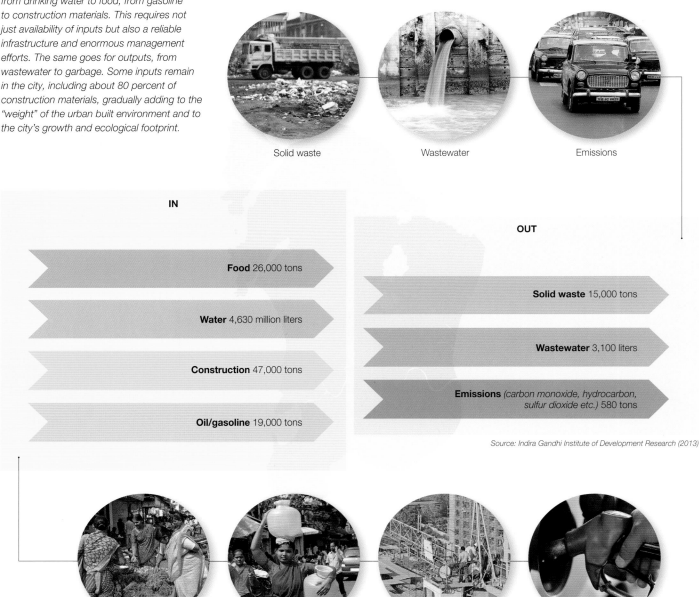

Solid waste

Wastewater

Emissions

IN

Food 26,000 tons

Water 4,630 million liters

Construction 47,000 tons

Oil/gasoline 19,000 tons

OUT

Solid waste 15,000 tons

Wastewater 3,100 liters

Emissions *(carbon monoxide, hydrocarbon, sulfur dioxide etc.)* 580 tons

Source: Indira Gandhi Institute of Development Research (2013)

Food

Water

Construction

Oil/gasoline

rely on wells, from which another 350 million cubic meters is pumped up every year—and that water is not clean. And as a result of the overuse of local wells, the groundwater table beneath Dhaka is dropping at an alarming rate. In Jakarta or Mexico City or Mumbai, many slum dwellers have no access to piped water or wells and are forced to pay high prices to the water trucks that come by on a daily basis.

Sewage is a major problem, too. Mexico City discharges about 2.5 billion cubic meters of wastewater, of which only about 10 percent is treated. The city emits an estimated 300 metric tons of hazardous waste annually and most of that is discharged into the municipal sewage system, too. In Mumbai, open sewers are common in many parts of the city, and this is especially problematic in the low-lying slum areas that have poor drainage and become flooded during the monsoon rains. The city has separate sewage and storm water systems but they are connected and overflow routinely during the rainy season.

Another key aspect of urban metabolism is solid waste disposal. Mumbai generates over 15,000 tons of garbage daily with only three dumping grounds. Garbage collection requires a herculean effort: it involves some 3,800 personnel and 800 vehicles, and about 2,000 truck dumpings per 24-hour period. It is estimated that about 95 percent of all generated waste is collected, which is in itself an amazing feat—but that leaves at least around 300–400 tons of uncollected garbage every day. Much of that is burned locally or deposited illegally in the city's creeks and other sites, causing a range of pollution problems.

The famous Indian architect Charles Correa once described Mumbai as a "great city, terrible place." The megacities of the Global South, such as Mumbai, manage to keep going. Every day, people all over this vast metropolis rise, get to work, eat, drink, use energy, excrete, and produce trash. But the fact that Mumbai keeps going does not mean all is well and many pay the price for its strained metabolism. The sustainability of this and other megacities remains in question.

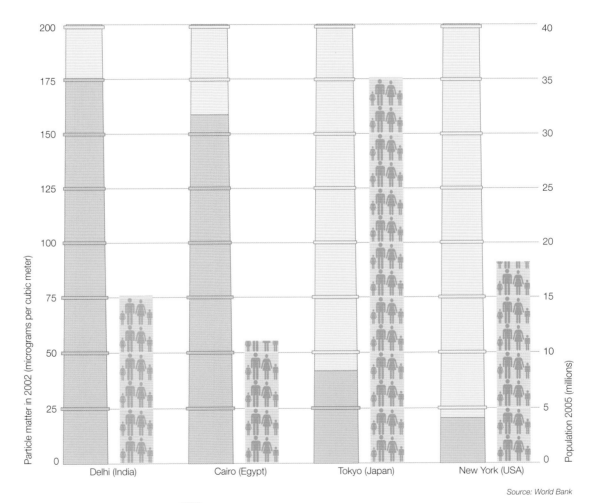

Source: World Bank

Megacity pollution

Delhi and Cairo are among the worst cities in the world when it comes to air quality, along with Beijing, Mexico City, and others. Air quality is generally a function of local emissions, climate, and physical geography. Pollution does not necessarily correlate with size, however. The air in New York and Tokyo–Yokohama is much better despite their bigger size, and here again, megacities tend to divide according to development levels.

Pollution level

Population level

Planning China's Megacities

China's urbanization has proceeded at an amazing pace in the past few decades. More than half the Chinese population is now living in cities. There are over 160 cities with more than a million inhabitants and at least six megacities: Shanghai (22 m), Beijing (18 m), Guangzhou (18 m), Tianjin (13 m), Chengdu (12 m), and Shenzhen (12 m). Shenzhen is often held up as the poster child of China's revolutionary urban transformation: it went in three decades from a cluster of small fishing villages to a megacity.

Chinese megacities are different from those in the Global South, or those in the United States, in that so much of their development is government planned. This applies to massive residential areas, industrial zones, and business districts in existing cities but it also involves, even more spectacularly, the creation of entirely new cities from scratch, such as Ordos in the province of Inner Mongolia. Another example of a jaw-dropping megaproject is Yujiapu: the construction of a vast complex of some forty-seven skyscrapers outside Tianjin nicknamed "China's new Manhattan," a huge new district of finance and producer services planned to be finished in 2019.

It is estimated that from 2000 to 2012 China's construction industry built twice as many new homes as there are today in the

China's megacities
In 2013, China counted six megacities, more than any other country in the world, with another eight cities having populations somewhere between 5 and 10 million. Most of today's megacities emerged in the coastal provinces where urbanization and industrialization moved in tandem and at breakneck pace. The next generation of megacities, however, is likely to be found in China's interior.

Yujiapu
"China's new Manhattan" on the outskirts of the megacity Tianjin, about 100 miles south of Beijing.

Chengdu

Guangzhou

Megacities (10 million plus)

Cities (5–10 million)

Shenzhen

entire United Kingdom. And it's not just homes. The growth of China's megacities is accompanied by massive infrastructural investments in roads, highways, power grids, bridges, tunnels, airports, public transportation, high-speed rail, and so on. China is also in the middle of a huge south–north water diversion project, from the Yangtze River near Shanghai to the Yellow River, that feeds much-needed water to the megacities in the arid northeast, Beijing and Tianjin.

The dizzying pace of China's urban growth is fueled by the country's rapid industrialization and accompanying need for urban workers. But it also reflects a model of development where fast-increasing revenues are almost routinely channeled into construction and in which building companies have become powerful players; where local and regional governments are increasingly independent and invent their own pet projects; and where speculation in real estate has escalated and where the market is highly non-transparent. Urban growth in China, in this way, reflects a peculiar mix of central planning and capitalism—one that has in the past delivered unprecedented and spectacular growth but that may now be getting out of control in more ways than one. That debate is now in full swing.

Since late 2012 it has become clear that tens of millions of new high-rise apartments, from the residential suburbs of Zhengzhou to the brand new city of Ordos, are sitting empty. The price range of most apartments is US$60,000–120,000 which is way out of reach for the average Chinese. A good number of the apartments are actually sold, but to well-off members of the new urban middle class who have no intention of ever living there and who speculate that prices will continue to rise as they have done in the past. Ordos is now referred to as China's biggest ghost town. By early 2013 only 10 percent of the 300,000 new homes were occupied, while construction continued relentlessly.

China's construction boom may not be sustainable. Real estate bubbles are common to economies all over the world and certainly the United States has had its share. But in China, everything is bigger and if this bubble does burst, it will be the biggest real estate meltdown the world has ever seen. That will not do away with China's megacities, but it may change the way they are planned.

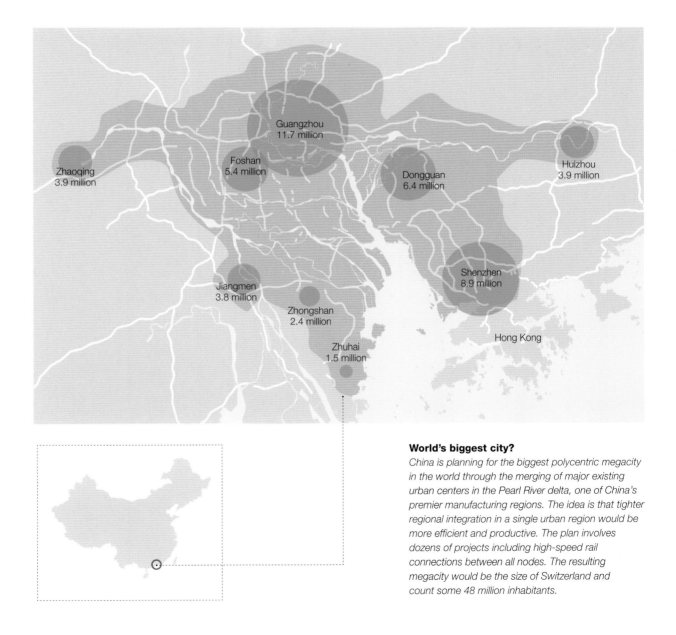

World's biggest city?

China is planning for the biggest polycentric megacity in the world through the merging of major existing urban centers in the Pearl River delta, one of China's premier manufacturing regions. The idea is that tighter regional integration in a single urban region would be more efficient and productive. The plan involves dozens of projects including high-speed rail connections between all nodes. The resulting megacity would be the size of Switzerland and count some 48 million inhabitants.

THE INSTANT CITY

LUCIA CONY-CIDADE

Core city
BRASILIA _____

Secondary cities
ABUJA _____
CHANDIGARH _____
CANBERRA _____

Left: Brasilia, Brazil

The Instant City: Introduction

Created out of political or economic imperatives and vested with transformative and symbolic expectations, instant cities are often planned and built to serve as national capitals. The capital city is important as the seat of the national government and the location of its higher administrative units, as well as representing national identity. Closely associated with the state, capital cities tend to work as a unifying core for disputing political forces and to convey the promise of future national achievements. As a result, a prerequisite is a level of urban quality—understood in terms of formal and functional aspects and symbolic forms situated in time and space—that is capable of facilitating the efficient operation of government activities.

"Many of the world's 200 national capitals are instant cities, devised to enable a swift transfer of functions from an old capital to a new center."

Perhaps not surprisingly, then, many of the world's 200 national capitals are instant cities, devised to enable a swift transfer of functions from an old capital to a new center. Brasilia, the capital of Brazil, is the pre-eminent case of a national capital built from scratch to an urban plan. Other examples are the planned capitals of Australia (Canberra) and of Nigeria (Abuja), and the city of Chandigarh, the capital of the Indian state of Punjab.

Brazil

Location of Brasilia

For countries with extensive territories, a strategic location might be in a relatively unpopulated region. The site approved for Brasilia by the federal government in 1954 was located in the sparsely occupied Brazilian central plateau, far from the main coastal cities. Replacing Rio de Janeiro, Brasilia became the new capital of Brazil in April 1960.

Le Corbusier and the Modernist city

Created following the partition of India and Pakistan in 1947, Chandigarh (capital of the state of Punjab) marked a break with tradition and made a bold statement about the nation's future. Invited to develop Albert Mayer's masterplan for the new city and to design a number of administrative buildings, the Swiss architect Le Corbusier produced one of the most internationally renowned centerpieces of modern urbanism. Functionalist, progressive urbanism focused on the principles of the Athens Charter, a document based on research by the CIAM (Congrès internationaux d'architecture moderne/International Congress of Modern Architecture) and published by Le Corbusier in 1943. Its main lines privileged the division of the city into sectors, with high-rise buildings and high densities, interspersed by parks. Emphasizing rationalism, the Modernist movement identified the city's main functions as housing, work, leisure, and transportation. Chandigarh and Brasilia, whose construction began only a few years apart (1951 and 1956, respectively), are the only two cities designed and built according to the principles of the Athens Charter. As instant cities, they broke new ground in representing the main tenets of Modernism and became icons of this challenging, creative, and controversial school.

Promoting development

Far from the densely occupied main cities, most of which are located on or near the coast, the new Brazilian capital also represented a national shift. Championing policies of industrialization and regional development, governmental discourse strongly dwelt on ideas of progress and the promotion of national growth. In a federation largely characterized by landed interests, the new Brazilian heartland capital carried not only the potential to symbolize national unity but also the promise of a coming era of dynamic modernity. Noteworthy for its modernist design and architecture and declared a UNESCO Heritage City in 1987, Brasilia grew to become a national metropolis.

Achievements and challenges

Chandigarh, Brasilia, and Canberra offer some of the highest per capita incomes, education levels, and quality of life in their respective countries. On the other hand, Abuja and Brasilia also suffer from the effects of large populations, informal employment, and wide income inequalities. As the urban area rapidly expanded into former rural areas, Brasilia soon faced a number of problems characteristic of the instant city. The Federal District has a disproportionate dependence on service employment located in the central area. Exorbitantly high land prices in the core oblige most of the working population to locate in peripheral areas, only a few of which are slowly becoming new sub-centers for commerce and services. The combination of excessive centrality with the steady formation of dormitory communities has contributed to imbalances in the supply of public services and a lack of infrastructure, especially in newly occupied low-income areas. In the instant city, the contrasts between wealth and poverty stand out in stark relief.

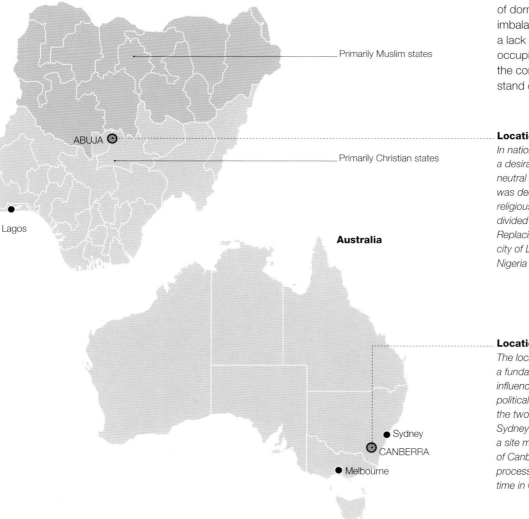

Nigeria

Primarily Muslim states

ABUJA

Primarily Christian states

Lagos

Australia

Sydney
CANBERRA
Melbourne

Location of Abuja

In nations with internal ethnic or religious rivalries, a desirable location for the national capital is in a neutral region. The site chosen for Abuja in 1976 was deemed a neutral territory vis-à-vis ethnic, religious, and political disputes in Nigeria that divided the country between north and south. Replacing the overcrowded and congested port city of Lagos, Abuja became the new capital of Nigeria in December 1991.

Location of Canberra

The location chosen for the new settlement is a fundamental strategic decision that may be influenced by a number of factors. In Australia, political disputes and economic rivalry between the two largest and most influential cities, Sydney and Melbourne, dictated the selection of a site midway between the two for the location of Canberra in 1908. After a lengthy construction process, the Federal Cabinet met for the first time in Canberra in January 1924.

Planning the Instant City: Modernist Utopia versus Thorny Reality

An opportunity to envisage a spatial organization that would transcend the problems typical of organic agglomerations, master plans for instant cities also represent the prospect of designing a social utopia. However, notwithstanding the idealist slants, economic, social, and cultural traditions remain fundamental in conditioning the unfolding of the built environment.

Brasilia was built and inaugurated between 1956 and 1960, in a record five years. Intended to represent the nation's new era of development,

the new capital soon revealed the shortcomings of a conservative modernization, marked by the maintenance of wide social and economic disparities. In this context, preserving the modern and selective character of the central Pilot Plan area, intended to house government employees, meant that deprived construction workers flowing into the new city settled in undeveloped peripheral areas. Borrowing the garden city taxonomy yet far from the main employment center and devoid of services, these neglected areas became known as the satellite towns. The Pilot Plan, the satellite towns, and newly occupied

The Pilot Plan

In the Pilot Plan, the eastern segment of the monumental axis was to gather the three instituted powers of the republic: the executive, the legislature, and the judiciary. The western section was to house the administrative buildings of the Federal District. The highway axis was the location for the superblocks, residential areas with six-story modern buildings separated by green spaces, and interspersed with local commercial blocks. Placed at the intersection of the axes, the bus station was to become a transport hub for different areas of the city, while special commercial and service sectors would provide an added attraction to the core area.

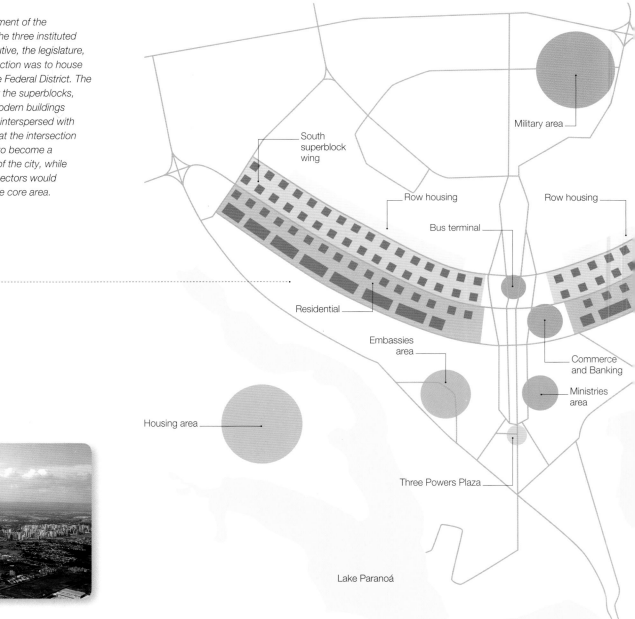

South superblock wing

Row housing

Row housing

Military area

Bus terminal

Residential

Embassies area

Commerce and Banking

Ministries area

Housing area

Three Powers Plaza

Lake Paranoá

Aerial view of Brasilia

neighborhoods, together with surrounding rural areas, make up the Federal District, a multi-nuclei distribution of densely populated residential areas with limited economic activity. Although some new commercial and services nuclei and a few robust sub-centers, such as Taguatinga and Guara, have begun to develop, the region remains disproportionately dependent on the Pilot Plan as the undisputed employment center.

The original planned area of Brasilia was intended to have an upper population limit of 500,000 inhabitants, but from the first this idea was demonstrably unrealistic, and the population of the Federal District has far outstripped this limit, reaching about 2 million inhabitants in 2000 and 2.5 million in 2010. The Federal District ranks fourth in terms of population centers in Brazil, after São Paulo (11.4 million), Rio de Janeiro (6.4 million), and Salvador (2.7 million). While the highly expensive residential areas in the Pilot Plan have led to a relative loss of population, the urbanized fabric has sprawled into peripheral areas including the surrounding municipalities. This sprawl includes not only low-income settlements but also new developments for middle and higher income families, with irregular land parceling and even the invasion of public land. In recent years, large-scale urban developers have launched a number of high-end projects with reference to the principles of New Urbanism on rural land on the outskirts of the urban area. Responding to political, demographic, and economic pressures, the modern instant city has been shown to be as unmanageable as any urban area in the globalized network.

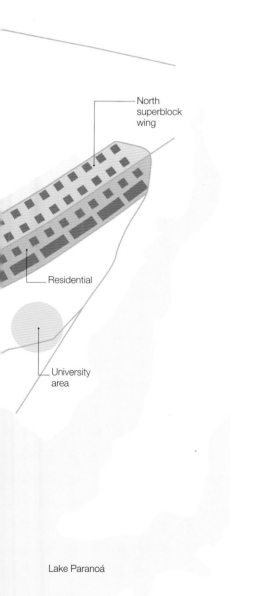

North superblock wing

Residential

University area

Lake Paranoá

Lúcio Costa's sketch

Running against a number of renowned architectural offices, Lúcio Costa (1902–98) won the national competition to design the new capital with a few unassuming yet ambitious sketches that became known as the Pilot Plan. An explicitly symbolic stance was emphasized throughout the project, which clearly privileged monumentality and open vistas to convey an image fit for a national capital. The original Modernist conception depicted two axes forming a cross, suggestive of the shape of an airplane or dragonfly. The bold axial crossing represented the taking hold of a place by a conquering people.

Populating the Hinterland

The intention behind placing the new capital in the central west of Brazil was not only to provide protection for the federal government apparatus in case of foreign invasion, but also to establish a base for taking control of a largely unoccupied and underexploited territory. By the mid-20th century, regional economic streams were largely focused on the main cities, a significant number of which were located along or near the coastline. The railroad network connected the main producing regions, such as the mining and farming zones, and most of the state capitals. Noteworthy were agricultural areas in the state of São Paulo, where coffee production attracted capital interested in building railroads directed to the port of Santos. Brazilian railroads did not serve the relatively isolated Amazonian states nor a considerable part of the hinterland.

Along with the existing railroad network, since the 1940s public policies had promoted the construction of highways. However, in 1956, when the construction of Brasilia started, the limited road transportation network in Brazil, part of which still consisted of dirt roads, extended mainly along the coast and to inland state capitals. Thus, the challenge of building a city in a sparsely populated farmland area poorly supplied with basic resources, much

Development of the road network
Facilitated by the creation of Brasilia, the evolution of the road network shows a steady progression from the coastline into the hinterland. In recent decades there has been a marked densification of highway connections, which suggests the prospect of increased Latin American integration. Part of a governmental strategy for progressive territorial control, the road network supported the dramatic expansion of the agricultural frontier, the establishment of agribusinesses, and the increased export of commodities. Growing urbanization of the countryside and large-scale environmental degradation ensued.

1964

1973

1980

1991

1997

less construction materials, called for a major logistical endeavor. During the construction of the new capital, the transportation of workers and building materials required, besides the construction of an airport, the deployment of highways and railroad lines linking Brasilia to nearby cities. Vital for territorial control, the expansion of the road network was also essential for the establishment of the fledgling Brazilian automotive industry. In addition, the new infrastructure was necessary to facilitate production flows from the growing manufacturing regions in the southeast and south into areas so far lacking incorporation into the emerging national market.

One of the first decisions taken after the commencement of the construction of Brasilia was the initiation in 1958 of the Belem–Brasilia road, to link the northern state of Para to the central western state of Goiás. The influence of the new capital was also felt in the construction of a number of other roads, such as Belo Horizonte–Brasilia (1959), Salvador–Brasilia (1970), Cuiaba–Santarem (1976), São Paulo–Brasilia (1978), and Cuiaba–Porto Velho–Rio Branco. In turn the railway network became secondary and was progressively neglected. Governmental planning also focused on equipping the territory with energy and communication networks as well as transportation. In the following decades, the consolidation of the new capital, with the ensuing expansion in the road network, stimulated the growth of hinterland cities as well as agricultural expansion in the central western states. Until then, regional archipelagos of traditional manufacturing had characterized relatively isolated and protected markets. The integration of the territory was to alter that equilibrium, facilitating the domination of the national market by capitalized southeastern companies. As a result, regional inequalities became even more accentuated.

In 1956 much of the road system consisted of dirt roads through the Brazilian hinterland. Most of the roads have been progressively tarmacked.

In 1957 the BR-040 was tarmacked and extended to Brasilia. It runs radially from the capital linking it to Belo Horizonte and Rio de Janeiro.

The BR-050 has been made a divided highway in the state of São Paulo and in the Federal District. Plans are in place for 2013 to improve the section which links Goiás in the central farm belt to the mineral-rich state of Minas Gerais. The road runs radially north–south from the national capital.

Sources: Déak/IBGE   2007

Mobilizing Development Inland

Far from being an independent singularity, the instant city often belongs to concerted and ambitious political endeavors. Since the colonial period, Brazil's national economy had been largely anchored in the export of primary resources, particularly sugar, gold, and coffee. The colossal profits from the coffee cycle provided a base for manufacturing activities, which in turn encouraged an unforeseen growth that leveraged São Paulo into first place in terms of population and economic production. In the mid-20th century, public policies were increasingly aimed at supporting incipient manufacturing activities. Dependent on markets and agglomeration economies, these shifts contributed to reinforce the main urban centers located in the southeastern and southern states.

A foundation for expanding the internal market was the establishment of urban bases inland. Efforts included the economic strengthening of existing cities, such as Volta Redonda in the state of Rio de Janeiro, which received a steel mill in 1941. The foundation of Goiânia, since 1935 the modern planned capital of the central western state of Goiás, provided an opportunity for a move inland. The city became not only a significant commercial and services center, but also a supporting nucleus for an expanding agricultural and farming area.

Brasilia–Anápolis–Goiânia axis

The articulation of Brasilia, Goiânia, and Anápolis, a dynamic transportation junction near Goiânia, has produced one of the most visible effects in the region. In recent years, a vigorous regional cities system includes what has been called the Brasilia–Anápolis–Goiânia axis, a stream of towns and agricultural areas concentrating economic activities and population in the central plateau area. The population in the three main agglomerations in the axis, the Goiânia metropolitan region, the Anápolis microrregion, and the integrated development region of the Federal District and surroundings has been growing significantly. While, in 1970, this area represented 1.63 percent of the population in Brazil, it grew continuously to reach 2.29 percent in 1980, 2.61 percent in 1991, 3.01 percent in 2000, and 3.34 percent in 2010. The three main cities in the axis taken together comprised, in 2010, 2.21 percent of the population and 4.89 percent of the GDP in Brazil. In the same year, the three cities comprised 30 percent of the population and 52 percent of the GDP in the central west region.

1970	1,521,545
	93,134,846
1980	2,725,072
	119,011,052
1990	3,826,528
	146,825,475
2000	5,109,795
	169,799,170
2010	6,373,261
	190,755,799

Brazilian population
Axis population

Sources: Haddad/IBGE (2010)

The creation of an industrial district in nearby Anápolis in the 1970s contributed to reinforce an incipient urban network to coalesce with Brasilia. Numerous towns arose along the highways linking the new capital to cities in the interior. In a number of cases, these towns became supporting centers for mining and agricultural activities.

Among the effects of the development plans associated with the new capital was the expansion of the agricultural frontier. Cattle farming, the planting of corn, beans, cotton, and especially the soybean complex followed by sugar cane became dynamic processes occupying lands toward the central west and the north. The modernization and technical advancement of agricultural production as well

as the establishment of agricultural complexes reinforced the concentration of landed property and the exclusion of traditional populations. The release of labor by both capitalized and stagnant traditional agriculture together with the growth of manufacturing employment and the perceived wealth in cities hastened migration flows to urban centers. The expansion of agricultural activity that was a significant factor in the development of the central west region has been accompanied by the degradation of natural resources in enormous areas in the cerrado and Amazonian ecosystems, led by the clearing of forests for cattle farming. In spite of its significant contribution to Brazilian economic growth, the extensive environmental impacts of this

agricultural drive have stimulated political debate and the demand for policies to curb these negative effects.

The new capital was one component in a set of innovative policies to bring improved economic development, stimulating not only an increase in urbanization, but also industrialization and agribusiness. However, unwelcome effects included excessive population growth and unemployment in cities, the landlessness of large numbers of the population and environmental degradation. In recent years, as in other large metropolitan areas, the national capital has felt the strain of decisions past.

Soybeans in a storage facility waiting to be loaded

Brazilian trucks being loaded with soybeans en route to the port and shipment to the United States and Europe

Growth of agribusiness

The main agricultural product in the export register, soy represents one of the driving forces in the expansion of the Brazilian agricultural frontier. Supported by demand increases in the international market, government policies, and technological improvements, the soybean complex has grown enormously over the last decades. From a total of 660 sq. miles (171,440 ha) in the 1959/60 harvest, soybean planting expanded to occupy a total area of 5,100 sq. miles (1,318,809 ha) in 1969/70, 44,600 sq. miles (11,551,400 ha) in 1989/90, 52,750 sq. miles (13,662,900 ha) in 1999/2000, and 90,600 sq. miles (23,467,900 ha) in 2009/10. Over that period total production grew from 226,793 tons (205,744 tonnes) to 75,715,780 tons (68,688,200 tonnes). The soybean territory occupies wide areas, particularly in the state of Mato Grosso, and proceeds toward the Amazonian rainforest.

Brasilia/Anápolis/Goiânia axis

Soybean cultivation areas 1970

Soybean cultivation areas 2003

Soybean cultivation areas 2009–2010

Source: IBGE, Brazilian Ministry of Agriculture

Decision-making and Political Capacities

Relocating the functions of the national capital to an instant city planted in a sparsely occupied agricultural area 750 miles inland from Rio de Janeiro was a highly political endeavor. Having faced opposition, at the 1960 inauguration of Brasilia President Juscelino Kubitschek was able to install the executive branch, the congress, and the judiciary in their respective buildings. Private support came in the form of the first newspaper and television station, as well as hotels and businesses. The first executive act was a message to congress proposing the creation of the federal university (*Universidade de Brasilia*).

From the beginning, taking the place of an established, cherished, and world-famous capital city, Rio de Janeiro, was an enormous challenge. Criticism stressed the enormous costs involved in construction; and the ensuing rise in inflation bequeathed to incoming national governments. While the consolidation of the new capital oscillated during the first years following the Kubitschek term (1956–60), after two decades of military rule (1964–84) the irreversibility of the move was clear. In 1988 the new national constitution was one of the democratic achievements emanating from the capital. Over the subsequent decades, while a few public enterprises kept their main branches in Rio de Janeiro, all the chief government

BRASILIA

Rio de Janeiro

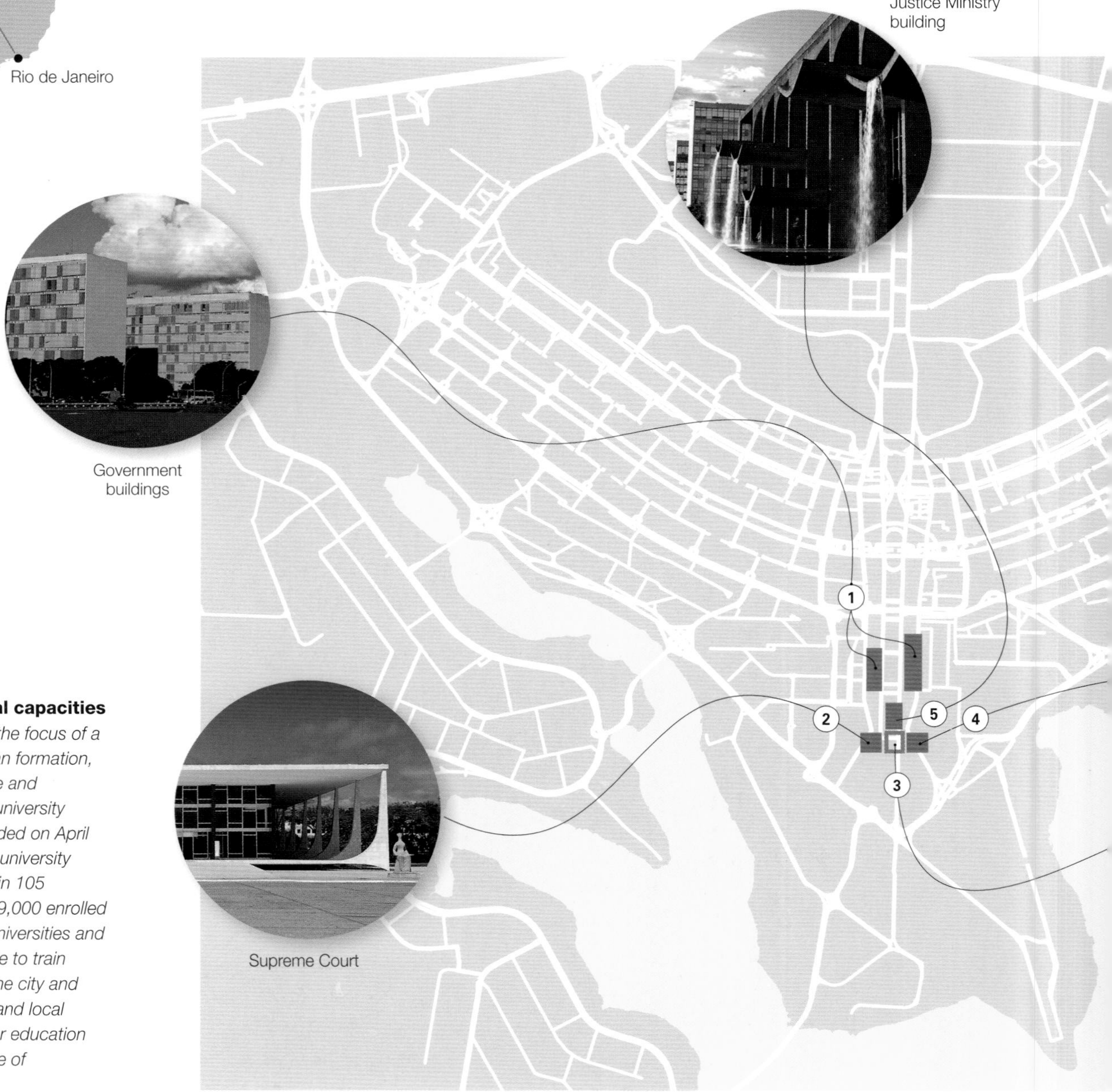

Justice Ministry building

Government buildings

Supreme Court

Administrative and educational capacities

As an instant city transformed into the focus of a contemporary if uneven metropolitan formation, Brasilia operates around knowledge and information exchange. The federal university (Universidade de Brasilia) was founded on April 21, 1962. In 2012 the fifty-year-old university had over 27,000 students enrolled in 105 undergraduate courses and nearly 9,000 enrolled in 147 graduate programs. Other universities and a number of colleges also contribute to train people for different professions in the city and in other regions, and in the federal and local government. The proximity to higher education centers has fostered the emergence of specialized activities.

institutions were installed in the capital. By its fiftieth anniversary in 2010, Brasilia had long become the indisputable capital of Brazil.

Within the Federal District, knowledge-based products and services, such as information and communication technologies, pharmaceuticals, logistical services, and civil construction are significant, with many being focused on energy efficiency and low environmental impact. The ongoing digital technology park (*Parque Tecnologico Capital Digital*) and the recycling center (*Polo de Reciclagem*) represent a vision of the future which aims to turn the capital into a metropolis whose economy is based on knowledge and innovation and which is a world leader in environmental sustainability.

As a multicultural setting with strong international connections, the city is a focus for international events. With a population drawn from the different Brazilian regions, the capital expresses a myriad of cultural influences. Movie, music, dance, and gastronomy festivals take place regularly in the city. The Brasilia Festival of Brazilian Movies (*Festival de Brasilia do Cinema Brasileiro*) has been held since 1965 and the inaugural Brasilia International Film Festival (*Festival Internacional de Cinema de Brasilia*) took place in July 2012. Other festivals include the Brasilia International Arts Festival (*Festival Internacional de Artes de Brasilia*), organized by the Federal District government with the support of a number of embassies,

first held in January 2012; the Brasilia Popular Culture Festival (*Festival Brasilia de Cultura Popular*); the Brasilia International Festival of Puppet Theatre (*Festival Internacional de Teatro de Bonecos*); and the Brasilia Music Festival, which also began in 2012. The government has also encouraged incoming sports mega-events, such as the 2014 soccer World Cup. One of the civil construction projects is the national stadium (*Estadio Nacional*), which, in spite of controversy, is intended to become the world's first ecological arena to be certified by the U.S. Green Building Council.

University

6

Plaza and presidential buildings

Congressional buildings

INTERNATIONAL ARTS FESTIVALS IN BRASILIA

With its celebrated modernist architectural ensemble, the capital city offers an appropriate context for multicultural and artistic expression.

Arts
Brasilia International Arts Festival (*Festival Internacional de Artes de Brasilia*)

Culture
Brasilia Popular Culture Festival (*Festival Brasilia de Cultura Popular*)
Festclown (*Festival Internacional de Palhaços*)

Dance
Novadanca Internacional Festival (*Festival Internacional da Novadanca*)

Music
Brasilia Music Festival—BMF
International Festival I Love Jazz (*Festival Internacional I Love Jazz*)

Movies
Brasilia Festival of Brazilian Movies—FBCB (*Festival de Brasilia do Cinema Brasileiro*)
Brasilia International Film Festival—BIFF (*Festival Internacional de Cinema de Brasilia*)
International Children Film Festival—FICI (*Festival Internacional de Cinema Infantil*)

Theater
Brasilia International Festival of Puppets Theater (*Festival Internacional de Teatro de Bonecos*)
Brasilia International Theater Festival (*Festival Internacional de Teatro de Brasilia—Cena Contemporanea*)

The Built Environment

Since the Industrial Revolution, problems of accelerating urban growth had preoccupied not only government administrators but also a number of architects and planners. In tune with an ideology of progress, modern planning envisaged urban design as a lever for ingraining rationalism into a chaotic built environment as well as for fostering the attainment of an idealized future. Creating wide boulevards and open spaces in an effort to help control popular rebellions and to bolster the real estate market, Haussmann's mid-19th-century renovation of Paris (see The Rational City, pages 88–105) represented a bold if controversial reference point for instant cities.

As a reflection of the actual pressures of a highly uneven and economically disparate society upon a utopian project, during and after the construction of the originally planned area of the Federal District a number of popular settlements were established. Located at a distance from the privileged core of the city and interspersed out into the agricultural periphery, suffering from poor infrastructure and scant employment, the satellite towns became a sort of a gray zone in the imagery of the capital. Even after decades of steady population growth and gradual service provision in the satellite towns, as well as the emergence of new middle-class high-quality land developments in the peripheral areas, the dominating image of the capital remains the original and celebrated Pilot Plan.

Highly structured and planned center
Four perspectives integrate Lúcio Costa's urban design for the Pilot Plan: the monumental, the residential, the gregarious, and the bucolic. Conceived to convey the image of a capital city and unfolding along the wide monumental axis, the monumental scale showcases an array of public buildings. Initially intended to house government employees, the residential scale encompassed superblocks with buildings up to six stories high, interspersed with local access streets and greenery. Aimed at promoting gatherings and social interaction, the gregarious scale unfolded around the main bus station, including entertainment, service, and shopping areas. Ensuring the presence of nature and open spaces, the bucolic scale included green areas, reservoirs, and parks distributed across the city. Acknowledging the value of Brasilia as paradigm of modern urban design, in 1987 UNESCO included the city in its World Heritage list.

- Residential
- Ministerial/Governmental
- Military/Industrial/Residential/Recreational
- Commercial/Cultural/Transport hubs
- Recreation areas

Under the influence of Modernism and subsidiary to a national developmental project that was geared toward heavy manufacturing and the motor vehicle industry, Brasilia's originally planned central area clearly privileged the automobile. Evoking both a cross and an airplane, the basic urban design flowed from two intersecting transportation axes, with adjoining sectors fulfilling different city functions. Two main perpendicular highways linking the center with surrounding areas and with the national road system structured the project. Conceived to fit the developments of the industrialization era, the street system in the Federal District's urbanized areas by and large favors cars, justifying the popular image of a city "without sidewalks." Operational since 2001, the subway service links the most populated neighborhoods in the city to the central area. However, in spite of being one of the three most extensive subway systems in the country, the Brasilia network is poorly integrated with train lines and especially with bus routes, although there are now initiatives to encourage urban mobility projects to integrate the subway to the bus network.

In tune with the government's commitment to universal telecommunications, Brasilia participated significantly in the expansion of telephony and access to digital computer networks such as the Internet. As a metropolitan center with multiple functions, the capital has modern transport and communications facilities. Linking the city to national and overseas destinations, Brasilia International Airport is one of the main airports in Brazil and Latin America. Often congested and having long since reached capacity, the airport has been expanded. Without the option of a rail link for passengers to reach the central area, the airport is to be served by a rapid transit bus route.

Demographic density and social inequality

In Brasilia, as in many other large cities, areas with better infrastructure and services, rapid access to the central business district and therefore higher land prices correspond to populations in the higher income brackets. Reinforced by territorial management actions, such as the offering to poor populations of land in peripheral areas with scant infrastructure, the income gradient noticeably decreases as distances from the Pilot Plan increase. By and large, higher density areas correspond to low-income sectors.

Residential section

Spatial distribution of average household income in terms of minimum wages in the Federal District, 2010/2011

Source: GDF

- 1–3 x minimum wage
- 3–5 x minimum wage
- 5–10 x minimum wage
- 10–15 x minimum wage
- greater than 15 x minimum wage

Population density, 2009

Source: GDF

- High
- Medium
- Low
- Very low
- Area of environmental interest

Residential superblock layout

Economy and Population

An active economic environment, Brasilia has evolved as a markedly tertiary city, dominated by public administration and services, and having little in the way of manufacturing activities. As a result of the public nature of most of the employment, the capital has stood out as relatively resistant to economic variations and has displayed privileged wage levels. In 2010 the Federal District had the highest per capita GDP in the country, almost three times the Brazilian average and twice as much as that of the state of São Paulo, placed second.

Between 2004 and 2008, in the Federal District, all manufacturing activities grew, particularly transformation industries. Wage improvements in low-income sectors trickled down to branches such as food, clothing, and civil construction, while increases in the purchasing power of the labor force stimulated sales in commerce and manufacturing. Industrial production in the Federal District is weighted toward graphical activities and information technology, with the public sector as the main client. The most significant sector of the economy remains services. With the third-highest gross value added in services when compared to state capitals, after São Paulo and

Employment in Brasilia, 2010

As a capital city, Brasilia grew around a service economy dominated by government functions and commercial businesses. Laid out in a sensitive physical environment, Brasilia had to focus on tertiary activities and non-polluting industries. As the heart of the federal government, Brasilia draws together a number of direct administrative functions as well as public and semi-public enterprises. Relatively well paid and by and large resistant to crises, public employment has fostered the creation of a steady market for services and commercial activities. Corresponding to about 16 percent of the employment in the Federal District, public administration is a powerful magnet for businesses willing to participate in public bidding for products and services.

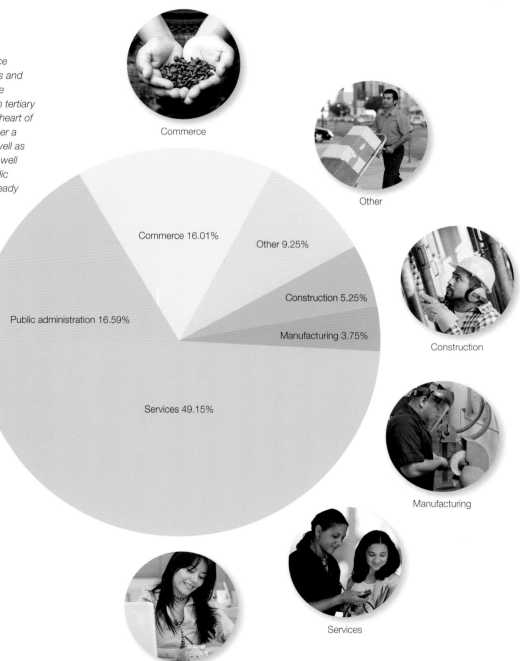

Commerce

Other

Construction

Manufacturing

Services

Public administration

Commerce 16.01%

Other 9.25%

Construction 5.25%

Manufacturing 3.75%

Public administration 16.59%

Services 49.15%

Source: Brazilian Ministry of Labor and Employment

Rio de Janeiro, Brasilia represented in 2008 5.7 percent of the total. During the period 2004–08, public administration, public health and public education, and social security accounted for as much as 50 percent of the economic structure in the Federal District. Out of around a million workers employed in 2010 in the Federal District, 49.15 percent were in services, while 16.59 percent were in public administration, and 16.01 percent in commerce. Construction contributed 5.25 percent, while manufacturing represented only 3.75 percent. Other employment contributed 9.25 percent.

Attracted by an affluent and dynamic milieu, a steady influx of migrants arrived in the capital from its inception. Although the rate of immigration has slowed, the numbers of incoming workers, many barely trained, remains high. Some have been employed in the construction industry, traditionally an absorber of unqualified workers. Another significant group has been absorbed by the informal market, while still others had to face unemployment. A growing metropolis whose workers were among the best paid in the country, Brasilia has also become one of the most economically unequal cities in Brazil.

Brasilia's catchment area embraces 298 municipalities, an area of 670,000 square miles, and a population in 2007 of 9.7 million inhabitants. In spite of its privileged position, Brasilia's urban network is small relative to those of São Paulo and Rio de Janeiro, representing only 2.5 percent of the Brazilian population and 4.4 percent of national GDP. With limited extension, the Brasilia network reaches the west of Bahia, as well as some municipalities in Goiás and in the northwest of Minas Gerais. There is a notable concentration of population and income in the center, which constitutes 72.7 percent of the population and 90.3 percent of the GDP in Brasilia's network. Of all Brazil's urban networks, this one has the highest GDP per capita.

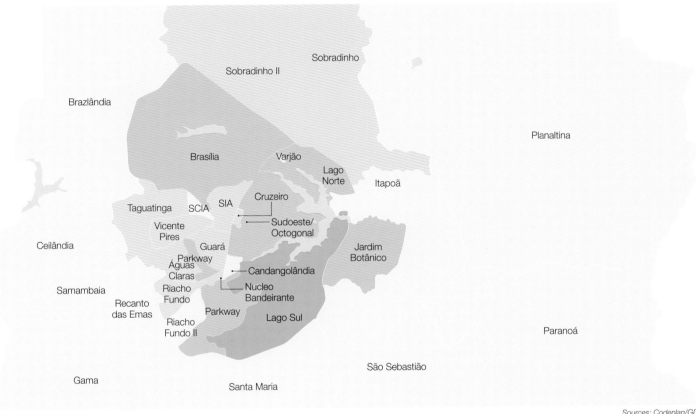

Sources: Codeplan/GDF

Per capita income (R$—Brazilian real) 2010
- 250–999
- 1,000–2,999
- 3,000–4,999
- 5,000 and above

Relative income distribution

In the Federal District, income distribution is highly skewed, with the administrative region of Lago Sul displaying the highest per capita income (R$ 5,420.00), approximately eighteen times the value for the poorest popular settlement SCIA/Estrutural (R$ 299.00) in 2010.

Sustainability

The instant city is obliged to develop according to the environmental conditions of its surrounding area. Inevitably the pressures of urbanization affect natural sites and impose on the use of resources. Located in the fragile savanna of the central plateau, the area in which the new Brazilian capital was to emerge had to be able to offer all the necessary support functions for a national capital. Interspersed with a number of watercourses and springs, the area is also the location where the three main watersheds in Brazil coincide: the Parana, the Araguaia/Tocantins, and the São Francisco. Because springs tend to start off feebly, trickling down to lower levels, the availability of water sources in the highlands depends largely on their protection. Due to the need to preserve not only water sources but also other natural features, the Federal District includes several conservation units.

The capital has a number of protected areas, including the Brasilia National Park, with around 90 percent of the territory covered by some kind of legal instrument. This might lead to the impression that the environment is highly conserved. However, the environment in the Federal District is not in fact well protected, while biodiversity is often threatened. This is because the creation and acknowledgment of

Lake Paranoá environmental protection area

One of the most striking features of Brasilia is Lake Paranoá. Built from the embankment of the Paranoá River, the dam was to provide water and energy for the initial construction years as well as to contribute to raising humidity levels in an area with a long dry winter. The lake was also intended as a public access leisure area. However, in spite of legislation guaranteeing public access, in practice only a few areas are open to all. The occupation of the margins by high-income residential plots, private clubs, and select restaurants has contributed to restrict access to the main part of the population. Distance from the satellite towns and the limited availability of public transport has also contributed to restrict access to the lake. While attachment to Lake Paranoá is deep-seated among the population, the perception remains that the lake is not in reality a public resource.

Central Brasilia

Lake Paranoá

Sources: GDF/IBRAM (2011)

- Wildlife preservation zone
- Wildlife conservation zone
- Water surface area zone
- Lake consolidated settlement zone
- Brasilia consolidated settlement zone
- Bananal special settlement zone
- Environmental interest special settlement zone
- Paranoá special settlement zone
- Taquari special settlement zone
- Varjão special settlement zone

protected areas has not been accompanied by effective management policies. Apart from the lack of human, financial, and legal resources, the main problems are the lack of land regularization; the lack of equipment and infrastructure; low incentives for research; inordinate use of public land; land speculation; lack of environmental education; and the low value attributed to local biodiversity. Two main deficiencies have weakened the effective implementation of conservation and protected units in the Federal District: juridical and legal aspects, and technical and operational aspects. In the latter case, there is the problem of the small number of management councils that have actually been established, and the limited effectiveness in terms of preventive

action of those that do exist. Many of the difficulties have to do with political and administrative outlooks as well as a lack of interest at the federal and district level. The main problem, however, seems to be a lack of data on the land situation and land registers, as well as a lack of management plans and management councils in these areas. To tackle these problems, the government has commissioned detailed studies which are included in the economic ecological zoning.

As Brasilia expanded into its natural surroundings without the necessary controls, the city soon started to produce environmental degradation. One particular feature is the disorderly urban occupation and pressure upon watersheds. The Federal District and its

adjoining area are reaching the limits of sources of water for consumption. Although the capital has efficient citywide garbage collection, it still lacks an effective system for garbage recycling. The area also needs a sustainable disposal system given that, in spite of relocation plans, a substantial part of the garbage is still dumped at a site near the protection area for the National Park—the Estrutural landfill. Latterly the large numbers of automobiles and rush-hour traffic jams associated with a lack of adequate public transportation have contributed to increased air pollution in a city hitherto known for the beauty of its sky and open horizon.

Rural

Urban

Protected

Sources: GDF/Seduma (2012)

Rural, urban, and integral protection

Unfolding into a predominantly rural area and somewhat restricted by protected zones, the urban fabric progressively extends toward the limits of the Federal District in a northeasterly direction and also in a southern and western direction. Although much of the incorporation of rural areas to urban uses was the product of low-income land parceling, middle-income developments and lately high-end condominiums have followed. Part of the urban growth stretches along highways leading to adjoining cities in the metropolitan ensemble and to the main state capitals.

THE TRANSNATIONAL CITY

JAN NIJMAN
MICHAEL SHIN

Core city
MIAMI _____

Secondary cities
VANCOUVER _____
HONG KONG _____
DUBAI _____
SINGAPORE _____
DUBLIN _____
LOS ANGELES _____

Left: Miami, USA

The Transnational City: Introduction

Transnational cities and their regional intersections

Transnational cities like Hong Kong (a former colony of the United Kingdom), Vancouver, and Beirut facilitate interactions and exchanges between different world regions. Miami connects the United States with South and Central America, as well as the Caribbean, and is often referred to as the "capital" of Latin America. It is precisely these global linkages that shape the cosmopolitan culture and urban landscape of the transnational city.

At the intersection of different world regions, the transnational city is where people, cultures, and ideas from different countries converge, collide, and flourish. This convergence produces social tensions, spawns new economic opportunities, and continuously redefines culture as unique with a "local flavor." The transnational city of the 20th century was simply called "multicultural"—the transnational city of the 21st century is more connected, more sophisticated, and more desirable as both destination and aspiration. The transnational city defines cosmopolitanism—it is the cosmopolis.

Owing much to their geographical position, transnational cities have always been central nodes between regional trade and migration networks. To facilitate this interregional exchange of people, goods, services, and ideas, transnational cities require diverse, foreign-born populations. Moreover, as the global economy shifts and as networks of production are reconfigured, the transnational city, its composition, and its very position are ever-changing. For instance, Hong Kong, the British colony where west met east in Asia, once epitomized the transnational city. This distinction is being challenged, if not redefined and replaced, by Vancouver, where east now meets west in North America.

World regional intersections

Transnational cities exhibit a particular dynamism, fortitude, and resilience, in large part due to their internal diversity, their agile response to external social, political, and economic pressures, and their geographical fixity. Beirut, the pearl of the Middle East, ravaged by decades of civil war, has been reconstructed and has once again re-emerged as a cosmopolitan tourist destination, a cultural center, and a city of commerce where Europe and the Middle East intersect.

Nowhere in the world is such cosmopolitanism more visible, embraced, or flaunted than in Miami. Though comparatively young for a transnational city in historic terms, Miami has defined and continuously redefines the transnational and cosmopolitanism. With over half of its resident population being foreign-born, Miami is more Latin American than any U.S. city. To meet the demands and requirements of these citizens of the world, contemporary transnational cities like Miami must offer cultural, culinary, and commercial amenities unlike those available elsewhere. Expatriate networks and linguistic social circles, fusion cuisine and local authentic tastes, and retail chains from "home" create a cosmopolitan urban landscape and vibe that is neither here nor there.

The provenance of cosmopolitan interlopers contributes to the emergence, persistence, and sustainability of the transnational city. As the second-busiest gateway for international travelers into the United States (behind New York's JFK), Miami International Airport annually welcomes over 1.5 million visitors from Brazil, over 1 million from Mexico and Colombia, respectively, and over 750,000 from the United Kingdom, Canada, Venezuela, and the Dominican Republic. Miami is also home to the third-largest consular corps in the USA, with over seventy foreign consulates. Of course, the lines between visitor, resident, expatriate, and local are very blurry for many in Miami and other transnational locales.

The transnational city is also one of deep and marked contradictions. Coupled with the best that cosmopolitanism has to offer, inequalities in income, status, and housing are thrown into sharp relief in the transnational city. Moreover, ambiguity, ignorance, and arrogance surrounding standards of authority, jurisdiction, and the rule of law make the transnational city a hub for illicit and illegal activities.

As borders become more porous, as people move about more freely, and as the global economy churns, what will become of the transnational city? Will new ones emerge? How will cities like Miami respond and be redefined? This chapter explores the complex and often contradictory facets of urban cosmopolitanism in an attempt to understand and map the transnational city.

Airline routes to Miami International Airport from Latin America

MIA is second only to New York's John F. Kennedy (JFK) International airport in terms of international passenger traffic, which exceeded 19 million passengers in 2012. MIA ranks first in international freight, and number three in total cargo compared to all other U.S. airports. The thickness of the lines on this map is proportionate to the number of passengers from each location.

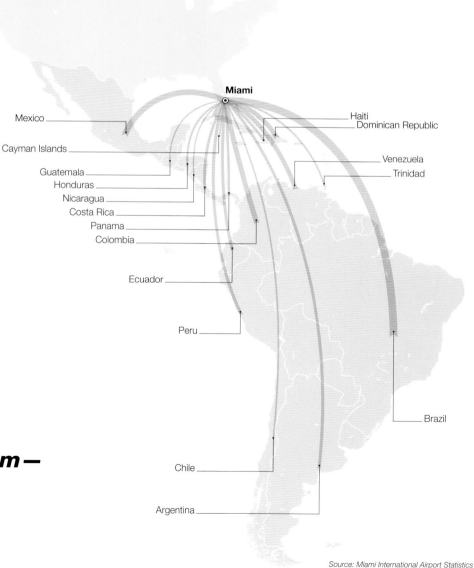

"The transnational city defines cosmopolitanism — it is the cosmopolis."

Source: Miami International Airport Statistics

Migrant Destinations

Transnational cities are prime destinations for international migrants and they are highly diverse. The mobilizing force of the transnational city is primarily expressed in its regional appeal: it is a node in the global landscape, highly visible, attractive for various reasons, and drawing in hundreds of thousands of migrants. The migrants come for economic reasons, most often, but they also choose these cities because of their openness and because they offer the opportunity of finding a relatively comfortable space, with good survival odds, amid already present immigrant communities.

Relative to its size, Miami receives more foreign immigrants than any other city in the United States. It is like a high-pressure valve in a system of global flows of people. In an average five-year period, about 285,000 foreign immigrants pour into the city, and many stick around. During the same period of time, Miami receives about 270,000 newcomers from elsewhere in the United States. This adds up to more than a half-million immigrants in a metro area of about 4.2 million.

Situated on the southern edge of the United States, it is no surprise that Miami's foreign-born population hails mainly from Central and South America. It is best known, of course, for its large Cuban presence (growing toward

Metropolitan Miami as a people "router"

Foreign and domestic migrant flows are enormous relative to the size of the city (shown here for an average five-year period in the past two decades). In the past half-century, the city's growth has been fed mainly through net foreign in-migration. Domestic in-migration is considerable, too, but domestic out-migration is even greater.

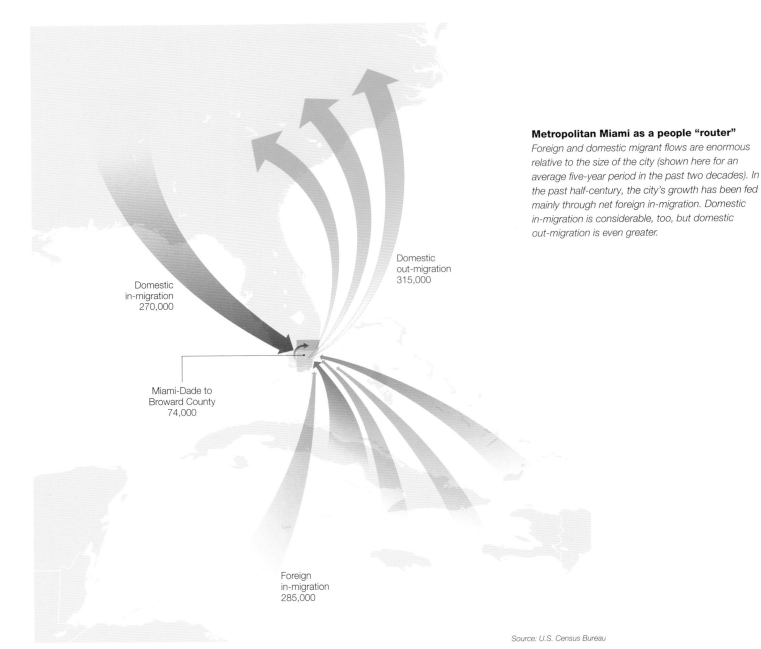

Domestic
out-migration
315,000

Domestic
in-migration
270,000

Miami-Dade to
Broward County
74,000

Foreign
in-migration
285,000

Source: U.S. Census Bureau

700,000 now) but there are many other groups from a wide range of countries, with especially large numbers of Haitians, Colombians, Nicaraguans, and Jamaicans.

Miami's newcomers could not possibly all be accommodated if some people did not also leave: in the same average five-year period, 315,000 people depart for other destinations in the USA. Those who leave are predominantly former domestic in-migrants and locals who decide to opt for more homogeneous and quiet pastures up north. Within the Miami urban region, there has for years been a net flow of people (around 74,000 in an average five-year period) from Miami-Dade County to more suburban Broward County. However, that intra-metropolitan distinction has been on the wane for some time: Broward County itself is increasingly international and diverse. Broward's population is 32 percent foreign-born, nearly three times as many as the average U.S. city—not what most people would consider a predictable suburb.

Whether or not, and how, global migration will create new transnational cities—or change and reshape ones like Miami—remains to be seen. Given the ever-increasing flows of people around the world, the question is not when such urban transformations will occur, but where.

Miami as a people magnet

Sitting on the edge of the United States but with Florida's southern tip protruding into the Caribbean and Latin America, Miami is an attractive destination for migrants from all over South and Central America and the Caribbean. The map shows the origins of Miami's main foreign-born populations.

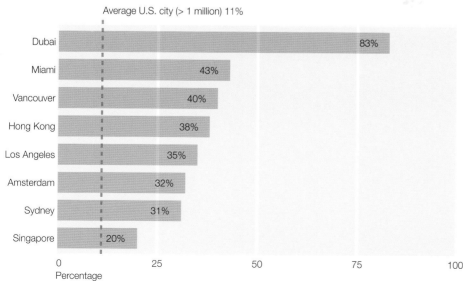

TOP TEN NATIONAL ORIGINS OF FOREIGN MIGRANTS TO MIAMI, 2010

Cuba	669,681
Haiti	157,597
Colombia	143,147
Jamaica	107,054
Nicaragua	83,680
Dominican Republic	53,954
Peru	52,296
Honduras	56,102
Venezuela	67,193
Mexico	41,166

Source: 2010, U.S. Census

Foreign-born as percentage of metro population in selected transnational cities, 2013

Average U.S. city (> 1 million) 11%

City	Percentage
Dubai	83%
Miami	43%
Vancouver	40%
Hong Kong	38%
Los Angeles	35%
Amsterdam	32%
Sydney	31%
Singapore	20%

Percentage: 0 25 50 75 100

Source: Metropolitan areas, estimates for 2013, various sources

Cities of strangers

Dubai is exceptional in that migrants typically are temporary workers and do not qualify for citizenship (over three-quarters of Dubai's population is male). Among "regular" transnational cities where migrant populations are more fully incorporated into the urban fabric, Miami leads with 43 percent foreign-born.

Miami: Transnational World City

Comings and goings

The strategic location of transnational cities makes them ideal ports of entry and embarkation for people, goods, and exchange-related services. Over half of all exports leaving Miami are headed to Latin America, via Miami International Airport or the Port of Miami.

World cities serve as the primary nodes of the global economy. From facilitating and regulating the flow of money between financial markets to serving as the preferred locations for multinational corporate headquarters, world cities are simultaneously products and patrons of contemporary economic globalization. It is precisely the transnational character of the world city that makes it an attractive location for business. Not only are they connected to other world cities, but the world itself can be found within them. The convergence of people from different places and cultures fosters transnational, multi-ethnic, and cross-cultural exchanges. Fluency in multiple languages, knowledge of local customs and international business practices, and the presence of ethnic cuisine are not merely luxuries, but are requirements in the 21st-century world city.

The hybridization of economics, politics, and culture defines transnational world cities like Miami, Hong Kong, and London. Though each is a market for luxury goods and services, the test bed of innovative design, and the site of tomorrow's next merger or acquisition, each also retains a distinct regional flair. Whether it is branded as Latin American cosmopolitanism or flexible citizenship in Hong Kong, the transnational world city is a product of the region, and the people who live and pass through it.

Cities like Miami, Hong Kong, and Dublin are considered contemporaries, but their emergence and ascendancy as world cities occurred under different circumstances and conditions. For instance, both Hong Kong and Miami experienced huge influxes of refugees, from mainland China in the 1960s, and from Cuba in the 1980s, respectively. These inflows became part of the broader geopolitical narrative of the Cold War, but were also crucial for both cities because they brought with them

Regional export shares for Miami, Hong Kong, and Dublin, 2012 *(approximate figures)*

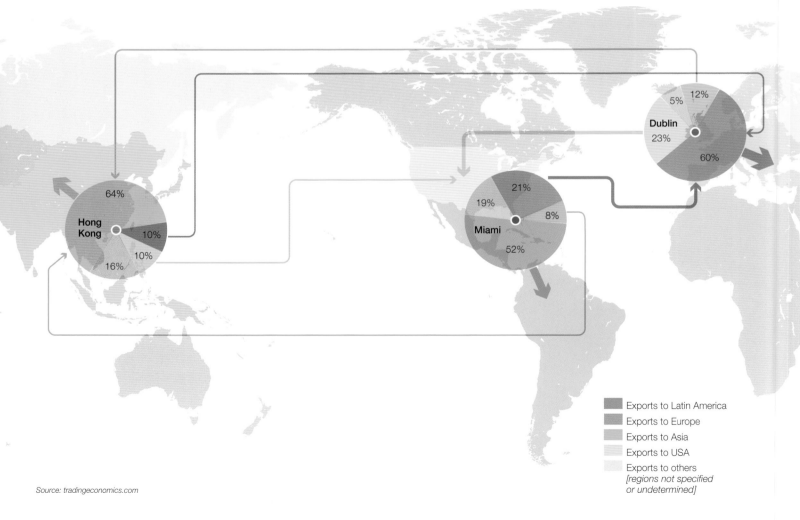

Exports to Latin America
Exports to Europe
Exports to Asia
Exports to USA
Exports to others
[regions not specified or undetermined]

Source: tradingeconomics.com

money, business acumen, and, most importantly, extra-local connections. The desire and ability of these immigrants and refugees to maintain these linkages facilitated the transnational character of these cities and the world city network itself. In contrast to Miami and Hong Kong, where global status was less planned and in some respects contested, Dublin's ascendancy was more recent and far more manufactured through policies and strategies to attract foreign investment. Such efforts, combined with a highly educated, skilled, and English-speaking workforce, paid off to make Dublin a destination and darling of globalization in the 1990s.

Regardless of their histories and origins, every city within the world city network depends upon the timely and efficient exchange of goods, services, and people. Though advances in information and communication technology introduce significant business efficiencies, the timely movement of goods and, in particular, people is critical to the operation of the world city network. For the transnational and ethnic global elite coming and going to places like Miami and Hong Kong, business remains a full-contact sport that requires in-person, face-to-face communication and interaction. Miami International Airport (MIA) ranks second, only behind New York's JFK, in terms of international traffic volume. Combined, MIA and the Port of Miami are responsible for over US$21 billion in imports and nearly US$40 billion in exports to places such as China, Colombia, Brazil, Switzerland, Venezuela, and France. With over seventy consulates, twenty-one foreign trade offices, and more than forty bi-national chambers of commerce, Miami is the hemispheric center for business in the Americas.

Though the geographical location of cities like Hong Kong and Miami is critical and advantageous to their success, it is the transnational character, demands, and orientation of the business elite and local populations in such places that reinforce the status of each city within the world city network.

Intensity of corporate linkages to Miami

In terms of corporate influence, Miami certainly punches above its weight as a source and destination for business. It is an attractive and familiar location for headquartering Latin American companies or business divisions, and is recognized to be a critical business hub within the Latin American market.

Cities with the greatest corporate influence on Miami
The ten cities with the largest number of headquarters of transnational companies active in South Florida

Madrid (28)
Chicago (27)
Tokyo (28)
São Paulo (12)
Amsterdam (11)
Atlanta (10)
Zurich (10)
Paris (40)
New York (66)
London (45)

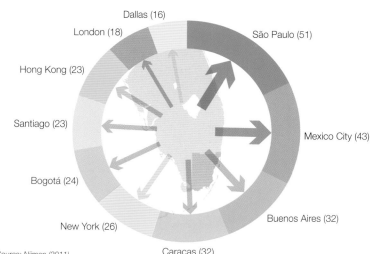

Dallas (16)
São Paulo (51)
London (18)
Hong Kong (23)
Santiago (23)
Mexico City (43)
Bogotá (24)
New York (26)
Buenos Aires (32)
Caracas (32)

Source: Nijman (2011)

Cities most influenced by Miami-based corporations
The ten cities with the largest number of branches of transnational companies headquartered in South Florida

Miami: Locals, Exiles, and Mobiles in the Transnational Landscape

One of the defining characteristics of the transnational city is the diversity of its inhabitants. This diversity is expressed in many ways and at different levels. Consider the linguistic diversity that is found in a city like Miami. The predominance of a Spanish-speaking population sets it apart from other cities in the United States, and colors it as an "exotic" or even "foreign" place to many Americans up north. At the same time, it is precisely this quality that makes Miami an attractive destination for Latin American nationals and businesses to the south.

Though English is spoken by many people in Miami, fluency in Spanish has its advantages when shopping, dining out, or applying for a driver's license. But merely speaking Spanish is not enough. The *kind* of Spanish that one is able to speak simultaneously defines one, and can just as quickly open or close doors of opportunity. There is Spanish with an American accent that identifies the eager outsider, the Latin American dialects (e.g., Colombian) that are often promoted and taught as "business Spanish," and, of course, the Cuban dialect that defines and reproduces membership within the Cuban community in Miami. Within each dialect there are even more variants, idioms, and gestures that are used for purposes of inclusion and exclusion. The evolution of

Languages spoken in Miami, 2011

A variety of languages can be heard and are spoken in transnational cities. According to American Community Survey estimates reported by the U.S. Census Bureau, nearly two-thirds of Miami residents consider Spanish their lengua materna, *or mother tongue. That said, several variations of the Spanish language, including the blend of Spanish and English referred to as "Spanglish," are spoken throughout the city.*

Languages spoken at home—one dot = 25 people

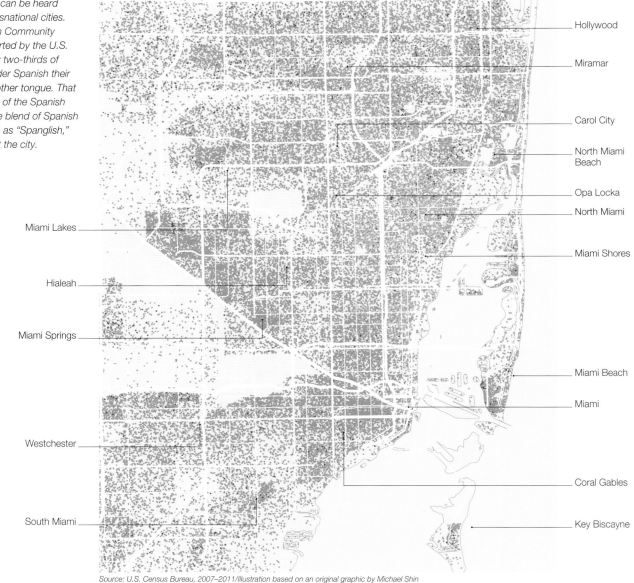

Hollywood

Miramar

Carol City

North Miami Beach

Opa Locka

North Miami

Miami Shores

Miami Beach

Miami

Coral Gables

Key Biscayne

Miami Lakes

Hialeah

Miami Springs

Westchester

South Miami

● Spanish
● English
○ Indo-European
● Asian

Source: U.S. Census Bureau, 2007–2011/Illustration based on an original graphic by Michael Shin

language is also a function of the transnational and transient character of cities like Miami. For instance, and depending upon who you ask, the hybridization—or bastardization—of Spanish and English into "Spanglish" can be considered a cosmopolitan inevitability or a tragedy for linguistic purists.

This hybridization of language, culture, business, and nearly every other aspect of life in the transnational city is fueled by transience, the ceaseless movement of people in and out of the city. Fewer than 20 percent of its residents were born or raised from an early age in Miami, and many of these children were born to non-locals who may not stay and raise their children in the city. For the children of the foreign-born who remain, and the relatively

small number of "locals," the blending of and tensions between cultures is the norm.

Miami is also a popular destination for "exiles." Though the Cuban exile community receives the most attention, political and economic exiles from Nicaragua, Haiti, Venezuela, and other parts of Latin America make up about one-third of Miami's population. For the exile, Miami is not really "home," but is a pit-stop or temporary residence. The aspirations of the exile to return home, whether realistic or not, play a major part in the exile's identity and the exile community's relationship with the city—or lack thereof. Then there are the "mobiles" who tend to be affluent and who come and go as they please. Throughout Miami's history, such mobiles have played

an important part in the city's ever-changing evolution and image. Once the destination for vacationers, retirees, and "snowbirds" from the northern USA, Miami now draws mobiles from much more global backgrounds. For them, Miami is often little more than a *pied-à-terre*, and their affluence and independence seem to militate against communal involved citizenship.

Diversity in culture and language in transnational cities like Miami is often framed as a benefit, and expressed as an aspiration for planners in other cities. More often than not, however, cultural identities are also fragmented through language and politics and class. The way in which the transnational city embraces, confronts, and addresses such issues continues to evolve.

Residential locations for particular identity groups in Miami

The identities of residents and particular neighborhoods in transnational cities are shaped by the constant ebb and flow of people. Although the Cuban exile community once defined Miami, the city is being reshaped by newer generations of migrants and ever-increasing amounts of wealth from Latin America and Europe.

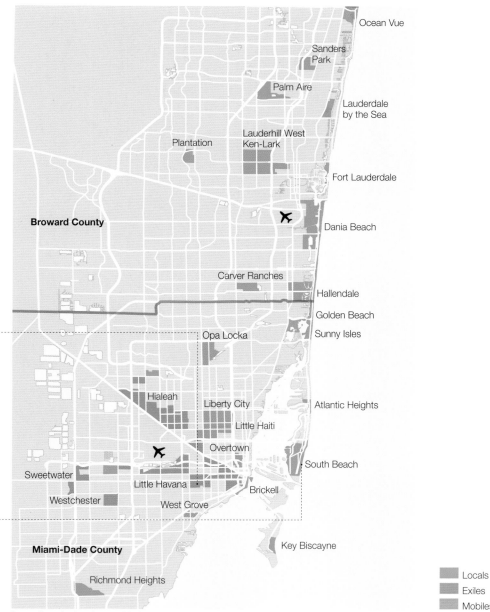

The Freedom Wall in Little Havana

South Beach skyline

Source: Illustration based on an original graphic by Jan Nijman

Ocean Vue
Sanders Park
Palm Aire
Lauderdale by the Sea
Lauderhill West
Ken-Lark
Plantation
Fort Lauderdale
Broward County
Dania Beach
Carver Ranches
Hallendale
Golden Beach
Sunny Isles
Opa Locka
Hialeah
Liberty City
Atlantic Heights
Little Haiti
Overtown
South Beach
Sweetwater
Little Havana
Westchester
Brickell
West Grove
Miami-Dade County
Key Biscayne
Richmond Heights

Locals
Exiles
Mobiles

Transnational Iconographies: From Chinatown to Little Havana

One of the defining features of the transnational city is that you can find the world within it. Through its geographical position within a region, the transnational city is promoted simultaneously as familiar and exotic. It is a multicultural melting pot where the global elite come to dine, do business, and play among the multi-ethnic locals. According to glossy in-flight magazines, these are the places and lifestyles that you too can experience if you are fortunate enough to have an overnight layover, or as United Airlines' *Hemispheres* magazine puts it, "Three perfect days."

The image projected by the transnational city is sometimes defined by the ethnic enclaves found within it. One of the most iconic ethnic enclaves is Chinatown. But which Chinatown are we talking about? Is it the one in Vancouver, Milan, or Bangkok? The ubiquity of Chinatowns around the world speaks not only to the transnational character of the Chinese, but to the dynamic nature of transnationalism in general. Though older Chinatowns are built around culinary stereotypes, dragon festivals, and kitsch, the new Chinatowns in places like Lagos are less about tourism and more about serving Chinese transnationals.

Vancouver

London

San Francisco

Chinatowns of the world

The most archetypical and stereotypical ethnic enclaves of the world are Chinatowns. While some Chinatowns are seen and promoted as tourist destinations, others serve a more functional role for Chinese transnationals. The size of the circles on this map is proportional to the significance of the Chinatowns in particular world regions. There is no Chinatown in Miami, the nearest being, perhaps unsurprisingly, in Havana, Cuba.

In stark contrast to the ubiquity of Chinatowns are the geographically specific enclaves that reflect particular regions of the world and help to distinguish one transnational city from another. Miami's Little Havana exemplifies how a single ethnic enclave can shape a city, its economy, its politics, and its urban landscape like no other. As Miami's largest and best-known ethnic group, only a minority of Miami's 700,000-plus Cubans now actually live in Greater Miami. Miami's Little Haiti is overshadowed and lesser known than its Cuban counterpart. Fewer in number than Cubans, Haitians also have a different and less

privileged social, political, and economic profile (to do with U.S. asylum policies). Consequently, the geographical manifestation of Little Haiti is less defined and less iconic than Little Havana.

The imagery and iconography of the transnational city is often based on the contradictions found across the urban landscape. Ethnic enclaves can be considered one form of spatial contradiction where a transnational group converges to create and reproduce locally a community and cultural identity that is rooted in a faraway place. Whether or not such enclaves truly capture the essence of those places is open to debate. Just

as the forces of globalization create a sameness across many transnational urban landscapes (Starbucks in Ho Chi Minh City, anyone?), ethnic enclaves can serve as geographical reminders of just how out of place or close to home we may find ourselves.

Kobe, Japan

Singapore

Sydney

Lemon City (Little Haiti)

Little Havana

Miami's ethnic enclaves

Although Miami lacks a Chinatown, its ethnic enclaves, and in particular, Little Havana and Little Haiti, are recognized around the world. Despite the small and defined geographical footprint of Little Havana, the Cuban exile community has successfully penetrated all aspects of life in Miami, from business to local government, and now extends throughout and beyond the greater Miami area.

Transnational Tourism

Cruise ships embarking from the Port of Miami

Miami ranks first in the world in total number of cruise ship embarkations. It is also a global tourist destination in its own right. Cruise ship passengers frequently arrive a few days before departure and remain a few days after a cruise ends to take advantage of Miami's upscale shopping centers, tropical culture, and vibrant nightlife.

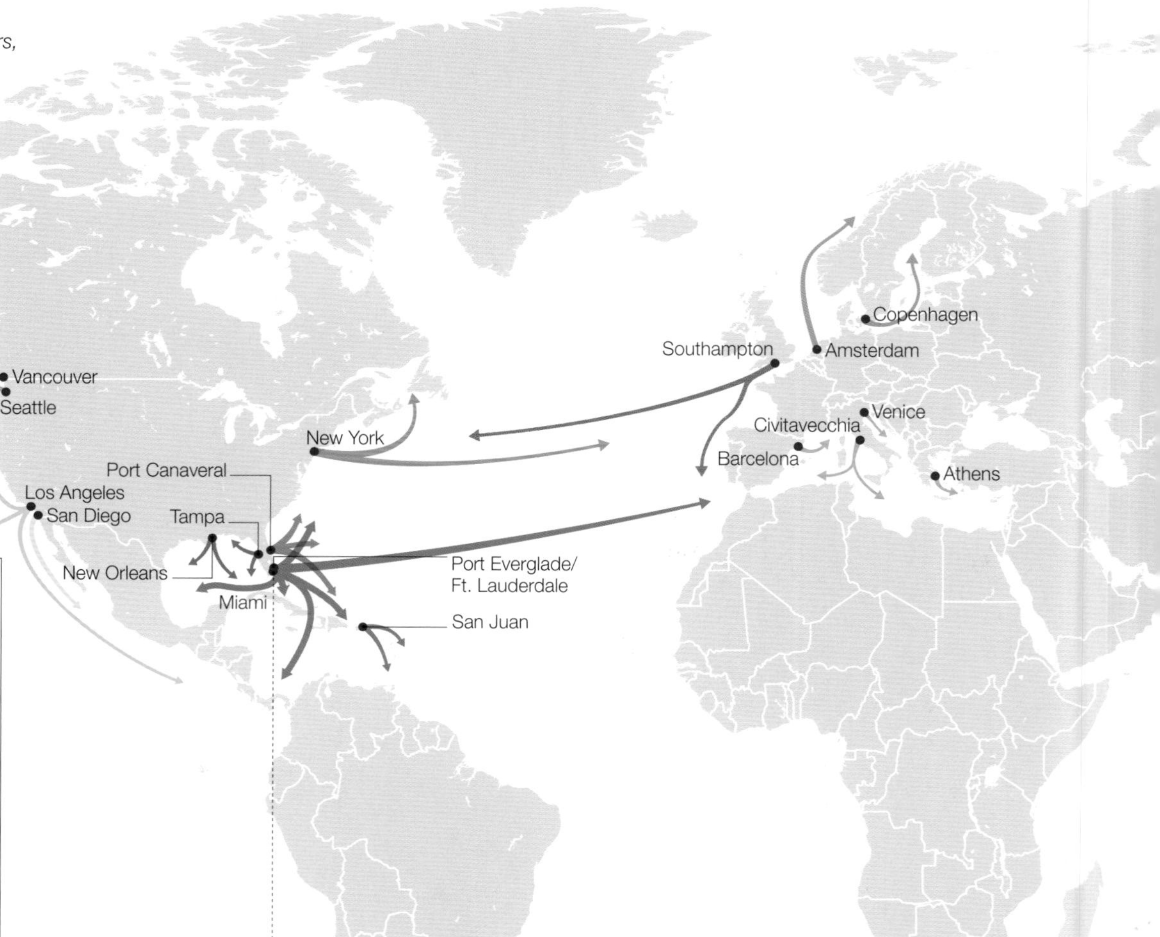

The locations of transnational cities between key world regions make them ideal points of departure for vacationers and tourists. Miami, for instance, is home to the biggest cruise port in the world and bade farewell to over 3.7 million multiday cruise passengers in 2012, many of them foreigners. This number is equivalent to two-thirds of the total population of the greater Miami urbanized area, and it creates numerous externalities that make Miami, already a popular vacation site, and other transnational cities like it, tourist destinations in their own right.

In addition to being a hub and point of transfer for vacationers, the transnational city offers incomparable opportunities to shop and consume. Singapore, Dubai, and Miami are all recognized as regional shopping epicenters where foreign consumers flock to luxury retail outlets, famous fashion houses, restaurants run by celebrity chefs, and duty-free shopping malls. This link between retail, dining, and leisure is often blurred in the transnational city, and is frequently used to promote such cities as attractive destinations for visitors and for those in transit.

EMBARKATIONS IN 2011	
Points of Embarkation	**Number of cruise ships**
Miami	781
Port Everglade/Ft. Lauderdale (within Miami metro area)	671
Port Canaveral	446
Venice	324
Los Angeles	297
Barcelona	289
Civitavecchia (Rome)	265
San Juan	227
New York	220
Seattle	217
Tampa	193
Vancouver	168
New Orleans	164
Amsterdam	134
San Diego	123
Athens (Piraeus)	102
Copenhagen	100
Southampton	100
Hong Kong	70
Sydney	58

Source: CLIA (2011)

Cruise ship in Miami port

Complementing shopping tourism in the transnational city is medical tourism, which refers to patient travel for health and medical care purposes. Offering affordable, high-quality medical treatments ranging from facelifts to organ transplants, and affordable full-service patient recovery options in convenient and sometimes exotic and tropical locales, medical tourism is well established in cities such as Singapore and Miami. In fact, thousands of international patients come to Miami every year for medical treatment and are enticed with a range of services such as VIP mall discounts, limousine service, medical visa assistance, and global package discount rates.

Medical tourism is also a legitimate economic development strategy for many cities around the world. The potential revenues associated with becoming a transnational medical destination are significant. What is more, the development of a medical tourist industry requires a highly skilled labor force (e.g., medical professionals), lower-skilled workers (e.g., post-treatment caregivers), and significant investments (e.g., medical and recovery facilities), all of which are readily available to the well-positioned transnational city.

Shopping and medical tourism speak to the continuous evolution of the transnational city and its shifting place within regional urban

hierarchies, and the global economy at large. Tourism for tourism's sake is now passé. Why even bother traveling unless you can (window) shop with the rich and famous, experience a meal at a restaurant with a celebrity chef's name on the menu, or revisit the fountain of youth with a tummy tuck or rhinoplasty?

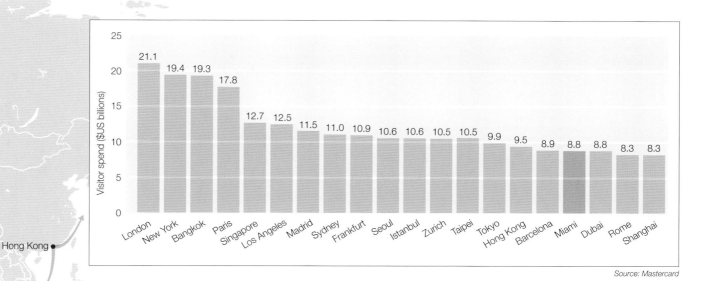

Source: Mastercard

International visitor spending in the transnational city, 2012

The total visitor spend in many transnational cities exceeds the annual GDP of several countries. Whether spent on hotels, restaurants, shopping duty free, or purchasing a pied-à-terre, money from such transactions is recirculated among other transnational cities, and in turn is used to attract even more visitors and more spending.

Transnational Economy: Drugs, Banks, and Real Estate

As ports of call for people, goods, and services from different world regions, transnational cities are also the repositories of enormous sums of wealth. Such wealth is typically concentrated in the hands of the few, and in only certain parts of the city. Though such disparities are common across most urban landscapes, in the transnational city the rich seem richer and the poor seem poorer.

The international transactions that generate such wealth also demand their own set of specialized services. From financial services to international and private banking, money is big business in the transnational city. While much of this wealth is generated legitimately, some of it is not. The cocaine trade of the 1970s and 1980s, with its origins in South America and Colombia in particular, propelled Miami on to the international scene and flooded the city with enormous amounts of cash. The laundering of these funds was facilitated by an already large Spanish-speaking population and co-culture in Miami, which helped to establish the city as an international banking center.

Linked directly to Miami's rise at this time was the fact that the currency of the narco-trade was the U.S. dollar. Recognized and accepted everywhere, and immune from the inflationary pressures of the Latin American debt crisis of the 1980s, the dollar was—and still is—the preferred currency of the global economy. Despite its illicit foundations and history, Miami's banking system and the U.S. dollar remain a much sought-after safe haven for foreign nationals in good times and bad.

Given the vast amounts of wealth within the transnational city, conspicuous consumption and investment is also a favorite pastime. Real estate is an indicator both of wealth and of

| 1971 $89 million | 1974 $924 million | 1979 $5.5 billion | 1982 $8 billion | 1985 $5.9 billion |

Source: Nijman (2011)

Cash surplus of banks in the Miami area
The combined cash surplus of Miami banks in selected years, as calculated by the Federal Reserve. There is a given amount of cash dollars in the U.S. economy and most cities on a yearly basis tend to have close to a neutral balance. The Miami surpluses were attributed to massive private deposits of cocaine dollars, most of them in the form of $20 notes. Miami was during those years the country's main distribution center of cocaine and most of the revenues returned to Miami.

The financial district of Brickell, Miami

financial savvy, at least for those with means. Those who consider the transnational city a temporary or secondary home tend to be the most affluent and seek out prime real estate (e.g., coastal locations, luxury high-rise condos). Foreign-owned second homes are common in Miami, and such homes are frequently among the most expensive and located in the most exclusive areas of the city. The demand to be in, and to own a piece of, the transnational city has driven real estate prices beyond the reach of most locals. For instance, prices per square foot in desirable areas of Beirut and Hong Kong are higher than those found in New York City.

Desirable real estate, easy and cheap money, and a culture of conspicuous consumption can also lead to a cycle of speculation. Though such speculation is not restricted to the transnational city, the housing bubbles that are inflated in such locations tend to be bigger and the meltdowns more severe. Though Miami's

first housing bubble in the 1920s was largely a domestic affair, the bubble that burst in the early 21st century was certainly fueled by the city's position as a transnational center. The cycle continues, however, as wealth from Brazil, Colombia, Venezuela, and other Latin American countries seeks a safe haven, political stability, and physical assets. The latest bust of Miami's housing market has once again made it an attractive location for foreign investors with strong currencies seeking real estate and driving prices to new heights.

The economy of the transnational city is a complex and ever-changing mix of financial flows and deposits, some legitimate and others not. The juxtaposition of extremes in wealth and in poverty both highlight and reinforce the contradictions behind capitalistic cosmopolitanism that form the transnational city.

Miami's real estate

Miami's prime real estate areas are found mainly along the waterfront, with more than half of all second homes owned by transnationals. In 2013 the Wall Street Journal *reported that over 85 percent of new construction buyers in Miami were foreign. Many of these deals were made in cash, with foreign investors seeking physical assets in Miami in light of economic uncertainty.*

Non-primary residences
█ 50–60%
▒ More than 60%

Sunny Isles

Atlantic Heights

South Beach

Brickell

Key Biscayne

Sunny Isles

South Beach

Brickell

Source: Nijman (2011)/Illustration adapted from an original by Jan Nijman

Life and Death in the Transnational City

In October 2012 a raft carrying twenty-three Cuban refugees on its way to Miami capsized and a reported fourteen people drowned. It had happened to hundreds more before them, and they surely will not be the last. Every year more than 1,000 Central Americans die trying to illegally cross the U.S. border. The transnational city is a place to die for. Ironically, however, once established in the transnational city, few envision staying there until their last breath. For many, it is a temporary venue, whether as a place of exile, a springboard for upward mobility, or a playground until new opportunities beckon. Few imagine dying there and, as the moment draws near, many make plans to go home.

In the transnational city, which is home to a disproportionate number of the foreign-born and expatriates, death and repatriation are a steady business. The bodies of an estimated 20 percent of South Florida's deceased are shipped out, more than from any other region in the USA. Most of the HRs (industry shorthand for human remains) going abroad depart from Miami International Airport. According to the CEO of Pierson, a leader in this business since 1964, around 80 percent of business is international, with the company shipping to a range of foreign destinations across Central and South America and a number of European countries as well.

The cost of shipping a body is not cheap, ranging from about US$500 to well into the thousands of dollars. The requirements for the

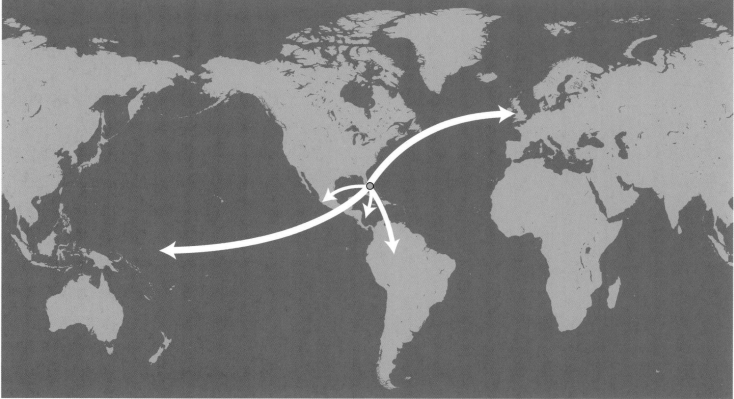

Source: American Airlines

Cost of shipping human remains internationally from Miami

As more and more migrants move to transnational cities, they too die there. And even in death, there are still costs to return home. Miami is the hub for American Airlines in Latin America, and the figures in the table are the airline's rates for repatriating human remains in 2013.

Country of origin	Destination	Uncremated remains		
USA		1–75 lbs	76–500 lbs	501+ lbs
	Europe/Pacific	$500	$2,500	$3,000
	Caribbean/Central America	$300	$900	$1,200
	Mexico	$225	$1005	$1,255
	South America	$400	$1,200	$1,600

shipment and delivery of HRs also vary for religious, cultural, and public health reasons. Given the expense and the lack of government assistance to repatriate the dead, who are often young and uninsured, immigrant communities in transnational cities sometimes organize burial societies to help offset costs. The origins of some credit unions and informal health insurance programs can be traced back to such societies established by Italians, Jews, and Greeks in New York, who were among the first transnationals in America. Newer generations of Mexicans, Chinese, Filipinos, and Bangladeshis are now doing the same in several transnational cities.

Clearly, dying abroad does not come without complications because few expats intend or plan to make the transnational city their eternal home. For instance, in Dubai, in the absence of a will for a deceased expat, Sharia law is applied and supersedes the laws governing inheritance in the deceased's home country. All assets, if there are any, are frozen and subsequently dispersed at the discretion of the Sharia court.

The thought of dying rarely enters the minds of those passing through or living in the transnational city. On the contrary, becoming an expat or immigrant in the transnational city is an open declaration about how one views life, not death. Yet it is in the approach of death that the transnational city offers the foreign-born its most stark and ultimate choices of belonging—between the local and global, between cosmos and earth, and between the transient and the eternal.

Returning home

The extent of the human remains repatriation network (c. 2013) of the Dublin-based airline Aer Lingus reflects the transnational character of the city and of the Irish. At one time discontinued, the human remains service was reinstated by the airline in 2004 after condemnation by emigrant groups.

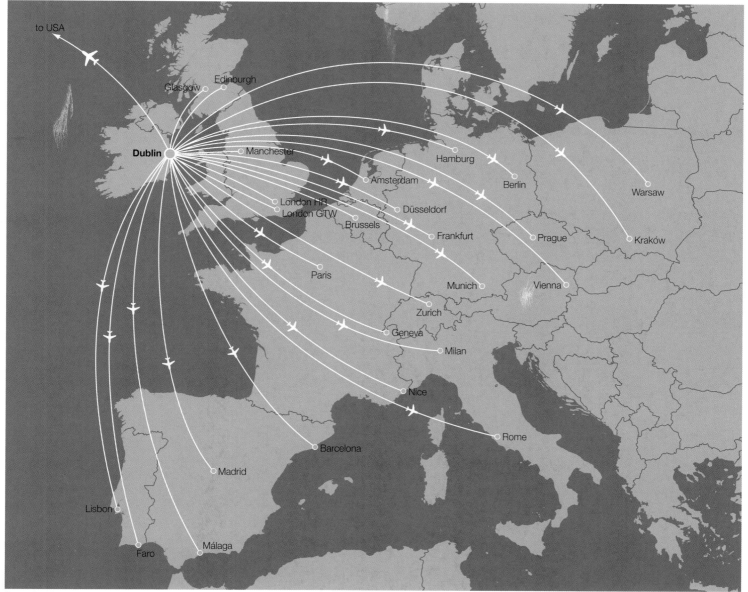

Source: Aer Lingus

THE CREATIVE CITY

PAUL KNOX

Core city
MILAN ____

Secondary cities
PARIS ____
NEW YORK ____
LONDON ____
PORTLAND ____
LOS ANGELES ____

The Creative City: Introduction

" In places where various branches of creative industries engage one another, sharing ideas and resources, a 'creative buzz' develops."

Large cities have long been recognized as important arenas of cultural production: hotbeds of cultural innovation, centers of fashion, and arbiters of taste. The density and diversity of large cities generates serendipity, hybridity, unexpected encounters, and new combinations of ideas that contribute to the generative and transformative processes that make cities such exciting places. In the past the creative milieux developed in some cities—Athens, Rome, Kyoto, Florence, Vienna, London, Paris, and New York—has been intense enough to have produced a distinctive "golden age" of innovation and creativity.

In recent times, much emphasis has been given to the importance of contemporary creative industries and the role of the "creative class" of workers to economic prosperity and urban

vitality. Western society has developed a much stronger emphasis on pleasure, experience, and aesthetics than ever before—a trend that has given rise to a "dream economy" oriented toward goods and services that are perceived to enhance people's self-image, express their identity, and mediate their social relations. The most dynamic metropolitan areas in Europe and North America consequently have post-industrial economies that rely heavily on technology-intensive manufacturing; advanced business, financial, and personal services; cultural products industries (such as media, film, music, and tourism); and design- and fashion-oriented forms of production such as clothing, furniture, product design, interior design, and architecture.

Richard Florida has defined the creative class as a broadly defined group of new-economy middle classes. Noting that a significant positive correlation exists between local economic growth and the incidence of this creative class

Innovative design cities

The density and diversity of big-city populations generate serendipity, unexpected encounters, and new combinations of ideas that often lead to innovation. In some cities the mix of innovative designers, entrepreneurs, and manufacturers has led to unique local design cultures and the creation of distinctive styles and iconic products that result in the city itself—like Vienna in the 1900s and Paris in the 1930s—becoming established as a global tastemaker.

London
1850s

Vienna
1900s

Paris
1930s

in different cities, he has suggested that urban economic development will depend increasingly on cities' ability to attract and retain significant numbers of this mobile but choosy class.

Creative industries

In the United States, there are about 600,000 design professionals. Without exception, these jobs are highly localized in major metropolitan areas. New York, Chicago, Los Angeles, Boston, and San Francisco dominate, especially with regard to concentrations of architects; but Detroit and San Jose host prominent concentrations of industrial designers, while Seattle tops the list among graphic designers. In the United Kingdom, about 200,000 people are employed in design, accounting for an estimated turnover of £15 billion. Almost half are located in London and metropolitan southeast England, with secondary concentrations in Manchester, Birmingham, Leeds, and Bristol. Elsewhere in Europe, there are major concentrations of designers and creative industries in Barcelona, Berlin, Milan, and Paris, with secondary concentrations in Amsterdam, Helsinki, Madrid, Prague, Rome, and Vienna.

The creative milieux in these cities seem to have certain things in common, including a marked interdisciplinarity. This is because separate industries—film, fashion, graphic design, architecture, photography, etc.—operate best within a context that allows them to collaborate with one another, review each other's products, and offer jobs that cross-fertilize and share skill sets. In such contexts, where the various branches of creative industries constantly engage one another, sharing ideas and resources, a "creative buzz" develops that often flowers into a distinctive local vibe, with lifestyles, music, aesthetics, décor, and clothing all typically reflecting cool, edgy, and neo-bohemian elements. The co-mingling of artists, artisans, designers, photographers, actors, students, educators, and writers in cafés, restaurants, and clubs and—for some—gallery openings, fashion after-parties, music release events, and celebrity events contributes to a blurring of the social worlds of work and lifestyle that is a distinctive dimension of creative-industry clusters in larger cities.

Creative spaces

All this seems to require a rich, old-fashioned, even overcrowded setting. The agglomeration inherent to cultural milieux is important because it provides visibility that can advance a city's brand identity as a center of creativity. Some cities derive a strong competitive advantage as a result of agglomerations of particular products and firms: fashion and graphic design in New York; architecture, fashion, and publishing in London; furniture, industrial design, and fashion in Milan; *haute couture* in Paris; sportswear in Portland, Oregon, and so on. Large clusters of cultural products professionals and firms also establish these cities as global tastemakers, with the result that they become, cumulatively, still more attractive to creative types and design professionals.

In many metropolises, the growth of creative activities has resulted in (and been facilitated by) the selective reorganization of land use, together with significant changes in urban infrastructure and the built environment. In addition to creative districts and design districts themselves, these outcomes include gentrified neighborhoods, large-scale urban regeneration projects, museum districts, iconic buildings designed by star architects, and luxury retail districts with flagship stores of exclusive fashion brands, high-end restaurants, cafés, art galleries, antique stores, and luxury boutiques.

Milan provides clear examples of all of this. The city has a long history of specialization in certain aspects of design but it was only in response to the deindustrialization of the 1970s that the city embarked on a deliberate strategy of remaking and rebranding itself as a design city. The success of the strategy is already evident in its built environment, its politics, its educational institutions, its design districts, its luxury fashion retailing in the "Quadrilatero d'Oro," and its fashion weeks.

The potency of design in strategies of urban regeneration, the increasing role of design services in adding value (and profit) in urban economies, the increasing importance of city branding, and the seductive idea of promoting urban economic growth through attracting a "creative class" means that more and more cities are actively promoting design. Johannesburg, for example, has established a branded Fashion District; Antwerp has opened Mode Natie, a multifunctional building that houses a Fashion Academy, a Fashion Museum, and the Flanders Fashion Institute; and Seoul is building the Dongdaemun Design Plaza, designed by Zaha Hadid, which will incorporate a design museum and design library as well as designer-oriented office and retail space. Other cities actively promoting design and creativity as a strategy for economic development include Bangkok, Colombo (Sri Lanka), Copenhagen, Helsinki, Istanbul, Kuala Lumpur, Manila, Melbourne, Pune, Sydney, and Toronto.

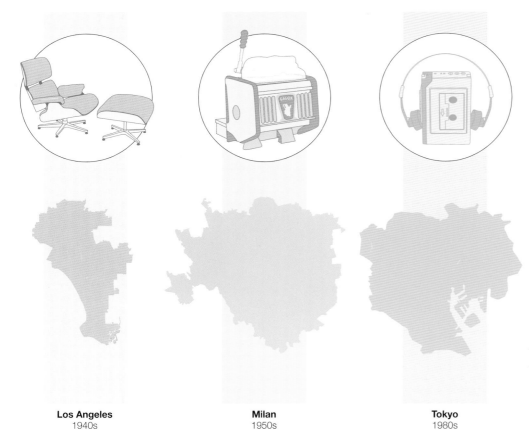

Los Angeles
1940s

Milan
1950s

Tokyo
1980s

The Creative City-Region

Every metropolitan area has an extensive hinterland: an extended territory that is economically interdependent with the metropolis itself. Milan's hinterland extends to most of Lombardy, including a host of small towns and several larger ones such as Bergamo, Brescia, Como, Cremona, and Varese. Closely integrated in terms of workforce and employment, infrastructure, services, policy, and politics, the city-region also shares a common history.

The economic roots of the region date from the Middle Ages, when flourishing agriculture, trade, and banking activities helped make it one of the most prosperous regions in Europe. In the process, Milan also became an intellectual and cultural center. Renaissance nobles sponsored the arts and brought Leonardo da Vinci to the city. In the modern era the city became the center of both Italian lyric opera and the Futurist avant-garde. Industrialization brought an influential publishing sector as well as manufacturing and engineering. Meanwhile, the smaller places around the city-region had

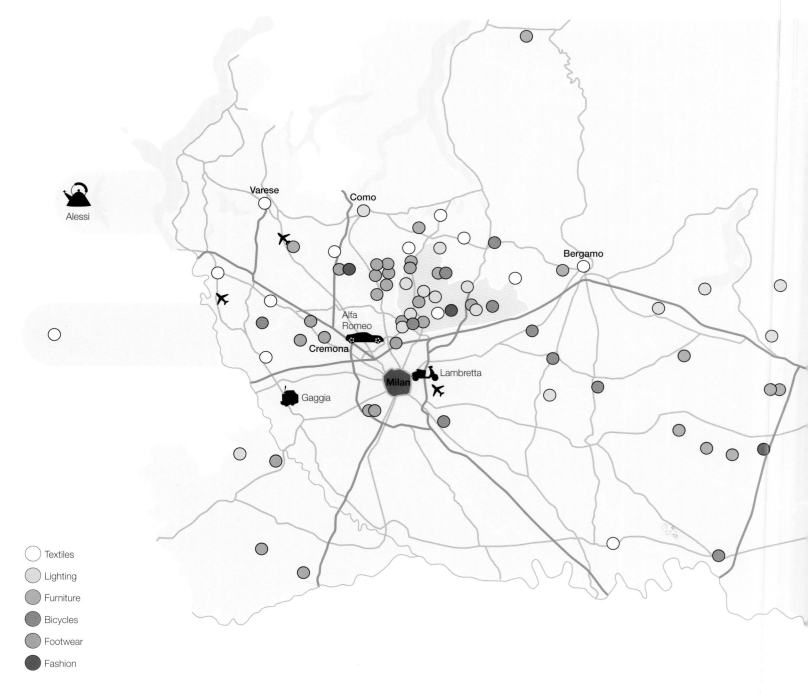

Alessi

Varese

Como

Bergamo

Alfa Romeo

Cremona

Lambretta

Milan

Gaggia

○ Textiles

○ Lighting

○ Furniture

○ Bicycles

○ Footwear

● Fashion

developed their own specializations: silk production in Como; wool and cotton weaving in Bergamo, Biela, and Varese; knitwear in Carpi; hosiery in Castelgoffredo; and furniture and wood-based craft products in the Brianza district that extends northwards from Milan to Monza and beyond.

The workshops and skilled workers associated with these specializations were the cradle of what would come to be a distinctive "Italian" design aesthetic. As large-scale industry continued to relocate to countries with cheaper labour and less regulation, the focus within the Milan city-region shifted from production to product design and product development, taking advantage of the combination of the intellectual and professional milieu that had emerged among architects, graphic designers, industrial designers, and the region's distinctive mixture of small firms, artisans, and workshops.

This remarkable transformation, together with the emergence of Milan itself as a major center of fashion and high-end *prêt-à-porter* menswear and womenswear, has led to one of the greatest concentrations of creative workers (more than a quarter of a million in the region as a whole) and firms (more than 80,000) in Europe. The region's fashion supply chain alone represents more than 60,000 workers, around 7,000 production firms, and a similar number of retail firms. A large component of this economy of creativity and innovation resides in the hinterland of the city, and in particular in the Brianza district, which has developed a highly fragmented but very flexible and innovative array of small and medium-sized firms geared to furniture production, textiles, apparel, and specialized textile machinery.

Brescia

Lake Garda

Major center of fashion

Architecture

Iconic manufacturing

Workshops

Art and design

Milan's creative city-region

Many of the iconic products of 20th-century Italian design were manufactured in Milan's extended city-region, including Alfa Romeo cars (in Arese), Bianchi bicycles (Treviglio), Gaggia espresso machines (Robecco sul Naviglio), Lambretta scooters (Lambrate), Alessi domestic ware (Omegna), and Artemide lighting (Telgate). By the 1970s, when much of Milan's heavy engineering and manufacturing was in decline, the city and its surrounding territory had developed into a distinctive ecology of specialized manufacturers, public institutions, trade magazines, design studios, educational programs, and research institutes.

Urban Infrastructure and Creativity

Since the mid-1970s, urban governance in cities around the world has become increasingly concerned with providing a "good business climate" that might attract investment. The increasing entrepreneurialism of urban governance has made rebuilding, repackaging, and rebranding the urban landscape a common priority among large cities. Flagship cultural sites, signature skyscrapers, conference centers, large mixed-use developments, warehouse conversions, waterfront redevelopments, heritage sites, and major sports and entertainment complexes have appeared in many cities. Often geared toward consumption rather than production, these settings are designed to provide a new economic infrastructure suited to the needs of a post-industrial economy.

In this context, the iconic buildings of celebrity architects—"starchitects"—have become increasingly important as cities compete for status and identity. The ability of a high-profile building of radical design to put a city on the global map was demonstrated by Sydney Opera House, designed by Danish architect Jørn Utzon in the late 1950s and completed in 1973. More recently (in the 1990s), the city of Bilbao, Spain, embarked on a high-profile strategy based around physical regeneration,

Regenerated Milan

Along with the regenerated art and design projects in Bovisa and Bicocca, the new exhibition area west of the city center in Rho replaced the old site located at the Fiera in the northwest suburbs. The site amounts to a self-contained town, with hotels, shopping mall, police station, chapel, mosque, restaurants, cafés, and metro and mainline high-speed train stations. The annual International Furniture Fair is the world's premium promotional event. Started in 1961, the fair has developed into a family of concurrent trade fairs (branded Milan Design Week) covering furniture as well as lighting, kitchens, bathrooms, office furniture and fittings, interior textiles, and accessories. During Design Week, Milan's main fairground accommodates all seven trade fairs and the rest of the city is given over to ancillary design events with around 350,000 trade visitors.

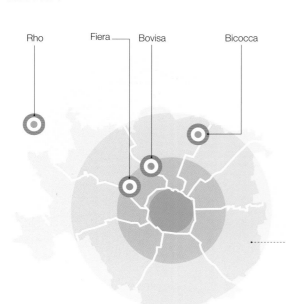

Rho Fiera Bovisa Bicocca

featuring signature structures as symbols of modernity in the hope of transforming the city into a flourishing international hub of culture, tourism, and advanced business services. The centerpiece of the strategy was the Bilbao Guggenheim Museum, designed by Frank Gehry, and its notoriety has encouraged many other cities to pursue strategies of physical regeneration. The potency of the symbolic capital of cities is now derived in part from their association with starchitecture. Stardom and city branding become mutually self-reinforcing as real estate developers realize that celebrity architects can add value to their projects, city leaders compete to acquire the services of the top names to design signature buildings that

will keep their city on the map, and the signature buildings of starchitects provide the backdrop for fashion shoots, movie scenes, TV commercials, music videos, and satellite news broadcasts.

Milan's regeneration strategies have been framed in similar vein, with an explicit focus on creative industries. Large parts of the city and its infrastructure have been redrawn by a coalition of city and regional authorities and private-sector developers. Most significant in this context is a new trade fair center, the Fiera, with more than 5 million square feet of exhibition space, designed by architect Massimiliano Fuksas at a cost of €750 million. Meanwhile, part of the old exhibition complex, closer to the

city center, is being redeveloped into the "CityLife" residential and business district with skyscrapers by architects Daniel Libeskind, Zaha Hadid, and Arata Isozaki. Other culture-led regeneration projects in the city include extensive facilities for the design faculties of the Politecnico di Milano in the former industrial district of Bovisa, and the redevelopment of another derelict industrial district, Bicocca, around the campus of the new University of Milan-Bicocca, a new theater, and space for arts facilities and cultural and creative industries.

Starchitecture

Just as star architects derive some of their standing through the visible presence of their work in major cities, so the image of world cities is derived in part from their association with "starchitects" and "starchitecture." The repeated appearance of a select group of architects right across the world shows how design stardom and city branding become mutually self-reinforcing.

ATLAS OF STARCHITECTURE

1 **New York**, Hearst Tower, *Foster & Partners*

2 **Dallas Perot**, Museum of Nature & Science, *Thom Mayne*

3 **Abu Dhabi**, Zayed National Museum, *Frank Gehry*

4 **Kuala Lumpur**, Petronas Towers, *César Pelli*

5 **Singapore**, Reflections at Keppel Bay, *Daniel Libeskind*

6 **Milan**, Il Dritto, *Arata Isozaki*

7 **Paris**, Tour Carpe Diem, *Robert A.M. Stern*

8 **Nanjing**, Sifang Art Museum, *Steven Holl*

9 **Doha**, Museum of Islamic Art, *I.M. Pei*

10 **Las Vegas**, Vdara Hotel and Spa, *Rafael Viñoly*

11 **London**, The Shard, *Renzo Piano*

12 **Bilbao**, Guggenheim Museum, *Frank Gehry*

13 **Los Angeles**, Walt Disney Concert Hall, *Frank Gehry*

14 **San Francisco**, San Francisco Museum of Modern Art, *Mario Botta*

15 **Beijing**, Galaxy Soho, *Zaha Hadid*

16 **Rio de Janeiro**, Cidade da Musica, *Roberto Marinho & Christian de Portzamparc*

17 **Seoul**, The Blade, *Dominique Perrault*

18 **Berlin**, Reichstag, *Foster & Partners*

19 **Rome**, National Centre of Contemporary Arts, *Zaha Hadid Architects*

20 **Marseilles**, CMA CGM Headquarters, *Zaha Hadid Architects*

21 **Hamburg**, Elbe Philharmonic Concert Hall, *Herzog and de Meuron.* Hamburg Science Centre, *Rem Koolhaas*

22 **Moscow**, Rossiya Tower, *Foster & Partners*

Mobilizing Creativity: Design Districts

Big-city environments are crucibles of creativity. They are forcing houses of cultural innovation and important arenas for the creation of taste. Creative industries themselves can only really flourish, though, in settings where knowledgeable professionals are in close contact with one another, with clients, and with other creative individuals. That is because innovation in creative industries usually results from the combination of a wide range of different types of knowledge. Because various design services and creative-products industries need to engage one another, sharing ideas and resources, they tend to be localized, in distinctive districts. Such districts are reinforced by the sociality and buzz, the dense interpersonal contacts and opportunities for informal information exchange that is important to cultural production.

Zona Tortona design district

Located next to Milan's defunct Naviglio canal and the railway lines that lead to the city's Porta Genova railway terminus, the district known as Zona Tortona, originally dominated by heavy engineering works and cheap housing, has become the world's definitive design district. The commingling of artists, artisans, designers, photographers, actors, students, educators, and writers contributes to a blurring of the social worlds of work and lifestyle that is so important to the social production of knowledge and diffusion of innovation in design and design-related professions.

- Fashion design/retail
- Design, arts, branding
- Interior design
- Events, spaces

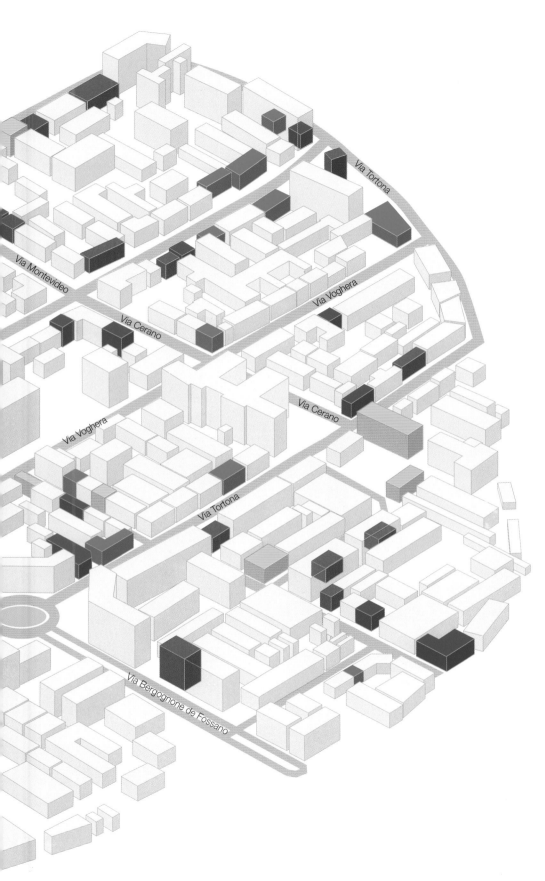

Individuals and small firms involved in art, architecture, graphic design, product design, interior design, lighting, set design, music, fashion, and photography tend to seek lower-cost accommodations in central rather than suburban locations. That means that they gravitate toward older working-class and/or former industrial districts. Their interdependence is facilitated by the emergence of associated agencies and services, and the result is a distinctive cultural quarter. The corollary of this process is the "gentrification" of the neighborhood as more affluent young professionals move in, seeking the character and sociability of the district, and consequently displacing poorer households as rents and property prices escalate.

This is what happened in Milan's Zona Tortona, an inner-city locality that was initially developed in the 19th century as a working-class factory and warehouse district. It prospered for a while after the Second World War as big engineering firms like Ansaldo, General Electric, Osram, and Riva Calzoni clustered around the nearby railyards of Porta Genova. But a classic process of deindustrialization left the district with abandoned factories and decaying housing.

The transformation of Zona Tortona began in the mid-1980s when Italian *Vogue* art director Flavio Lucchini and the photographer Fabrizio Ferri set up Superstudio in a former bicycle factory. Other photographic studios soon appeared and the district promptly attracted young artists, architects, and design consultants. In 1990 the city of Milan purchased the former Ansaldo engineering complex for the Teatro alla Scala's wardrobe and prop storage, workshop, and rehearsal stage. Subsequently, the city commissioned the British architect David Chipperfield to transform the huge complex into a "city of culture" to house a number of major city museum institutions. Galleries, bookshops, trendy restaurants, bars, and cafés followed, along with fashion showrooms, editorial offices, fashion and design schools, a super-chic designer hotel, and exhibition space for sculpture. The status of the district as the world's definitive design district was ensured in 2002 when the former Nestlé factory, remodeled by Japanese architect Tadao Ando, reopened as the corporate headquarters of Giorgio Armani.

Promoting Creativity: Place Marketing

Celebrating and promoting innovation and creativity has been an important aspect of the competitiveness of cities ever since the Industrial Revolution triggered the serial realignment of the world economy. Today, place marketing has become a central task of urban design and planning, while many city governments have adopted intensive city branding campaigns that draw on their image as centers of design and creativity. Many cities have long had

promotional magazines, vehicles for "urban imagineers" who not only propagate a city "brand" but also help to construct and impose sanitized and commodified urban identities.

Some of the earliest examples of the promotion of innovation and creativity were the World Expositions, "spaces of triumph" that were based on the French tradition of national exhibitions. The first World Exposition was held in London in 1851. The original Crystal Palace,

EU Capitals of Culture

Since the mid-1980s the European Union has sponsored urban brand management and the promotion of culture and design to support both regional development and the notion of a common European cultural heritage. Its Capitals of Culture program was conceived in 1983 by Melina Mercouri, then Greek Minister for Culture; Athens was duly appointed the first European Capital of Culture in 1985. Financial support from the EU for these cities amounts to only a few hundred thousand euros in each case, but the real value is in the rebranding and place marketing afforded by EU recognition.

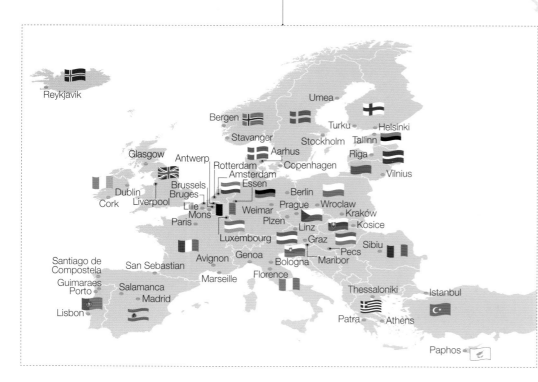

built to house the "Great Exhibition of the Works of Industry of All Nations," was the first spectacular urban megastructure. Understandably, the early Expositions were framed around creativity and innovation in the context of industrialization and modernization; since the 1980s, however, the emphasis has been more on branding and promoting both the host city and the host nation.

Milan has built and consolidated its image as a city of fashion, design, and creativity in various ways. In 1881 it hosted a national exposition, and in 1906 the city hosted a World Exposition that attracted more than 4 million visitors. In 1923 the Triennale was established in Monza as a showcase for modern decorative and industrial arts, with the aim of stimulating relations among the industry and applied arts. It moved to central Milan in 1933 and its subsequent conferences, experimental architectural projects, and international exhibitions of art, architecture, and design provided an important platform for Italian design to become known internationally. In 2015 Milan will host the next World Exposition, an event that has already prompted a great deal of urban regeneration as well as a new platform for city branding. Meanwhile, the success of Milanese fashion and design firms has itself reached the point where their products collectively brand the city, while the city in turn reinforces the brand of the products. In this way, Milan, along with cities like London, Paris, New York, and Los Angeles, has become a global tastemaker, a design object in itself.

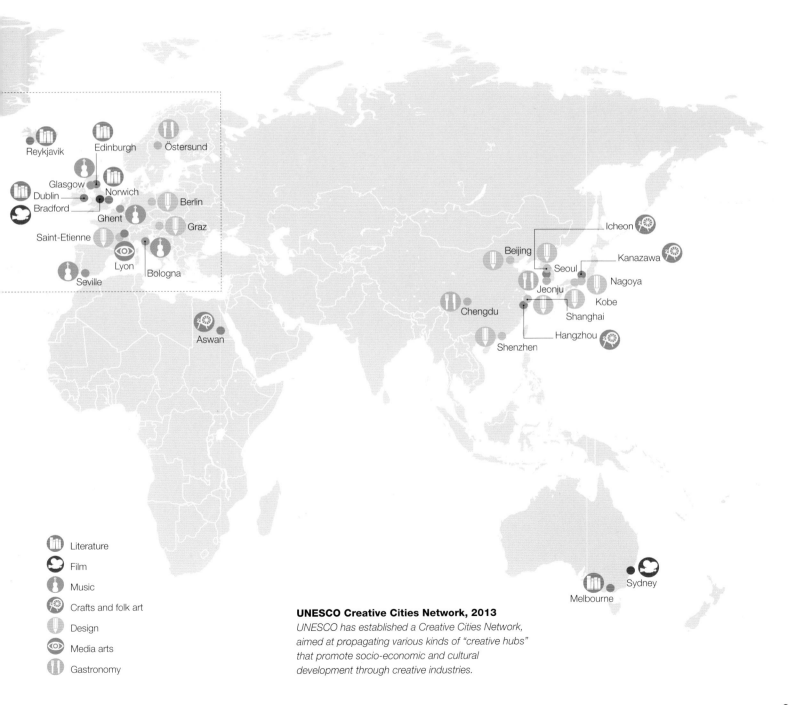

UNESCO Creative Cities Network, 2013
UNESCO has established a Creative Cities Network, aimed at propagating various kinds of "creative hubs" that promote socio-economic and cultural development through creative industries.

The Creative City

205

The Geography of Fashion: Cities as Brand Platforms

Until the 1950s, Paris was unrivaled as *the* city of high fashion. Charles Frederick Worth, an English designer, moved to Paris in 1848 and effectively created the first designer brand, inventing the role of the couturier as arbiter of style and taste. By the early 20th century, thanks largely to the availability of fashion imagery and the introduction of factory-based production, there had developed a democratized international fashion system, with Parisian style as the principal point of reference. But the comparative advantage enjoyed by Paris was severely diminished after the Second World War as a result of the Nazi authorities' attempt to move the entire business of *haute couture* to Berlin and Vienna, and of postwar rationing of materials and the effects of a general drop in personal incomes.

With the subsequent emergence of *prêt-à-porter* designs and the expansion of global consumer markets, fashion became an important feature of global competition among cities, part of broader strategies of metropolitan branding and boosterism. New York and London were the first to benefit from the decline of Paris, whose couturiers suffered from high production costs and persisted in focusing on luxury collections rather than the expanding *prêt-à-porter* market. London emerged, in the

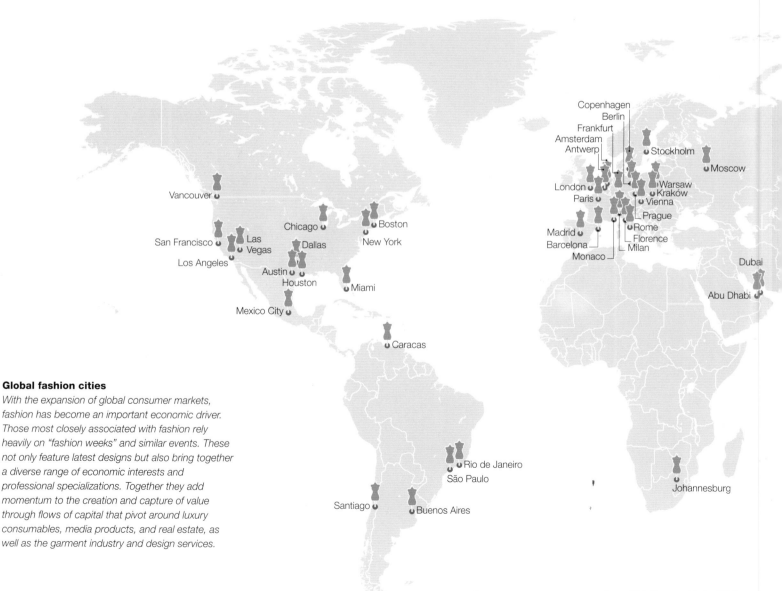

Global fashion cities

With the expansion of global consumer markets, fashion has become an important economic driver. Those most closely associated with fashion rely heavily on "fashion weeks" and similar events. These not only feature latest designs but also bring together a diverse range of economic interests and professional specializations. Together they add momentum to the creation and capture of value through flows of capital that pivot around luxury consumables, media products, and real estate, as well as the garment industry and design services.

Source: Global Language Monitor (2011)

"Swinging Sixties," as a hub of edgy and innovative fashion, while New York emerged as a center of leisurewear and "business casual" design.

Milan took advantage of its tradition of craftsmanship in making high-quality fabrics and millinery, its relatively low costs, and its strong international reputation in furniture and product design. Its status as a fashion city was first announced in the 1970s when it hosted the first catwalk shows, breaking with the suffocating *haute couture* traditionalism of Florence. The meteoric rise of Milanese designers—Giorgio Armani, Stefano Dolce, Gianfranco Ferré, Elio Fiorucci, Domenico Gabbana, Miuccia Prada, and Gianni Versace—and their *prêt-à-porter* brands meant that the city quickly became a magnet for photographers, models, buyers, manufacturers, commercial traders, and journalists.

Today, the city hosts the corporate headquarters of many of the largest international luxury goods and fashion conglomerates. Altogether, Milan has some 12,000 companies involved in fashion production, along with hundreds of showrooms, seventeen educational institutions with a focus on fashion and design, and an extensive fashion press with close connections to the corporate world. Women's and men's Fashion Weeks dominate Milanese commercial life and attract buyers and fashion journalists from all over the world. The fall week for Milano Moda Donna, for example, typically involves around 20,000 trade visitors and 2,000 accredited journalists covering more than 100 runway shows in various settings across the city. Fashion weeks have become critical to reinforcing claims to "world city" status. They structure the global fashion industry's work and production cycles, bringing together fashion designers, fashion retailers and wholesalers, clothing manufacturers, textile makers, event organizers, the fashion media, and other specialized fashion intermediaries. Cities like Milan, Paris, New York, London, and Tokyo thus function as global showcases for fashion. As backdrops to fashion and design, their image and the brands of their principal fashion corporations are closely intertwined.

Seoul
Tokyo
Shanghai
New Delhi
Hong Kong
Mumbai
Bangkok
Singapore
Bali
Sydney
Melbourne

● Fashion houses
○ Design schools
● Fashion agencies

Fashion industry in Milan
Milan has self-consciously recast its economy and remade its image through a strategic alliance between the city's administration and the fashion and design industries. The process began in the 1970s, with Milan making its public spaces, from La Scala to the Triennale to the Stock Exchange and the Central Station, available for the fashion shows of up-and-coming Milanese designers. Subsequently, the city has attracted a significant concentration of fashion houses, educational institutions with strong concentrations on fashion and design, and photographic and fashion agencies.

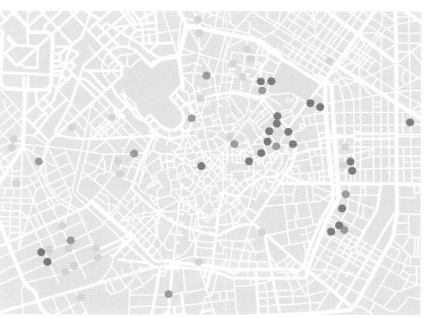

The Infrastructure of Consumption

Cities are settings for consumption as well as production. With the emergence of a new middle class in the 19th century, cities developed a new infrastructure for consumption. The *passages couverts* of Paris and the arcades and gallerias of Brussels, Milan, London, and Naples were the precursors of modern upscale shopping malls. As mass consumption became a central driver of Western economies, every large city developed a downtown retail district, while smaller towns developed high streets and main streets dominated by retailing.

In the largest cities of the world there emerged exclusive shopping districts that cater for a national and international clientele. In Paris, for example, the triangle of luxury stores between the Avenue des Champs-Élysées, the Avenue Montaigne, and Avenue George V in the 8th *arrondissement* has been called a *griffe spaciale*—a "griffe," in the language of fashion, being the designer label affixed to a branded luxury product.

VIA MANZONI
Seventy
Simonetta
Martinelli
7 for all mankind
Partizia Pepe
Twin Set
Paul Smith
Driade
Pal Zileri
Scappino
Radaelli
Inghirama
Alessi
Bijoux de Paris

VERRI VIA S. ANDREA
Vannucci
Baldinini
Canali
Tom Ford
Tumi
Berluti
Il Gufo
Espresso

SAN PIETRO ALL'ORTO
Hermès
Miu Miu
Barbara Bui
Roger Vivier
Gianfranco Ferre
Antonio Fusco
Church's
Armani Casa
Trussardi
Ludicious
Eres
Guido Pasquali
Jimmy Choo
Casadei

GALLERIA VITTORIO EMANUELE
Ruggieri Man
Grimoldi
Currado
Mejana
Piumelli
Church's
Gucci
Zadi
Louis Vuitton
Ricordi
Oxus
Vigano
Dutti
Rizzoli
Fans shop
Luisa Spagnoli
Leo-Pizzo
Prada
Tod's
Swarovski
Bernasconi
Mercedes Benz
Stefanel
Nara
Cadei

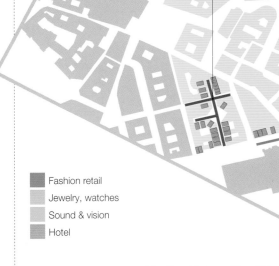

- Fashion retail
- Jewelry, watches
- Sound & vision
- Hotel

The *Quadrilatero d'Oro*, Milan

In the 1980s, retail districts in larger cities developed into "brandscapes" dominated by specialized luxury fashion stores like Cerruti, Coach, Fendi, Ferragamo, Furla, Marc Jacobs, Missoni, Moschino, Prada, and Valentino, supported by expensive restaurants, cafés, art galleries, and antique shops. It was a direct consequence of the affluence of the upper-middle classes, bolstered by the credit industry, by booming financial markets, and by the escalating salaries of the new economy.

Milan, self-consciously establishing itself as a global capital of fashion and design, took advantage of the trend toward competitive and conspicuous consumption to market itself as a destination for luxury shopping. The signature styles of Milanese fashion and design—Modernist-flavored elegance and luxury on the one hand and the ostentatious bling of Versace on the other—were ideally suited to the "dream economy" of the 1980s and 1990s. High-end fashion stores populate the city's principal downtown area around the Galleria Vittorio Emanuele II and Corso Vittorio Emanuele II, while the importance of luxury fashion to the city is reflected by billboards on every available surface, from the gable ends of city blocks to the interior spaces of the city's railway stations and airports. Even the Duomo has sported huge fashion billboards (including, notoriously, an advertisement featuring Madonna as the face of the Swedish fashion firm H&M) on scaffolding during repair and restoration work.

The *Quadrilatero d'Oro*

The growth of luxury fashion retailing has been reflected in the city's branded fashion retail district, the Quadrilatero d'Oro, located a few blocks away from the Duomo and the Galleria. The Quadrilatero, formerly a district dominated by antique dealers, now contains several hundred upscale fashion outlets, many of them unwelcoming and exclusive. Many of the fashion boutiques are divided into two sections: a first floor showroom to attract tourists and window shoppers, and discreet private showrooms upstairs or to the rear, catering to an exclusive cadre of high-spending consumers drawn from around the world. Embedded among the stores and showrooms are several five-star hotels, including the Four Seasons Hotel, occupying a renovated 14th-century monastery. More ostentatious is the Grand Hotel et de Milan just across from the Armani megastore and hotel complex: 8,000 square feet of Armani retailing, including Armani Casa furniture and accessories, an Emporio Café and a branch of New York's Nobu sushi bar, with the five-star Armani hotel grafted on to the top floors.

VERRI VIA S.ANDREA

Hermès	Ludicious
Miu Miu	Eres
Barbara Bui	Guido Pasquali
Roger Vivier	Jimmy Choo
Gianfranco Ferre	Casadei
Antonio Fusco	Fendi
Church's	M. Kors
Armani Casa	Moschino
Trussardi	Chanel
	Iris
	Ballantyne
	Banner
	Cesare Paciotti
	Doriani
	Missoni
	House
	Miki

VIA DELLA SPIGA

Douglas	Mega Fashion
Harmont & Blaine	Nilufar
Byblos	Cuccinelli
Colombo	Blumarine
Piquadro	Moschino
Roccobarocco	Dolce & Gabbana
Sette Carmice	Tod's Man
Rucoline	Tod's Woman
Lanvin	Sport Max
Daad	Prada
Rocca	Colombo
Tiffany & Co	Gio Moretti Baby
Franck Muller	Malo
Rivolta	Monyclear
Fay	Gilli
B. Cucinelli	Stuart Weitzman
Miu Miu	Car Shoe
Chopard	Chimento
Gherardini	Falconeri
Pasquale Bruni	

VIA MONTENAPOLEONE

Cusi	Frette	Valentino Woman
Galasso	A.Testoni	A. Ferretti
Bucellati	Agnona	Drumohr
Jacente Piombo	Larusmiani	Cartier
Hogan	Gucci	Paul & Shark
Tosca Blu	Pederzani	Emilio Pucci
Omega	Paul & Shark	Swatch
Toy Watch	La Perla	Dior Man
Celine	Ferragamo	Dior Woman
Miss Sixty	Dior	Iceberg
Yves Saint Laurent	Mantellassi	Damiani
Mont Blanc	Bottega Veneta	Prada
Loro Piana	Etro	Ars Rosa
Vertu	Nara Camice	Fedeli
Sergio Rossi	F.lli	Bally
Vierre	Rossetti	Sabbadini
Zegnaman	Bruno Magli	Seia-Montenap
Fabi	Corneliani	Camper
Faraone	Geox	Cielo
Aspesi	Rolex	Prada Man
Versace	Zanotti Giuseppe	Audemas Piguet
Venini	Design	Ralph Lauren
G. Lorenzi	Vetrerie di Empoli	Armani
Paul & Shark	Ferragamo Man	Louis Vuitton
Baldinini	Valentino Man	Bulgari
		Boss

CORSO VENEZIA

Allegri
Dolce & Gabbana
Uomo
Burberry Brit
Henry Cottons
D & G
Celestani
Cos
Prada U/D
Pirelli
Zara Home

CORSO VITTORIO EMANUELE

Pollini	Boggi
Solaris	Moreschi
Jdc	Intimissimi
H&M	Camicissima
Celio	Morellato
Terranova	Varpisa
Tezenis	Alcott
Furla	Nara
Marella	Yamamay
Golden Point	Motivi
Penny Black	Vergelio
Max & Co.	Bershka
Benetton	Sephora
Pica	Replay
Calzedonia	Mango
Zara	Banana Republic
Mc Kenzy	Gap
Marilena	Foot-Locker
Gobbi	Liu Jo
Swatch	Marina Rinaldi
Geox	Luisa Spagnoli
Dutti	Oysho
Diesel	Stroili Oro
Bagatt	Nadine
Phard	Sisley

THE GREEN CITY

HEIKE MAYER

Core city
FREIBURG _____

Secondary cities
STOCKHOLM _____
PORTLAND _____
CURITIBA _____
MASDAR CITY _____
GÜSSING _____
WILDPOLDSRIED _____

Left: Freiburg, Germany

The Green City: Introduction

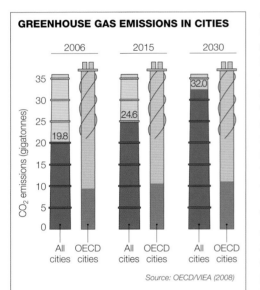

GREENHOUSE GAS EMISSIONS IN CITIES

CO₂ emissions (gigatonnes)

2006: All cities 19.8
2015: All cities 24.6
2030: All cities 32.0

All cities / OECD cities

Source: OECD/VIEA (2008)

Global greenhouse gas emissions have dramatically increased since the early 1970s, driven by economic growth and resulting energy use in developing countries. Producing electricity and heat for residential and commercial buildings is one of the main contributors to greenhouse gas emissions. Many green cities aim to reduce heat loss through energy-efficient building standards, but also through alternative ways of producing heat. Another main contributor to greenhouse gas emissions is transportation. Efforts to reduce emissions from transportation include the promotion of public transport, cycling, and walking.

> **"Green cities are places where people are working toward a more resilient urban environment."**

Cities are at the forefront of efforts related to ecological conservation and sustainability. Over the past decades, both large and small cities have followed the goal of transforming themselves into green cities. Such cities are places in which politicians, urban planners, and citizens are working toward developing more resilient infrastructures, institutions, and behaviors to help them face the problems associated with climate change.

Why should cities be at the forefront of fighting climate change? Cities occupy only about 2 percent of the world's landmass, but they consume 80 percent of global energy and produce 75 percent of global greenhouse gas emissions. In terms of climate change impacts, cities leave a large footprint. However, even though cities are part of the problem, urban leaders and politicians are increasingly becoming aware that they can be integral to solving issues related to climate change. Cities might indeed be in a better position to address climate change than, for example, national governments. City governments are generally more nimble than national authorities and can react more quickly to opportunities and threats that their population might be facing. Because cities are dense and compact, innovative technologies to improve mobility or produce more sustainable energy can be implemented more quickly. Urban residents can be mobilized to adopt new behaviors and more sustainable lifestyles. In sum, cities are complex systems and their social and physical infrastructures provide opportunities to create integrated solutions that help adapt to climate change. Scholars and policymakers agree that local action is critical to solve the negative effects of climate change.

New York/Newark
Virginia Beach
New Orleans
Miami

Cities in danger

Climate change is threatening the world's urban population in particular. According to the Intergovernmental Panel on Climate Change, average global temperatures rose by 1.3 degrees Fahrenheit (0.74 degrees Celsius) between 1906 and 2005. The global mean surface temperature has increased at a more alarming rate over the past two decades, by 0.6 degrees Fahrenheit (0.33 degrees Celsius) since 1990. As a result of these temperature changes, sea levels have risen by 6.7 inches. These changes lead to higher climate variability and extreme weather events. As urbanization increases, more and more cities will experience climatic changes such as more frequent hot days and nights, heavier precipitation, severe droughts, dangerous floods, and rising sea levels. Such extreme weather events will affect the social and physical infrastructure of cities. Hurricanes like Sandy, which swept over New York City in late October 2012, not only damage transportation systems and electricity supply,

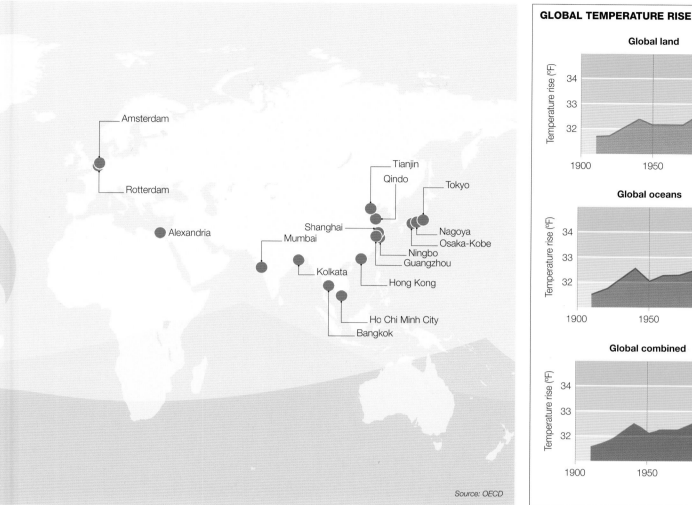

Source: OECD

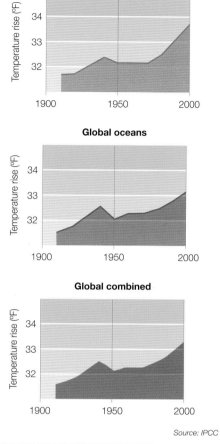

GLOBAL TEMPERATURE RISE

Source: IPCC

---

but also severely disrupt local economies and people's livelihoods. Cities like New York, which are located in low-elevation coastal zones, will be most vulnerable to climate change effects. Megacities with a total population of more than 10 million will be affected in particular. For example, the cities that will be most exposed to coastal flooding by 2070 are expected to be Kolkata, Dhaka, Guangzhou, Ho Chi Minh City, Shanghai, Bangkok, Rangoon, Miami, and Hai Phong. With the exception of Miami, all of these cities are located in developing countries in Asia and many of them account for a very large population.

Cities contribute in significant ways to greenhouse gas emissions, which are responsible for climate change. Greenhouse gases are produced in cities primarily through the consumption of fossil fuels. Energy used for electricity generation, transportation, industrial production, and buildings is the main source of greenhouse gases in urban areas. The levels of greenhouse gas emissions a city produces vary depending, among other things, on its

population density, but also on the efforts it has made toward more sustainable ways of producing and consuming energy.

Meeting the challenge

Many cities are mobilizing against climate change. In the absence of federal action, more than 1,054 mayors in the United States have signed an agreement that commits their cities to meet and exceed the greenhouse gas emission targets set in the Kyoto protocol. Large and small cities have joined this movement and are urging higher levels of government to pass legislation to support their local action. In Europe, the Sustainable Cities and Towns Campaign has been urging the implementation of the Aalborg Charter since 1994. The Charter calls for the development and implementation of local sustainability programs, the Local Agenda 21 process. More than 2,500 local and regional governments from thirty-nine countries have committed to the Charter. Since 2005, the C40 network has convened the world's megacities, which are committed to reduce greenhouse gas

Global warming will impact cities

Cities will experience the effects of climate change primarily through changes to the average weather or increased weather variability. Between 1906 and 2005 average global temperatures have risen by 1.3°F (0.74°C). Global ocean temperatures have also risen. The Intergovernmental Panel on Climate Change (IPCC) states that rising temperatures are most likely associated with the increase in greenhouse gases produced by humans.

emissions. These examples show that many large and small cities are committed to a greener future.

What does it take to become a green city? Leadership from politicians and policymakers is instrumental. Planning and policies in support of sustainable ways of life are critical. Changes in urban lifestyle and behavior and alternative ways of developing a city economy are needed. There are several examples that lead the way. Freiburg is a pioneer in the green city movement. So are Portland and Curitiba. These and many others are presented in this chapter.

Green Visions and Sustainable Planning

Freiburg is a picturesque city of about 220,000 residents in the south of Germany. It is not only a green city because of its location near the Black Forest, but also because city leaders and politicians have followed an ambitious goal of turning the city into one of the most sustainable places in the world. Freiburg has gained international recognition for the implementation of sustainable urban development concepts. In order to reach the goal of reducing carbon emissions by 40 percent by the year 2030, the city employs a unique mixture of environmental, economic, and social policies.

Freiburg's efforts to develop as a green city go back to the postwar era. City planners decided to rebuild the destroyed city center following its traditional medieval pattern. Contrary to many other German cities, Freiburg consciously avoided more Modernist redevelopment paradigms that would have given priority to automobiles. Instead it retained its charming character of narrow streets and alleys. An active environmental movement began to form in the mid-1970s as a response to plans to build a nuclear power plant in a small community nearby. By the 1980s Freiburg was one of the first cities to establish an environmental protection agency and the city pledged to support solar energy after the Chernobyl nuclear power plant disaster in 1986. In 1996

Conventional housing development

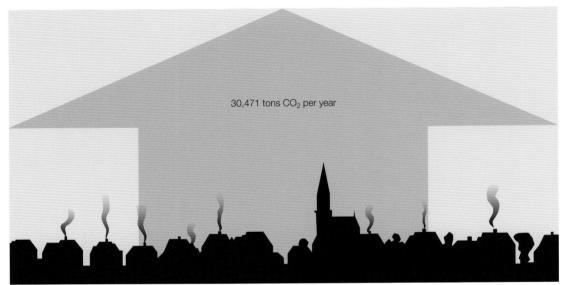

30,471 tons CO_2 per year

Rieselfeld district

Rieselfeld is a new urban district in Freiburg. The neighborhood was planned and built according to strict ecological standards and regulations. This graphic illustrates measures designed to reduce CO_2 emissions in Rieselfeld and compares them to a conventional housing development. Through the use of greater density, low-energy housing standards, combined heating and power systems, energy conservation measures, and improved public transit, it is possible to reduce carbon emissions by more than 50 percent.

Rieselfeld development

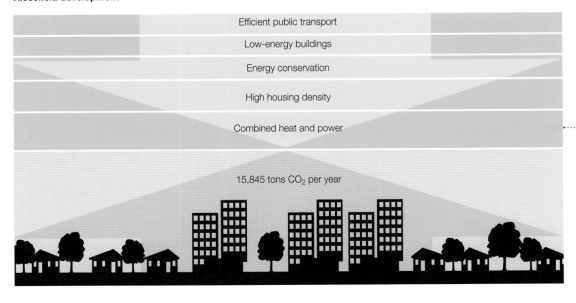

Efficient public transport

Low-energy buildings

Energy conservation

High housing density

Combined heat and power

15,845 tons CO_2 per year

Source: City of Freiburg

Freiburg's city council passed a climate protection resolution that called for the reduction of carbon emissions by 25 percent by the year 2010. By 2009 the city had reduced its emissions by 18 percent. Even though the reductions were respectable, they fell short of the goals set out more than ten years earlier. However, city leaders and politicians did not give up, and instead they set themselves an even higher goal; Freiburg is aiming for a reduction in emissions of 40 percent by 2030.

Freiburg has followed its green vision with rigorous urban planning and environmental protection strategies. Traffic and transportation policies encourage environmentally friendly mobility such as walking, cycling, or public transport. The city's energy policy encourages the use of renewable resources such as solar, wind, or biomass and sets standards for the use of energy in housing developments. As a result of its proactive support of solar energy, Freiburg is home to many businesses operating in environmental industries such as photovoltaic. Due to strong growth and resulting pressures on the housing market, Freiburg has developed two new neighborhoods that follow strict ecological standards. Rieselfeld, a new 170-acre (70-hectare) large urban district for 10,000 to 12,000 residents, is easily accessible by public transport and the houses are built to low-energy standards using photovoltaic and solar thermal technology. The nearby district of Vauban is home to 5,000 residents, many of them car-free, and planning regulations also prescribe low-energy construction methods. Developing such ecologically sensitive neighborhoods is central to turning a green city vision into a success, and Freiburg's track record illustrates that it works: Rieselfeld's housing, for example, emits 20 percent less carbon dioxide than conventional housing developments in Germany.

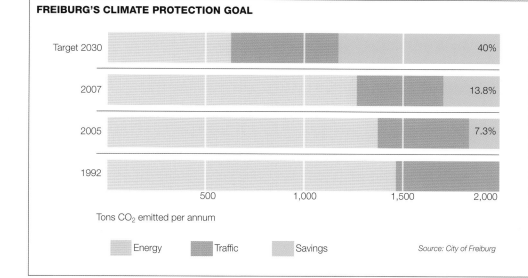

FREIBURG'S CLIMATE PROTECTION GOAL

Target 2030	40%
2007	13.8%
2005	7.3%
1992	

500   1,000   1,500   2,000

Tons CO_2 emitted per annum

Energy   Traffic   Savings

Source: City of Freiburg

Freiburg's goal is to reduce carbon emissions by 40 percent by 2030. From 1992 to 2005 the city reduced its carbon emissions by 7.3 percent. The reductions doubled to almost 14 percent by 2007. Most savings have come from shifting to renewable energy sources, the promotion of energy conservation, and stricter energy-efficiency standards for buildings. The city also introduced a program called CO_2-Diet with which residents can calculate their own carbon footprint and receive hints on how to reduce it.

Efficient public transport   **Environmental mobility**   **High-density housing**   **Low-energy housing**   **Renewable resources**

Sustainable Design and Transportation

Green cities like Freiburg pay a lot of attention to the ways in which the built environment facilitates sustainable development. How a city's built environment is arranged and how buildings use and save energy are important components of sustainable architecture in green cities. The use of alternative transportation modes such as walking, cycling, or public transport not only changes mobility patterns, but also reduces carbon emissions. In addition, the use of renewable energy makes cities less dependent on imported oil.

Sustainable urban design starts at the scale of the neighborhood. Ecological urban districts like Freiburg's Rieselfeld or Stockholm's Hammerby Sjöstad integrate land use with transportation planning and ensure easy access to public transport. Their compact urban design focuses on mixing different kinds of uses. These neighborhoods also incorporate public green spaces, which often link nearby conservation areas with smaller green spaces interspersed throughout the urban fabric. Such dense and ecologically smart neighborhoods are not only attractive to residents, they also provide living spaces for plants and animals.

Green urban design

There are multiple ways of designing and building more sustainable houses. Rainwater can be collected on the roof and used to water plants or wash cars. Solar technology can be used to heat water. Small wind turbines set on the roof may generate electricity. Insulated glass helps reduce the loss of heat, and energy-efficient appliances conserve energy use. The higher costs of a green building can be compensated by the power and water savings. An example of green design is Hammerby Sjöstad, a new environmentally friendly urban district in Stockholm. Houses here are built in a dense block pattern and the main axes are designed as public parks that are free of cars. Green building techniques and the use of renewable energy sources help reduce the carbon footprint of an urban district, since buildings consume a lot of energy.

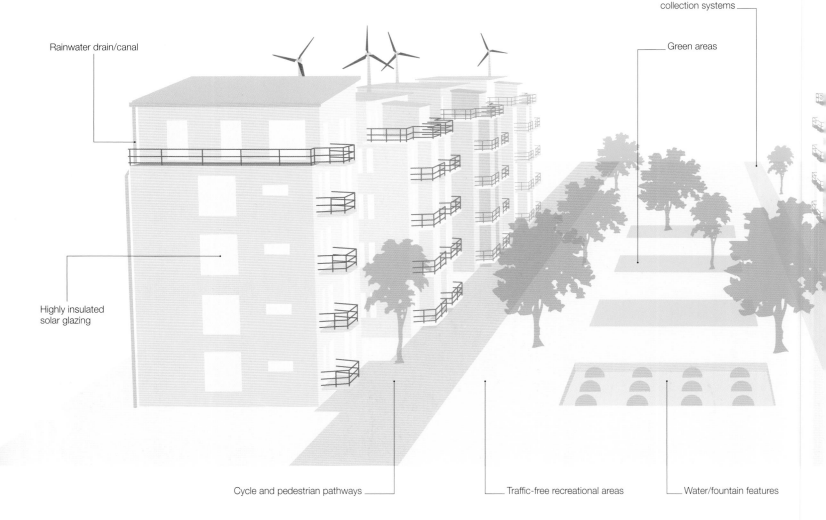

Rainwater drain/canal

Highly insulated solar glazing

Rainwater collection systems

Green areas

Cycle and pedestrian pathways

Traffic-free recreational areas

Water/fountain features

Green cities also pay attention to the ways in which buildings are constructed and how the built environment uses energy. Green architecture uses sustainable materials and eco-friendly products such as wood and stone that are free of chemicals or other contaminants. New building standards ensure energy savings or even energy generation. Freiburg, for example, places a heavy emphasis on the use of solar technology. To reach its goal of reducing carbon emissions, the city supports the use of all kinds of projects that utilize the power of the sun. There are more than 400 photovoltaic installations, water is heated through solar thermal technology, and many houses are built using passive solar design.

While the use of energy in buildings is one important component by which a green city can reduce its carbon footprint, another important element is the way a city manages mobility. Green cities like Freiburg, Stockholm, Copenhagen, Portland, and also those in emerging countries like Curitiba in Brazil, develop a wide variety of alternative transportation opportunities ranging from "slow transport" like walking or cycling to the use of different forms of public transport like buses, light rail, or streetcars.

Green cities are pioneering the use of renewable energies like sun, wood, and water. Often they implement integrated and decentralized solutions. In Stockholm's Hammerby Sjöstad district, for example, heat is extracted from wastewater, and in the small town of Waldkirch near Freiburg, small decentralized woodchip heating systems produce heat not only for a high school but also for an entire neighborhood.

Wind turbines on roof tops

Solar panel roofing

Highly insulated walls

Share of trips by public transport, cycling, and walking in Freiburg

	Vehicles	Vehicles shared	Public transport	Pedestrians	Cycles
1982	29%	9%	11%	35%	15%
1999	26%	6%	18%	23%	27%
2020 projected	24%	5%	20%	24%	27%

Vehicles · Vehicles shared · Public transport · Pedestrians · Cycles

Source: City of Freiburg

Alternative transportation

Green cities like Freiburg are working toward shifting transportation from individualized motor vehicles to alternative forms such as public transport, cycling, or walking. Even though Freiburg has grown over the past thirty years and the mobility of its citizens has increased in general, the city was able to increase the use of alternative transportation between 1982 and 1999. Key to this shift is the integration of land use planning with transport planning to create a compact city in which alternative forms of transportation are comfortable and easy to use.

Sustainable Lifestyles

A green city is only as sustainable as its residents' lifestyles. Lifestyles and consumption habits are a critical element in the ways in which humans impact the environment. The European Union Sustainable Lifestyles 2050 project defines the material footprint of a sustainable lifestyle at 8.8 tons (8,000 kg) per annum for one person. This material footprint measures all the resources that a person consumes, such as housing, food, transport, etc. The current average of a European lifestyle ranges from 29.7 to 44 tons (27,000 to 40,000 kg). To achieve the dramatic reduction required to meet the sustainable lifestyle target, consumption habits have to change. There are already some promising trends such as those toward more localized production and consumption and the formation of so-called local resource loops.

Taqwa Community Farm

Discovery Hill School

Urban farms in New York City's Bronx, 2011

Tremont Community Gardens

Garden of Happiness

Garden of Youth

River Garden

C.S. 211 Garden

Rincon Criollo Cultural Center

The Point's Riverside Farm

El Flamboyan Community Garden

Padre Plaza Community Garden

La Finca del Sur

Brook Park

One trend that is emerging in cities is urban gardening, which is sometimes also referred to as urban agriculture. The idea is to use open green spaces in the city for the cultivation of fruit and vegetables. Produce grown in the city can be consumed by those who grow it or sold at local farmers' markets. The argument is that food produced locally is more fresh, often more healthy, and easily available to a wide range of urban residents including those who normally do not have access to good food. Vacant lots in shrinking cities like Detroit and Cleveland have been turned around to grow foodstuffs like lettuce, rhubarb, and potatoes. Detroit is home to the world's largest urban farm. Urban agriculture is one example of how urbanites can create local resource loops in an effort to reduce their material footprint.

Another way to change a lifestyle toward sustainability is to renounce individual car ownership and join a car-sharing program. Car-sharing has gained in popularity since the mid-1990s. Even in the United States, where owning a car is still very important, alternative mobility through car-sharing is growing. Many cities have started local bike-sharing programs, which offer residents, visitors, and tourists the opportunity to rent a bike. Milan, for example, started offering bike-sharing in 2008 and the program now has more than 3,000 bicycles at 173 stations throughout the city. Car- and bike-sharing have one thing in common: they are social innovations that aim at changing local lifestyles and consumption habits.

Car-sharing and urban agriculture are only two ways in which lifestyles are changing. Environmental values and goals are starting to change behaviors in many more ways. Trends like green fashion, carbon-neutral beer, sustainable local foods, and music venues that use solar panels for their power illustrate how green lifestyles are taking hold.

Urban farm key

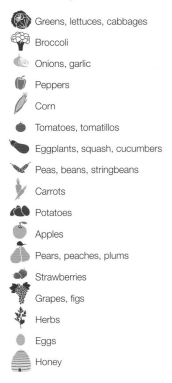

- Greens, lettuces, cabbages
- Broccoli
- Onions, garlic
- Peppers
- Corn
- Tomatoes, tomatillos
- Eggplants, squash, cucumbers
- Peas, beans, stringbeans
- Carrots
- Potatoes
- Apples
- Pears, peaches, plums
- Strawberries
- Grapes, figs
- Herbs
- Eggs
- Honey

Urban farms in New York City's Bronx

Urban farms are emerging in many cities. There are, for example, more than 150 farms and community gardens in New York's Bronx. According to Bronx Green-Up, a program run by the New York Botanical Garden, 80 percent of these sites produce food. Each year, people can visit those farms on an annual tour. As the example of the Bronx shows, New York City's neighborhoods are greening. Brooklyn has about 290 school and community gardens and farms. Manhattan has about 165 such sites. Rooftop vegetable plots and small backyard gardens are also popular.

Car-sharing worldwide

Renouncing individual car ownership and joining a car-sharing program is becoming more and more popular. According to Berkeley's Transportation Sustainability Research Center at the University of California, more than 1.7 million people are members of car-sharing programs worldwide and they share over 43,550 vehicles. North America accounts for the largest proportion of car-sharing members, particularly young people in large cities such as New York City, Washington, D.C., or San Francisco. Programs in Europe generally use fleets of cars located centrally in cities, which can be used flexibly.

CAR-SHARING WORLDWIDE, 2012

Worldwide
Members 1,788,027
Vehicles 43,554
Ratio 41.1 / 1

North America
Members 908,584
Vehicles 15,795
Ratio 57.5 / 1

Europe
Members 691,943
Vehicles 20,464
Ratio 33.8 / 1

Asia
Members 160,500
Vehicles 6,155
Ratio 26.1 / 1

South America
Members 15,000
Vehicles 60
Ratio 25 / 1

Australia
Members 25,500
Vehicles 1,080
Ratio 23.6 / 1

Source: Berkeley Transportation Sustainability Research Center

Toward a Green Economy

Green cities can create economic benefits so that their economies develop in alternative ways. A green economy is defined as low-carbon, resource-efficient, and socially inclusive. Instead of always creating quantitatively more, a green economy puts an emphasis on qualitative economic development that is sustainable.

Through investment in sustainable urban design and infrastructure, green cities can create numerous economic benefits. New industry sectors emerge that develop and produce sustainable technologies. As a result new jobs are created and residents benefit economically. In Freiburg, for example, the green economy consists of about 2,000 businesses that employ nearly 12,000 people. As a result of its proactive solar policies, the solar sector by itself accounts for more than 100 businesses and 2,000 employees, three to four times the national average. Freiburg's green economy benefits from a range of research organizations and universities that develop new technologies.

A similar case is the city of Portland in the United States. As a result of policies in support of sustainable architecture, Portland is home

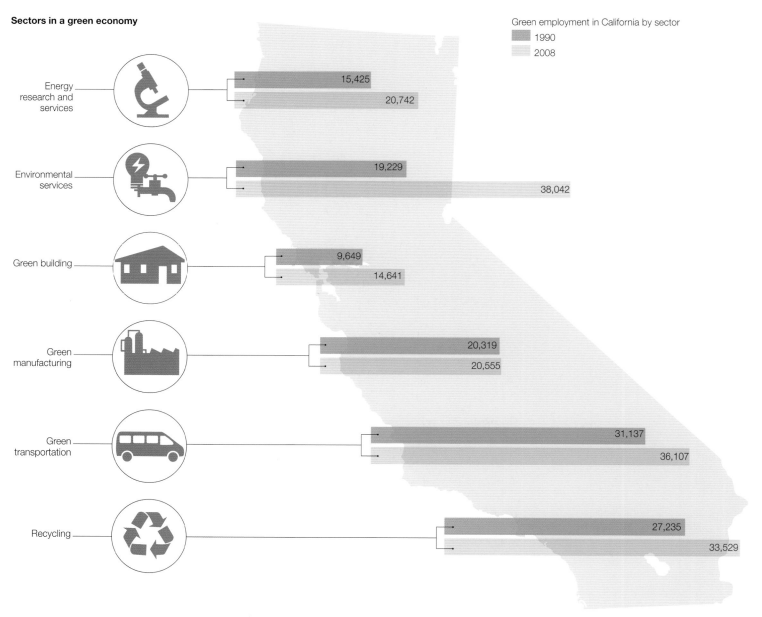

Sectors in a green economy

Green employment in California by sector
- 1990
- 2008

Energy research and services — 15,425 / 20,742

Environmental services — 19,229 / 38,042

Green building — 9,649 / 14,641

Green manufacturing — 20,319 / 20,555

Green transportation — 31,137 / 36,107

Recycling — 27,235 / 33,529

Source: UCB Center for Community Innovation, Berkeley

to a vibrant and growing cluster of firms active in the green building industry. Key to this development was the establishment of a green building technical assistance program which was pioneered by a volunteer citizen group. Today, the Green Building program focuses on technical assistance, financial incentives, education, and policymaking. The program helped create local competitiveness around green building techniques and gave local entrepreneurs a competitive edge.

The green economy not only produces innovations for more sustainable products and services, it also is a significant employment factor. Researchers at the University of California at Berkeley analyzed the size of the green economy and found that there are 163,616 workers employed in this sector. Even though the green economy accounts for a relatively small share of the overall economy of the state of California, it is rapidly growing. In addition, the green economy is concentrated in the largest metropolitan areas such as Los Angeles. In terms of producing innovations for the green economy, traditional high-tech regions like Silicon Valley are turning toward sustainable opportunities.

There are numerous ways to create a green economy. Efforts range from alternative and radical ways to create value such as local currencies to more conventional approaches like planning and building eco-industrial parks. What these efforts have in common is a focus on stimulating demand for environmentally friendly products and services and the creation of ecologically driven innovations.

Sectors in a green economy (left)

Defining the green economy and identifying the industry sectors that are part of such an economy can be very difficult. Both traditional and new industries make up the green economy. New and emerging industries are those that produce environmentally sensitive or low-energy technologies such as photovoltaic or biofuels. Yet traditional industries that are changing the ways in which they manufacture products or deliver services can also be part of this green economy. In addition, industries such as energy and utilities, green building, waste management and recycling, and transportation are key to the transformation of our economy toward a more sustainable future.

Portland's industry clusters with cleantech 2001–07

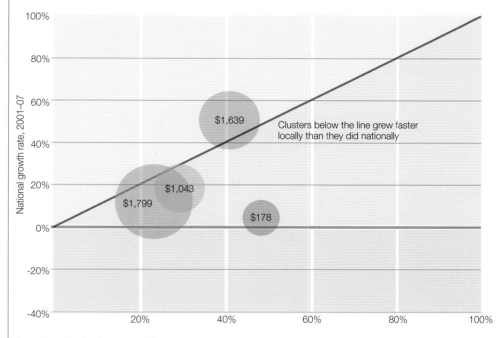

Growth rate Portland, 2001–07. The size of the bubble relates to the value added in 2007

Source: Portland Development Commission

- Advanced manufacturing
- Activewear and outdoor gear
- Cleantech
- Software

Portland's green economy

Portland is the largest city in the state of Oregon and is known for being the location of several well-known companies such as Nike and Intel. These firms are central to industry clusters that specialize in activewear and outdoor gear or advanced manufacturing. In recent years, the city has also become host to a range of firms that belong to the green economy. The city's economic developers call this concentration the cleantech industry cluster. The graphic to the right compares four industry clusters located in Portland. Even though Portland's cleantech industry grew more slowly than the national average, it shows significant value added and has become an important target industry for the city's economic developers.

Green Cities in Emerging Countries

Green cities like Freiburg or Portland are in industrialized countries. The challenge, however, will be to develop sustainable green cities in emerging countries where there are pressures from urbanization as well as challenges arising from high levels of poverty, limitations in terms of urban governance, and a scarcity of resources to implement green ideas. There are, however, numerous examples of how cities in developing countries are turning toward more sustainable development.

Curitiba bus system

Curitiba is known for its innovative bus rapid transit system, the Rede Integrada de Transporte, implemented in 1974. More than 1.3 million passengers a day utilize the system, which offers comfortable, cheap, and fast transportation throughout the city. Unique to the design are the dedicated elevated tubes that form the bus stops which make the buses more accessible to people with disabilities. The buses are long and drive on dedicated lanes, with a wait of as little as ninety seconds between buses. Combined with an easy and cheap fare structure (there is only one fare), the system is efficient and popular with all classes of society.

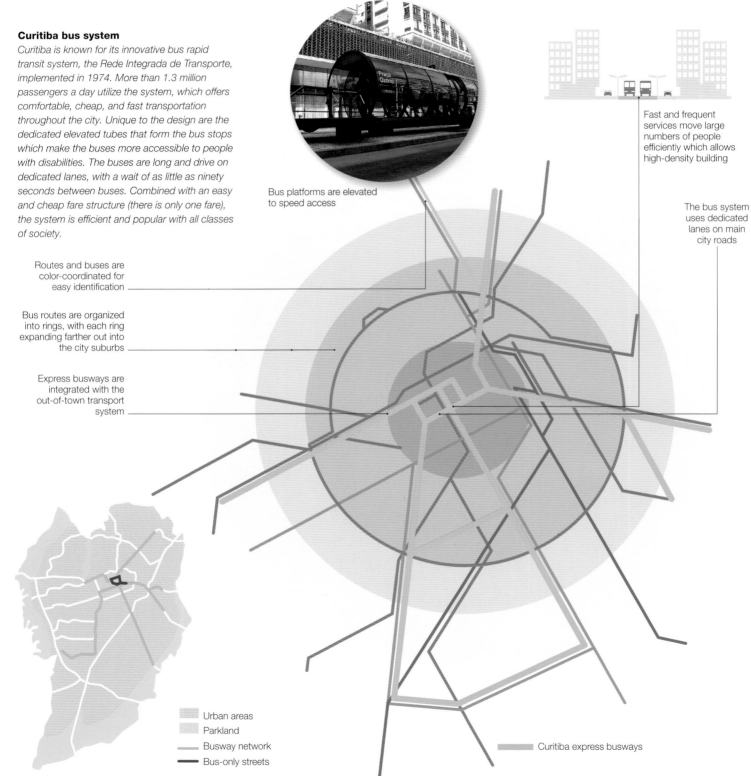

Bus platforms are elevated to speed access

Fast and frequent services move large numbers of people efficiently which allows high-density building

The bus system uses dedicated lanes on main city roads

Routes and buses are color-coordinated for easy identification

Bus routes are organized into rings, with each ring expanding farther out into the city suburbs

Express busways are integrated with the out-of-town transport system

Urban areas
Parkland
Busway network
Bus-only streets

Curitiba express busways

Curitiba in Brazil has won several awards for its transportation system, which is built around a large network of bus rapid transit. Buses run along the regular street network, which minimizes the costs of infrastructure, and stops are built as elevated tubes. Because the bus system is flexible and does not require large-scale fixed investments (compared to rail for example), the costs can be kept at a minimum and fares are low, making it accessible to most residents. The system has inspired many other cities such as Mexico City, Jakarta, and Kuala Lumpur. As a result of introducing the bus rapid transit system, Curitiba successfully shifted mobility from automobile travel to bus travel. Today, the bus system offers about 12,500 trips a day and serves more than 1.3 million passengers. Moreover, the system addresses a social sustainability goal as the residents of Curitiba spend only about 10 percent of their income on travel.

In the Middle East, a promising project aims at building a green city in the middle of the desert from scratch. Abu Dhabi is planning Masdar City, an eco-city for about 47,500 residents. Once it is built, the city promises to use only renewable natural resources (solar power) to produce its energy. The plans call for a desalination facility that is powered by solar energy. The built environment is inspired by the traditional Arab city, which is arranged and built in such a way as to minimize sun exposure. Masdar City has been planned by the English star architect Norman Foster and it is planned to go live by 2025. Critics, however, claim that the building of Masdar City is merely an experiment, and that its character as a gated community does not help in generalizing this kind of green city model.

Developing green cities in emerging and developing countries will be an important challenge in the future. As more people come to live in urban areas in these countries, they will face greater vulnerability as a result of climate change. The international community recognizes that making these cities resilient to environmental risks and dangers is among the most important tasks of the future.

Conventional city vs Masdar CO_2 emission

Conventional city: 1,100,000 tonnes CO_2 per year

- 80% — Conventional design/oil & gas — Building design energy generation
- 13% — Landfill — Waste
- 7% — Fossil fueled — Transport
- Carbon offsetting

- Highly efficient design −56%
- Renewable energy −24%
- Recycled −12%
- Transport −7%
- −1%

Masdar City: carbon neutrality—zero CO_2

Source: www.rpd-mohesr.com

Masdar City

Masdar City is located in Abu Dhabi in the United Arab Emirates. It will be developed as an eco-city by Masdar, a subsidiary of Mubadala Development Company, which is financed mostly by the government of Abu Dhabi. The city will utilize solar energy and the goal is to achieve zero waste. It will host the International Renewable Energy Agency and developers hope that it will become a hub for numerous other green economy players. It will be interesting to see whether the idea of a green city can be implemented in a desert environment.

Masdar City locator

Abu Dhabi — United Arab Emirates — Abu Dhabi — Masdar City

Small Town Sustainability

The greening of a large city has to be addressed at the neighborhood level. How this might work is demonstrated in many small towns across the world. Small towns play an important role in national urban systems. In some countries in Europe, at least half of the population lives in small to medium-sized towns of no more than 50,000 residents. In countries like the United States or China, small towns play an important role as anchors of more peripheral regions. Unlike large cities, which are often integrated into global networks, small towns are struggling to respond to a variety of challenges.

Growing small towns near large urban agglomerations struggle to contain urban sprawl and have to work to retain their identity and heritage. Shrinking small towns are struggling to keep residents and many small town policymakers are working toward creating a viable community with jobs and services for the residents. There are many examples of how small towns are developing strategies to foster a more sustainable and stable economy, to respond to challenges originating from climate change and other environmental problems, and to foster a more equitable society. Many small towns in Italy, Germany, Switzerland, the United States, China, and Korea have joined international networks whose work aims toward

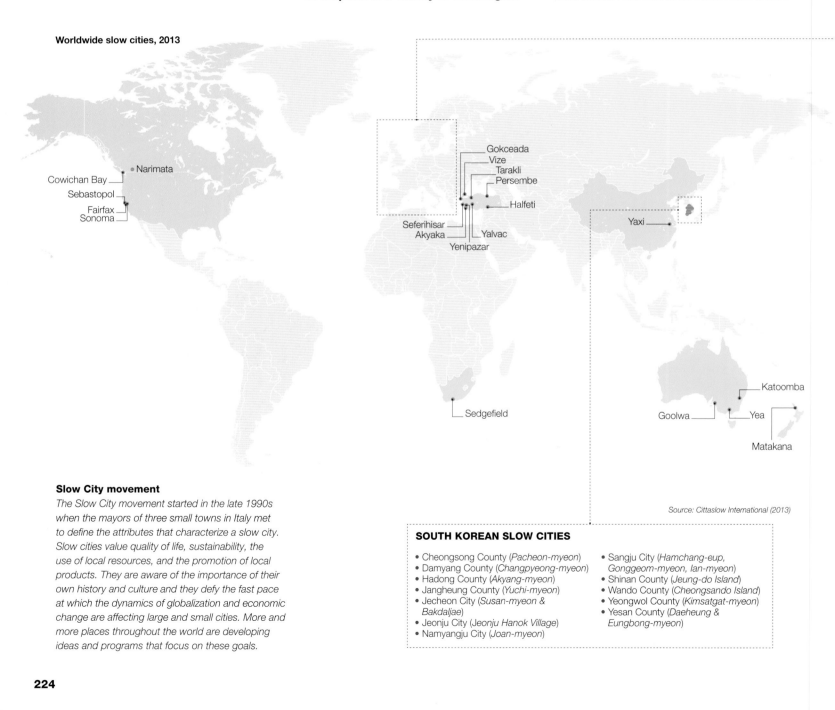

Worldwide slow cities, 2013

Narimata
Cowichan Bay
Sebastopol
Fairfax
Sonoma

Gokceada
Vize
Tarakli
Persembe
Halfeti
Seferihisar
Akyaka
Yalvac
Yenipazar

Yaxi

Katoomba
Goolwa
Yea
Matakana

Sedgefield

Source: Cittaslow International (2013)

Slow City movement

The Slow City movement started in the late 1990s when the mayors of three small towns in Italy met to define the attributes that characterize a slow city. Slow cities value quality of life, sustainability, the use of local resources, and the promotion of local products. They are aware of the importance of their own history and culture and they defy the fast pace at which the dynamics of globalization and economic change are affecting large and small cities. More and more places throughout the world are developing ideas and programs that focus on these goals.

SOUTH KOREAN SLOW CITIES

- Cheongsong County (*Pacheon-myeon*)
- Damyang County (*Changpyeong-myeon*)
- Hadong County (*Akyang-myeon*)
- Jangheung County (*Yuchi-myeon*)
- Jecheon City (*Susan-myeon & Bakdaljae*)
- Jeonju City (*Jeonju Hanok Village*)
- Namyangju City (*Joan-myeon*)

- Sangju City (*Hamchang-eup, Gonggeom-myeon, Ian-myeon*)
- Shinan County (*Jeung-do Island*)
- Wando County (*Cheongsando Island*)
- Yeongwol County (*Kimsatgat-myeon*)
- Yesan County (*Daeheung & Eungbong-myeon*)

sustainable development. Examples of networks include the international Slow City movement, the Eco City movement, the mountain town network, Alliance in the Alps, or the Fairtrade Town movement. Small towns that join these movements commit to specific sustainability goals. Through their affiliation in an international network, they are able to learn from each other and exchange ideas about what works and what does not.

The Slow City movement encompasses small towns no larger than 50,000 residents. More than 166 cities in twenty-five countries have joined the movement, and they are implementing a 54-point charter that outlines efforts to produce a calmer and less polluted environment, conserve local heritage, foster local crafts and cuisine, create more sustainable economies, and foster a less hectic way of life. The Italian town of Orvieto, for example, has created a more sustainable public transport system that uses electric buses. The German town of Waldkirch, which is located near the Black Forest, is known for fostering social programs to support families, youths, immigrants, and unemployed people. The first Chinese slow city, Yaxi, is working toward sustainable tourism. While the Slow City movement benefits from its prominent label, more and more small towns are taking the philosophy seriously and implementing a variety of sustainability initiatives.

Small towns can be pioneers when it comes to developing solutions to sustainability issues. Wildpoldsried in southern Germany only has about 2,500 residents, yet it produces more than 320 percent of the energy it needs. As a result the town's income from feeding the national grid is about 4 million euros. This initiative dates back to 1999 when the town adopted the goal of energy independence. The town supports numerous alternative energy sources such as biogas, windmills, and solar panels. The town uses water as a renewable energy source and has built a parking structure from regionally available wood. Wildpoldsried received the European Energy Award in 2009 for its integrated climate protection efforts.

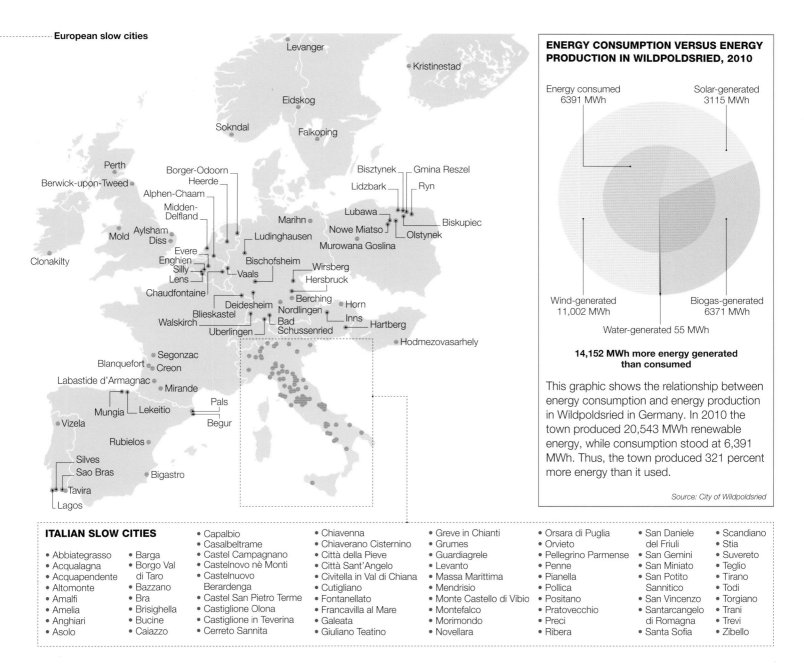

European slow cities

ENERGY CONSUMPTION VERSUS ENERGY PRODUCTION IN WILDPOLDSRIED, 2010

Energy consumed 6391 MWh
Solar-generated 3115 MWh
Wind-generated 11,002 MWh
Biogas-generated 6371 MWh
Water-generated 55 MWh

14,152 MWh more energy generated than consumed

This graphic shows the relationship between energy consumption and energy production in Wildpoldsried in Germany. In 2010 the town produced 20,543 MWh renewable energy, while consumption stood at 6,391 MWh. Thus, the town produced 321 percent more energy than it used.

Source: City of Wildpoldsried

ITALIAN SLOW CITIES

- Abbiategrasso
- Acqualagna
- Acquapendente
- Altomonte
- Amalfi
- Amelia
- Anghiari
- Asolo
- Barga
- Borgo Val di Taro
- Bazzano
- Bra
- Brisighella
- Bucine
- Caiazzo
- Capalbio
- Casalbeltrame
- Castel Campagnano
- Castelnovo nè Monti
- Castelnuovo Berardenga
- Castel San Pietro Terme
- Castiglione Olona
- Castiglione in Teverina
- Cerreto Sannita
- Chiavenna
- Chiaverano Cisternino
- Città della Pieve
- Città Sant'Angelo
- Civitella in Val di Chiana
- Cutigliano
- Fontanellato
- Francavilla al Mare
- Galeata
- Giuliano Teatino
- Greve in Chianti
- Grumes
- Guardiagrele
- Levanto
- Massa Marittima
- Mendrisio
- Monte Castello di Vibio
- Montefalco
- Morimondo
- Novellara
- Orsara di Puglia
- Orvieto
- Pellegrino Parmense
- Penne
- Pianella
- Pollica
- Positano
- Pratovecchio
- Preci
- Ribera
- San Daniele del Friuli
- San Gemini
- San Miniato
- San Potito Sannitico
- San Vincenzo
- Santarcangelo di Romagna
- Santa Sofia
- Scandiano
- Stia
- Suvereto
- Teglio
- Tirano
- Todi
- Torgiano
- Trani
- Trevi
- Zibello

THE INTELLIGENT CITY

KEVIN C. DESOUZA

Core city
LONDON _____

Secondary cities
AMSTERDAM _____
TOKYO _____
NEW YORK _____
SINGAPORE _____
SEOUL _____
SAN FRANCISCO _____
CHICAGO _____
SYDNEY _____
VIENNA _____

Left: London, England

The Intelligent City: Introduction

"Intelligent cities empower their residents with information and resources to improve their own quality of life."

A city, like any organization, thrives or fails depending on its capacity to process signals from its environment. The management of infrastructures, processes, and events within a city has traditionally been inefficient because of an inability to harness data toward real-time decision-making. This has led to significant wastage of resources and squandering of opportunities. Furthermore, until recently most citizens have been passive recipients of programs devised by their elected officials. Urban planners and designers have historically focused on innovating for citizens rather than with citizens, or, better, providing citizens with the resources and capabilities to innovate for themselves.

Today, following advances in communication and computational technologies, cities are harnessing data and information with a view to becoming more "intelligent." The adoption of mobile technologies and the diffusion of Internet connectivity has made information accessible to most individuals, even the poorest of the poor. Cities are embedding a wide assortment of technologies within their physical and social spheres so as to enable real-time processing of data to further the goal of smarter decision-making. In addition, cities are liberating data that was previously withheld from the public. Citizens, in turn, are playing a more active role in shaping the future of their environments. Citizens are not only creating mobile apps that promote smarter ways of conducting various functions, but are also building online platforms so as to source problems and solutions from their fellow dwellers.

Through the gathering and analysis of information, the situational awareness of cities

1. San Francisco
San Francisco implemented its intelligent parking system, SF Park, which allows the city to redistribute the parking demand throughout the city. Web and phone apps allow citizens to locate parking by spot and price. (Intelligent Parking)

2. Chicago
Chicago has deployed "Virtual Shield," one of the world's largest video security deployments. This unified fiber network will deploy a wireless surveillance strategy infrastructure to capture and monitor video for real-time and forensic-related safety applications. (Intelligent Security)

3. New York
New York has entered into numerous partnerships to expand wireless and broadband connectivity in New York City that is free and open to the public to encourage growth and entrepreneurship. (Intelligent Connectivity)

has increased, which allows them to make real-time decisions aimed at furthering the quality of life of their citizens. Consider the case of Amsterdam which, in collaboration with the network computing company Cisco, has deployed an Urban EcoMap. An Internet-based tool, the Urban EcoMap enables citizens to visualize the impact of their activities on their

4. London
London has made public data free and available to citizens through the London Datastore. Much of the data consists of civil service data, updates on traffic congestion and tube operations. (Intelligent Access)

5. Amsterdam
Amsterdam's Utrechtsestraat Climate Street is an initiative to develop Utrechtsestraat, a popular shopping and restaurant street, into an energy-saving and environmentally conscious area with sustainable waste collection, smart meters, tram stops, and street lighting. (Intelligent Streets)

city in terms of carbon emissions. Data is visually displayed at the district level and suggestions are offered toward lowering emissions through conducting activities in a more sustainable manner. Cities such as London use CCTV and sophisticated image- and video-processing technologies to monitor activities within their perimeters. Through sensors on various artifacts from cars to roads and even ID badges carried by citizens, the city can fuse data from various sources to guide real-time decisions. Through the deployment of information technologies such as urban mesh networks, cities enable interconnectivity via wireless Internet connections between devices and individuals. Cities such as Seoul have used wireless mesh networks to monitor critical infrastructure to promote public safety.

6. Seoul
Seoul Metropolitan Government has developed a "Smart Work Center" scheme which allows government employees to work from ten offices located closer to their homes with access to sophisticated groupware and teleconferencing systems. (Intelligent Work)

7. Tokyo
Tokyo is transforming itself into a "smart energy city" that enhances low-carbon capabilities and disaster resistance at the same time through sustainable energy-saving measures that eliminate waste and are easy to implement. (Intelligent Saving)

8. Singapore
Singapore's real-time traffic information in GPS-enabled taxi cabs, integrated public transportation system, and Electronic Road Pricing (ERP) system have advanced transportation in the metro. (Intelligent Transportation)

9. Sydney
Sydney has implemented the "Smart Grid, Smart City" to test a series of smart grid technologies to gather information on the benefits and costs associated with implementing the technology. (Intelligent Metering)

The most common domain in which we see the deployment of technologies to make a city intelligent is "energy," in order to enable judicious decisions about scarce resources. Singapore launched a ten-year $3.2 billion master plan in 2006 to transform itself into an "intelligent nation." Smart metering systems provide real-time information to consumers about their energy consumption and allow customers to modify their behavior. In addition, smart grid systems allow customers to sell unused energy back to the service provider so that it can be re-routed.

Existing cities are on the path toward becoming more intelligent through innovative implementation of technologies. These cities are retrofitting their infrastructures, automating their processes, and even empowering their citizens through information provision. We are also seeing the development of "new" intelligent cities, cities built from scratch with intelligent capabilities. Consider the case of Fujisawa city (about twenty-five miles southwest of Tokyo), a project led by the electronic giant Panasonic. The city will consist of over 1,000 smart houses, each of which has advanced sensor and information technologies to optimize resource consumption and provide residents with real-time information on events in the city. The houses will be built in a sustainable manner, and will use information networks to promote smart use of household appliances to promote energy efficiency.

Intelligent cities are hotbeds for innovation, especially when it comes to designing technologies to address urban challenges. This chapter considers the range of challenges that can be addressed through the use of "intelligent" technologies.

World map of intelligent cities
The intelligent city senses data from objects, actors, and events within and beyond its environment to arrive at actionable knowledge, which is then leveraged for management of its space, its processes and practices, its citizens and organizations, and the present and future. Open data programs exist in many major cities through which data on a wide variety of operations and governance mechanisms are being made widely available, so as to maximize the potential for this information to be deployed in the design, planning, and governance of resources and environments.

Liberating Data

Intelligent cities endeavor to promote smarter living through multifaceted uses of technology. Citizens are active participants in creating innovative solutions for their cities, not only working collaboratively with public agencies, but also creating partnerships with their fellow residents to leverage their creativity, expertise, and insights. To facilitate this, cities are liberating data buried in administrative, urban, infrastructure, and service systems. Opening up data serves to mobilize the creative class toward designing intelligent urban spaces. It provides citizens with the opportunity to

contribute creative technology-based solutions ranging from mobile apps to crowdsourcing platforms.

London has been at the forefront of merging current resources and technology for maximum utility. In 2010 London made government data available to the public by opening the London Datastore. Managed by the Greater London Authority, the London Datastore offers citizens the opportunity to view and use raw data released from city agencies and civil servants. Information distributed includes data on crime, economics, budgeting and resource priorities, and real-time data from transit systems. The wisdom behind offering such powerful

London bike hire app
This is a fast and user-friendly app for the Barclays Cycle Hire scheme in London. Citizens can use the app to locate one of the 400 cycle docking stations in Central London, get cycling directions between bike hire stations, and use maps that are preloaded to the app so as to be accessible without Internet access.

GROSVENOR SQ
11 bikes available
10 empty spaces

AVAILABLE　　　NO DOCKING　　　NO BIKES

informational tools to citizens is twofold: open data sources increase transparency among public officials and also encourage entrepreneurship, which can benefit the city by reducing costs. An important form of entrepreneurship that has resulted from London's open data system has been the development of software applications that can be run on a variety of electronic devices. Matthew Somerville, a web developer, created an online map app of the London underground which received over 250,000 hits in a matter of days. Likewise, Ben Barker, an electronics engineer and cyclist, created a bike map with information pulled from the London Datastore. Apps like these endeavor to provide information in a usable and digestible format for the public.

The city of New York has not only made data on a range of urban services available to the public but has incentivized the creation of mobile applications that make this data usable. The NYC Big Apps competitions (http://nycbigapps.com/) have led to a range of creative solutions such as tools to find parking efficiently within the city, to repurpose vacant property, and to effectively use public transportation. In addition, New York City's mayor, Michael Bloomberg, has a "geek squad" that works to find creative solutions to urban problems by mining city data. NYC's Office of Policy and Strategic Planning houses the "geek squad" which is made up of tech-savvy experts who have strong quantitative and analytical skills. They plow through the vast amounts of data the city collects on a daily basis to make sense of it. Citizens leverage this data to create technologies that advance urban governance. Citizens have created mobile apps to increase public transit ridership, increase awareness of criminal activity in localities, facilitate real-time problem identification and routing for municipalities, optimize trash collection, and reduce inefficiencies and corruption in local government, among others. Through mobile apps citizens can plug directly into a city's fabric and interact with the city in a more meaningful and richer manner as they conduct their daily activities.

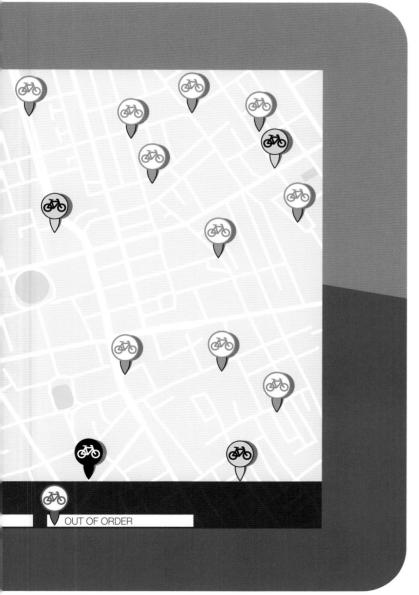

OUT OF ORDER

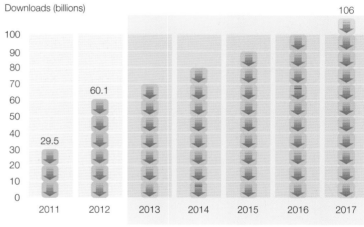

Annual app downloads

Downloads (billions)

106

100
90
80
70
60.1
60
50
40
30 29.5
20
10
0

2011   2012   2013   2014   2015   2016   2017

Projected figures to 2017

Source: Berg Insight

Increasing use of apps

People are increasing the use of apps in their day-to-day lives because of their portability, convenience, and rapid information production. One of the most appealing aspects of apps in terms of intelligent living is the ability to personalize them to fit one's daily needs. This means that sacrifices to live a smart and sustainable lifestyle are easier to coordinate and maintain.

Infrastructure

Smart infrastructure innovations can improve a city's capacity to meet the needs of the public. Examples of smart infrastructure are roads that monitor how congested they are and where accidents are most likely to occur, and that can adjust the recommended traffic speed accordingly; bus systems that can run different-sized buses at different times of day to meet demand changes; and energy grids that have better real-time and predictive features to meet demand. For instance, real-time and predictive parking reduces the frustration of residents and improves the quality of life. Sensors placed in the roadway identify whether a parking place is vacant and drivers can access this information via an app on their smartphone. This opens up the city for many who might otherwise avoid visiting for fear of not finding parking and increases accessibility to local merchants, which can boost the local economy. The reduced occurrence of "circling the block" to find a parking space results in reduced CO_2 emissions, reduced traffic, and fewer vehicle miles.

Smarter infrastructures have embedded information appliances which citizens can employ as they conduct their daily activities. An example of an information appliance that is embedding intelligence within a city is the next-generation telephone booth created by Telecom Italia. The prototype was deployed in

Smart roads

Wireless sensor networks in or near roads can help the maintenance and development of cities' transportation infrastructure. Wireless sensors can monitor the state of road surfaces, air quality in tunnels, and weather conditions for the safety of travelers and economic efficiency.

High-power LED lamps, partially wind powered.

Temperature-reactive road surface displays potentially slippery conditions.

Small, self-contained, high-efficiency wind turbine.

Sensors detect vehicles to activate lighting.

Below-surface induction grid for electric vehicle use.

Marked priority induction lane for electric vehicles.

Turin, just outside the Turin Politecnico. The telephone booth can be used to make traditional phone calls, but it also allows the user to find information about local attractions, shopping, public services, and even social networks. Visitors to Turin do not have to rely on static maps to navigate the city but can use these information kiosks to access dynamic, location-specific, and real-time information.

Financial institutions in Tokyo are developing smarter ATMs that enable customers to conduct transactions using fingerprint authentication rather than a traditional plastic card. Customers can access their finances by placing their hands on a scanner and entering an identifying code such as date of birth or a PIN. The technology matches a combination of three fingerprints with palm-vein data to filter millions of possible identities down to a few thousands in a matter of seconds, after which detailed pattern recognition takes places that relies on parallel processing using multiple servers. Given the fact that Tokyo is subject to natural disasters in which individuals may lose all of their personal belongings or face challenges accessing them, the use of fingerprints offers a more user-friendly and resilient way to access funds.

A critical aspect of designing intelligent infrastructures is the need to promote bottom-up designs and plans that originate from citizens, since urban development affects many aspects of citizens' everyday lives and impacts the lives of future generations. Helsinki chose to invest in a process that encouraged collaboration and idea development for more sustainable and innovative options for the future. In 2009, in collaboration with Sitra's Finnish Innovation Fund, Helsinki launched the Low2No competition, a sustainable development design competition. The competition directed teams to design buildings using four central principles: energy efficiency; low/no carbon emissions; high architectural, spatial, and social value; and sustainable materials and methods. This competition was not an architectural competition or a competition about ideas. It was to find the team that had the best sustainable development plan based on the four central principles to design a large building complex in Jätkäsaari, a precinct of the city.

Predictive parking

Predictive parking systems count open spaces as well as predicting when lots will have free spaces. They use algorithms that combine historical data such as previous parking patterns and current events such as sporting events and concerts.

Sensors in parking bays detect the presence of cars. When no car is present signal is sent to central computer.

With a suitable app, a mobile device will display vacant spaces within predetermined city areas.

Sustainability

Intelligent cities are deploying a range of technology and policy innovations to become more sustainable. Technologies equip individuals and organizations to monitor how their individual actions impact their local environment. Through provision of real-time information, cities are able to encourage citizens and organizations to modify their behavior to reduce their negative impacts on the environment. Policy interventions are focused on modifying the economics of how citizens consume and access resources.

Promoting sustainability through innovative technology is central to Amsterdam's efforts to become an internationally recognized sustainable city by the year 2040. An important initiative targeted a popular and busy street in the city center, Utrechtsestraat. The

Utrechtsestraat Climate Street project was a two-year pilot initiative that featured electrically powered garbage collection vehicles, smart metering, energy display, electric vehicle charge ports, street light dimming at night, and remote access to control electrical equipment in shops so as to reduce the carbon footprint in one of the city's busiest areas. The primary goals of the Utrechtsestraat Climate Street initiative were to create a sustainable environment in the city center, to educate citizens about their energy consumption, and to encourage entrepreneurship and collaboration for greater adoption of sustainable technologies.

As an innovative answer to traditional garbage trucks, electric garbage collection vehicles have a number of benefits in terms of sustainability. They do not pollute or emit CO_2 into the atmosphere, and they have been designed to be energy efficient with special features such as an energy-recovery braking

A smart micro-grid

Smart micro-grids are a sub-element of the smart grid. They locally generate, distribute, and regulate the flow of electricity to consumers. This is done through the use of renewable sources, energy storage, and a distribution system carried out by an intelligent power device that balances the energy load and source. This enables greater reliability, carbon emission reduction, diversification of energy sources, and cost reduction for the community being served.

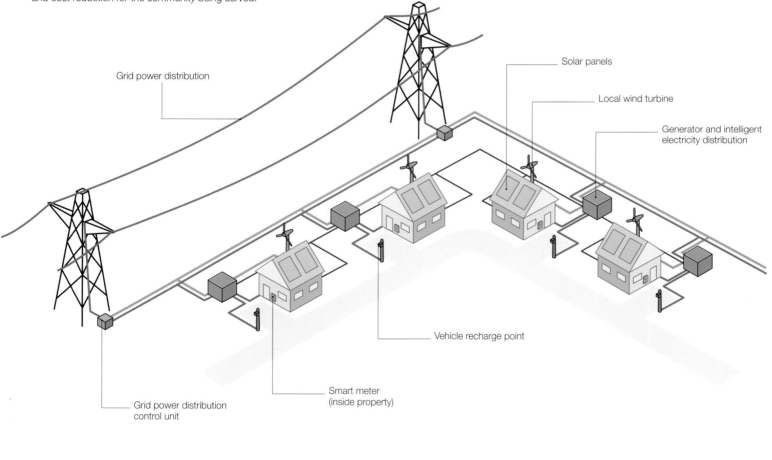

Grid power distribution

Solar panels

Local wind turbine

Generator and intelligent electricity distribution

Vehicle recharge point

Grid power distribution control unit

Smart meter (inside property)

	Power drawn from grid
	Power sent to grid
	Current sharing

system that reduces energy consumption by up to 30 percent, which is significant for continuous "stop and go" garbage truck movements. Electric garbage vehicles are equipped with special cooling systems to help them operate in high temperatures and on tough terrain. They can lift garbage and recycling bins alike and can dump the contents directly into waste compacting machines. All these features lead to less energy being used and a smaller environmental impact. At the end of the pilot scheme in 2011, Amsterdam officials announced that CO_2 emissions had been reduced by 8 percent through energy saving and that a further 10 percent was saved by switching to green energy.

In Australia, Sydney is making strides toward becoming a smart city. In an effort to save power and create a domestic, renewable energy source, the Australian government implemented a commercial-scale smart grid program in Newcastle and Sydney. Smart grids offer consumers and cities the ability to access real-time information about energy usage. This information allows users to modify their behavior regarding the ways in which they consume energy. If smart grid applications were adopted throughout Australia, the government estimates that Australians could cut carbon emissions by 3.5 megatonnes a year. In Newcastle and Scone in New South Wales, sixty homes were chosen to link up in a trial micro-grid. The micro-grid is a self-sufficient network of locally connected energy sources. Each property has a five-kilowatt zinc-bromide battery, about the size of a small refrigerator, installed outside. The micro-grid can draw power from the main electricity network during off-peak periods and store it for use, so that properties in the grid are shielded from power outages and can make independent use of other energy sources such as solar. Keeping with the trend of moving toward energy efficiency, Sydney has become the first city in Australia to use new energy-efficient LED street lights. An eighteen-month trial in various neighborhoods around Sydney suggested that the energy-efficient street lights would reduce emissions and lessen energy usage by 50 percent. As a part of a A\$7 million three-year project, energy companies GE and UGL Ltd. began installing new LED lights on George Street, in front of Sydney Town Hall. This project indicates that small changes can make a big difference when cities are committed to making smarter living choices.

Amsterdam Climate Street, Utrechtsestraat
Innovative technologies such as sustainable street lighting using energy-saving lamps, solar-powered waste bins with built-in garbage compacters, and energy displays providing feedback on energy consumption are just a few ways entrepreneurs and community members on Utrechtsestraat are making strides toward using less energy.

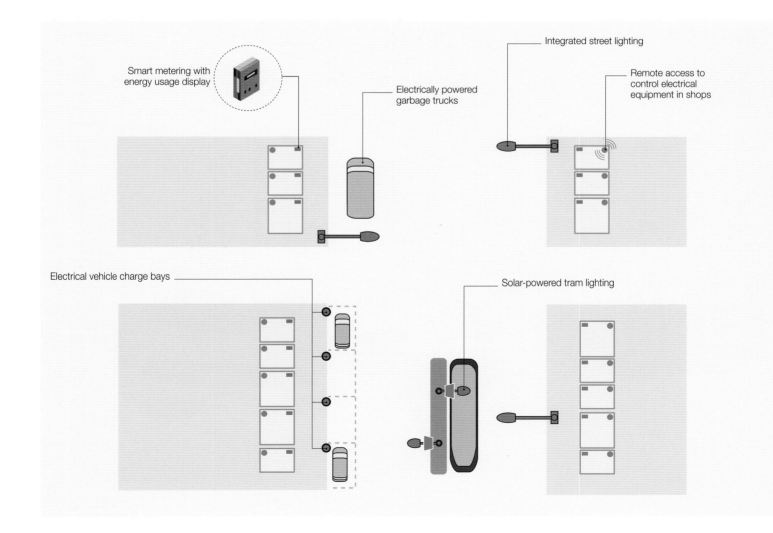

Smart metering with energy usage display

Electrically powered garbage trucks

Integrated street lighting

Remote access to control electrical equipment in shops

Electrical vehicle charge bays

Solar-powered tram lighting

Mobility

Commuting is not a trivial issue. The Texas Transportation Institute estimates that across the USA in 2015 the average commuter will waste $900 in fuel and time due to gridlocks (this is up from $750 in 2010). Fuel burned in gridlocks will amount to 2.5 billion gallons in 2015 (up from 1.9 gallons in 2010). The pressure to address this issue increases when we consider the fact that the number of cars will double worldwide in 2020 from 1 to 2 billion. Moreover, given the fact that, according to the World Health Organization, over 100,000 people per month are killed in traffic accidents across the world and 90 percent of these are due to human error, it is not surprising that we are seeing research and development into driverless cars.

These technologies have benefits beyond the reduction of accidents, including reducing congestion and lowering pollution through more efficient routing. Most major car manufacturers have already developed technologies that get us closer toward driverless vehicles, including adaptive cruise control, lane-keeping systems, self-parking systems, and automated braking based on laser or camera obstacle detection. BMW and Audi, among other car manufacturers, have already tested driverless cars in Europe and the USA. Driverless cars use an assortment of technologies including LIDAR (which measures distance by illuminating a target with laser light and analyzing the reflected light), video cameras, GPS, ultrasonic sensors, radar sensors, vehicle-to-vehicle communication systems, accelerometers, and gyroscopes, among

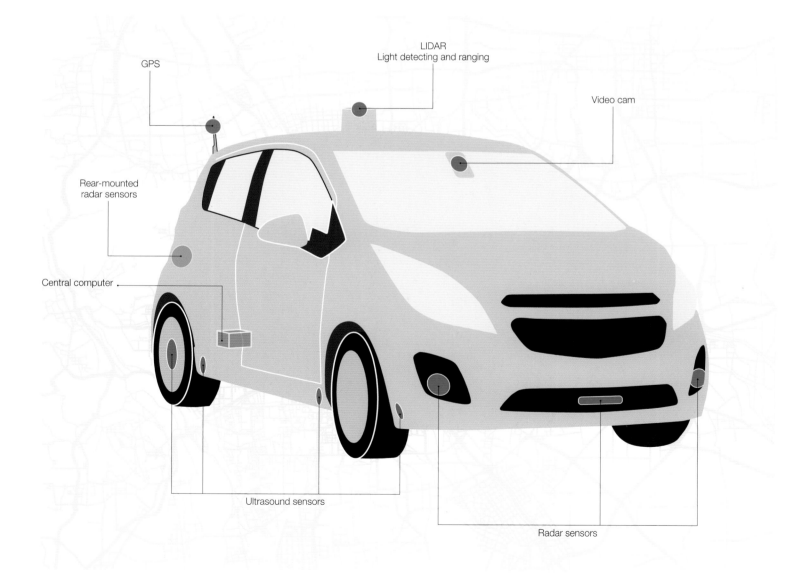

GPS

LIDAR
Light detecting and ranging

Video cam

Rear-mounted
radar sensors

Central computer

Ultrasound sensors

Radar sensors

others. Google is investing in devising software solutions to process information from the multiple sensors on cars to make driverless cars a reality. Key to the development of driverless cars are advances on our current state-of-the-art in image and pattern recognition.

London has a range of measures to address the challenge of mobility for its citizens. The city implemented a congestion charge in 2003 using automated license plate readers to levy a standard charge of £10 ($16) a day on vehicles entering the congestion zone. London's congestion charge encourages less use of private vehicles and fewer CO_2 emissions, and also raises funds for London's public transportation system. The use of private automobiles has fallen to levels last seen in the mid-1980s. In 2003 London introduced a payment system valid for all modes of public

transport in the city using a pre-paid card, the Oyster card, to speed passenger access to trains, trams, and buses. Today, 5.7 million people use an Oyster card weekly and over 80 percent of bus and tube payments are made by Oyster card. In another endeavor to increase accessibility and decrease traffic, London developed the Barclay's Cycle Hire program in 2010. The program allows members and casual users to register online and rent a bicycle and retrieve it twenty-four hours a day/seven days a week. As of April 2013 over 21.2 million cycle hires had been made. During the London 2012 Olympic Games, the program reported 47,105 cycle hires in a single day. The success of the cycle program is an example of an innovative use of technology to respond to the need for improved and more sustainable mobility.

Singapore has used a variety of financial policy tools to discourage its citizens from using automobiles in the city. Citizens have to enter an auction for the right to purchase an automobile. The fees paid for an entitlement certificate range from about $50,000 to $75,000 a year. In addition, the government imposes severe taxes (most of the time over 100 percent) on the sale price of vehicles. Singapore also uses technologies such as electronic road pricing systems to control traffic in the city through differential tolls based on road usage.

Commuter pain index, 2010

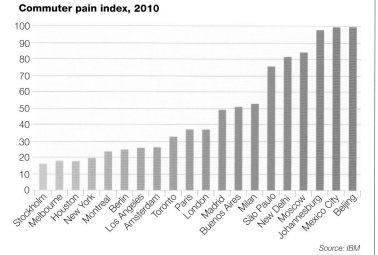

Source: IBM

Driving problems in cities and intelligent solutions

The IBM Global Commuter Pain Survey ranks the emotional and economic toll of commuting in some of the world's most economically important cities on a scale of 1 to 100, 100 being onerous. Although high in some areas, particularly in newly developing cities in the Global South, commuter pain has decreased in some Western cities as they have increased their infrastructure investments in areas such as targeted traffic decongestion and improving public transportation networks.

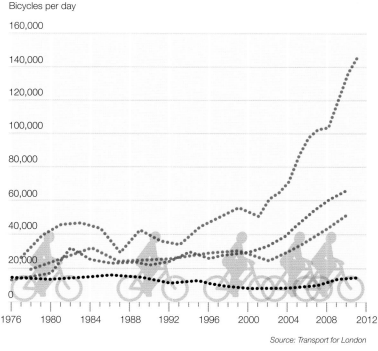

Source: Transport for London

····· Central London
····· Thames screenline (covering all Thames crossing from Runnymede)
····· Inner London
····· Greater London boundary

Cycling boom in London

London has made great strides in improving bike accessibility and bike safety. In addition to the Cycle Hire program, Barclays has sponsored Cycle Superhighways that were developed to connect inner and outer London as well as provide safe cycle zones around urban centers.

Entrepreneurship

Intelligent cities are taking active steps to bring together creative and talented professionals around the development of innovative technologies. This creative class comprises workers in science and engineering, design, education, arts, and entertainment, whose economic function is to generate new creative content. Within a city the creative class plays a vital role in designing the city, organizing activities and events that spur innovation, and promoting an entrepreneurial culture that acts as a catalyst for economic development.

In London, East London Tech City, modeled after Silicon Valley in California, has brought together technology giants such as Cisco, Facebook, Intel, Google, and Vodafone. Situated near the Old Street roundabout, the number of technology-focused startups and established players has grown from about fifteen in 2008 to 200 in 2011. Unique in its beginnings as a government-developed startup, Tech City received a £50 million government investment which contributed to its increasing global technology profile and its recognition as an important international tech hub. Many innovations have sprung from Tech City's development; Cisco's equipment maker, Telecom, created a research center of "smart infrastructure" with Imperial College London and University College London, while Intel created a high-performance computing cluster to offer local firms the opportunity to sample new technologies. Tech City allows companies and

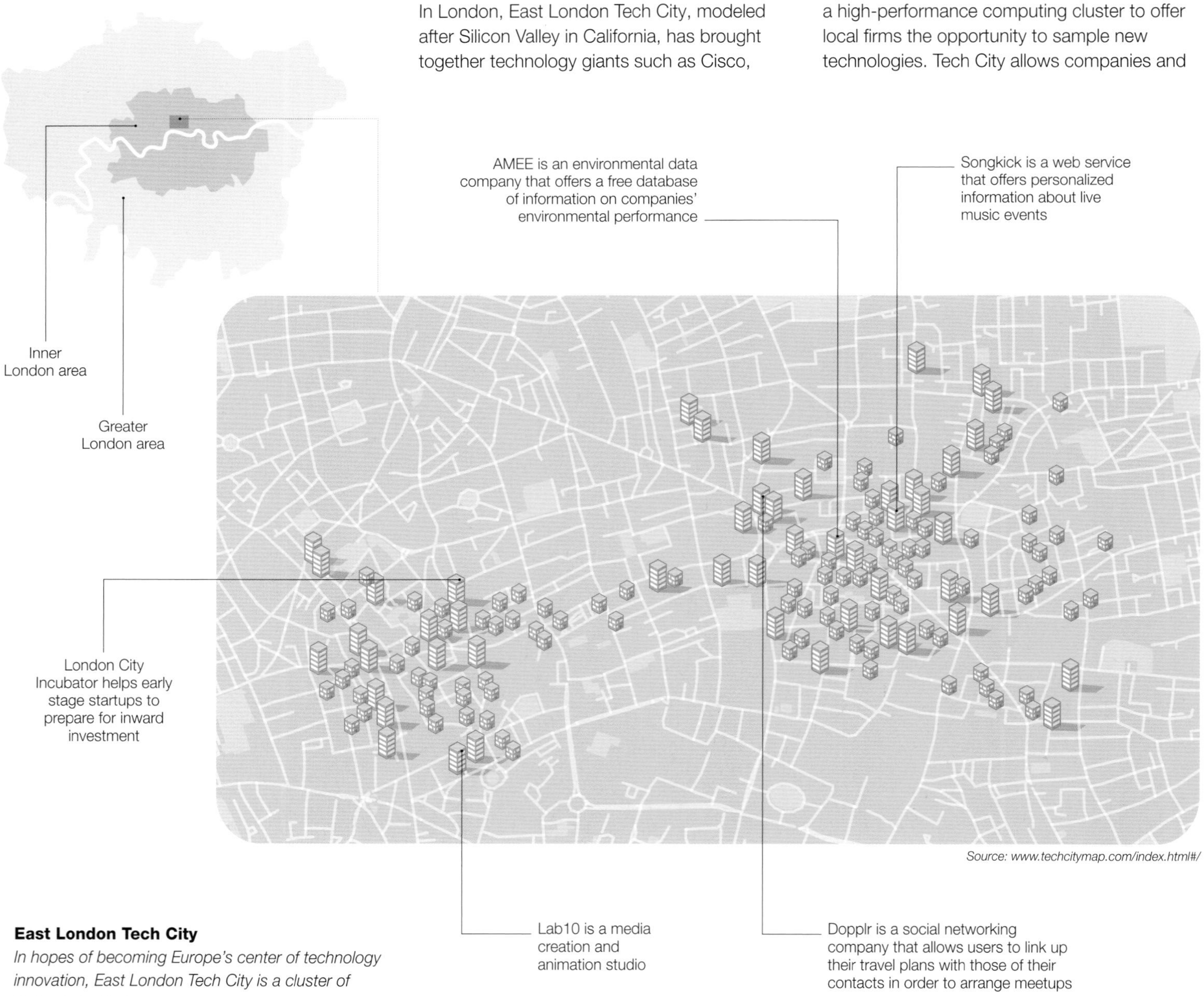

Inner
London area

Greater
London area

AMEE is an environmental data company that offers a free database of information on companies' environmental performance

Songkick is a web service that offers personalized information about live music events

London City Incubator helps early stage startups to prepare for inward investment

Source: www.techcitymap.com/index.html#/

East London Tech City

In hopes of becoming Europe's center of technology innovation, East London Tech City is a cluster of technology startups.

Lab10 is a media creation and animation studio

Dopplr is a social networking company that allows users to link up their travel plans with those of their contacts in order to arrange meetups

professionals to come together for greater collaboration and innovation that will attract more professional talent and technology innovations for the future.

Cities have to be entrepreneurial themselves so as to avoid falling prey to decline. As the social and economic environments around a city change, the city must take proactive steps to recognize these signals, understand their implications, and make the necessary innovations in response. Turin, once a city in decline, is today a leading intelligent city. As the Italian car capital, with major producers such as Fiat, Turin suffered mightily during the decline of the automotive sector in Italy. When the automobile industry began to decline, Turin's leaders saw the need for diversification in production and in how it presented itself to

businesses outside of its primary industry. Instead of marketing itself as the "Italian car capital," Turin redirected its efforts to international marketing, urban planning, and investments in innovation. The city authorities also provided support for the development of food and tourism sectors.

During Turin's repurposing and redirecting phase, the city transformed into one of the most dynamic cities in Italy. Experiencing an increase in per capita GDP more than 10 percent higher than the national average in 2012, Turin is now on an upswing. Many of the old industrial complexes were transformed into thriving commercial areas such as shopping centers, hotels, art galleries, and restaurants. Turin creatively marketed itself as a "total package" of businesses that could offer a one-stop

shopping experience to fulfill multiple needs. This approach boasted the strength of multiple businesses in Turin instead of solely promoting one large business. It proved to be beneficial. The Politecnico di Torino played a crucial role in ensuring that graduates had relevant skills to contribute to the local economy and hosted the I3P incubator, a nonprofit consortium of educational, commercial, and governmental institutions that fosters entrepreneurship by supporting startups with a networked collection of resources including funders, subject-matter experts, and consultants.

Top ten technology startups in the USA, 2012

The United States is home to many of the most capital-rich tech startups in the world. Tech startups are a mix of education, talent, financing, and environments that are conducive to production. Each of these cities possesses attributes that are appealing to budding entrepreneurs looking for success.

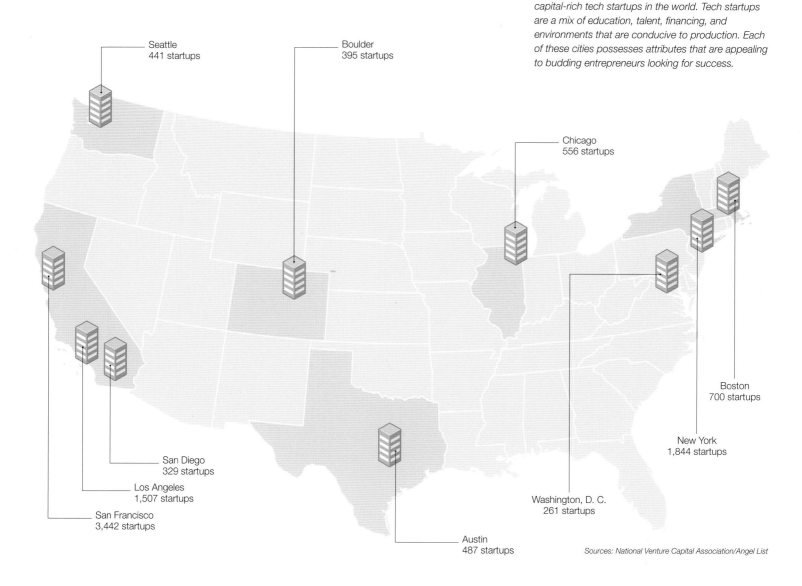

Seattle
441 startups

Boulder
395 startups

Chicago
556 startups

San Diego
329 startups

Los Angeles
1,507 startups

San Francisco
3,442 startups

Austin
487 startups

Washington, D. C.
261 startups

New York
1,844 startups

Boston
700 startups

Sources: National Venture Capital Association/Angel List

Quality of Life

Intelligent cities work creatively to ensure that their citizens enjoy a high standard of living. Critical to achieving this goal is the use of technologies to keep the city's infrastructure up to date. This requires a city to consider not only its present but also what it wants as its future. Transitional states—cities that are undergoing a period of change—are viewed as experiments where feedback is sought from citizens.

Consider the case of Vienna. Vienna is consistently ranked as having one of the best standards of living of any city in the world. By 2050 the city will have gone through a significant demographic shift from being one of the oldest regions in Austria to one of the youngest (currently, just over 20 percent of all Viennese are over 60). In keeping with this demographic shift, Vienna is already making itself more accessible and friendly to the

Smart City Vienna
Vienna's city authorities are improving the design, development, and perception of their city. Vienna is looking to advance the quality of life for its citizens by making long-term infrastructure, energy, and mobility improvements.

Car-free residential zones
Residents commit to not owning or operating a vehicle of their own. Instead, they walk or use public transport or bicycles.

Bike city
The former Nordbahnhof (northern station) area is to become an entirely new urban quarter by the year 2025.

CLUE
Climate Neutral Urban Districts in Europe improve their carbon footprint using innovative new technologies and building techniques.

Solar power plants
Viennese citizens have the opportunity to invest in community-funded solar power plants. Shares in the Vienna Citizens' Solar Power Plants can be acquired by any private individual living in Austria.

younger generation. The "Smart City Wien" project focuses primarily on devising models to promote intelligent urbanity with a focus on reducing the city's impact on its environment and planning for rapidly changing population demographics. One major effort toward this goal is to make the city more bike friendly. The city government has committed Vienna to doubling cycling's overall transport share by 2015 from 5.5 percent to 10 percent. Vienna is focusing on creating "bicycle-friendly streets," the upgrading of main routes like the Ring-Rund-Radweg which has peak user volumes of more than 7,000 cyclists per day, further enlargement of cycle parking facilities (there are over 30,000 slots at the moment), and new solutions for the combination of cycling and public transport. Investments in cycle parking facilities, especially at railway stations, are also being made.

A critical aspect of maintaining a good quality of life is ensuring that a city remains accessible to its residents and visitors. Tokyo leads all cities when it comes to creating innovative solutions to combat high real-estate prices. As with most cities, real estate is expensive in Tokyo, which makes it inaccessible to the average citizen or tourist. Hotels are therefore experimenting with offering capsule-style accommodation. A traditional hotel room in Tokyo will run to about $250 a night. By contrast, for about $35 a night, you can rent a capsule with a bed, a small TV, wi-fi, an alarm clock, and programmable lighting that aligns with one's biorhythms. A traditional hotel room will accommodate about eight capsules. Communal facilities are provided for showers and luggage storage. These capsules are increasing in popularity as they provide a means to increase access to the city.

THE TOP FIFTY LIVEABLE CITIES, 2012
From the Mercer Quality of Living Survey

1	**Vienna**	Austria
2	Zurich	Switzerland
3	Auckland	New Zealand
4	Munich	Germany
5	Vancouver	Canada
6	Düsseldorf	Germany
7	Frankfurt	Germany
8	Geneva	Switzerland
9	Copenhagen	Denmark
10	Bern	Switzerland
10	**Sydney**	Australia
12	**Amsterdam**	Netherlands
13	Wellington	New Zealand
14	Ottawa	Canada
15	Toronto	Canada
16	Berlin	Germany
17	Hamburg	Germany
17	Melbourne	Australia
19	Luxembourg	Luxembourg
19	Stockholm	Sweden
21	Perth	Australia
22	Brussels	Belgium
23	Montreal	Canada
24	Nurnberg	Germany
25	**Singapore**	Singapore
26	Canberra	Australia
27	Stuttgart	Germany
28	Honolulu	United States
29	Adelaide	Australia
29	Paris	France
29	**San Francisco**	United States
32	Calgary	Canada
32	Helsinki	Finland
32	Oslo	Norway
35	Boston	United States
35	Dublin	Ireland
37	Brisbane	Australia
38	**London**	United Kingdom
39	Lyon	France
40	Barcelona	Spain
41	Milan	Italy
42	**Chicago**	United States
43	Washington, D.C.	United States
44	Lisbon	Portugal
44	**New York City**	United States
44	Seattle	United States
44	**Tokyo**	Japan
48	Kobe	Japan
49	Madrid	Spain
49	Pittsburgh	United States
49	Yokohama	Japan

Aspern
One of Europe's largest urban developments, Vienna's Urban Lakeside will be a city within a city. Intended to be complete by 2028, it will boast 8,500 housing units that will accommodate 20,000 people and is expected to develop 20,000 jobs.

Smile
SMILE—Smart Mobility Info and Ticketing System—is a multi-modal mobility platform for all of Austria providing comprehensive information for public and individual mobility services.

Marxbox
Austria's First "Green" Laboratory Building with a LEED Gold certification (Leadership in Energy and Environmental Design) by the U.S. Green Building Council.

Source: smartcity.wien.at/site/

Living Labs

Intelligent cities are turning themselves into living labs where experimentation with new technologies can take place with ease. Living labs embrace the city as an environment in which individuals and organizations can run field experiments to test new technologies and generate knowledge that advances the planning and design of cities, administrative systems, processes, and infrastructures.

A living lab is a real-life testing and experimental environment where innovations are co-created for user-driven innovation. Living labs utilize co-creation, exploration, experimentation, and evaluation for the development of solutions. Each of these activities can be performed in a variety of scenarios with a variety of outputs. Living labs increase the potential success of an idea because it is tested and scrutinized by users, producers, and the public. Amsterdam developed one of the first living labs in Europe, the Amsterdam Living Lab (ALL). ALL is focused on developing sustainable ideas that assist in the delivery of effective services, such as large-scale mobility management to reduce traffic congestion, gaining better energy efficiency through intelligent surroundings and feedback, and facilitating the creation of

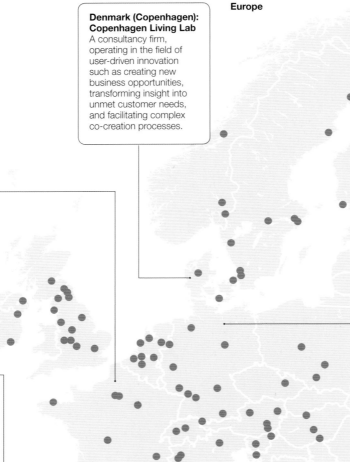

Europe

Denmark (Copenhagen): Copenhagen Living Lab
A consultancy firm, operating in the field of user-driven innovation such as creating new business opportunities, transforming insight into unmet customer needs, and facilitating complex co-creation processes.

France (Paris): Universcience Living Lab
A public science museum whose visitors can attend 60 daily science shows with real experiments carried out by scientists dealing with the basics of science, and exhibits and workshops to discuss the latest scientific issues.

Germany (Sankt Augustin): Virtual Research & Innovation Cooperation Lab
This connects technology support for the European Research & Innovation Community with the user-centered methodology framework created and applied within different European and national research projects to further the development of future cooperation.

Portugal (Chamusca): ECO LivingLab@ Chamusca
This supplies innovative goods and services, in accordance with the paradigm of industrial ecology, through the development of innovative businesses that create jobs while safeguarding the area's ecological equilibrium.

Italy (Rome): Space2Land Living Lab
This aims to improve public services for citizens, stimulate research, and enhance industrial regional systems through the development and implementation of the living labs platforms and related services.

Source: www.openlivinglabs.eu

change between people living in the same city area with the help of media. Amsterdam has focused its living lab on understanding the intersection between quality design and real-life behaviors of users. This attention to finding the utility in ideas is what makes living labs integral to the quest for success through collaboration, innovation, and technology.

Living labs also involve crowdsourcing ideas and actively engaging citizens in the experimentation and solution development processes. As Amsterdam continues to confront the challenges that face citizens, community leaders develop new ways to engage a variety of stakeholders in finding solutions to improve the quality of life. Amsterdam's quest to become a smart city hinges on its desire and commitment to find innovative ways to confront ongoing community issues through collaboration and technology. In a crowdsourcing pilot in 2010, the city presented the community with three local policy challenges that required attention: 1) the bike storage problem in Amsterdam; 2) a redesign and repurposing of the red light district to attract new businesses; and 3) a way of convincing homeowners to produce energy. The municipality received 100 ideas that were considered in terms of their usefulness as solutions to community challenges and as an experiment in the feasibility of crowdsourcing as a policymaking tool.

Due to the need to generate new knowledge and test out cutting-edge concepts, many of which reside in R&D labs, cities often partner with academic institutions. Some living labs start out within universities, while others are sponsored by industries that are keen to explore new ideas. Singapore has teamed up with MIT to create the Singapore-MIT Alliance for Research and Technology (SMART). The project, funded by Singapore's National Research Foundation, has attracted over 500 researchers who are focused on designing technologies to tackle myriad urban challenges.

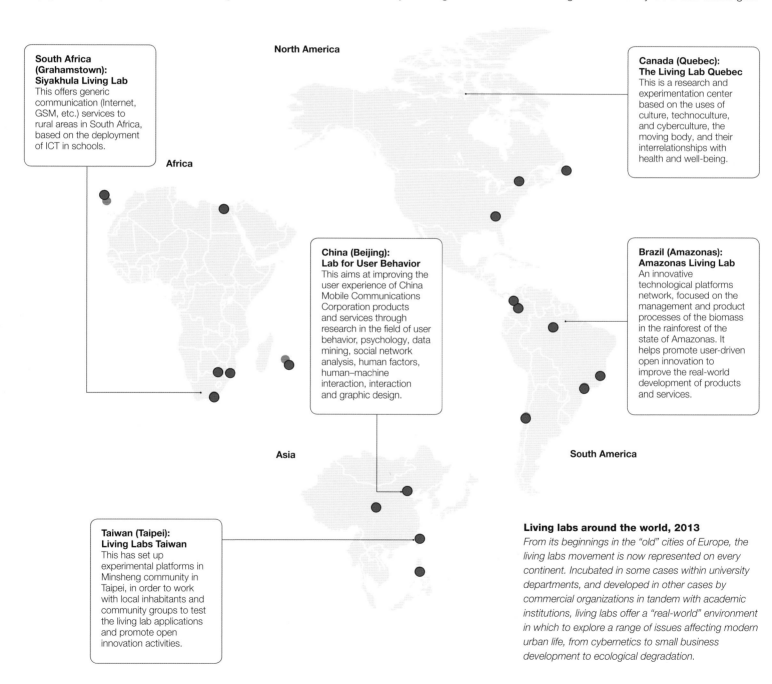

South Africa (Grahamstown): Siyakhula Living Lab
This offers generic communication (Internet, GSM, etc.) services to rural areas in South Africa, based on the deployment of ICT in schools.

North America

Africa

Canada (Quebec): The Living Lab Quebec
This is a research and experimentation center based on the uses of culture, technoculture, and cyberculture, the moving body, and their interrelationships with health and well-being.

China (Beijing): Lab for User Behavior
This aims at improving the user experience of China Mobile Communications Corporation products and services through research in the field of user behavior, psychology, data mining, social network analysis, human factors, human–machine interaction, interaction and graphic design.

Brazil (Amazonas): Amazonas Living Lab
An innovative technological platforms network, focused on the management and product processes of the biomass in the rainforest of the state of Amazonas. It helps promote user-driven open innovation to improve the real-world development of products and services.

Asia

South America

Taiwan (Taipei): Living Labs Taiwan
This has set up experimental platforms in Minsheng community in Taipei, in order to work with local inhabitants and community groups to test the living lab applications and promote open innovation activities.

Living labs around the world, 2013
From its beginnings in the "old" cities of Europe, the living labs movement is now represented on every continent. Incubated in some cases within university departments, and developed in other cases by commercial organizations in tandem with academic institutions, living labs offer a "real-world" environment in which to explore a range of issues affecting modern urban life, from cybernetics to small business development to ecological degradation.

Glossary

acropolis: from the Greek meaning "highest city," an acropolis is a fortified citadel built on a hill which was a central feature of many ancient cities across the Mediterranean, constituting a refuge for the citizens in times of war. The most famous acropolis is that of Athens.

agora: in ancient Mediterranean cities the agora was an open space where citizens would gather to hear pronouncements from the ruling authority or to report for military duty. The agora was also a marketplace, and the open plaza or square remains a feature of Mediterranean cities.

agribusiness: the business of producing and distributing food crops, particularly used of large-scale mechanized operations based on intensive farming and the widespread use of chemical fertilizers and pesticides.

alderman: a member of the governing council of a town or city, sometimes a senior member elected by the council itself rather than the populace. The title originated in the UK, though it is no longer in use there; many U.S. cities are governed by a board of aldermen.

bill of exchange: a binding agreement that obliges one party to pay a fixed sum to another party at a specific future date. The introduction of these instruments in Europe during the Middle Ages, made possible by reliable courier services, facilitated trade since they removed the necessity for face-to-face interactions and the transporting of actual cash.

biomass: biological material derived from plants that can be used as fuel; wood is an obvious example, but sugar cane residue, rice husks, and algae are also actual or potential biomass fuel sources.

boosterism: the process of "talking up" the merits of a particular town or city, which might involve simple rhetorical gestures such as speeches by the mayor or publicity stunts, or large-scale municipal investments such as hosting an international sports event or erecting an eye-catching building.

bourgeoisification: also called "gentrification," this is the process by which working-class urban areas that have lost their original function as a result of, for example, deindustrialization are repurposed to suit the residential or business needs of middle-class incomers who have been priced out of other areas of the city.

built environment: the entirety of the human-made spaces in which people live and work. This includes not only buildings and roads but also parks and open spaces, infrastructure, and services such as entertainment or retail units.

Chicago School: a group of sociologists centered on the University of Chicago in the 1920s and 1930s who examined and theorized the effects of the urban environment on the culture and behavior of those who lived in it. Notable members of the Chicago School were Louis Wirth, Frederic E. Clements, and Robert E. Park.

city-state: in the classical period and in subsequent periods, many cities exercised command and control functions over the surrounding region so as to form mini-states, for example the Greek city-states of Asia Minor or Renaissance Milan and Venice.

cleantech: a general term for the development of technologies that make use of renewable energy sources, that are efficient and productive, and that reduce waste products or pollution.

clustering: the process by which companies offering services or products within a particular sector come together in particular locations for mutual benefit, a process that is self-supporting and that over time often works to exclude other locations from taking part in those activities. Also referred to as "agglomeration."

containerization: the process of packing goods into standard-size steel boxes for transport and distribution, which allows for mechanization of port city activities and resulted in large-scale changes in employment patterns in cities such as Liverpool and Rotterdam during the 1960s.

creative class: a population identified by the urban theorist Richard Florida that comprises workers in science and engineering, architecture and design, education, arts, music, and entertainment whose economic function is to create new ideas, new technology, and new creative content.

demographics: the statistically quantifiable subsets into which a given population can be divided, in terms of, for example, age, gender, income, ethnicity, education, mobility, and so on.

designscape: the result of a planned effort to mold the built environment through striking or integrated building projects to create a specific image, for example to project an impression of creativity or commercial vibrancy or cultural excellence.

diseconomy of scale: an adverse effect resulting from increasing the size of an organization, the opposite of an economy of scale.

dormitory town: a community that functions solely as a living place for its inhabitants, who work in another, often larger conurbation. Dormitory towns have few if any local employment sources, other than retail outlets, and residents derive their income from another location.

dystopian: the opposite of "utopian," designating a place where living conditions are far from ideal, sometimes applied to cities when highlighting such aspects as crime, overcrowding, environmental degradation, economic inequalities, or homelessness.

ecological footprint: the total environmental impact of individual or collective human activities, including energy consumption and waste disposal. Calculating the ecological footprint of a population is a means of assessing whether that population's lifestyle is sustainable in terms of the biosphere's available or potential resources.

enclosure: the process by which common land or open pasture in England was fenced off and entitled to specific landowners from the 16th century onward; this consolidated land into larger parcels and restricted the common rights of agricultural workers, contributing to the migration of rural populations into the new industrial centers in search of work.

externality: an externality is a cost or benefit resulting from an activity that affects a third party who did not take part in that activity. An obvious example is environmental pollution from industrial or agricultural activities, which imposes a cost (whether social or economic) on parties other than the producers or consumers of the products of such activities.

garden city movement: initiated by Ebenezer Howard in the late 19th century, this was an urban planning concept that envisaged highly planned towns of about 30,000 people with open spaces and a surrounding green belt; these communities were intended to be self-sufficient, with agriculture and industry being incorporated into the plan.

geopolitics: the study of the effects of geographical issues on political relationships between states, which might take account of such things as physical location, access to communications routes, natural resources, and demographics.

greenhouse gases: gases in the earth's atmosphere that absorb and emit thermal radiation, chiefly carbon dioxide and methane; without these gases the earth's surface would be appreciably cooler since the thermal radiation from the sun would not be recycled in the atmosphere and re-radiated toward the earth. The burning of fossil fuels has increased the amount of carbon dioxide in the atmosphere, and thus contributed to the process of global warming.

guild: an association of artisans or craftspeople which controls the practices of their particular trade, prescribing standards of qualification, and protecting their common interests. In medieval Europe, guilds held exclusive privileges over their particular trades, which meant they had a powerful voice in municipal politics.

hinterland: strictly speaking this refers to the region from which a port receives products for shipment. More broadly it suggests the region surrounding a conurbation that falls under its influence in terms of commerce, culture, or politics.

infrastructure: the basic facilities that are required for an organization or society to function. For urban spaces this would include water supply, sewerage, power supplies, roads and railways, and telecommunications systems: the elements that are necessary in order for productive economic activities to take place.

local resource loops: cooperative projects aimed at developing a degree of local self-sufficiency in key resources, products, and services, for example urban farms that supply their immediate area or local currencies that can be exchanged for goods and services within a specific community.

Luddites: a movement of skilled textile workers in 19th-century England who protested against the introduction of machinery that could be operated by unskilled workers, thus threatening their livelihood.

megacity: usually defined as a city which has a population of 10 million inhabitants or more. The majority of megacities are found in the developing world.

mesh network: a wireless communication network made up of a mesh of radio nodes that transfer information from one to another; within the network the nodes (for example laptops or smart phones) can share information over a large area through a series of short links, and if one node falls out of the network a different route can be found that bypasses the failed node.

metropolis: from the Greek meaning "mother city," a metropolis was originally a city from which settlers departed to establish a colony. In modern usage a metropolis is a large city that has a significant political, economic, and cultural influence over a region; many countries have a specific definition of a metropolis that has administrative implications.

monocentric: used of a city that has developed from a single originating settlement, as opposed to a city formed from the gradual coalescing of several originally spatially separate urban centers, a "polycentric" city. Generally speaking Western cities tend to be polycentric, while cities in the developing world are more usually monocentric.

neoliberalism: in its most recent incarnation this refers to a form of laissez-faire capitalism that promotes free trade, deregulation, and extremely limited government intervention in the economy.

New Urbanism: an urban design movement that promotes walkable neighborhoods that do not privilege the automobile, freely accessible open spaces, mixed residential types, community institutions, and local businesses and services. Its aim is to reduce urban sprawl and create self-organizing and self-governing communities.

node: a point in a network where two or more linkages meet which is capable of receiving, sending, or forwarding information.

oligarchy: a form of governing structure in which a small group of people exercise power, usually but not always because they control wealth.

pull factors: circumstances that draw people to a location, for example employment opportunities or better housing.

push factors: circumstances that cause people to leave a location, for example overcrowding or lack of fertile land.

service sector: broadly speaking, this is the sector of the economy which involves people supplying services of some kind; this includes public administration, healthcare and education, financial and legal services, retail, and media and hospitality. Also referred to as the tertiary sector, in distinction from the primary sector (agriculture, fishing, mineral extraction) and the secondary sector (manufacturing).

slave mode of production: according to Marxist theory, various modes of production (a combination of the means of production and the legal and social structures that obtain in a particular society) have characterized particular periods of human history. In the ancient world, the slave mode of production required that certain classes of people, often foreigners captured in war, be recognized as property, and these people supplied productive labor.

smart grid: an electricity supply grid that uses IT systems to gather data on energy usage and automatically makes adjustments according to circumstances, for example redistributing power across the grid, allowing take-up of power from distributed sources, or alerting users or devices attached to the grid to the variable costs of using energy at different times to encourage more efficient energy use.

snowbird: a person from the northern USA or Canada who habitually spends the winter months in a warmer, more southerly location, typically Florida, Arizona, California, or the Caribbean.

suburbanization: the process by which wealthier sectors of a population gravitate from the center to the periphery of an urban area, often to escape overcrowding, pollution, or other perceived quality of life disadvantages. Among the consequences are the stratification of social classes with poorer people left in the depopulated city center, urban sprawl, and an increase in traffic as people commute to work in the urban center.

transaction cost: the cost of performing or participating in some kind of economic activity, for example the opportunity cost of finding a particular thing you want to buy, a commission fee payable to a broker, or the cost of drawing up a contract that specifies the details of the activity being undertaken.

transformation industries: the sector of manufacturing which involves the processing of raw materials into secondary materials that can then be used to make finished goods.

transitional state: in urban terms, this is a period during which a city is adapting to changes in, for example, its demographic profile or its economic well-being, a process that presents opportunities as well as threats.

urbanization: broadly, the process by which a population moves from a rural location and lifestyle to an urban location, driven by, for example, economic and educational opportunities. In the developing world this process is advancing at an unprecedented rate.

Resources

THE FOUNDATIONAL CITY

Image references

p. 18: Toynbee, A. ed., 1967. *Cities of Destiny*. London: Thames & Hudson; Leontidou, L., 2011 (in Greek). *Ageographitos Chora [Geographically illiterate land]: Hellenic idols in the Epistemological Reflections of European Geography*. Propobos, Athens; Dimitrakos, D. & Karolides, P. 1950s (in Greek). *Historical Atlas*, vol. 1. D.&V. Athens: Loukopoulos Editions.

p. 19: Benevolo, L., 1993. *The European City*. Oxford: Blackwell; Pounds, N. J. G. 1990. *A Historical Geography of Europe*. Cambridge University Press.

p. 20: Pavsanias, 1974 edn. (in Greek) *Pavsanias' Hellenic Tour: Attica*. Papachatzis, N. D. (ed. 1974), Ekdotiki Athens; Travlos. I., 1960 (in Greek). *Urban Development of Athens*. Athens: Konstantinides- Michalas.

pp. 21–3: Travlos, I., 1960 (in Greek). *Urban Development of Athens*. Athens: Konstantinides-Michalas; Biris, C. 1966 (in Greek) *Athens – From the 19th to the 20th Century*. Athens: Foundation of Town Planning and History of Athens.

pp. 24–5: Based on Leontidou-Emmanuel L., "Working Class and Land Allocation: The Urban History of Athens, 1880–1980," PhD dissertation, London School of Economics, 1981, p. 66, 290; also Leontidou, L. *The Mediterranean City in Transition: Social Change and Urban Development* (Cambridge: Cambridge University Press, 2nd edn, 2006 [1990]), p. 55 Fig. 2.1, p. 150 Fig. 4.8; page 25 also: Couch, C., Leontidou, L. & Petschel-Held, G. (eds) 2007. *Urban Sprawl in Europe: Landscapes, Land-use Change and Policy*. Oxford: Blackwell.

p. 30: Based on Benevolo, L., 1993. *The European City*. Oxford: Blackwell; Pounds, N.J.G. 1990. *A Historical Geography of Europe*. Cambridge University Press; also Wikimedia commons: Andrei Nacu: http://upload.wikimedia. org/wikipedia/commons/b/bb/Roman_ Empire_125.png

pp. 32–3: Adapted from Leontidou, L., 2011 (in Greek). *Ageographitos Chora [Geographically Illiterate land]: Hellenic Idols in the Epistemological Reflections of European Geography*. Athens: Propobos; Demand, N. H., 1990. *Urban Relocation in Archaic and Classical Greece: Flight and Consolidation*. Norman: University of Oklahoma Press; Dimitrakos, D. & Karolides, P.,1950s (in Greek). *Historical Atlas*, vol. 1. D.&V. Loukopoulos editions, Athens.

Text references and further reading

Bastea, E., 2000. *The Creation of Modern Athens: Planning the Myth*. New York: Cambridge University Press.

Couch, C., Leontidou, L. and Petschel-Held, G. (eds), 2007. *Urban Sprawl in Europe: Landscapes, Land-use Change and Policy*. Oxford: Blackwell.

Demand, N.H., 1990. *Urban Relocation in Archaic and Classical Greece: Flight and Consolidation*. Norman: University of Oklahoma Press.

Diamantini, D. and Martinotti, G. (eds), 2009. *Urban Civilizations from Yesterday to the Next Day*. Napoli: Scriptaweb.

Lefebvre, H., 1991. *The Production of Space*. Oxford: Blackwell.

Leontidou-Emmanuel, L., 1981. *Working Class and Land Allocation: The Urban History of Athens, 1880–1980*. Ph.D Dissertation, University of London.

Leontidou, L., 1990/2006. *The Mediterranean City in Transition: Social Change and Urban Development*. Cambridge: Cambridge University Press.

Leontidou, L., 2009. "Mediterranean Spatialities of Urbanism and Public Spaces as Agoras in European Cities" in Diamantini, D. & Martinotti, G. (eds), 2009. *Urban Civilizations from Yesterday to the Next Day*. Napoli: Scriptaweb, 107–126.

Leontidou, L., 2011 (in Greek). *Ageographitos Chora [Geographically illiterate land]: Hellenic Idols in the Epistemological Reflections of European Geography*. Athens: Propobos.

Leontidou, L., 2012. "Athens in the Mediterranean 'Movement of the Piazzas': Spontaneity in Material and Virtual Public Spaces" in *City: Analysis of Urban Trends, Culture, Theory, Policy, Action*, vol. 16, no 3: 299–312.

Leontidou, L., 2013. "Mediterranean Cultural Identities Seen through the 'Western' Gaze: Shifting Geographical Imaginations of Athens" in *New Geographies* (Harvard University Press), vol. 5, 14.3.2013: 111–122; 27–28, 46–47.

Loukaki, A., 2008. *Living Ruins, Value Conflicts*. Aldershot: Ashgate.

Martinotti, G., 1993. *Metropoli: La nuova morfologia sociale della citta*. Bologna: Il Mulino.

Martinotti, G. and Diamantini, D., 2009. Preface in Diamantini, D. and Martinotti, G. (eds) *Urban Civilizations from Yesterday to the Next Day*. Napoli: Scriptaweb, 5–22.

Martinotti, G., 2012. "La fabbrica delle città, Postfazione" in Hansen, M. H. *Polis. Introduzione alla città-stato dell'antica Grecia* (trsl. McClintock, A.), Milano: UBE-Egea, pp. 221–259.

THE NETWORKED CITY

Image references

p. 36: Abu-Lughod, J. L., 1989. *Before European Hegemony. The World System A.D. 1250–1350*. New York: Oxford University Press, p. 34: "Figure 1. The eight circuits of the thirteenth-century world system."

p. 38: Seibold G.,1995. *Die Manlich. Geschichte einer Augsburger Kaufmannsfamilie*. Sigmaringen: Jan Thorbecke Verlag.

p. 39: Hanham, A., ed., 1975. *The Cely Letters 1472–1488*. London: Oxford University Press.

p. 40: Bairoch, P., Batou, J., and Chèvre, P., 1988. *La Population des villes européennes: Banque de données et analyse sommaire des résultats, 800–1850*. Geneva: Librairie Droz.

p. 41: Lane, F. C., 1973. *Venice, A Maritime Republic*. Baltimore and London: Johns Hopkins University Press, pp. 339–41: "Merchant galley fleets in the fifteenth century."

p. 42: Melis, F., 1973. "Intensità e regolarità nella diffusione dell' informazione economica generale nel Mediterraneo e in Occidente alla fine del Medioevo" in *Mélanges en l'honneur de Fernand Braudel. Histoire économique du monde méditerranéen 1450–1650*. Toulouse: Edouard Privat, pp. 389–424/b.

p. 43: Laveau, G., 1978. *Een Europese post ten tijde van de Grootmeesters van de familie de la Tour et Tassis (Turn en Taxis)*. Brussels: Museum van Posterijen en van Telecommunicatie, p. 54: "Wegenkaart van de Internationale Post georganiseerd door de Tassis (1490–1520)."

p. 44: Dollinger, Ph., 1970. *The German Hansa*. Translated and edited by D. S. Ault and S. H. Steinberg. London: Macmillan.

p. 45: Verlinden, Ch., 1938. "La Place de la Catalogne dans l'histoire commerciale du monde méditerranéen médiéval" in *Revue des Cours et Conférences*, 1st series, 39.8: 737–54.

p. 46: Ryckaert, M., 1991. *Historische stedenatlas van België. Brugge*. Brussels: Gemeentekrediet, p. 172.

p. 47: Mack, M., 2007. "The Italian Quarters of Frankish Tyre: Mapping a Medieval City" in *Journal of Medieval History* 33: 147–65.

p. 48: Epstein, S. R., 2000. *Freedom and Growth. The Rise of States and Markets in Europe, 1300–1750*. London: Routledge, pp. 120–1.

p. 49: Spufford, P., 2002. *Power and Profit. The Merchant in Medieval Europe*. London: Thames & Hudson, p. 75: "Princes and their Paris palaces c. 1400."

p. 50: McNeill, W. H., 1976. *De pest in de geschiedenis*. Amsterdam: De Arbeiderspers, p. 6. Translated from McNeill, W. H., 1976. *Plagues and Peoples*. New York: Doubleday.

p. 51: Reith, R., 2008. "Circulation of Skilled Labour in Late Medieval and Early Modern Central Europe" in S. R. Epstein and M. Prak, eds., *Guilds, Innovation, and the European Economy, 1400–1800*. New York: Cambridge University Press, p. 120.

Further reading

Grafe, R. and Gelderblom, O., 2010. "The Rise and Fall of Merchant Guilds: Re-thinking the Comparative Study of Commercial Institutions in Premodern Europe" in *Journal of Interdisciplinary History* 40.4: 477–511.

Hunt, E. S. and Murray, J. M., 1999. *A History of Business in Medieval Europe (1200–1550)*. Cambridge: Cambridge University Press.

Jacobs, J., 1969. *The Economy of Cities*. New York and Toronto: Random House.

Lane, F. C., 1973. *Venice, A Maritime Republic*. Baltimore and London: Johns Hopkins University Press.

Lapeyre, H., 1955. *Une Famille de marchands: Les Ruiz. Contribution à l'étude du commerce entre la France et l'Espagne au temps de Philippe II*. Paris: Librairie Armand Colin.

Spufford, P., 2002. *Power and Profit. The Merchant in Medieval Europe*. London: Thames & Hudson.

Taylor, P. J., 2013. *Extraordinary Cities: Millennia of Moral Syndromes, World-systems and City/State Relations*. Cheltenham: Edward Elgar.

Taylor, P. J., Hoyler, M., and Verbruggen, R., 2010. "External Urban Relational Process: Introducing Central Flow Theory to Complement Central Place Theory" in *Urban Studies* 47.13: 2803–18.

Van der Wee, H., 1963. *The Growth of the Antwerp Market and the European Economy (Fourteenth–Sixteenth Centuries). II. Interpretation*. Louvain: Université de Louvain.

Verbruggen, R., 2011. "World Cities before Globalisation: The European City Network, A.D. 1300–1600." PhD thesis, Loughborough University.

THE IMPERIAL CITY

Image references

p. 65: Kara, M., "The Analysis of the Distribution of the Non-Muslim Population and their Socio-Cultural Properties in Istanbul (Greeks, Armenians and Jews), in the Frame of 'Istanbul: European Capital of Culture 2010,'" Masters thesis, 2009.

p. 66: *Vatan* newspaper, October 17, 2010, http://ekonomi.haber7.com/ekonomi/haber/624733-istanbuldaki-kentsel-donusum-projeleril

p. 67 United Nations, Department of Economic and Social Affairs, http://esa.un.org/unup/CD-ROM/Urban-Agglomerations.htm

Further reading

Driver, F. and Gilbert, D., 1999. "Imperial Cities: Overlapping Territories, Intertwined Histories" in F. Driver and D. Gilbert, eds., *Imperial Cities: Landscape, Display and Identity*. Manchester: Manchester University Press, pp. 1–17.

Freely, J., 1998. *Istanbul: The Imperial City*. London: Penguin Books.

Hall, P., 1998. *Cities in Civilization*. New York: Pantheon Books.

Harris, J., 2007. *Constantinople: Capital of Byzantium*. London: Continuum Books.

Kirecci, M. A., 2011. "Celebrating and Neglecting Istanbul: Its Past vs. Its Present" in M. A. Kirecci and E. Foster, eds., *Istanbul: Metamorphoses in an Imperial City*. Greenfield, MA: Talisman House Publishers, pp. 1–17.

Kuban, D., 1996. "From Byzantium to Istanbul: The Growth of a City." *Biannual Istanbul* (Spring 1996): 10–42.

Mansel, P., 1996. *Constantinople: City of the World's Desire 1453–1924*. New York: St. Martin's Press.

Mumford, L., 1961. *The City in History*. New York: Harcourt.

Seger, M., 2012. "Istanbul's Backbone – A Chain of Central Business Districts (CBDs)" in S. Polyzos, ed. *Urban Development*. s.l.: InTech, pp. 201–16.

Other resources

Byzantine Constantinople: http://en.wikipedia.org/wiki/Constantinople

The Silk Road: http://en.wikipedia.org/wiki/Silk_Road

Via Egnatia: http://en.wikipedia.org/wiki/Via_Egnatia

THE INDUSTRIAL CITY

Image references

p. 75: (bottom right) *Spinning the Web — The Story of the Cotton Industry*, http://www.spinningtheweb.org.uk/m_display.php?irn=5&sub=cottonopolis&theme=places&crumb=City+Centre

p. 76: Lancashire County Council: Environment Directorate: Historic Highways, http://www.lancashire.gov.uk/environment/historichighways/

p. 77: Chicago Urban Transport Network, Lake Forest College Library special collections, http://www.lakeforest.edu/library/archives/railroad/railmaps.php/

p. 84: Chicago Census map, http://www.lib.uchicago.edu/e/collections/maps/ssrc/

p. 85: Marr Map of Manchester Housing, 1904, Historical Maps of Manchester, http://manchester.publicprofiler.org/

p. 87: (top graph) Manufacturing output as share of world total, http://fullfact.org/factchecks/Growth_Labour_manufacturing-28817, original source UN National Accounts Database

p. 87: (bottom graphs) *Spinning the Web — The Story of the Cotton Industry*, UK imports of cotton piece goods 1937–64, http://www.spinningtheweb.org.uk/web/objects/common/webmedia.php?irn=200106; exports of cotton and manmade fibre piece goods 1851–64, http://www.spinningtheweb.org.uk/web/objects/common/webmedia.php?irn=2001062

Other resources

Historical Maps of Manchester, http://manchester.publicprofiler.org/

University of Manchester Library online map collection, http://www.library.manchester.ac.uk/searchresources/mapsandatlases/onlinemapcollection/

THE RATIONAL CITY

Image references

p. 94: Small graph, based on Harvey, D., 2003. *Paris: Capital of Modernity*. New York and London: Routledge.

p. 97: Sewer maps. Gandy, M., 1999. "The Paris Sewers and the Rationalization of Urban Space" in *Transactions of the Institute of British Geographers*, New Series, 24.1: 23–44.

p. 99: Growth of railways maps. Clout, H. D., 1977. *Themes in the Historical Geography of France*. New York: Academic Press.

Other resources

The City of Paris's official web site: www.paris.fr (in French)

Turgot map of Paris, 1739, http://edb.kulib.kyoto-u.ac.jp/exhibit-e/f28/f28cont.html; the Turgot map is a highly detailed street map of mid-18th century Paris, before the changes inaugurated by the French revolutionaries and Napoléon III.

University of Chicago Library web site "Paris in the 19th Century," with many maps of the city: www.lib.uchicago.edu/e/collections/maps/paris

"Paris Marville ca. 1870 & Today," a web site showing photographs taken by Charles Marville, a photographer engaged to record scenes of Paris before the city's redevelopment by Haussmann, together with what the places look like today: http://parismarville.blogspot.com/p/map.html

Further reading

Ferguson, P. P., 1994. *Paris as Revolution: Writing the 19th Century City*. Berkeley, CA: University of California Press.

Gluck, M., 2005. *Popular Bohemia: Modernism and Urban Culture in Nineteenth-Century Paris*. Cambridge, MA: Harvard University Press.

Harvey, D., 2003. *Paris, Capital of Modernity*. New York and London: Routledge.

Kennel, S., 2013. *Charles Marville: Photographer of Paris*. Chicago: University of Chicago Press.

Sramek, P., 2013. *Piercing Time: Paris after Marville and Atget, 1865–2012*. Bristol: Intellect.

Truesdell, M., 1997. *Spectacular Politics: Louis-Napoleon Bonaparte and the Fête Impériale, 1849–70*. Oxford: Oxford University Press.

Weeks, W., 1999. *The Man Who Made Paris Paris: The Illustrated Biography of Georges-Eugene Haussmann*. London: London House.

THE GLOBAL CITY

Image references

p. 110: http://www.gsma.com/latinamerica/aicent-ipxs-vision

p. 111: CAPA Centre for Aviation, http://centreforaviation.com/data/

p. 112: Wall, R. S. and Knaap, G. A. v.d., 2011. "Sectoral Differentiation and Network Structure within Contemporary Worldwide Corporate Networks" in *Economic Geography* 87.3: 266–308.

p. 114: Emporis Skyline Ranking, http://www.emporis.com/statistics/skyline-ranking

p. 115: Lizieri,C. and Kutsch, N., 2006. *Who Owns the City 2006: Office Ownership in the City of London*. Reading: University of Reading Business School and Development Securities, pp. 27 + iii.

p. 116: Walker, D. R. F. and Taylor, P. J., 2003. "Atlas of Economic Clusters in London. Globalization and World Cities Research Network, http://www.lboro.ac.uk/gawc/visual/lonatlas.html

Resources

p. 117: Pain, K., 2006. "Policy Challenges of Functional Polycentricity in a Global Mega-City Region: South East England" in *Built Environment* 32.2: 194–205.

p. 118 Fiscal Policy Institute, 2008. "Pulling Apart in New York: an Analysis of Income Trends in New York State," http://www.fiscalpolicy.org/FPI_PullingApartInNewYork.pdf

p. 119: http://www.globalpropertyguide.com/Europe/United-Kingdom/Price-History

p. 120–1: http://www.plutobooks.com/display.asp?K=9780745327983

p. 123 Office of Travel and Tourism Industries, U.S. Department of Commerce, http://travel.trade.gov

Further reading

Burn, G., 2000. "The State, the City and the Euromarkets" in *Review of International Political Economy* 6: 225–61.

Lai, K., 2012. "Differentiated Markets: Shanghai, Beijing and Hong Kong in China's Financial Centre Network" in *Urban Studies* 49.6: 1275–96.

Sassen, S. ,1999. "Global Financial Centers" in *Foreign Affairs* 78: 75–87

Wójcik, D., 2013. "The Dark Side of NY-LON: Financial Centres and the Global Financial Crisis" in *Urban Studies*. doi:10.1177/0042098012474513.

THE CELEBRITY CITY

Image references

pp. 128–9: County Business Pattern Industry Data, BLS 2008/County Business Pattern Industry Data, BLS 2007 (businesses) and 2008 (payroll); Currid-Halkett, E., 2010. *Starstruck: The Business of Celebrity*. New York: Faber & Faber.

p. 130: Currid-Halkett, E. and Ravid, G., 2012. "'Stars' and the Connectivity of Cultural Industry World Cities: An Empirical Social Network Analysis of Human Capital Mobility and its Implications for Economic Development" in *Environment and Planning A* 44.11: 2646–63.

p. 131: Lorenzen, M. and Täube, F. A., 2008. "Breakout from Bollywood? The Roles of Social Networks and Regulation in the Evolution of Indian Film Industry" in *Journal of International Management*, 14.3: 286–99; Lorenzen, M. and Mudambi, R., 2013. "Clusters, Connectivity and Catch-up: Bollywood and Bangalore in the Global Economy" in *Journal of Economic Geography* 13.3: 501–34.

pp. 132–3: Ravid G. and Currid-Halkett, E., 2013. "The Social Structure of Celebrity: An Empirical Network Analysis of an Elite Population" in *Celebrity Studies* 4.1 : 182–201.

pp. 135–7: Currid-Halkett, E. and Ravid, G., 2012. "'Stars' and the Connectivity of Cultural Industry World Cities: An Empirical Social Network Analysis of Human Capital Mobility and its Implications for Economic Development" in *Environment and Planning A* 44.11: 2646–63.

pp. 138–9: Currid, E. and Williams, S., 2010. "The Geography of Buzz: Art, Culture and the Social Milieu in Los Angeles and New York" in *Journal of Economic Geography* 10.3: 423–51.

Further reading

Adler, M., 1985. "Stardom and Talent." *The American Economic Review* 74.1: 208–12.

Boorstin, D., 1962. *The Image*, New York: Atheneum.

Braudy, L., 1986. *The Frenzy of Renown: Fame and its History*. Oxford: Oxford University Press.

Currid, E., 2008. *The Warhol Economy: How Fashion, Art and Music Drive New York City*. Princeton, NJ: Princeton University Press.

Currid-Halkett, E., 2010. "Networking Lessons from the Hollywood A-list" in *Harvard Business Review*, October 25th.

Currid-Halkett, E., 2011. "How Kim Kardashian Turns the Reality Business into an Art" in *Wall Street Journal*, November 2nd.

Currid-Halkett, E., 2011 "Where Do Bohemians Come From?" in *New York Times*, Sunday Review, October 16th.

Currid-Halkett, E., 2012. "The Secret Science of Stardom." Salon.com, February 24th.

Currid-Halkett, E. and Scott, A., 2013. "The Geography of Celebrity and Glamour: Economy, Culture and Desire in the City" in *City, Culture and Society* 4.1: 2–11.

Gamson, J.,1994, *Claims to Fame: Celebrity in Contemporary America*. Berkeley, CA: University of California Press.

McLuhan, M., 1964. "The Medium is the Message" in *Understanding Media: Extensions of Man*. New York: Signet.

Mills, C. W., 1956. *The Power Elite*. Oxford: Oxford University Press.

Rosen, S., 1981. "The Economics of Superstars" in *American Economic Review* 71.5: 845–58.

THE MEGACITY

Image references

p. 147: Demographia, 2013, http://www.demographia.com

pp. 150–1: Various sources, including U.S. Census Bureau data. Total number of slum dwellers estimated from various publications of Cities Alliances NGO; population density for Dharavi based on Nijman, J., 2010. "A Study of Space in Mumbai's Slums" in *Tijdschrift voor Economische en Sociale Geografie* 101: 4–17.

p. 153: Various sources including Globescan and MRC McLean Hazell, 2012. "Megacity Challenges: A Stakeholder Perspective." Munich.

p. 154: Indira Gandhi Institute of Development Research, 2013, http://www.igidr.ac.in

p. 155: The World Bank, http://www.worldbank.org

THE INSTANT CITY

Image references

pp. 164–5: Brazil, paved roads (1964), Professor Csaba Déak, Universidade de São Paulo, http://www.usp.br/fau/docentes/depprojeto/c_deak/CD/5bd/2br/1maps/m02rd64-/index.html; evolution of the road network (1973, 1980, 1991, 1997, and 2007), IBGE – Instituto Brasileiro de Geografia e Estatística. Atlas Nacional do Brasil 2010., ftp://geoftp.ibge.gov.br/atlas/atlas_nacional_do_brasil_2010/4_redes_geograficas/atlas_nacional_do_brasil_2010_pagina_282_evolucao_da_rede_rodoviaria.pdf

p. 166: Population of Brasilia-Anápolis-Goiania axis as percentage of Brazil, 1970–2010, IBGE—Instituto Brasileiro de Geografia e Estatística. Census—2010, http://www.ibge.gov.br/cidadesat/topwindow.htm?1; raw data for 1970–2000: Marcos Bittar Haddad, "Eixo Goiânia—Anápolis–Brasília: estruturação, ruptura e retomada das políticas públicas," Eixo Goiânia–Anápolis–Brasília: estruturação, ruptura e retomada das políticas públicas Seminário Nacional Governança Urbana e Desenvolvimento Metropolitano, 1–3 September 2010, UFRN, Natal, RN, Brasil, http://www.cchla.ufrn.br/seminariogovernanca/cdrom/ST1_Marcos_Haddad.pdf

p. 167: Data for 1959/1960 and 1969/1970: Bonato E. R. and Bonato, A. L. V., *A soja no Brasil: história e estatística* (Londrina, PR: Embrapa—Empresa Brasileira de Pesquisa Agropecuária/CNPSo—Centro Nacional de Pesquisa de Soja, 1987), http://www.infoteca.cnptia.embrapa.br/handle/doc/446431; data for 1989/1990: Brasil. Ministério da Agricultura, Pecuária e Abastecimento. Companhia Nacional de Abastecimento—Conab. SIGABrasil—Sistema de Informações Geográficas da Agricultura Brasileira, http://www.conab.gov.br/OlalaCMS/uploads/arquivos/60b1081123ce2c30f1940d73a0ca3319.jpg; data for 1999/2000: Brasil. Ministério da Agricultura, Pecuária e Abastecimento. Companhia Nacional de Abastecimento—Conab. SIGABrasil—Sistema de Informações Geográficas da Agricultura Brasileira, http://www.conab.gov.br/OlalaCMS/uploads/arquivos/d73c1ab59b310194ebfba21dc8407175..jpg; data for 2009/2010: Brasil. Ministério da Agricultura, Pecuária e Abastecimento. Companhia Nacional de Abastecimento - Conab. SIGABrasil – Sistema de Informações Geográficas da Agricultura Brasileira, http://www.conab.gov.br/OlalaCMS/uploads/arquivos/13_08_19_17_37_07_brsoja2010.png

p. 171: GDF—Governo do Distrito Federal. Seduma—Secretaria de Desenvolvimento Urbano e Meio Ambiente; Greentec Tecnologia Ambiental. Zoneamento Ecológico-Econômico do DF. Subproduto 3.5—Relatório de potencialidades e vulnerabilidades. Subproduto 3.5—Relatório de potencialidades e vulnerabilidades, p. 77, http://www.zee-df.com.br/Arquivos%20e%20mapas/Subproduto%203.5%20-%2Relat%C3%B3rio%20

de%20Potencialidades%20e%20Vulnerabilidades.pdf; Federal District, demographic density: GDF—Governo do Distrito Federal. Seduma—Secretaria de Desenvolvimento Urbano e Meio Ambiente. PDOT—Plano Diretor de Ordenamento Territorial do Distrito Federal; Documento técnico. Brasília, novembro de 2009. Mapa 5—Densidade Demográfica (densidade bruta ocupação), http://www.sedhab.df.gov.br/images/pdot/mapas/mapa5_densida_bruta_ocupacao.jpg

p. 172: Pesquisa de emprego e desemprego no Distrito Federal - PED. Brasil. Ministério do Trabalho/FAT; GDF/Setrab; SP/Seade; Dieese. Maio, 2010, p. 4, http://portal.mte.gov.br/data/files/FF8080812BA5F2C9012BA5F3890A05D1/PED_DF_ma_2010.pdf

p. 173: GDF. Seplan. Codeplan. Delimitação das Regiões Administrativas. PDAD/DF—2011: Nota metodológica. Brasília: 2012, p. 17, http://www.codeplan.df.gov.br/images/CODEPLAN/PDF/Pesquisas%20Socioecon%C3%B4micas/PDAD/2012/Nota%20Metodologica_delimitacao2013.pdf

p. 174: GDF. Ibram. Plano de manejo da APA do Lago Paranoá. Produto 3. Versão resumida revisada. Março de 2011. (Technum Consultoria). Mapa de Zoneamento Ambiental da APA do Lago Paranoá, p. 6, http://www.ibram.df.gov.br/images/Unidades%20de%20Conserva%C3%A7%C3%A3o/APA%20do%20Lago%20Parano%C3%A1/PLANO%20DE%20MANEJO%20PARANO%C3%81.pdf

p. 175: GDF—Governo do Distrito Federal. Seduma—Secretaria de Desenvolvimento Urbano e Meio Ambiente; Greentec Tecnologia Ambiental. Zoneamento Ecológico-Econômico do DF. Subproduto 3.5—Relatório de potencialidades e vulnerabilidades. Subproduto 3.5—Relatório de potencialidades e vulnerabilidades. Brasília: 2012, p. 46, Padrões de uso predominante do território com o limite das 19 Regiões Administrativas que possuem limites oficialmente definidos, http://www.zee-df.com.br/Arquivos%20e%20mapas/Subproduto%203.5%20-%20Relat%C3%B3rio%20de%20Potencialidades%20e%20Vulnerabilidades.pdf

THE TRANSNATIONAL CITY

Image references

p. 179: MIA Passenger Services brochure, http://www.miami-airport.com/pdfdoc/MIA_Passenger_Services_brochure.pdf

p. 180: Average of aggregated figures for 1995–2000 and 2004–2009, U.S. Census.

p. 181: National origin of foreign-born population in Miami-Dade and Broward counties, 2010, U.S. Census.

p.182: Trading Economics, http://www.tradingeconomics.com

p.183: Nijman, J., 2011. *Miami: Mistress of the Americas*. University of Pennsylvania Press.

p. 184: U.S. Census Bureau, American Community Survey, 2007–2011, American Community Survey 5-Year Estimates, http://www.census.gov/geo/maps-data/data/tiger-data.html

p. 188: 2010 Cruise Lines International Association Destination Summary Report, http://cruising.org/regulatory/clia-statistical-reports

p. 189: Mastercard Global Destination Cities Index, http://insights.mastercard.com/wp-content/uploads/2013/05/Mastercard_GDCI_Final_V4.pdf

pp.190–1: Nijman, J., 2011. *Miami: Mistress of the Americas*. University of Pennsylvania Press.

p. 192: American Airlines: https://aacargo.com/learn/humanremains.html

p. 193: Aer Lingus, 2013, http://www.aerlingus.com/help/help/specialassistance/

THE CREATIVE CITY

Image references

p. 206: Global Language Monitor, http://www.languagemonitor.com/fashion/london-overtakes-new-york-as-top-global-fashion-capital/

Further reading

Foot, J., 2001. *Milan Since the Miracle*. Oxford: Berg.

Knox, P., 2010. *Cities and Design*. London: Routledge.

THE GREEN CITY

Image references

p. 212: OECD/VIEA, 2006; World Energy Outlook, 2008; see also p. 25 in http://www.unhabitat.org/pmss/getElectronicVersion.aspx?nr=3164&alt=1

p. 213: p. 25 in the UN Habitat report, http://www.unhabitat.org/pmss/getElectronicVersion.aspx?nr=3164&alt=1

pp. 214–15: City of Freiburg.

p. 217: City of Freiburg.

p. 218: http://online.wsj.com/article/SB10001424053111904888304576476302775374320.html#

p. 219: Transportation Sustainability Research Center, University of California at Berkeley.

p. 220: Chapple, K. 2008. *Defining the Green Economy: A Primer on Green Economic Development*. Center for Community Innovation, University of California, Berkeley.

p. 221: Portland Development Commission.

p. 223: www.rpd-mohesr.com

pp. 224–5: Cittaslow International, http://www.cittaslow.org

p. 225: City of Wipoldsried, http://www.wildpoldsried.de/index.shtml?Energie

Further reading

Knox, P. L., and Mayer, H., 2013. *Small Town Sustainability: Economic, Social, and Environmental Innovation*. 2nd edn. Basel: Birkhäuser.

Beatley, T., 2012. *Green Cities of Europe*. Washington, D.C.: Island Press.

Birch, E. L., and Wachter, S. M., 2008. *Growing Greener Cities: Urban Sustainability in the Twenty-first Century*. Philadelphia: University of Pennsylvania Press.

Kahn, M. E., 2006. *Green Cities: Urban Growth and the Environment*. Washington, D.C.: Brookings Institution Press.

THE INTELLIGENT CITY

Image references

p. 231: EWeek/Berg Insight, http://www.eweek.com/mobile/mobile-app-downloads-to-hit-108-billion-in-2017/

p. 237: (left) Commuting pain, http://www-03.ibm.com/press/us/en/pressrelease/32017.wss#resource

p. 237: (right) Transport for London, http://www.tfl.gov.uk/assets/downloads/corporate/tfl-health-safety-and-environment-report-2011.pdf

p. 238: Techcity, http://www.techcitymap.com/index.html#/

p. 239: Top ten technology start-ups in the US, http://usatoday30.usatoday.com/tech/columnist/talkingtech/story/2012-08-22/top-tech-startup-cities/57220670/1

pp. 240–1: Smart City Vienna, https://smartcity.wien.at/site/en/

pp. 242–3: Living Labs, http://www.openlivinglabs.eu/livinglabs

Further reading

Desouza, K. C., 2011. *Intrapreneurship: Managing Ideas within Your Organization*. Toronto, CA: University of Toronto Press.

Desouza, K. C. (Editor), 2006. *Agile Information Systems: Conceptualization, Construction, and Management*. Boston, MA: Butterworth-Heinemann.

Desouza, K. C. and Paquette, S., 2011. *Knowledge Management: An Introduction*. New York, NY: Neal-Schuman Publishers, Inc.

Desouza, K. C. and Flanery, T., 2013 "Designing, Planning, and Managing Resilient Cities: A Conceptual Framework" in *Cities*, 35 (December), 89–99.1.

Desouza, K. C. and Bhagwatwar, A., 2012. "Citizen Apps to Solve Complex Urban Problems" in *Journal of Urban Technology*, 19 (3), 107–136.

Contributors

JANE CLOSSICK trained as an architect at the University of Sheffield and the University of East London and has worked for practices in London and Manchester. She completed an MA in Urban Design in 2008, and began her doctoral studies with Peter Carl at the Cass School of Architecture in 2010. Her Ph.D. research explores the structure of communication, linking macro and micro scales of social, spatial, and political involvement in London. She also teaches on the undergraduate architecture Critical and Contextual studies course at London Metropolitan University. She lives and works in East London with her husband, Colin O'Sullivan, and small son Tomás.

LUCIA CONY-CIDADE is an Associate Professor at the Universidade de Brasília. As a member of the Department of Geography, she teaches courses in urban geography and in Brazilian territorial formation as well as a doctoral seminar in the preparation of research projects. She was a visiting researcher and a lecturer at Cornell University, Department of City and Regional Planning. She is a co-editor of *Brasília 50 anos: da capital a metrópole* (UnB, 2010) and author of several book chapters and articles in academic journals. She was a research fellow of the Conselho Nacional de Desenvolvimento Científico e Tecnológico. She has served as a member of the board of the Associação Nacional de Pós-Graduação e Pesquisa em Planejamento Urbano e Regional– Anpur (2009–2011).

ELIZABETH CURRID-HALKETT is an Associate Professor at USC's Price School of Public Policy. She is the author of *The Warhol Economy: How Fashion, Art and Music Drive New York City* (Princeton University Press, 2007) and *Starstruck: The Business of Celebrity* (Faber & Faber, 2010). Currid-Halkett is a frequent commentator in major newspapers and magazines around the world. Her work has been featured in the *New York Times*, *Wall Street Journal*, the *Washington Post*, *Salon*, the *Economist*, *Elle*, the *New Yorker*, *Times Literary Supplement*, *Financial Times*, and the BBC, among others. Currid-Halkett has written pieces for the *New York Times*, *Wall Street Journal*, *Los Angeles Times*, and *Harvard Business Review*, among other mainstream and academic publications. She is regularly invited to speak at venues such as Google, Harvard University, 92nd Street Y/Tribeca, and at other universities and locations around the world. She is currently working on a book on American

consumer patterns and the evolution of conspicuous consumption, forthcoming with Princeton University Press. Currid-Halkett received her Ph.D. from Columbia University. She lives in Los Angeles with her husband Richard and son Oliver.

BEN DERUDDER is Professor of Human Geography at Ghent University, and an Associate Director of the Globalization and World Cities (GaWC) research network. As a Marie Curie Research Fellow under the European Union's 7th Framework Programme, he is presently also affiliated with Monash University's School of Geography and Environmental Sciences. His research focuses on the conceptualization and empirical analysis of transnational urban networks in general, and its transportation and production components in particular. His work on transnational urban networks has been published in leading academic journals, and he has co-edited a number of books on this topic, including *Cities in Globalization* (Routledge, 2006, with P.J. Taylor, P. Saey, and F. Witlox) and a recent volume entitled *International Handbook of Globalization and World Cities* (Edward Elgar, 2012, with P.J. Taylor, F. Witlox, and M. Hoyler).

KEVIN C. DESOUZA is Associate Dean for Research at the College of Public Programs and is an Associate Professor in the School of Public Affairs at Arizona State University. He has held faculty and/or research appointments at the University of Washington, London School of Economics and Political Science, University of the Witwatersrand, Virginia Tech, and the University of Ljubljana. Desouza has authored, co-authored, and/or edited nine books, the most recent being *Intrapreneurship: Managing Ideas within Your Organization* (University of Toronto Press, 2011). He has published more than 150 articles in scientific journals across a range of disciplines from software engineering, to information science, public administration, political science, technology management, and urban affairs. Desouza has received over $1.7 million in research funding from both private and government organizations. For more information, please visit http://www.kevindesouza.net.

ANDREW HEROD is Distinguished Research Professor in the Department of Geography at the University of Georgia. He writes mostly on matters of globalization and labor but is also interested in the intersections between political praxis and spatial form. He runs a study abroad program in Paris, having fallen in love with the city the first time he visited it nearly four decades ago.

MICHAEL HOYLER is a Senior Lecturer in Human Geography at Loughborough University, UK, and an Associate Director of the Globalization and World Cities (GaWC) research network. He is an urban geographer interested in the transformation of cities and metropolitan regions in globalization. His recent research has focused on the conceptualization and empirical analysis of contemporary (world) city and city-regional network formation. He has published widely in the field of urban studies, including the co-edited books *Global Urban Analysis: A Survey of Cities in Globalization* (Earthscan, 2011), *The International Handbook of Globalization and World Cities* (Edward Elgar, 2012), *Cities in Globalization* (Routledge, 2013), and *Megaregions: Globalizations New Urban Form?* (Edward Elgar, 2014).

PAUL KNOX is a Distinguished Professor and Co-Director of the Global Forum on Urban and Regional Resilience at Virginia Polytechnic Institute and State University. As a member of the Department of Urban Affairs and Planning he teaches courses on European urbanization and on cities and design. He is the author or editor of a dozen books, including *Palimpsests: Biographies of 50 City Districts* (Birkhauser, 2012), *Cities and Design* (Routledge, 2011), and *Urban Social Geography* (with Stephen Pinch, Longman, 2010). He is a member of the editorial board of seven international journals and has served as co-editor of *Environment and Planning A* and the *Journal of Urban Affairs*. He has received numerous honors and awards, including the 2008 Distinguished Scholarship Award of the Association of American Geographers.

LILA LEONTIDOU is Professor of Geography and European Culture at the Hellenic Open University (EAΠ), Director of Studies in European Culture and Director of the GEM Research Unit of EAΠ. She has been a Senior Fellow of the LSE since 2012 and of the JHU since 1986, has held permanent university posts in Greece (AUTH and NTUA, 1980s) and the UK (KCL, 1990s), and was a founding member (Senate and first Chair) of the first Greek Department of Geography at the University of the Aegean (1990s). In 2002 she moved to the Hellenic Open University, where she was twice elected Dean of the School of Humanities. She has published in Greek, English, and French, and her work has been translated into Spanish, Italian, German, and Japanese. She is author of *The Mediterranean City in Transition* (Cambridge University Press, 1990/2006), *Cities of Silence* (in Greek, 1989/2001/2013), *Geographically Illiterate Land* (in Greek, 2005/ 2011), co-editor of *Mediterranean Tourism* (Routledge, 2001) and *Urban Sprawl in Europe* (Blackwell, 2007), and eight other books. She has also published over 180 research papers, articles, textbooks, and monographs. She has been member of editorial advisory boards of four international academic journals and several Greek ones. She is fluent in three languages and reads three more.

GUIDO MARTINOTTI, one of the last scholars to be called "maestro," as he opened up new theoretical and methodological approaches to sociology and the study of cities, died suddenly in Paris on November 5th, 2012. He was one of the most important Italian sociologists with an international career in the EU, where among others he chaired the Standing Committee for the Social Sciences of the ESF, and in the USA, where he taught at, among others, the University of Michigan, NYU, and the University of California. Martinotti also taught in several universities in Italy (Naples, Turin, Pavia, Milan, Florence) and in France. He was a founding member of the University of Milano-Bicocca, where he taught until his retirement, and of the European Consortium for Sociological Research. He authored, among other books, *Metropolis: The New Social Morphology of the City* (Il Mulino, 1993; trans. Princeton, 1993), he edited *The Metropolitan Dimension and Development of the New City Government* (Il Mulino, 1999) and *Atlas of the Needs of the Milanese Suburbs* (Municipality of Milan, 2001), and he co-edited *Education in a Changing Society* (Sage Publications, 1977).

HEIKE MAYER is Professor of Economic Geography in the Institute of Geography and co-director of the Center for Regional Economic Development at the University of Bern in Switzerland. Her primary area of research is in local and regional economic development with a particular focus on the dynamics of innovation and entrepreneurship, place making, and sustainability. She started her career in the United States, where she completed a Ph.D. in Urban Studies (Portland State University) and held a tenured professorship at Virginia Tech University. She is the author of *Entrepreneurship and Innovation in Second Tier Regions* (Edward Elgar, 2012) and co-author of *Small Town Sustainability* (with Paul Knox, Birkhäuser, 2009).

JAN NIJMAN is Director of the Center for Urban Studies at the University of Amsterdam. His research interests are in urban geography, globalizing cities, and urban development/ planning with a regional focus on North America, South Asia, and West Europe. He has over fifteen years of fieldwork experience in urban India, mostly in Mumbai. In North America, most of his work focuses on Miami. His latest book is *Miami: Mistress of the Americas* (University of Penn Press, 2011). He is a former Guggenheim Fellow and he currently chairs the National Geographic's Global Exploration Fund in Europe.

ASLI CEYLAN ONER is an Assistant Professor in the School of Urban and Regional Planning at Florida Atlantic University. She teaches graduate and undergraduate courses on urbanization and historical development and planning of cities. Her research interests include globalization, planning and governance of global cities, comparative urbanization, built environment, and metropolitan area growth. She has published journal articles and book chapters related to these topics and participated in many conferences in Europe and the USA. She is a member of the Globalization and World Cities Research Group (GaWC).

MICHAEL SHIN is Associate Professor of Geography at the University of California, Los Angeles (UCLA). His work applies geospatial information technology and geo-visualization techniques to questions and datasets in economic, political, and health geography. He is also Director of UCLA's program on Geospatial Information Systems and Technology, and has published extensively on Italy and Italian politics.

PETER TAYLOR is Professor of Human Geography at Northumbria University (UK) and the Founding Director of the Globalization and World Cities (GaWC) Research Network. He is author or editor of over thirty books, the most recent being *Extraordinary Cities* (Edward Elgar, 2013), *Cities in Globalization* (Routledge, 2012), *Seats, Votes and the Spatial Organization of Elections* (European Consortium of Political Research, reprinted 2012), *International Handbook of Globalization and World Cities* (Edward Elgar, 2011), *Political Geography: World-Economy, Nation-State, Locality* (Longman, 2011, 6th ed.), and *Global Urban Analysis: a Survey of Cities in Globalization* (Earthscan, 2011). He was a founding editor of both *Political Geography* and *Review of International Political Economy*. He is a Fellow of the British Academy, has been awarded Distinguished Scholarship Honors by the Association of American Geographers, and has honorary doctorates from Oulu (Finland) and Ghent (Belgium) universities.

RAF VERBRUGGEN is Doctor in Historical Urban Geography. He wrote his Ph.D. on the late medieval and early modern European city network at the Globalization and World Cities research network at the Geography Department of Loughborough University (UK). He has co-authored several papers on historical globalization. He currently works as a policy consultant on spatial planning for the Flemish Youth Council (Belgium).

FRANK WITLOX holds a Ph.D. in Urban Planning from Eindhoven University of Technology and is Professor of Economic Geography at Ghent University. He is also a Visiting Professor at ITMMA (Institute of Transport and Maritime Management Antwerp), and an Associate Director of GaWC (Globalization and World Cities). Since 2010 he has been Director of the Doctoral School of Natural Sciences at UGent. Since August 2013 he has been an Honorary Professor in the School of Geography at the University of Nottingham. He has been a guest lecturer at Lund University-Campus Helsingborg (Sweden), University of Tartu (Estonia), and Chongqing University (China). His research focuses on travel behavior analysis and modeling, travel and land use, sustainable mobility issues, business travel, cross-border mobility, city logistics, global commodity chains, globalization and world city-formation, polycentric urban development, contemporary challenges in agricultural land use, and locational analysis of corporations.

Index

Index

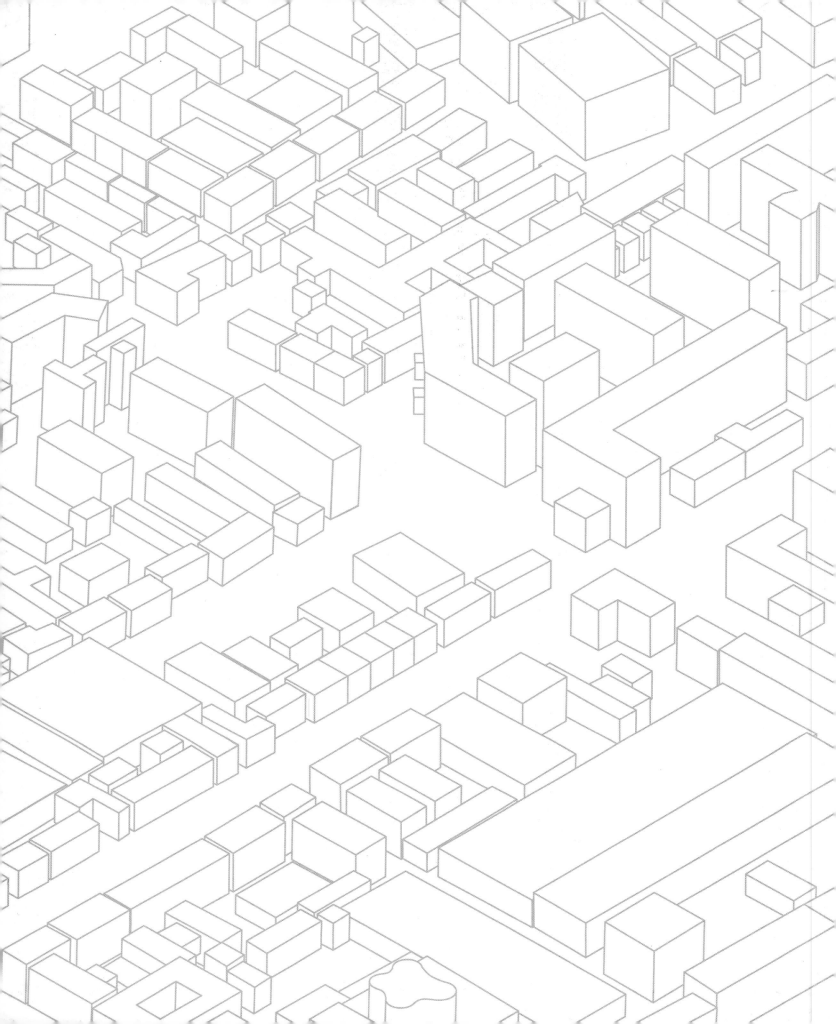